Obama's Fractured Legacy

New Perspectives on the American Presidency
Series Editors: Michael Patrick Cullinane and Sylvia Ellis,
University of Roehampton

Published titles
*Constructing Presidential Legacy: How We Remember the
American President*
Edited by Michael Patrick Cullinane and Sylvia Ellis

Presidential Privilege and the Freedom of Information Act
Kevin M. Baron

Donald Trump and American Populism
Richard S. Conley

Trump's America: Political Culture and National Identity
Edited by Liam Kennedy

*Obama's Fractured Legacy: The Politics and Policies of an
Embattled Presidency*
Edited by François Vergniolle de Chantal

Obama v. Trump: The Politics of Rollback
Clodagh Harrington and Alex Waddan

Forthcoming titles
The White House, the War on Poverty and the GOP
Mark McLay

Midterms and Mandates
Patrick Andelic, Mark McLay and Robert Mason

Harry S. Truman and Higher Education
Rebecca Stone

Series website: https://edinburghuniversitypress.com/new-
perspectives-on-the-american-presidency.html

OBAMA'S FRACTURED LEGACY

The Politics and Policies of an Embattled Presidency

Edited by François Vergniolle de Chantal

EDINBURGH
University Press

Edinburgh University Press is one of the leading university presses in the UK. We publish academic books and journals in our selected subject areas across the humanities and social sciences, combining cutting-edge scholarship with high editorial and production values to produce academic works of lasting importance. For more information visit our website: edinburghuniversitypress.com

Edinburgh University Press Ltd
The Tun – Holyrood Road
12(2f) Jackson's Entry
Edinburgh EH8 8PJ

Typeset in 11/13 Adobe Sabon by
IDSUK (DataConnection) Ltd

A CIP record for this book is available from the British Library

ISBN 978 1 4744 5493 3 (hardback)
ISBN 978 1 4744 5495 7 (webready PDF)
ISBN 978 1 4744 5494 0 (paperback)
ISBN 978 1 4744 5496 4 (epub)

Contents

v

Contributors

David Bensman, in memoriam: Professor of History at Rutgers University where he studied American labor history, education reform, and the impact of global economic integration on working people. He was the author of *Central Park East and its Graduates: Learning by Heart* (Teachers College Press, 2000) and of *Rusted Dreams: Hard Times in a Steel Community* (McGraw-Hill, 1987). He was also one of the co-authors of *Who Built America? Volume II* (Bedford/St Martin's, 2007).

Audrey Célestine is Associate Professor in Political Science at Lille 3 University (CERAPS – UMR 8026) and a junior member of the Institut Universitaire de France (2016–2021). In 2018, she published *La fabrique des identités. L'encadrement politique des minorités caribéennes à Paris et New York* (Paris, Karthala) and *Une famille française. Des Antilles à Dunkerque en passant par l'Algérie* (Paris, Textuel).

Frédérick Douzet is Professor of Geopolitics at the University of Paris 8, Director of the French Institute of Geopolitics research team (IFG Lab) and Director of the Center Geopolitics of the Datasphere (GEODE). She is a Commissioner of the Global Commission on the Stability of Cyberspace. In 2017, she was part of the drafting committee for the Strategic Review of Defense and National Security. Frédérick was nominated junior member of the Institut Universitaire de France (2006–2011) and received several awards for her research, including three book prizes (Society of

Geography, Academy of Moral and Political Sciences, International Cybersecurity Forum), the France-Berkeley Fund Award for Outstanding Young Scholar (2014), and the best paper award from the Urban Affairs Association (2009). Her current research deals with the geopolitics of cyberspace.

Aude Géry is a PhD candidate in international law at Rouen University (France) and is affiliated to the Castex Chair in Cyberstrategy. Her research deals with the consequences of cyber weapons for international law.

Michael Kazin is Professor of History at Georgetown University and co-editor of *Dissent*. He specializes in the history of politics and social movements in the United States. Kazin writes frequently for such publications and websites as *The New York Times*, *The Washington Post*, *Foreign Affairs*, *The Nation*, and *The New Republic*. His most recent book is *War Against War: The American Fight for Peace, 1914–1918* which was awarded the Elise M. Boulding Prize for the best book on peace history published in 2017 and 2018 by the Peace History Society. It was also an Editor's Choice of *The New York Times Book Review*. Kazin is also the author of *American Dreamers: How the Left Changed a Nation*, *A Godly Hero: The Life of William Jennings Bryan*, *The Populist Persuasion: An American History*, *Barons of Labor: The San Francisco Building Trades and Union Power in the Progressive Era*, and, with Maurice Isserman, *America Divided: The Civil War of the 1960s* (6th edition, 2020). He was also editor-in-chief of *The Princeton Encyclopedia of American Political History*. Kazin has lectured widely in the United States, Europe, and Japan and has received various honors, including a Guggenheim Fellowship, an NEH Fellowship, a fellowship from the Woodrow Wilson Center, two Fulbright fellowships, and a fellowship from the Institute of Advanced Study at Princeton. Kazin is currently at work on a history of the Democratic Party, under contract with Farrar, Straus and Giroux.

Donna Kesselman is Professor of American Studies at Université Paris-Est Créteil (UPEC – IMAGER – EA 3958). Her research deals with the evolution of work and social rights in the United

States and in a comparative perspective. She was project manager for a French national grant program (ANR) on new employment norms in France, the United States, and Brazil. Her most recent publication is a co-edited e-book *Women at Work in the Americas Today* (Presses Universitaires de Provence, 2016).

Thad Kousser is a Professor and Chair of the Department of Political Science at UC San Diego. He has authored or edited *The Logic of American Politics*, 9th edition (CQ/Sage, 2019), *Politics in the American States*, 11th edition (CQ/Sage, 2018), *The Power of American Governors* (Cambridge University Press, 2012), *The New Political Geography of California* (Berkeley Public Policy Press, 2008), *Term Limits and the Dismantling of State Legislative Professionalism* (Cambridge University Press, 2005), and *Adapting to Term Limits: Recent Experiences and New Directions* (Public Policy Institute of California, 2004).

Nelson Lichtenstein is Distinguished Professor of History at the University of California, Santa Barbara. There he directs the Center for the Study of Work, Labor, and Democracy. He is the editor, with Gary Gerstle and Alice O'Connor, of *Beyond the New Deal Order: U.S. Politics from the Great Depression to the Great Recession* (University of Pennsylvania Press, 2019). He is writing a book on the economic policy of the Clinton administration.

Nicolas Martin-Breteau is Associate Professor of US History at the University of Lille 3, France. He specializes in contemporary African American history, on which he has published several articles in peer-reviewed journals. He has recently translated and published the first French edition of W. E. B. DuBois's 1899 classic *The Philadelphia Negro* (Paris, La Découverte, 2019). He is currently editing the manuscript of his forthcoming book, tentatively entitled *Bodies Politic: Sport in African American Struggles for Justice in Washington, D.C.* (Paris, EHESS, 2020).

Alix Meyer is Associate Professor of American Politics and Government at the Université de Bourgogne France Comté (Dijon, France). After graduating from Sciences Po Lyon, he passed the

Agrégation d'anglais and received a PhD from the Université Lumière Lyon 2. A former Fulbright fellow, his research focuses on US political institutions. He recently published *The Obama Presidency (2009–2017)* (Paris, Belin, 2019) and he is a member of the editorial board of *Politique Américaine*.

Sidney M. Milkis is the White Burkett Miller Professor in the Department of Politics and a Faculty Associate at the Miller Center at the University of Virginia. His most recent publications are *Rivalry and Reform: Presidents, Social Movements and the Transformation of American Politics* (Chicago Press, 2019) and *The American Presidency: Origins and Development, 1776–2018* (SAGE, 8th edition, 2019), co-authored with Michael Nelson.

Andrew Rudalevige is the Thomas Brackett Reed Chair of Government at Bowdoin College in Brunswick, Maine, and former Chair of the Presidents and Executive Politics section of the American Political Science Association. He is a graduate of the University of Chicago and Harvard University. His books include *Managing the President's Program, The New Imperial Presidency: Renewing Presidential Power after Watergate*, and the forthcoming *Executive Orders and the Executive Branch*, along with the textbook *The Politics of the Presidency*, and edited volumes on the Bush and Obama presidencies.

Elizabeth T. Shermer is an Associate Professor of History at Loyola University Chicago. She is the author of *Sunbelt Capitalism: Phoenix and the Transformation of American Politics* (University of Pennsylvania Press, 2013), editor of *Barry Goldwater and The Remaking of the American Political Landscape* (University of Arizona Press, 2013), and co-editor, with Nelson Lichtenstein, of *The Right and Labor in America: Politics, Ideology, and Imagination* (University of Pennsylvania Press, 2012).

Stephen Skowronek is the Pelatiah Perit Professor of Political and Social Science at Yale University. His most recent book, with Karen Orren, is *The Policy State: An American Predicament* (Harvard, 2017). It was followed by a companion piece, "The Adaptability

Paradox: Constitutional Resilience and Principles of Good Government in Twenty-First-Century America" (*Perspectives on Politics*, 2019). He has worked extensively on the development of American national institutions and the politics of presidential leadership. His books on the American presidency include *The Politics Presidents Make* (Harvard, 1993) and *Presidential Leadership in Political Time* (Kansas, 3rd edition, 2020).

Thomas Sugrue is Professor of Social and Cultural Analysis and History at NYU. He is the author of *Not Even Past: Barack Obama and the Burden of Race* (Princeton University Press, 2010) and *Sweet Land of Liberty: The Forgotten Struggle for Civil Rights in the North* (Random House, 2008). He co-edited *Immigration and Metropolitan Revitalization in the United States* with Domenic Vitiello (Penn Press, 2017). He is currently engaged in a research project on race, ethnicity, and citizenship in France and the United States.

Isabelle Vagnoux is Professor of American History and Politics at Aix Marseille Université (France). Her research deals with American foreign relations as well as Hispanics in the United States. She is also co-editor of the online journal *IdeAs* (Institute of the Americas) and the online blog on the foreign relations of the English-speaking world, OREMA. She co-edited (with Michel Bertrand, Jean-Michel Blanquer, and Antoine Coppolani) a dictionary on *Les Amériques* (Paris, Robert Laffont, 2016). Her latest edited book is *Obama et le monde: quel leadership pour les Etats-Unis?* (La Tour d'Aigues, L'Aube, 2013).

François Vergniolle de Chantal is Professor of American Politics and Government at Université de Paris (France). His most recent publications include *L'impossible présidence impériale* (Paris, CNRS Editions, 2016) and *Leadership and Uncertainty Management in Politics* (with Agnès Alexandre-Collier, Palgrave, 2015). He co-directed (with Alexandra de Hoop Scheffer) *Politique Américaine*, a French academic review in political science. He is working on comparative republican traditions in France and the United States in the twentieth century.

Jean-Christian Vinel is Associate Professor in American History at Université de Paris (France). In 2013 he published *The Employee. A Political History* (University of Pennsylvania Press). He also co-edited (with Clarisse Berthezene) *Conservatismes en movement* (Editions de l'EHESS, 2016).

Acknowledgments

This edited volume has its origins in a December 2016 international symposium "Obama's Legacy: Tensions and Reconfigurations after the Presidential Elections" held at Paris Diderot University (now Université de Paris) in France. The three-day event gathered some forty scholars of American history and politics from both sides of the Atlantic, who were tasked with assessing the eight-year Obama legacy as president, barely two months after Trump's presidential victory still bewildered many analysts and even the world at large. With the benefit of hindsight and in light of new circumstances like the failed impeachment attempt and the worldwide COVID-19 pandemic, *Obama's Fractured Legacy: The Politics and Policies of an Embattled Presidency* is the long-awaited and long-matured output of the symposium.

Neither the conference nor the edited volume could have seen birth without steadfast institutional support. I would first like to express my gratitude to my research center, LARCA (Laboratoire de Recherches sur les Cultures Anglophones – UMR/CNRS 8225), to the US Embassy in Paris, and also to the German Marshall Fund of the United States which initially supported the 2016 conference and later covered the republication fee for the chapters by Michael Kazin and Tom Sugrue that were first published in another collection of essays edited by Julian Zelizer in 2018. Let me extend my gratitude to Princeton University Press for making this republication possible.

My warmest thanks go to all the contributors who agreed to participate in this project in spite of their busy schedules. Their generous dedication made it possible to keep chapters updated in

ACKNOWLEDGMENTS

the context of a Trump presidency that promised to reject each and every achievement of the Obama administration. This collection of essays has thus constantly improved since the papers were first delivered in 2016 and they present an assessment of Obama's legacy while including constant references to Trump. Let me also thank Jean-Christian Vinel, Associate Professor in American History, my colleague at Université de Paris, with whom I had the pleasure of co-organizing the conference and who co-signs the introduction to the volume. And, finally, heartfelt thanks to the 'New Perspectives on the American Presidency' series editors at Edinburgh University Press for responding so positively to such a book project initially and throughout.

As always, the outcome of this project benefitted from the full and dedicated support of my ever-attentive insightful *Zelie*.

François Vergniolle de Chantal
Full Professor of American Politics and Government
(Université de Paris)
Paris, August 19, 2020

xiv

Introduction: Obama and the exhaustion of progressive presidentialism

François Vergniolle de Chantal and Jean-Christian Vinel

> *Now that all the smoke is gone,*
> *And the battle's finally won,*
> *Victory is finally ours,*
> *History, so long, so long . . .*

If popular culture has a way to convey the particular mood of a moment, then rap singer Jay-Z's song "History," which he performed at the pre-inauguration ball in Washington DC on January 19, 2009, offers an important window through which to grasp the expectation of change that Obama's own campaign slogans – from "Hope" to "Yes, We Can" – encapsulated. Jay Z and his wife Beyoncé were important donors to the Obama campaign – artists who had transcended race themselves to occupy prominent places once reserved to white singers in the American cultural apparatus.[1] Beyond their individual support, the song held particular resonance because it was a tale of rupture and empowerment suggesting that the election was the dawn of a new era during which African Americans could at last remove the shackles of the past and start writing their own history.[2] Echoing the song, one observer noted that the election of the first African-American president seemed to have sent civil rights history into "obsolescence."

To be sure, the campaign had not been free from racial tensions, but its outcome suggested to many the reality of a post-racial America, one that Obama embodied by offering a tale of both continuity and discontinuity.[3] Early in the campaign,

1

particularly at an event in Selma in March 2007, Obama had regularly framed his own career in the context of the history of race in the US, suggesting that he "stood on the shoulders" of former civil rights leaders such as Martin Luther King Jr. Even so, as the controversy over the pastor Jeremiah Wright suggested, Obama had carefully – and successfully – left racial grievances aside, holding the promise of a rupture, a grand reconciliation enabling whites and blacks to move beyond racial consciousness and focus on pursuing a renewed national purpose around important issues such as healthcare, education, jobs, and the protection of the environment.[4]

Indeed, while race thus put the relationship between the past and the present at the forefront of interpretations of the election, so did political economy. Analogies with the New Deal abounded at the time of the election, the most famous one being a *Time* magazine cover featuring a well-known picture of Franklin D. Roosevelt in an open limousine with a picture of a smiling Obama pasted on the face of the president who had once told Americans that the only thing they had to fear was fear itself. Not only did Obama's election in the fall of 2008 take place at the moment when the worst economic crisis since the Great Depression had reignited a debate on the role of the federal government in the economy, but it also came after two decades of increased discussion of class and inequality in the US, one symbolized by the emergence of the living wage movement in the 1990s and the publication of best-sellers on the working poor such as Barbara Ehrenreich's celebrated *Nickel and Dimed*. The grassroots surge that accompanied the election and the president elect's ambitious agenda, whether in labor law or healthcare reform, cemented the analogy so firmly that the phrase "New Deal" was still a fixture of early book titles analyzing the Obama presidency.

In point of fact, Obama himself at times claimed the legacy of the New Deal, either by explaining how his grandfather had benefitted from the G.I. Bill or, as in a speech given in June 2008, by eulogizing the Americans who went through the great depression as "the greatest generation . . . that conquered fear itself, liberated a continent from tyranny, and made this country home to untold opportunity and prosperity."[5] There was more than a hint

2

of irony in this use of the New Deal as a guiding light, for the
New Deal's racial politics had been checkered at best, and had left
most black Americans in its shadow by extending its protective
hand only to industrial workers employed full time, and by failing to challenge segregation – be it in the South or in the North.
Yet, as historian William Jones explained in *The Nation* in 2008,
Obama was ideally suited to fuse the New Deal and civil rights
traditions, building progressive and race-neutral policies dealing
with healthcare, jobs, or education where Roosevelt and the New
Dealers had failed.[6]

Underwriting the faith that the economy had created a liberal
moment similar to the 1930s was the notion that the 2008 election was a realignment – albeit one whose importance remained
to be determined. In an article entitled "America the Liberal,"
historian John Judis explained that the 2008 election revealed the
political dynamics of a post-industrial economy centered in large
urban-metropolitan areas. According to Judis, professionals were
thus the core of Obama's electoral bloc (he won the nineteen states
with the largest number of people with an advanced degree) along
with minorities and women. Unlike the white working class, Judis
sanguinely noted, the numbers of these workers would grow, and
a new political worldview –more culturally liberal and more open
to government intervention in the economy – would gradually
run deeper and deeper roots, cementing a new electoral map that
differed from previous ones because the post-industrial economy
was not limited to any region.[7]

All in all, however, what made Obama's rhetoric of hope and
change truly inspirational was his unique political background.
Indeed, Obama's resume combined an education at elite universities with an experience of activism at the grassroots that set him
apart from previous trustees of the nation's stewardship. In 1985,
after graduating from Columbia University, Obama was trained
as a community organizer in Chicago's South Side, where he
was employed by the Calumet Community Research Conference
(CCRC) – a group of inner-city churches – to work on housing
issues such as jobs, banks and asbestos removal. There, representing poor black Americans in a city that had just ended the Daley era
by electing Harold Washington – Chicago's first African-American

3

mayor – Obama not only found a connection to the black struggle that he had long needed, but he also became immersed in a tradition harkening back to the teachings of Saul Alinsky and the strategies of CIO unions of the 1930s. This tradition saw grassroots organizing as the source of radical politics, but it also focused on achieving concrete results in a specific environment rather than building idealistic movements.[8]

Even as we reconstruct these dynamics, however, one must see that to a large extent, change remained at best an amorphous concept. If Obama sounded like Roosevelt, it was the Roosevelt of 1932 who promised experimentation and pragmatism, but not the Roosevelt who attacked the "privileged princes of the new economic dynasties" in Philadelphia in 1936, and who contended that "political equality" had been made "meaningless in the face of economic inequality." Throughout the campaign, Obama presented himself as a post-partisan candidate, one who could transcend ideological boundaries and bring Americans together after the divisions that had riven American politics since the 1990s. There was of course a long history of presidential candidates and presidents contending that they stood above parties before Obama entered politics, but nonetheless, there was a noticeable gap between partisan expectations that Obama's term would lay the basis for a liberal realignment and his avowed pragmatism.

In retrospect, however, it is striking that Obama's campaign followed the analysis he had offered in *The Audacity of Hope*, in 2006, in which he vowed to distance himself both from Democratic "centrists" who ended up "with each passing year ceding more and more ground" and from the Democrats who "still championed the old time religion, defending every New Deal and Great Society program from Republican encroachment" but did not see that their efforts were "exhausted and bereft of energy and new ideas." Echoing E. J. Dionne's famous *Why Americans Hate Politics*, which argued that Americans were tired of being locked in either/or politics and longed for a new political center, Obama further criticized the Democratic Party for having become "the party of reaction," one that failed to see that compromise and the making of large majorities of Americans were necessary to implement the policies required to meet contemporary challenges.[9]

4

As law professor (and former colleague) Cass Sustein argued during the Democratic primaries, Obama was best seen as a "visionary minimalist":

> Barack Obama is widely regarded as a visionary because of his emphasis on "change" and his soaring rhetoric, but he also has strong minimalist tendencies . . . Like all minimalists, Obama believes that real change usually requires consensus, learning, and accommodation – a belief directly reflected in many of his policies . . . "Visionary minimalist" may sound like an oxymoron, but in fact – and this is the key point – Obama's promise of change is credible in part because of his brand of minimalism . . . For him, reconciliation is change, and it is also what makes change possible.[10]

Sustein, who went on to be Obama's choice to lead the powerful Office of Internal and Regulatory Affairs (OIRA), exemplified the ideological ambiguity that attended the election of Barack Obama. He had once advocated returning to Roosevelt's 1944 economic Bill of Rights, but by the 2008 election he had tempered this enthusiasm for FDR's unfinished agenda, and he was much better known for "libertarian paternalism," the notion that government should rely on behavioral economic to develop regulatory policies "nudging" people to make the right economic decisions rather than forcing them on individuals.[11]

Quite beyond the minimalism and moderation which Sunstein saw as the basis of Obama's political agenda, one important question was whether the progressive presidency remained the powerful instrument celebrated by John Morton Blum in his 1980 classic *The Progressive Presidents*. If, on an individual level, Obama was misread and misunderstood as a politician seeking to effect profound changes by many of his supporters as well as many adversaries, when he actually favored "nudges," his moderation did not rhyme with inaction. Obama was a skilled policy-maker whose record with the 111th Congress was exceptional by contemporary standards.[12] Even after the 2010 "shellacking," he succeeded in bypassing conservative opposition in Congress by relying on executive power, as shown in the environmental or immigration fields. Obama thus had a number of significant accomplishments. Despite the fierce opposition he faced, he is probably the most successful domestic president of the past half-century. Even so, Obama failed to fundamentally change the condition and direction of American politics. This begs the question which is at the forefront of this collection of essays, namely why did Obama's legacy turn out to be a mixed bag, especially for his most enthusiastic supporters of 2008?

We suggest that these policy moves and outcomes can be seen as illustrations of the changing nature of the presidential institution itself, as an engine for social reform. This second line of inquiry focuses on the limits of presidential power: to what extent were Democrats victim of a presidential illusion that Ted Lowi had analyzed more than thirty years ago when comparing the president to the Wizard of Oz, namely a man who cannot deliver on his promises? Or, rather, is the modern presidency, as Stephen Skowronek has argued, an exhausted institution?[13] This institutional entry point questions the assumption of an omnipotent presidency inherited from the New Deal. Franklin D. Roosevelt towered over many of the limits on executive power; he placed the president in charge of countless agencies, programs, and projects across the country and he spoke directly to citizens through the radio, motivating them to act on his behalf. In other words, FDR did more for the presidency than any other leader in American history. His impact on institutional arrangements and political expectations was such that Bruce Ackerman in 1995 famously depicted the New Deal as no less than a "constitutional moment" in its own right.[14]

Since then, the promise of presidentially led political breakthroughs has run deep in American imagination. This is the model that remains the standard against which presidential leadership is judged. As William Leuchtenburg wrote in his 1983 classic on presidential power, all presidents operate "in the shadow of FDR" and always fall short. None of FDR's successors replicated the unsurpassed first New Deal and its fifteen new sweeping legislations adopted in Congress within three months. The assumption here is that FDR's successors did not benefit from the same reconstructive opportunities and consequently never towered over institutional constraints the way FDR did. If an exceptional conjunction of factors created a powerful "plebiscitary executive" that successfully enacted major social reforms

in the 1930s, it would also appear that the president's political capacities to repudiate and reconstruct weakened over the
course of the twentieth century.[15]

With the benefit of hindsight, it appears Obama's presidency
did not escape this trend, as exemplified in this collection of essays.
Paradoxically though, conditions for a wave of presidentially led
progressive reforms seemed to be ripe in 2008, after decades of
Republican dominance. After a nomination campaign which testified to the massive grassroots support Obama enjoyed,[16] he swept
his party into full control of the governmental apparatus at a
time when an economic crisis resulting directly from the outgoing
administration was plaguing the country. From a purely electoral
point of view, Obama's victory in 2008 was thus impressive on
all counts: with a turnout of 63 percent – the highest percentage
in fifty years – Obama gained almost 53 percent of the popular
vote (and 365 electoral votes), thus becoming the first Democrat
to be elected with a majority since Carter's 50.1 percent in 1976.
On top of that, Democrats in Congress gained eight seats in the
Senate (standing officially at fifty-seven, but reinforced by two
Independents caucusing with them, Bernie Sanders from Vermont
and Joe Lieberman from Connecticut), and twenty-one seats in the
House of Representatives (totaling 233 seats). The results pointed
to a "mandate" from the American people and invited all sorts of
expectations from Obama's supporters – Henry Louis Gates Jr.
called Obama's victory "a magical transformative moment"[17] –
as well as fears from his opponents. On the Republican side, the
results were a massive repudiation that pundits, journalists, and
talking-heads were quick to relate to the 1932 disaster of Herbert
Hoover. For some, like Samuel Tanenhaus, these results were not
merely an electoral defeat but rather a philosophical repudiation:
conservatism was declared "dead" as a political ideology.[18] Public
opinion was also shifting on the progressive side: government activism was called for by many.[19] The alignment of political stars – a
charismatic candidate with grassroots support, electoral victories,
and ideological shifts – seemed to be perfect and to call for proactive presidential reforms. All the more so that another element, this
time institutional, favored a potential twenty-first-century replay
of the major waves of progressive reforms that swept the country

three times in the twentieth century: the reconstruction of presidential power inherited from the Bush administration. Indeed, George W. Bush had surrounded himself with a team of advisers who were dedicated to a "post-Watergate" reconstruction of the presidency. As Andrew Rudalevige documented, an obsession among the most influential presidential advisers was to overcome what they saw as a trauma for the presidency, namely the weakening of the presidency in the wake of Nixon's 1974 resignation. After the 9/11 attacks and the fight against terrorism, the presidential branch was thus strengthened thanks to the commitment of people like Vice-President Richard Cheney, Secretary of Defense Donald Rumsfeld, who both started off in politics in the Nixon administration and witnessed first-hand the Watergate scandal unfold, chief of staff Andrew Card, and legal scholars like John Yoo who pondered over the notion of a "unitary Executive."[20]

But paradoxically none of these factors prevented Obama from being on the defensive during his two terms. Even between 2008 and 2010, when public opinion seemed to believe Obama had a mandate[21] and when the 111th Congress was made up of Democratic majorities, Republicans remained steadfast in their opposition to Obama. Few were willing to cross the aisle and work with a Democratic administration. Indeed, the Obama agenda triggered a grassroots opposition, known as the Tea Party movement, that quickly became the engine behind the Republican Party. Initially a fiscally conservative movement, little interested in social issues such as abortion or gun rights, they were adamant that the "Washington Establishment," President Obama, and the Democratic Congress needed to be stopped at all costs. The "post-partisan" order that Obama wanted to promote came at a steep cost for the most progressive Democrats: typically, President Obama was indeed willing to give away the most progressive provisions of a bill to gain a very limited number of Republican votes or none at all. Even though the "public option" (a governmental public healthcare program) was dropped by Obama, the Affordable Care Act of 2010, Obama's signature issue, was adopted without a single Republican vote in either chamber, which was a major defeat for the administration. After the 2010 Republican electoral victory, Republicans in Congress, fueled by the freshmen class of Tea Party members, clearly signaled they wanted no collaboration with the administration.[22] The budget battles in 2011 showed that Republicans were willing to send the entire government into default, which shocked the Obama administration by providing a clear sense of just how far right the congressional Republicans had moved.[23] The 2013 government shutdown was a prime example of the budget impasse created by this congressional polarization.

Following Skowronek's work, we argue that this evolution is symptomatic of the new shape of presidential power and goes far beyond the constraints in a checks and balances system.[24] It is well known, for instance, that Reagan, who came into power with an ambitious transformative agenda of his own, was dependent on Democrats in the House of Representatives; so was Nixon in 1968. Conservatives were in a position to start reshaping public policy only when they finally dominated Congress in 1994. Clinton and Obama were also hindered by divided government and the latter's lawmaking abilities were greatest with the Democratic 111th Congress. The mix of partisan and institutional checks, however, is only part of the story. These constraints are part and parcel of American politics, and even FDR, who built the Presidency as it exists today, had to face his share.[25]

Nevertheless, none of these Presidents had to face the level of party polarization that Obama was confronted with. In the 1930s, for instance, the lay of the political land was characterized by a bipartisan conservative coalition in Congress rather than a polarized Republican party as it is today. Even Reagan and Clinton were able to craft bipartisan legislations, such as the social security amendments of 1983 or the 1996 welfare reform. However, Obama operated in a political environment characterized by partisanship and extreme polarization.[26] The extent to which polarization has grown since the 2000s sets the Obama presidency apart from his most immediate Democratic predecessor, Bill Clinton. Even though polarization was already high in the early 1990s – Clinton had to face a Republican wall of obstruction for both his 1993 budget and the 1994 healthcare reform – it was in no way near to what Obama experienced. Obama came to power talking of "post-partisan" politics, seeking comity, and trying to bridge the political divide,[27] but this resulted in nothing. Spurred by the Tea Party movement, Republicans in Congress were locked in a tactic of systematic obstruction against all major presidential initiatives. In 2008, Obama was thus the first president to be in a position to govern following the pattern set by the great progressive presidents of fore, but in a context of extreme party polarization.

In such an unfavorable partisan configuration, institutional power cannot secure legislative achievements. In other words, the omnipotent presidency inherited from the 1930s becomes an embattled executive in the context of a polarized politics. To use an expression applied to the Supreme Court, the presidency seems to generate "hollow hopes," an assessment that perfectly fits Obama's administration.[28]

This partisan configuration shows the extent to which liberals – Obama too – erred in trying to go back to the model of the progressive president.[29] None of them had to confront the same degree of polarization than Obama. Franklin Roosevelt operated in a bipartisan context, so that all of his legislative achievements were passed thanks to a majority of progressives from both the Republican and the Democratic Parties. Lyndon Johnson, arguably the last transformative president on the Democratic side, was able to swing large numbers of Republican votes in the House and the Senate to his side. Even Clinton was able to rally Republicans to his centrist policies. In other words, there was no precedent against which the inherited constraints Obama had to face could be meted. This is true in most of the literature as well. The classical analytical framework of modern presidential power is made up of three major books – Richard E. Neustadt's *Presidential Power* (1960), Arthur M. Schlesinger, Jr.'s *The Imperial Presidency* (1973), and Theodore J. Lowi's *The Personal President* (1985) – and none of them anticipated the current level of party polarization. Rather, they tend to downplay the part played by political parties and highlight the "plebiscitary" link between the president and public opinion so as to impose the presidential program on Congress. For instance, as Arthur Schlesinger wrote, Nixon was "moving toward (. . .) a plebiscitary Presidency. His model lay not in Britain but in France – in the France of Louis

Napoléon and Charles de Gaulle (. . .) Certainly after his reelection he began what can profitably be seen as an attempt to establish a quasi-Gaullist regime in the United States."[30] In Lowi's account, the weakening of "the one type of group that stood between the government and the masses, the political parties" is one of the core challenges for the American republic, next to the concentration of government in the presidency and the focusing of mass expectations on the president, which, altogether, make up the "second Republic of the United States."[31] As for Neustatdt, a former adviser to Kennedy on executive organization, presidential power bypassed parties altogether, since it was merely a "power to persuade" individual Congress members.[32] In Neustadt's analysis, a president acts somewhat like a magnet under a sheet of paper that has each filling move in the desired direction. In the wake of these analyses, many authors emphasized presidential leadership and presidential ability to "go public" and rely on the "bully pulpit."[33] Since none of the three standard analysis of presidential power took party polarization into account, this begs the question of what happens to the modern presidency, especially its progressive version, in a polarized context?

So far, political science has shown that presidential powers are extremely circumscribed in a polarized context.[34] Against the conventional understanding of presidential leadership, it can be argued that presidents do not succeed in persuading others to support them, but rather by recognizing and exploiting effectively opportunities already present in their environments. To put it differently, presidents cannot create opportunities for change. Instead, they are dependent on exploiting the opportunities at hand. As explained by George C. Edwards, "a common premise underlying the widespread emphasis on political leadership as the wellspring of change is that some leaders have the capability to transform policy by reshaping the influences on it."[35] But this traditional view paves the way for presidential "overreach," i.e. "when presidents propose policies that lack substantial support in the public or Congress, expecting to create opportunities for change by persuading a majority of the public and the Congress to support their policies." As a result, these presidents typically suffer heavy political losses that eventually undermine their ability to govern. Think Bill Clinton's healthcare reform

11

in 1994 or George W. Bush's Social Security reform in 2005. In a polarized context, argues Edwards, "presidents are not in strong positions to create opportunities for legislative success by persuading others to support their policies."[36] Instead, they must evaluate the opportunities for change in their environments and exploit opportunities that already exist. This of course is a risky enterprise since the context of any presidency is complex. But the starting point is clear enough: in a polarized context, presidents can first exploit opportunities essentially by maintaining their coalitions, meaning that they need to mobilize their core supporters and not try to persuade the skeptical, much less convert the opposition. Yet, as illustrated by his numerous "post-partisan" calls, Obama seems to have overestimated the opportunities for change in his environment and his ability to create new opportunities. Edwards emphasizes that "effective leaders" are first and foremost "facilitators who work at the margins of coalition-building"; in other words, "effective [presidential] leadership involves exploiting rather than creating opportunities."[37] To that extent, Obama's calls to go beyond partisanship made for good campaigning but fell on deaf ears once governing was the issue. Obama behaved as if a New Deal-type presidency were still possible. And he was certainly not alone in that. As the British magazine *The Economist* noted two weeks after the election, "Barack Obama talked about people getting their hands on the arc of history" and added:

> Many liberals would like to turn it towards a "new new deal". Washington is currently buzzing with talk of Franklin Delano Roosevelt. Members of Obama's inner circle are reading up on FDR's first hundred days. No political conversation is complete without a knowing reference to the squire of Hyde Park. Both *Time* and the *New Yorker* feature pictures of Mr Obama as FDR, smoking a cigarette, driving an open top car and looking very much as though he has nothing to fear but fear itself.[38]

In truth, Obama occasionally cautioned against reading too much of the New Deal into his own election and plans, but he did claim a transformative agenda nonetheless – raising hopes that he might be able to rebrand the Democratic party as the party fighting both social and racial inequality, and push through reforms that would generate support at the polls to lead to a new era of Democratic dominance.

If party polarization quickly dashed these hopes, additional factors made progressive presidential activism even more difficult for Obama. For one thing, the Democratic Party was riven by inner tensions that grew more intense over the course of Obama's presidency. Since the late 1980s, centrist Democrats – aka the "New Democrats" and embodied by Bill Clinton – have gained the upper hand in the party apparatus. In 2008, Hillary Clinton was the party establishment's choice candidate and Barack Obama succeeded in derailing Clinton's candidacy only by relying on a grassroots progressive mobilization that none among the party elites had seen coming. Notwithstanding this posture, Obama governed from the center, which explains why many on the left were disappointed with yet another "neoliberal centrist with a smile,"[39] to use Cornel West's dismissive assessment of Obama. Between 2008 and 2016, the Democratic Party thus experienced a growing discontent from rank-and-file members, who have found themselves more progressive than the party establishment. Considering that centrist party elites have maintained strong control over presidential selections and continue to play a strong kingmaker role in selecting candidates for congressional, state, and sometimes local down-ballot elections, the gap with the base has become worrisome. The party establishment can wield great power over candidates through access to data, donors, media, and get-out-the-vote resources. These various tools of control mean that the Democratic Party significantly shapes the spectrum of candidates that voters may choose from. Yet, as demonstrated by Bernie Sanders's 2016 presidential campaign and the attempt since the mid-2000s of liberal political action committees to mount primary challenges against conservative Democrats, many Democrats are unhappy.[40] The share of voters who describe themselves as leaning Democratic has included a growing percentage of self-described liberals – from 27 percent in 2000 to 41 percent in 2015, and this trend shows no sign of abating. Having lost its more conservative voters since the 1960s and, thus, having consolidated its membership as a more progressive voting bloc, the Democratic Party is confronted with a major challenge, since its establishment is now at odds with much of its base.[41] Meanwhile, the decline in union membership means that there are few pre-organized, get-out-the-vote groups at a scale that Democrats can rely on separate from the party. Neither Obama's charisma nor his "reconstructive" calls had sufficient weight to overcome such obstacles. To some observers, Jimmy Carter, Calvin Coolidge, or Harry Truman are – albeit for very different reasons – thus more adequate comparisons than FDR.[42]

The idea behind this volume emerged at an international conference held in Paris Diderot University in France a few weeks after Trump's November 2016 election.[43] By that time, the literature on Obama, his intellectual background, the historical hopes he raised as a charismatic figure, his record, and his legacy had already been an expanding field for quite some time. Many studies had been published as early as the end of his first term in 2012.[44] Since then, the amount of publications has kept growing,[45] despite the unending record of gaffes, malapropisms, and scandals of the Trump administration that already checks the overflowing field of "Obama studies." This backdrop brings out a stark gap between frequent references to progressive values and reforms on the one hand (inspired by Obama as a leader and a campaigner), and just as many numerous difficulties encountered by Obama the President, especially when Democratic allies in Congress were in the majority (see Obamacare), on the other hand. Should one read this, along with James Kloppenberg, as the unstoppable outcome of "stubborn features of American culture: persistent localism, distrust of the federal government, a deep ambivalence about engaging in world affairs, and a racism that appears nearly as entrenched in the 21st century as it was in the 18th, 19th, and 20th?"[46] Or, rather, should one advance the moderation and pragmatism of Obama and his team as a more plausible explanation – which can combine with Kloppenberg's analysis? Or, again, was this the result of party configuration, ranging from divisions with the Democratic party to the advent of the Tea Party as a powerful social movement?

To fully understand the forces at play, our initial insight was to establish a dialog between political historians and political scientists, which is the leading scientific take that drives this edited volume. Known in American academic debates as "American Political Development" (APD), this perspective seeks to establish a genuinely historical political science and emphasizes boundary-crossing between history and social sciences. Chapters in this volume often draw on social scientific questions, propositions, theories, and methods without any sacrifice of their grounding in the particularities of time and space. This is particularly the case with the chapters by Stephen Skowronek, Michael Kazin, Tom Sugrue, Elizabeth Shermer, and Nelson Lichtenstein. In all of them, particularity and contingency are read in an analytical vein. For scholars of APD and the larger field of historical institutionalism within which it is embedded, the linkage between actors and structures is provided mainly by institutions, both formal and informal, and best grasped by analysis of institutions. This orientation "takes time seriously" and aims at specifying sequences and at tracing transformations and processes of varying scale and temporality.[47] The dual emphasis on institutions and on temporal sequences is a general characteristic of our collection of essays. Furthermore, the latter collectively emphasize or highlight the limits of Obama's presidential power – and more largely of American presidential power in a polarized context. As a result, they also indirectly question the larger notion of the current "political order" – namely the set of ideas, public policies, and political alliances shaping American politics over a long-term period. Despite its initial momentum, the election of the first black president did not trigger a "new New Deal,"[48] even though all political assets were with him. As James Kloppenberg writes,

> Successful reformist presidents, from Abraham Lincoln, Theodore Roosevelt, and Woodrow Wilson through Franklin D. Roosevelt, enjoy[ed] solid majorities in both houses of Congress when they achieved their legislative triumphs (. . .); they [also] had at their disposal a combination of carrots and sticks to persuade reluctant congressmen to vote for the measures they proposed. *For a variety of reasons, none of those strategies has worked for the Obama administration.*"[49]

As we contend, one of these reasons is of an institutional nature: the Obama administration illustrated the limits of social change in a polarized context, when initiated from the Oval Office.

Looking essentially at domestic policy, the book encompasses a wide range of actors both at the grassroots and in the political sphere to explain why this widely anticipated moment of change and reform did not fully materialize. The Obama presidency, these essays collectively show, navigated partisan and institutional obstacles and quickly lost its 2008 momentum. Despite its initial successes with the 111th Congress, the administration was unable to pass other legislative achievements. Many of the fault lines of American society, including race relations of course, were largely left unaddressed, thus paving the way for the populist Trump campaign in 2016. This is explored in the three successive sections of the book, namely institutions, public policies, and movement politics.

The volume opens with the chapter by Stephen Skowronek, one of the political scientists who pioneered the study of APD.[50] He makes a theoretical case to analyze Obama's presidency within the framework of presidential leadership he delineated in the now classic *The Politics Presidents Make* (1993). There, he explains that each presidency is defined by its relationship to the established political order. According to him, presidents exercise power and authority to create ("reconstruction"), defend and innovate ("articulation"), oppose ("preemption"), or bankrupt and end ("disjunction") the order. Assessing the Obama presidency, he concludes here that it should be primarily understood as "a pretty standard second-round preemption," (see p. 43) trying to oppose the inherited conservative political order, but ultimately encased in it.[51] In other words, politics under Obama played out in a framework in which Republicans retained significant ideological, institutional and electoral advantages. Chapters 2, 3, and 4 then go on to elaborate on the institutional aspects of Obama's legacy. They all point to an administration that found it most difficult to enact its priorities and, when it eventually did, to protect them versus states or the judicial branch. Andrew Rudalevige explores the administrative tactics extensively used by Obama, especially after the 111th Congress and the ensuing legislative gridlock; he also underlines the mixed results of these administrative decisions in courts. Alix Meyer then shifts the emphasis on what he calls a "conducive coalition" in Congress that sometimes bypassed gridlock. Following Rothenberg's analysis in 2018,[52] Meyer contends that there has actually been some level of cooperation between Democrats and Republicans, beyond the infighting, which led notably to the adoption of a major budget deal (Ryan-Murray) and a consequential reform of entitlements (Medicare "doc-fix"). Next, Thad Kousser elaborates on the unintended devolution revolution that took place under the Obama presidency. Through a series of intertwined policy victories, political defeats, and judicial decisions, the path toward uniform federal standards promoted by the administration was blocked. As a consequence, states were more powerful by the end of the Obama presidency than they were when it began, thus showing the extent to which federalism can still impact national policy-making.

Chapters 5, 6, 7, and 8 deal with policy outcomes, and here again the administrative tools were front and center. Isabelle Vagnoux describes the various forces at play on immigration issues during Obama's eight years in office and the limits to his policy-making power in that field, arguing that Obama did actually challenge the immigration consensus despite the lack of a major immigration overhaul. Addressing a totally different domain, cyberspace and the security of network and information systems, Frédérick Douzet and Aude Géry press that these probably rank as the field that has undergone the most dramatic and rapid evolutions under the Obama administration, in the broader context of global cyber infighting, regulations, and preoccupations. Thomas Sugrue then takes us back to a more domestic issue, urban policy, by emphasizing the contrast between the scope and scale of the administration's urban programs compared to the magnitude of social, economic, and educational problems that metropolitan America faced. Sugrue underlines the part played by neoliberalism in the 1990s and 2000s, as well as Obama's own personal caution when it came to pushing pro-integration policies. Nelson Lichtenstein's chapter on healthcare reform underlines how the ACA (Affordable Care Act) is structured in a radically discordant and contradictory fashion, exhibiting both highly progressive levels of taxation, regulation, and planning along with neoliberal, market-centric mechanisms that leave intact many of the most dysfunctional trajectories inherent in American politics and political economy.

The last part of the book, Chapters 9 through 12, deals with "movement politics." A whole series of social movements stepped in to try and make up for the lack of success at the governmental level. This last part starts off with a piece by Michael Kazin on the left during Obama's presidency. This chapter shows the relative lack of impact movements like Occupy Wall Street and #BlackLivesMatter had during Obama's presidency. It also assesses the future of the American left from a grassroots perspective and concludes on a paradox. If the left was somehow impotent under Obama, President Trump and his policies may succeed where Obama failed: by fueling the rise of a sizable movement of "resistance" to the Republican administration and its policies. In their joint contribution, Audrey Célestine and Nicolas Martin-Breteau zoom in on one of these movements, #BlackLivesMatter. They argue that #BlackLivesMatter impacted American politics in a decisive fashion: if not by creating a mass movement, at least by redefining the nature of racial minorities' struggles by combining multiple claims inherited from a wide array of oppressions and contexts into one single movement. Turning to another facet of movement politics, David Bensman and Donna Kesselman then analyze the Obama administration's labor and employment legacy. Starting with the fact that Obama continued to embrace neoliberal policies throughout most of his presidency and repeatedly disappointed labor allies (Obama did not try to push the Employee Free Choice Act, although he had supported it in Congress; nor did he ever pay a visit to Wisconsin in 2011 when it became the main battleground between conservatives and public-sector employees), they also see a silver lining in that progressive countermovements pushed back against precarization: protests organized by the Occupy movement were followed by progressive denunciations of worsening economic inequality and by the mobilization of workers in the fast food, home-care and domestic work industries. Accordingly, the Obama administration fitfully began adopting programs that departed from neoliberal orthodoxy. This part concludes with a chapter by Elizabeth Shermer entitled "Why wasn't there a Twenty-First-Century 'New' New Deal? Historical

Perspectives for the Hope for and Reality of Obama's Presidency." In it, she tends to downplay the opposition between a successful Franklin Roosevelt and an embattled Barack Obama by showing how decades of research has now shown that FDR also struggled to preside the country. As a historian, she underlines how persistently poor accounts of the past and present have only fed the frustration not to say the rage of many Americans who have been promised but have not received a lot of immediate change.

Finally, in the coda to the volume, Sidney Milkis ponders on "Obama's Fractured Legacy." Taking a long view, he argues that Obama's legacy – and the threat the 2016 election and Trump's presidency poses to it – should be viewed as a new and highly disturbing episode in an ongoing contest between liberalism and conservatism – one that can be traced back to the 1960s, but one that took more definite shape during the George W. Bush and Obama presidencies. Assessing the different policy fields covered in this book, he reminds us how in some areas – like healthcare reform – the Obama administration did achieve victories, but in other areas his administration made much less headway, even if administrative action allowed the president to press his agenda unilaterally. A fitting paradox: Obama left the White House very popular – more so than many of his predecessors – but the election of Donald Trump raised doubts about the imprint his administration has left on American society and politics, especially considering that Trump's first instinct was to try and erase everything his predecessor had done. Milkis stresses how the causes of America's present discontents are best understood as the consequence of critical changes over the course of the past five decades that have transformed the US – once praised or criticized for its centrist politics and pragmatism – into a deeply divided country rattled by widespread dissatisfaction with government, strong and intensifying polarization, and high-stakes battles over the basic direction of domestic and foreign policy. Paradoxically, what Milkis calls the "rise of the Blue and Red nation" (see p. 391) might prove to be the more lasting legacy of the president who vowed to promote post-partisanship. It could even be argued that by advocating a "post-racial" order and surfing on its appeal, while presiding as a color-blind unifier, the first black president inadvertently and unwillingly left the old, subterraneous racial wounds of American society to simmer,[53] thereby paradoxically easing the way for Trump's victory in 2016. To some extent, it may be that the first black president begot, as Ta-Nehisi Coates wrote in *The Atlantic*, the first "White" President.[54]

Notes

1. "Obama describes his bond with Jay Z," *The Washington Post*, June 16, 2017. Available at: https://www.washingtonpost.com/ gdpr-consent/?destination=%2fnews%2fmorning-mix%2fwp%2f 2017%2f06%2f16%2fobama-describes-his-bond-to-jay-z%2f%3f (accessed August 2019).

2. "Jay Z explains meaning behind Barack Obama 'History' Song," *NME*, January 21, 2009. Available at https://www.nme.com/news/ music/jay-z-135-1317967 (last accessed on April 8, 2019). Jay Z explained: "You know, if you listen to the record it's pretty much talking about trying to find victory, victory being a woman, and so me and victory can make a kid – the kid being history, and then history tells your legacy. It's deep but it's fun. It's not really that complicated."

3. The first black president seemed to fulfill, at least symbolically, the promises of Lyndon Johnson's Great Society. Obama's personal storytelling and his advocacy of a "post-racial" society were based on the integration of values and codes inherited from the civil rights struggles of the 1960s, as illustrated by his 1995 autobiography, *Dreams From My Father*. He also willingly displayed his sense of belonging to the black community by ticking the "Black/ African-American" box in the 2010 Census.

4. See Thomas J. Sugrue, *Not Even Past, Barack Obama and the Burden of Race* (Princeton, NJ: Princeton University Press, 2009), 13–15.

5. Barack Obama's Remarks in Saint Paul, *The New York Times*, June 3, 2008. Available at: https://www.nytimes.com/2008/06/03/us/ politics/03text-obama.html (accessed August 2019).

6. William Jones, "Obama's New Deal," November 13, 2008. Available at: https://www.thenation.com/article/obamas-new-deal/ (accessed August 2019).

7. John Judis, "America the Liberal," *The New Republic*, November 19, 2008. Available at: https://newrepublic.com/article/60995/ america-the-liberal (accessed August 2019).

8. Obama's days as a community organizer are recounted at length in *Dreams From My Father*. On Alinsky's principles see his *Rules for Radicals: A Pragmatic Primer for Realistic Radicals* (New York: Random House, 1971). See also Barack Obama, "Why Organize? Problems and Promise in the Inner City" in *After Alinsky: Community Organizing in Illinois*, Illinois Issues, Springfield, University of Illinois, 1990. Available at: http://garifunacoalition.org/yahoo_site_admin/ assets/docs/WhyOrganize-BarackObama.143111756.pdf (accessed August 2019). More generally, for Obama's relationship to Alinsky's legacy, see Ryan Lizza, "The Agitator: Barack Obama's Unlikely Political Education," *The New Republic*, March 19, 2007. Available at: https://newrepublic.com/article/61068/the-agitator-barack-obamas-unlikely-political-education (accessed August 2019). Chicago, Obama recalled later, was where he received "his best political education," and although he grew disillusioned with the potential for change it offered – he entered Harvard Law School in 1988 – he remained committed to organizing, leading a voter registration drive in 1992 that served as the basis for his first campaign in 1996. Notably, Obama at the time argued that there was no contradiction between his electoral ambitions and his past experience as an organizer. "What if a politician were to see his job as that of an organizer, as part teacher and part advocate, one who does not sell voters short but who educates them about the real choices before them? As an elected public official, for instance, I could bring church and community leaders together easier than I could as a community organizer or lawyer," he explained in 1995 in an interview with the *Chicago Reader*.

9. Barack Obama, *The Audacity of Hope* (New York: Crown Publishing, 2006), 38–39. See E. J Dionne, *Why Americans Hate Politics* (New York: Simon and Schuster, 1991).

10. Cass Sustein, "The Visionary Minimalist", *The New Republic*, January 29, 2008. Available at: https://newrepublic.com/article/ 62229/the-visionary-minimalist (accessed August 2019).

11. Richard H. Thaler and Cass R. Sunstein, *Improving Decisions about Health, Wealth, and Happiness* (New Haven, CT: Yale University Press, 2008). See also Robert Kuttner, "The Radical Minimalist," *The American Prospect*, March 19, 2009. Available at: https://prospect .org/article/radical-minimalist (accessed August 2019).

12. Barbara Sinclair, "Obama and the 111th Congress: Doing Big Things," pp. 198–222, in Bert Rockman, Andrew Rudalevige, and Colin Campbell (eds.), *The Obama Presidency: Appraisals and Prospects* (Washington, DC: CQ Press, 2012).

13. Stephen Skowronek (2014), "Twentieth Century Remedies," *Boston Law Review*, 94: 795. Theodore Lowi, *The Personal President: Power Invested, Promise Unfulfilled* (Ithaca, NY: Cornell University Press, 1985).

14. Bruce Ackerman, *We The People: Foundations* (Cambridge, MA: Belknap Press, 1995).

15. William Leuchtenburg, *In the Shadow of FDR: From Harry Truman to Ronald Reagan* (Ithaca, NY: Cornell University Press, 1983); Theodore Lowi, *The Personal President*.

16. During the nomination battle, Obama campaigned on the left, which allowed him to break all the calculations by the party establishment in favor of yet another Clinton.

17. Quote available at: https://www.npr.org/templates/story/story.php?storyId=96663680&t=1566764093129 (accessed August 2019).

18. Samuel Tanenhaus, "Conservatism is Dead," *The New Republic*, February 18, 2009. Available at: https://newrepublic.com/article/61721/conservatism-dead (accessed August 2019). Tanenhaus went on to explain that the conservative tradition in the US had been replaced by a "movement conservatism," which "defines itself not by what it yearns to conserve but by what it longs to destroy – 'statist' social programs; 'socialized medicine'; 'big labor'; 'activist' Supreme Court Justices, the 'media elite'; 'tenured radicals' on university faculties; 'experts' in and out of government.' Trump's victory in 2016 largely vindicated this early assessment.

19. See for instance Robert Kuttner, *Obama's Challenge: America's Economic Crisis and the Power of a Transformative Presidency* (White River Junction, VT: Chelsea Green Publishing, 2008).

20. Andrew Rudalevige, *The New Imperial Presidency* (Anne Arbor: University of Michigan Press, 2005). See also, Steven G. Calabresi and Christopher S. Yoo, *The Unitary Executive: Presidential Power from Washington to Bush* (New Haven, CT: Yale University Press, 2008). Domestically, Bush presided over a vast expansion of national and presidential powers: from education (No Child Left Behind in 2002) to Medicare (creation of "part D" in 2003), including of course anti-terrorism (Patriot Act in 2002); his domestic record was clearly the result of governmental activism. But, as always, American presidents are systematically stronger in the field of foreign relations. The Bush presidency confirmed the classic "two-presidencies" thesis by A. Wildavski (1966) in that presidential outreach was much more successful in foreign affairs: Congress basically agreed to grant Bush

carte blanche in the run-up to the 2003 Iraq War, in the War against Terror, and in the invasion of Afghanistan.

21. On this hazy and flexible notion by definition, see Lawrence J. Grossback, David A. M. Peterson, and James A. Stimson, *Mandate Politics* (New York: Cambridge University Press, 2nd ed. 2012).

22. All the more so that any Republican who strayed from the party line faced the threat of a primary challenge from the Tea Party.

23. Julian Zelier "Tea-Partied: President Obama's Encounters with the Conservative-Industrial Complex," pp. 11–29, in Julian Zelizer (ed.), *The Presidency of Barack Obama: A First Historical Assessment* (Princeton, NJ: Princeton University Press, 2018).

24. S. Skowronek, "Twentieth-Century Remedies", *art. cit.*; with Karen Orren, *The Policy State: An American Predicament* (Cambridge, MA: Harvard University Press, 2017).

25. Ira Katznelson, *Fear Itself: The New Deal and the Origins of Our Time* (New York: W. W. Norton & Company, 2013).

26. John Sides and Daniel Hopkins, *Political Polarization in American Politics* (New York: Bloomsbury, 2015); Alan Abramowitz, *The Disappearing Center: Engaged Citizens, Polarization and American Democracy* (New Haven, CT: Yale University Press, 2010) and *The Polarized Public: Why American Government is So Dysfunctional* (New York: Pearson Longman, 2013); see also his most recent, *The Great Alignment: Race, Party Transformation and the Rise of Donald Trump* (New Haven, CT: Yale University Press, 2019).

27. Obama's keynote during the Democratic Convention in Boston in 2004 was the first well-known statement of this "post-partisan" behavior.

28. Gerald N. Rosenberg, *The Hollow Hope. Can Courts Bring about Social Change?* (Chicago: Chicago University Press, 2nd ed. 2008).

29. John M. Blum, *Progressive Presidents: Theodore Roosevelt, Woodrow Wilson, Franklin D. Roosevelt* (New York: W. W. Norton, 1980).

30. Arthur M. Schlesinger Jr., *The Imperial Presidency* (Boston, MA: Houghton Mifflin Co., 2nd ed. 2004), pp. 254–255.

31. Theodore Lowi, *The Personal President*, p. 99. For a more historical account making a similar case, see Sidney M. Milkis, *The President and the Parties. The Transformation of the American Party System since the New Deal* (New York: Oxford University Press, 1993).

32. Richard E. Neustadt, *Presidential Power and the Modern Presidents. The Politics of Leadership from Roosevelt to Reagan* (New York: Simon and Schuster, 2nd ed. 1990), p. 32.

33. See for instance: James McGregor Burns, *Presidential Government: The Crucible of Presidential Leadership* (Boston, MA: Houghton Mifflin, 1965) and his *Leadership* (New York: Open Road, 1978); Fred Greenstein, *The Hidden-Hand Presidency* (New York: Basic Books, 1982) and *Leadership in the Modern Presidency*, ed., (Cambridge, MA: Harvard University Press, 1988); Samuel Kernell, *Going Public: New Strategies of Presidential Leadership* (Seattle: Washington Press, 1987).

34. See for instance the works by George C. Edwards III: *At the Margins: Presidential Leadership of Congress* (New Haven, CT: Yale University Press, 1990), *On Deaf Ears: The Limits of the Bully Pulpit* (New Haven, CT: Yale University Press, 2006), *The Strategic President: Persuasion and Opportunity in Presidential Leadership* (Princeton, NJ: Princeton University Press, 2012), and *Overreach. Leadership in the Obama Presidency* (Princeton, NJ: Princeton University Press, 2012).

35. Edwards, *Overreach*, p. 2.

36. Ibid., p. 5.

37. Ibid., p. 180.

38. "Lexington," *The Economist,* November 20, 2008. Indeed, "the new New Deal—What Barack Obama can learn from F.D.R.—and what Democrats need to do" was the feature story in the *Time* magazine issue of November 24, 2008.

39. Thomas Frank interview with Cornel West, *Salon*, August 24, 2014. Available at: https://www.salon.com/2014/08/24/cornel_west_he_posed_as_a_progressive_and_turned_out_to_be_counterfeit_we_ended_up_with_a_wall_street_presidency_a_drone_presidency/ (accessed June 2018).

40. Moveon.org, and many smaller organizations, began targeting primaries in the mid-2000s. The Progressive Change Campaign Committee, a progressive political action committee threatening more conservative Democrats with primary challengers, grew out of the 2011 Occupy movement. One indicator of Democratic Party strength, however, is that the party faces fewer primary challenges and fewer successful challenges than Republicans. See Robert Boatright, *Getting Primaries: The Changing Politics of Congressional Primary Challenges* (Ann Arbor: University of Michigan Press, 2013).

41. For more on the Democratic Party's consolidation of policy into a more progressive force, see Pew Research Center, "Political Polarization in the American Public," Pew Research Center, June 12, 2014. Available

at: http://www.people-press.org/2014/06/12/political-polarization-in-the-american-public/ (accessed August 2019).

42. Michael Kazin, "Obama is Good Company: All Presidents End Up Unpopular," *New Republic*, August 20, 2011. Available at: https://newrepublic.com/article/93961/failed-presidents-obama-history (accessed August 2019).

43. The Paris December 2016 international symposium, organized by the two authors of this introduction, was entitled "Obama's Legacy: Tensions and Reconfigurations After the Presidential Elections." This three-day event gathered some forty scholars from both sides of the Atlantic and obtained both French (*région Ile de France, Institut des Amériques, Sciences-Po*) and American (German Marshall Fund, Stanford University, US Embassy in Paris) financial support.

44. See among others: William Crotty (ed.), *The Obama Presidency: Promise and Performance* (Lanham, MD: Lexington Books, 2012); Gary Dorrien, *The Obama Question: A Progressive Perspective* (Lanham, MD: Rowman and Littlefield, 2012); James T. Kloppenberg, *Reading Obama: Dreams, Hope, and the American Political Tradition* (Princeton, NJ: Princeton University Press, 2012); Baodong Liu, *The Election of Barack Obama. How He Won* (New York: Palgrave Macmillan, 2010); Bert Rockman, Andrew Rudalevige, and Colin Campbell (eds.), *The Obama Presidency: Appraisals and Prospects* (Washington, DC: CQ Press, 2012); Theda Skocpol and Lawrence R. Jacobs, *Reaching for a New Deal: Ambitious Governance, Economic Meltdown, and Polarized Politics in Obama's First Two Years* (New York: Russell Sage, 2011); Theda Skocpol et al., *Obama and America's Political Future* (Cambridge, MA: Harvard University Press, 2012); Michael Tesler and David O. Sears, *Obama's Race: The 2008 Election and the Dream of a Post-Racial America* (Chicago: University of Chicago Press, 2010); Robert Watson et al. (eds.), *The Obama Presidency: A Preliminary Assessment* (Albany, NY: State University of New York Press, 2012); Pauline Peretz (ed.), *L'Amérique post-raciale?* (Paris : Presses Universitaires de France, 2013); Olivier Richomme and Vincent Michelot (eds.), *Le bilan d'Obama* (Paris: Presses de Sciences-Po, 2012).

45. See for instance: Edward Ashbee and John Dumbrell, *The Obama Presidency and the Politics of Change* (New York: Palgrave Macmillan, 2016); John David Graham, *Obama on the Home Front. Domestic Policy Triumphs and Setbacks* (Bloomington: Indiana University Press, 2016); Bert Rockman and Andrew Rudalevige (eds.), *The Obama Legacy* (Lawrence: University Press of Kansas, 2019); Louis Fisher,

President Obama Constitutional Aspirations and Executive Actions (Lawrence: University Press of Kansas, 2018); Steven E. Schier (ed.), *Debating the Obama Presidency* (Lanham, MD: Rowman & Littlefield, 2016); Michael Tesler, *Post-Racial or Most-Racial? Race and Politics in the Obama Era* (Chicago: Chicago University Press, 2016); Julian Zelizer (ed.), *The Presidency of Barack Obama: A First Historical Assessment* (Princeton, NJ: Princeton University Press, 2018).

46. James T. Kloppenberg, "Barack Obama and the Traditions of Progressive Reform," pp. 431–452, in Stephen Skowronek, Stephen M. Engel, and Bruce Ackerman (eds.), *The Progressives' Century. Political Reform, Constitutional Government, and the Modern American State* (New Haven, CT: Yale University Press, 2016). Quote p. 432.

47. Paul Pierson and Theda Skocpol, "Historical Institutionalism in Contemporary Political Science," pp. 693–721, in Ira Katznelson and Helen V. Millner (eds.), *Political Science: State of the Discipline* (New York: W. W. Norton, 2002). See also Ira Katznelson, "The Possibilities of Analytical Political History," pp. 381–400, in Meg Jacobs, William J. Novak, and Julian E. Zelizer (eds.), *The Democratic Experiment* (Princeton, NJ: Princeton University Press, 2003). See also the recent Richard M. Vallely, Suzanne Mettler, and Robert C. Lieberman (eds.), *The Oxford Handbook of American Political Development* (New York: Oxford University Press, 2016); especially the introduction by Suzanne Mettler and Richard M. Vallely, "The Distinctiveness and Necessity of American Political Development," pp. 7–24.

48. Michael Grunwald, *The New New Deal. The Hidden Story of Change in the Obama Era* (New York: Simon and Schuster, 2012).

49. James Kloppenberg, "Barack Obama and the Traditions of Progressive Reform," pp. 442–443; emphasis added.

50. Stephen Skowronek, *Building a New American State: The Expansion of National Administrative Capacities, 1877–1920* (Cambridge: Cambridge University Press, 1982).

51. Previous "preempting presidents" include people such as Dwight Eisenhower and Bill Clinton who exploited divisions within the established order.

52. Lawrence S. Rothenberg, "Policy Success in an Age of Gridlock," (Cambridge University Press, online series *Elements in American Politics*, July 2018). DOI: https://doi.org/10.1017/9781108628044

53. Fredrick Harris, *The Price of the Ticket: Barack Obama and Rise and Decline of Black Politics* (New York: Oxford University Press, 2012).
54. Ta-Nehisi Coates, "The First White President," *The Atlantic*, October 2017. Available at: https://www.theatlantic.com/ magazine/archive/2017/10/the-first-white-president-ta-nehisi-coates/537909/ (accessed August 2019).

Part 1

INSTITUTIONS

Barack Obama and the promise of transformative leadership

Stephen Skowronek

The movement candidate of 2008, Barack Obama mobilized voters behind a promise to transform America. Once in office, however, that promise became a rallying cry for a counter-mobilization against him. Conservatives rehabilitated their own movement by casting Obama as a threat to the nation's core values. They stymied his administration and used his alleged heresies to rework their old orthodoxies. At the end of his second term, Obama tried to leverage his still considerable popularity in an effort to pass power on to a chosen successor. But a candidate promising a very different kind of transformation built a movement of his own in 2016, and he trounced Obama's designated heir in the election. In transformational leadership 2.0, the first order of business was to erase everything that Obama accomplished.

So what are we to make of these two leaders, Barack Obama and Donald Trump, each peddling transformative leadership? Did either face a problem so serious that only fundamental changes could save the nation? Did they bring to office resources sufficient to effect change on that scale? Is change of that sort more feasible today from the right than it was yesterday from the left? These are the large questions hovering over Obama's political legacy. This first chapter will address them schematically, sorting through various historical dimensions of the situation.

Donald Trump's administration is virtually synonymous with his promise of a "great disruption," but that goes with the territory. The rise of a new president is always a disruptive event; every president intrudes upon the status quo and shakes things up; no president leaves American government and politics as they found it. Presidents disrupt things simply by setting up their own administration. Talk of transformation is, at least in part, prompted by the need to rationalize the inherently disruptive effects of exercising the powers of this office. Still, very few presidents become transformational.

The problem is that the presidential office is not very well equipped to control the meaning and political effect of the changes its incumbents set in motion. Getting things done is not their biggest problem. The hard part is convincing the nation of the legitimacy of the innovations made. To paraphrase Lincoln, people must buy into the president's definition of where Americans are as a nation and whither the country is tending. That means keeping people aligned with the president's view of the situation even as he changes it. As it turns out, the strongest political leaders in the American presidency, those who have had the most durable political impact, have been those, like Lincoln, who came closest to doing just that. And it is surely no coincidence that these are also the presidents who effected the most sweeping transformations in government and politics.

The paradox of presidential leadership – call it the Lincoln paradox – is that presidents are better able to control the meaning and political effects of change when they change just about everything. By reconstructing government and politics fundamentally, they marginalize those who would hold an alternative view, compelling their deference and setting a new standard of legitimacy. The most recent president to do something close to that was Ronald Reagan. The "Reagan Revolution" virtually expunged the word "liberal" from legitimate political discourse and brought a durable anti-tax, anti-government regime to power.

For people who study political leadership, the challenge is to figure out why some presidents are better able to do this than others and to think through the political consequences of success and shortfall. In a sense, this task is not unlike that of presidents themselves. Academics, observers, and analysts too are in the business of trying to tell time, to specify the long-running political patterns or historical currents that frame particular episodes and to draw insights from the ways in which these different currents interact in new combinations. In this chapter, I will stick with this macro historical/structural perspective, pointing to various currents that constructed Obama's historical moment and converged in a particular configuration.[1]

Political time, secular time and divergent expectations

All episodes in the politics of presidential leadership can be situated within two broad temporal frames. I call the first "political time." Political time refers to presidency-driven sequences of political change in which incumbents bid to define a compelling political project for themselves in reaction to the work of their predecessors. In the post-Reagan era, as in all prior sequences, we find two types of leaders: there are affiliated leaders like the two Bushes, presidents who affirmed the commitments and vitality of the Reagan Revolution and who pledged to continue, to extend, and to update the received agenda; and there are opposition leaders like Bill Clinton and Barack Obama. They preempted the conservative agenda, tried to exploit stresses and strains within the coalition that supported it, and tested the possibilities for reconstructing political priorities altogether. Affiliated leaders try to exercise the powers of the presidential office in their own right without betraying orthodoxy; opposition leaders challenge orthodoxy and try to broaden support for something else.

Candidates reach the presidency by providing a compelling account of their place in sequences like these, but they are not always comfortable with the boundaries of the situation they fashion for themselves. Bill Clinton, the fabled master of triangulation, found his leadership position exasperating, exclaiming at one point, "I hope you're all aware we're all Eisenhower Republicans."[2] He was referring back to the prior sequence, the New Deal sequence. Eisenhower was the first president elected in opposition to FDR's transformation of priorities. Clinton, the first Democrat to come to power since Reagan's reconstruction of priorities, was analogizing the constraints of his own situation to Eisenhower's by pointing back to the relative weakness of the alternative that Eisenhower was able to muster. He was thinking in political time.

But as presidential leadership unfolds in political time and the nation drifts away from the priorities stamped on government by last reconstruction, opportunities change. Affiliated leaders characteristically find it harder to hold the old regime together, and they act out increasingly convoluted renditions of orthodoxy. By the same token, opposition leaders find that they can mount more direct and fundamental challenges. Orthodox innovators and heterodox preemptors push and pull at the old formulas in this way. Together they drive American politics to flashpoints wherein a nominal affiliate of an old and fractured regime gets caught in a crisis that seals the opposition's case against the old orthodoxy. Characteristically, the old order falls apart from within, imploding under the hapless leadership of a late-regime affiliate. That crisis of legitimacy is disjunctive: it exposes the old priorities as bankrupt and old governing formulas as the very source of the nation's problems. It opens the door to an opposition leader who can finally forthrightly repudiate received commitments of ideology and interest, redefine the terms and conditions of legitimate national government, and reset the clock. These dynamics recur over the course of American political history. Political time accounts for that curious juxtaposition of incumbents – Adams and Jefferson, Adams and Jackson, Buchanan and Lincoln, Hoover and Roosevelt, Carter and Reagan – the first in each pair, an affiliated leader who appeared paralyzed and incompetent in political action; the next an opposition leader who stands out from the pack as a transformative leader and undisputed master of the leadership arts.

Presidents also act in "secular time." Whereas political time cycles, linking the experiences of presidents in different historical periods as they sought to lead at similar junctures in a political sequence, secular time registers the differences between leadership today and leadership in earlier eras. Secular time describes a universe of presidential action which has grown progressively more inclusive in its interests and purview, more interdependent in its operations, thicker in its institutional environment, and more reliant on central management. As we might expect, developments in secular time complicate the rhythms of political time. Affiliated leaders will find their leadership position bolstered by enhanced powers of their office in agenda setting, central management, and political mobilization. With more resources for independent action, they will find themselves less constrained by old orthodoxies and affiliation with received commitments. Opposition leaders, on the other hand, will find their efforts to challenge the established order hampered by the newfound interdependence of interests. In that regard, secular time would appear to dim the prospects for any abrupt repudiation or wholesale transformation of the terms and conditions of legitimate national government.

It is no accident that the clearest exemplars of reconstructive or transformative leadership are nineteenth-century incumbents – Jackson and Lincoln – presidents who in Bank Battle and in Civil War decisively dismantled the political and institutional supports for the politics of the past and reworked the foundations of government and politics. The twentieth-century exemplars of the type were less successful in marginalizing resistance and the results were notably messier: Franklin Roosevelt was defeated in his battle with the Court, defeated in his reorganization initiative, and defeated in his party purge. The Reagan reconstruction proved even less effective at displacing the programmatic commitments of the old order and configuring institutions. It was left instead to rework political coalitions, governmental priorities, and ideological advantage.

My interests lie here, in these contretemps of political and secular time. These two ticking clocks can be employed to think through the current juncture. We can begin with political time. If we superimpose the most recent sequence of presidents – the sequence which followed upon the Carter disjunction and the Reagan reconstruction – on the prior sequence – the one that followed upon the Hoover disjunction and the New Deal reconstruction – we will find that they align remarkably well. In both, the transformative leader passed power to an affiliate. After that there was an opposition victory, a first preemption; next, there was a second round of orthodox innovation, and then a second preemption. There is nothing iron clad about this; the post-Civil War sequence was more complicated. But the general patterns hold. If we reach back further still, we find that the sequence of presidents that followed upon John Quincy Adams's disjunction and the Jacksonian reconstruction followed the same rotation as the two most recent ones. On this grid, then, Barack Obama falls in a fairly standard line of rotation between affiliates preaching orthodox innovation and opposition leaders testing the strength of the established orthodoxy and the prospects for breaking free of it. His position as a second-round preemptor is a good starting point for assessing his leadership. His historical counterparts set a baseline of expectations against which we can identify deviations and developments of special note.

Before moving on, the tensions and contradictions implicit in these two frames of action should be underscored. Consider in this regard changes in the presidency inaugurated by American progressives in the early decades of the twentieth century. On the one side, the progressives set out to generalize the examples of Jackson and Lincoln. Indeed, Theodore Roosevelt celebrated what he called the "Jackson-Lincoln school" of leadership, elevating it into a national standard for judging all presidents.[3] The Jackson-Lincoln school taught that to be successful, a president must capitalize on the unique political capacities of office to break through the gridlock of constitutional constraints. Henry Jones Ford, a protégé of Woodrow Wilson, spoke similarly of tapping the potential power of the presidency to "extricate government from the control of established interests."[4] Accordingly, the progressive formulation carried with it heightened expectations for presidency-induced political change; the idea was that *every* president could and should reach to the foundations and try to transform the system, that Jackson and Lincoln should set the aspirations for all presidents. This idea took concrete institutional form in the gradual displacement of party conventions by primaries for the selection of presidential candidates and in the development of "presidential parties," personalized coalitions of intense policy demanders unmediated by strong organs of collective control and responsibility.

A second innovation of the progressive era looked in a different direction. The idea was that the presidency, not the Congress, should serve as the locus of responsible problem solving for the nation at large; that the presidency, not the Congress, should become "policy central" in service to all. Progressives wanted to expand the range of interests incorporated into government, to construct new tools of overhead management, to cast the president as a rational processor of expertise, and master orchestrator of national interests and institutions. They imagined the president as a policy entrepreneur who would foster coordination and collaboration among the several parts of government and negotiate pragmatic adjustments as needed in the national interest. This idea took concrete institutional form in creation of technocratic tools for overhead management in the Executive Office of the President.

In other words, the "modern presidency" has jumbled together idealized portraits of action in both political and secular time – at once routinizing the promise of transformative action and heightening expectations for managerial responsibility. On the one hand, we have created presidential parties to allow leaders to more forcefully disrupt and thoroughly transform the system, mobilizing voters to extricate interests and shake up the powers that be. On the other hand, we have created technocratic offices to encourage leaders to adjust interests to issues as they arise, to manage policy central for the government as a whole, to attend to best practice and make the system work. It has never been entirely clear how the competing demands posed along these two dimensions of action were to be reconciled with one another – how heightened expectations of mobilizing interests and targeting foundations would align with heightened expectations for responsible problem solving and political cooperation. Oddly enough, the assumption seemed to be that these ambitions were all one and the same.

In 2016, however, these ambitions came at us in starkly contrasting candidate caricatures – Hillary Clinton and Donald Trump – one all about problem solving and responsible management, the other all about populist mobilization and the great disruption. The incongruity has become glaring, as have the difficulties presented on both sides. It might not be too much to suggest that the contretemps of political time and secular time have put the modern presidency at cross purposes and that they are working to tear the nation itself apart.

Obama in political time

These various patterns and the political dynamics associated with them can be used to pull Obama's leadership more clearly into focus. The first, and to me the most striking, point is that political time still seems be doing a lot of the work. If the secular thickening of governmental affairs is having an effect, and I will suggest later how it might, the standard historical rhythms of presidency-driven regime change are still clearly in evidence. The clock at work in Obama's leadership was telling political time.

As I indicated with reference to Bill Clinton's frustration in feeling like Eisenhower, political time frames actions and their effects, not leadership as the president might wish it to be. There is no mistaking how Obama *presented* his case to the nation. He said explicitly he wanted to do for progressives what Ronald Reagan had done for conservatives. Indeed, he said he preferred the Reagan model of leadership to that of fellow Democratic Bill Clinton. Obama distinguished himself from Hillary Clinton as the movement candidate in the 2008 presidential race, setting himself against ideological trimming and triangulation and mobilizing voters around the prospect of delivering something of more historic proportions. He said the goal should be to "change [. . .] the trajectory" of national affairs, to put government and politics on a "new foundation," to "fundamentally transform [. . .] the United States of America." He launched his campaign on the capitol steps in Springfield, Illinois and, standing where Lincoln had stood, he urged the American people to grasp the standard of the great reconstructive leaders. That was a "change we can believe in."[5]

Obama had a keen sense of history, but this does not mean that analysts should take his rhetoric at face value. As indicated, the rhetoric of transformative leadership has been routinized in modern campaigns by progressive expectations for leadership. It is a commonplace by-product of the presidential parties of our day, a reflection of the efforts of candidates from the same party to differentiate themselves from one another and mobilize reform energies behind a personal brand. All that was clearly evident in Obama's effort to distinguish himself from Hillary Clinton in the 2008 primaries. So while Obama won a decisive victory, one that confirmed his party's majorities in both houses of Congress, we need to look beyond rhetoric. Taking the full measure of the situation in which he found himself, we might well ask whether this really was a transformative moment.

There is reason for doubt. On a strict reading of leadership in political time, Obama was a second-round opposition leader taking advantage of newfound stresses and strains on the political appeal of conservative orthodoxy as George W. Bush had rendered it. Looking at prior sequences, this would align Obama's leadership with the likes of Richard Nixon in the liberal era following the New Deal and Woodrow Wilson in the long Republican era following the Civil War. Note that Nixon delivered a more potent and sweeping indictment of the orthodoxy of the liberal era than had Dwight Eisenhower, and that Wilson delivered a more potent and sweeping indictment of the orthodoxy of the Republican era than had Grover Cleveland. So it should come as no surprise that Obama delivered a more potent and sweeping indictment of conservative orthodoxy than had Bill Clinton. The rhetoric of transformation signaled Obama's intent to deliver a more significant change than Clinton had, but the question remains: how far could he push? Neither Wilson nor Nixon delivered a decisive, knock-out blow to the previously established regime. In fact, no second-round opposition leader has been able to do that. In each case, these leaders quickly found that they were dealing with a still-resilient establishment, one that was down but not out, strained but not broken, threatened but able to bounce back and challenge the legitimacy of the interloper. It may be that Obama's promise of transformation was the one thing capable of snapping the battered ranks of conservatives back together in a last-ditch defense of their hold over the terms and conditions of legitimate national government.

Note as well how Obama's case for transformative action was further complicated by his status as the first African-American nominee, for that distinction argued strongly against pushing any direct connection between transformative ambitions and a frontal assault on the legitimacy of the establishment. An inspiring symbol of a more inclusive America, Obama was astute enough to strip the promise of transformation of any hint of repudiating anyone or anything. As bad as things had gotten under George W. Bush, Obama wisely steered clear of the historic equation of transformative leadership with a great disruption and a frontal assault on foundations. This muddied his intentions considerably, but Republican incompetence and insensitivity were safer charges for Obama to level against Republican rule than illegitimacy. When the federal response to Hurricane Katrina in 2005 faltered, a movement to make American government more effective gained wide appeal. Beyond that, Obama could ride a wave of anti-war sentiment, carefully parsing distinctions between the good Afghan War and the bad Iraq War.

What, then, about the system-shocking events of the final months of Bush's second term? There is no denying that the financial crisis which erupted late in 2008 left the foundations of conservative orthodoxy fully exposed. The meltdown threatened the whole of the national economy and in the process it opened the Republican establishment and its governing formulas to direct repudiation as the very source of the nation's problems. From the perspective of political time, however, the most significant feature of that crisis was precisely that it broke so late in the Bush presidency. Conservatives lost power before they themselves were forced to grapple at length with the failure of their governing formulas in the face of the crisis. They never had to stew in events that had exposed their regime's foundations. James Buchanan did. Herbert Hoover did. Jimmy Carter did. George W. Bush did not. As a consequence, conservatives never bore the political cost of trying to negotiate a path out of the crisis, a cost sure to be extracted at the level of core ideological commitments, programmatic pretensions, and political credibility. If political time tells us anything, it is that old orders disintegrate first from within by revealing their own incompetence in the exercise of power. Without a disjunction of that sort, there is no reconstruction.

Once in office, President Obama tried his best to lay the financial collapse at the doorstep of a Republican establishment. He blasted Republican mismanagement and inattention saying, "they drove our car into the ditch," that they left us with the "largest worldwide economic crisis since the Great Depression."[6] But unlike Franklin Roosevelt, Obama did not ride to power on the back of four years of Republican bungling, self-incrimination, and political implosion; there was no compelling public demonstration that their responses to the financial crisis were empty and bankrupt. Moreover, unlike Roosevelt, who in 1932 had refused to collaborate with Hoover in emergency response, Obama could not say that he came into office as a president with "clean hands."[7] On the contrary, he went to Washington in the last weeks of the Bush administration to enlist his party's support for the Republican president's emergency response legislation. In effect, Obama made the financial crisis a national problem, not a regime problem. So there was no disjunctive event, and short of that, conservatives retained the wherewithal to regroup and rebound. Indeed, they targeted Obama's own response to the economic crisis as misguided and inadequate, and they delivered a stunning blow to his leadership in the 2010 midterm. The absence of a disjunctive episode meant that Obama's opposition would remain preemptive.

Reading these events in political time, one is not led to conclude that Obama is a failed reconstructive leader. It would appear, rather, that he was dealt a relatively weak hand for a transformation of that sort. Nor is there much evidence that he wanted to play his hand that way. It is not what he failed to do that tells the tale in this regard, it is what he did. Notwithstanding his criticisms of Bill Clinton, the preemptive mode of opposition leadership was in full view from the very start of his administration, even in the first two years with Democratic majorities in Congress most fully supportive of his ambitions. The standard here is not the amount of legislation enacted. All presidents get a lot of things done, and so did this one. The hallmark of preemptive leadership is the advance of an opposition agenda that skirts the foundations of the old order. The preemptive style was evident in Obama's choice of a Clinton-era team with strong Wall Street ties to map his response to the financial crisis. It was evident in the selection of his primary opponent, Hillary Clinton, to head foreign policy at the State Department. It tells in his reluctance to go after the banks in financial reform even with the Occupy movement at his back. It registers in his retreat from the promise to end the wars in Afghanistan and Iraq. It fits his initial reluctance to go after the gun lobby and his embarrassing retreat from proposed gun controls, and it explains his efforts to solicit political support for immigration reform by accelerating the deportation of the undocumented.

The preemptive mode of opposition leadership is evident even in the administration's signature political departure, healthcare reform. Obama took the template for that proposal from a plan previously put forth by the Republicans. He assembled a grand coalition of all interests in the healthcare industry and pulled his movement supporters kicking and screaming behind an initiative that grew to be as complicated as it was ambitious. There was no assault on established institutions, no thought of starting afresh with the single-payer plan, and a potential opening to that goal, the public option, was quickly dropped. Obama's program was engineered to lay on top of healthcare arrangements already in place and to do so with as little disruption to those arrangements as possible. This was a big change, a major policy achievement, but it was not transformational, at least not as political transformation has been expressed historically. It is true Obama succeeded where other preemptive leaders have failed. These leaders usually find their signature programs defeated outright. Think about Cleveland and the tariff, about Wilson and the League, about Clinton and healthcare. But on this count Obama is the exception that proves the rule, for conservatives never accepted the legitimacy of his healthcare program. They began agitating for its repeal as soon as it was enacted, and President Trump put it first on the chopping block in the new administration.

For preemptive leaders the battle to define the situation is fierce and the situation volatile. Defenders of the old orthodoxy can still regroup even as the opposition leader exploits the vulnerabilities of their agenda. The president is taunting and goading a weakened establishment but also risking its fierce backlash. These presidents are forced to play a long game, presenting the political and policy outlines an alternative regime, even though they cannot dislodge the one in place. The agendas of preemptive leaders offer attractive policies that more orthodox innovators shun or ignore, and perhaps for that very reason they provoke increasingly anxious defenders of orthodoxy to engage in character assassination, impugning the authenticity and even legality of the incumbent's tenure. The Gingrich assault on Clinton gave us "Slick Willy," the liberal assault on Nixon gave us "Tricky Dick," the Republican assault on Woodrow Wilson gave us "Shifty Tom." For Obama, the birther movement gave that same impulse an ugly racial spin. The theme of the illegitimate, inauthentic interloper is part and parcel of preemptive politics; it is part of the battle over the meaning of the moment at hand, an effort to deny the opposition leader control over the terms and conditions of legitimate national government. A related aspect of this is that, in the face of resistance, preemptive leaders rely heavily on unilateral executive action to advance their agendas, and with that they become vulnerable to charges of abuse of power. In fact, preemptive leaders are historically the only presidents seriously threatened by impeachment. Obama avoided that, but charges of his abuse of executive power grew steadily through his tenure, and regime stalwarts availed themselves of their entrenched power in the judiciary to challenge the legality of his action and forestall his initiatives in court. Notably, the Republican Speaker of the House brought a suit against him for failure to faithfully execute the laws. There was a sharp rebuke on recess appointments in the *Noel Canning* decision, and a smack-down on his use of executive orders to change immigration policy in *United States* v. *Texas*.[8] Surely, had Justice Scalia not died before that ruling, the decision would have reached far more broadly.

On the basis of observations like these, the case is strong that the Obama presidency is not a failed transformation but a pretty standard second-round preemption, one which largely confirms what one would expect from prior sequences and the rhythms of leadership in political time. Obama, like Nixon and Wilson, was the harbinger of a reconstruction that still lay far off in the future. This leads directly to consideration of Obama's successor, and what we might expect from Donald Trump's promise of transformation. But before turning to that, we still have to consider "secular time." There is something more to be ventured about Obama's leadership on that front. What I have to say here sits comfortably within the boundaries of the preemptive type, but leaving it submerged there would be a mistake.

Obama in secular time

In considering Obama in secular time, it might be useful to return to his initial promise of transformation. Earlier, I argued that we cannot take transformative rhetoric at face value because presidential parties now routinely invoke that Jackson-Lincoln standard of leadership. Still, when Obama said that he wanted to "change the trajectory of national affairs" and set a "new foundation," he may have had something different in mind than resetting the clock that tells political time. There is reason to think that his "new foundation" was meant to abandon that time frame altogether, to break with the whole conception of great leadership as political repudiation and governmental reconstruction, and instead to make the case for the priority of governing in secular time.

In this respect, Obama's leadership presents an historic attempt to resolve the conundrum of modern presidency as the progressives bequeathed it to us. The insight we might draw from his leadership is that the progressive promise of transformative leadership will never be reconciled with the progressive promise of responsible problem solving so long it retains the Jackson-Lincoln standard of action. Obama has been called a progressive in the mold of William James and John Dewey, that is, an "anti-foundationalist" and "ruthless pragmatist."[9] There is in that description a different twist on his studied reluctance to repudiate anything fundamental. After all, there was one thing that Obama was willing to repudiate repeatedly: the stubborn refusal of Republicans to engage in pragmatic problem solving.

Obama's leadership stance speaks in this way to the peculiar character of the political orthodoxy he was preempting. The core message of the Reagan Revolution – that government is not the solution to our problems; that government *is* the problem – never squared with the realities of governing in a fully developed policy state. Reagan set forth a powerful mobilizing idea but it had no correlative formula for executive management. Indeed, the orthodoxy of the conservative establishment was always more forcefully expressed in Republican renunciations of Clinton and Obama than in Republican follow-through by the two Bushes. Obama's cool pragmatism – his insistence on problem solving plain and simple – was indeed ruthless, for it targeted the irrational drift of Republican orthodoxy toward the extreme obstructionism of the Freedom Caucus. "We cannot mistake absolutism for principle," he said in his second inaugural address. "We must act, knowing that today's victories will be only partial."[10]

Obama's pragmatic, problem-solving stance was, to be sure, part of the arsenal of preemptive leadership, political leverage to use against his opponents; but it was also an effort to expose the irrelevance and impossibility of conservative orthodoxy, and that nearly drove adherents to that orthodoxy crazy. Time and again – on issues like gun control, climate change, healthcare, and immigration – the president used their implacable resistance to problem solving to make the case for his own responsible management. Time and again – in the debt ceiling stand-off, the government shutdown, the sequester, and the siege-like investigations – he pushed the conservative regime to expose its most self-destructive tendencies.

This leads me to suspect that the "new foundation" Obama had in mind was one that would dispense altogether with the wrenching business of constructing a new regime. He wanted instead to make government safe for secular pragmatism, for problem solving in the moment. He ventured that the traditional American promise of redemptive leadership—redemption to be achieved through presidential repudiation and institutional reconstruction—now persists as a cultural affliction; that the Jackson model of leadership is a historical hangover, one that the cause of progressivism would do well to discard. He went willingly to the Bush administration to help save the nation from the financial crisis, even though that act relinquished his claim to deal with the crisis as a great repudiator with "clean hands." He stood apart from the fighting posture of Elizabeth Warren and Bernie Sanders, with its projection of a future in which the battle is decisively won. For the secular pragmatist that posture is wrong-headed, even a step backwards. Obama preferred the cool, self-assured confidence of tackling issues to the anger of visionaries and dragon slayers. There is no hint of repudiation in his oft-stated refrain: "we are all in this together."[11] Full inclusion all but precludes repudiation. The goal he said time and again was simply to "get stuff done," and to "move the ball forward."[12] When the Court turned back his immigration order, Obama insisted with steely resolve that there was really no alternative: immigration reform, he said, is "not a matter of if, it's a matter of when." Better sooner than later. The only real question at issue, he said, is will we tackle the problem in a "smart, rational, sensible way."[13] This is the voice of policy central, the presidency as the locus of responsible problem solving. The message is that resistance to pragmatic action is an annoying and dangerous distraction from the pressing business of running a policy state and keeping it up to date.

The anti-foundational qualities of secular pragmatism fit neatly within the preemptive type because preemptive leadership, by definition, skirts foundational issues. As a guide to the future, secular pragmatism is a formula for perpetual preemption, for preemptive leadership as the new normal. It would make American government safe for leaders who are untethered to orthodoxies of any kind and free to craft their agenda to the exigencies of the moment. The secular pragmatist can use the newfound institutional independence of the modern presidency to deal with issues as they arise. When institutional obstacles are thrown in their way, they can assert the primacy of problem solving, as Obama did when he rallied the nation to support unilateral action: "We can't wait for Congress to do its job, so where they won't act, I will."[14] The secular pragmatist can use the instrumentalities of the presidential party to justify his constant maneuvering, to monitor his supporters, and explain himself to his benefactors. That is just what Obama did through his personal political machine, *Organizing for Action*. OFA opened a continuous communication stream with followers, persuading them to stick with their leader as he navigated the exigencies of the moment.[15]

No president since Reagan dedicated as much energy as Obama did to securing his legacy through the election of a chosen successor. But if Hillary Clinton had won, I would not have retrospectively re-categorized Obama as a reconstructive leader. This was not transformative leadership as it has been understood historically. Nonetheless, a Clinton victory would have been something entirely new, a conspicuous wrinkle in political time, a stunning victory for secular pragmatism as the new standard, a harbinger of perpetual preemption. The fact is that no preemptive president has been able to turn power over to a handpicked successor. Bill Clinton nearly did it in 2000. Obama nearly did it in 2016. Al Gore and Hillary Clinton both won the popular vote. Both anticipated a new normal. But the rhythms of political time were not broken in either case. A Clinton victory, though considered by many as the expected outcome of the recent race, would have been odd from the perspective of political time, but consistent with a washing out of those patterns by secular change.

It is easy to see why Obama found Clinton an attractive successor. Here are adjectives *The New York Times*'s Paul Krugman used to praise her: "competent," "self-possessed," "calm under pressure," "deeply prepared," "poise[d] in stressful situations," able to follow "a strategic plan."[16] That was the legacy that Obama was intent to affirm in 2016. But the weaknesses inherent in that leadership stance were equally apparent. Hillary Clinton had no compelling answer of her own to the question: what time is it? She struggled in vain to articulate a vital project for the nation, to convey a compelling sense of what it meant to be Obama's successor, to define that moment politically.

Obama had passed to her a unique and tough challenge: to mobilize the electorate around the promise of pragmatism and responsible management. Clinton asked the electorate to rally to the cause of experience, of policy positions vetted by experts; of a promise to make the policy state work. Her defeat too is a telling marker of the contretemps of political and secular time. It indicates the stubborn limits of secular pragmatism and responsible management as mobilizing standards in American politics and sustainable premises for presidential leadership.

Donald Trump in political and secular time

That leads us finally to Donald Trump: what are we to make of the promise of transformation 2.0? In the twenty-seven years since I first published the political time thesis, the politics of leadership has unfolded pretty much true to type. Indeed, the familiar patterns have recurred in a more lock-step fashion than I could have ever imagined. But with the rise of Donald Trump, the thesis faces a more serious test. There is no mistaking Trump's own answer to the question: what time is it? He proposed a redemptive reconstruction. He declared the state corrupt. He charged it a betrayal of fundamental principles. He renounced it as a failure in practice. He promised to break it up and replace it with something that would "Make America Great Again."[17] His leadership posture was as clear and familiar as any stance marked in political time. It is unbridled Jacksonism. But is such a reconstruction in the cards? Or is this just more of the transformative hyperbole we have come to expect from contemporary candidates?

The first wrinkle to consider is that Trump's ambitions run hard against the guiding rule of leadership in political time. Call it the Jefferson rule, after Jefferson's reasoning in 1796 that he would ultimately be better off if Adams won that contest. This rule posits that the old order must first collapse internally, indicting itself in the exercise of power, before it can be reconstructed; that the leader cannot transform American government and politics without irrefutable evidence that there is no viable alternative. Unless there is a prior disjunction demonstrating beyond doubt that the old order is bankrupt, it will be difficult for the leader to maintain control over the meaning of a wholesale change in the course of trying to enact it.

So if we extend these historical patterns in the politics of leadership, we might be even more skeptical of the promise of transformational leadership under Trump than under Obama. Historically speaking, reconstruction has never been purely a matter of preference or will, and, on the face of it, Trump's political circumstances made a woefully weak case for a great repudiation and reconstruction. Evidence that the Obama presidency was a national calamity was thin to say the least and largely fabricated. The Obama years saw a slow but steady economic recovery; things were relatively stable, and Obama left office with resurgent popularity. In the 2016 election, Obama's chosen heir, Hillary Clinton, carried the popular plurality by a nearly three million votes. During his four years in office, Trump's popularity as president never broke 50 percent. All this promises to make Trump's drive to eradicate all traces of the Obama administration less transformative than divisive. Rhetoric aside, political time does not identify Donald Trump as Andrew Jackson nor for that matter as Ronald Reagan.

Stalwart conservatives scattered the field in 2016, opening the door to an outlier. Trump emerged from that crowded field as a third-round regime affiliate saddled with a set of commitments that no longer seemed to resonate. If the clock at work in presidential leadership is still telling political time, this was an unmistakable moment, albeit not the one Trump had in mind. In this frame, he appears as the Jimmy Carter of the conservative era. Like Carter, he is the one affiliated with a party that seemed to have lost its way. Like Carter, he is unwanted taskmaster of the old order, offering to save a battered establishment from itself. Like Carter, he is a leader only tangentially related to his own allies and touting a convoluted, nearly unrecognizable version of their orthodoxy. The characteristic premise of the late regime affiliate is that he has some uncanny and inimitable skill missing in the insiders, that only an outsider can update and revive the old formulas. Trump offered "the art of the deal."[18] His boast: "I alone can fix it."[19]

Success in these circumstances means recasting, rehabilitating, and repairing the establishment from within, and though the prospects for such presidencies are certainly disruptive, they do not portend success. No late regime affiliate has succeeded in delivering on that promise. None has been able to reconstruct an old establishment from within. Having seen this movie before, the only question is whether it will come to a different conclusion. The prospect is for a crisis of the conservative order, like the one that liberals experienced under Carter. In this case, that would mean a self-inflicted indictment and decisive implosion of conservative governance.

Signals of a disjunctive event of this sort are not hard to identify. They emerged early on in the "Never Trump" movement within the Republican Party and continued through the opening act of the Trump administration, the attempt to repeal and replace Obamacare. First, the Republican Party stripped the president of the pretense of offering a more attractive replacement; then it indicted itself by failing to pass a straight repeal. Simmering Republican discontent over the administration's trade, immigration policy, and foreign policy suggest other potential flashpoints that might trigger a political implosion. All this is true to type.

But note that this case also displays the countercurrents of secular time as well. The weakening of affiliation as a constraint on presidential action, already evident in the Carter presidency, is even more pronounced in the Trump presidency. The President's independence, anchored in his newfound capacities to mobilize a presidential party, is underscored by the relative weakness of the partisan push-back from stalwart conservatives. Ted Kennedy challenged Carter's new priorities head on; Paul Ryan retired.

The prospect that Trump might weather the disjunctive phase and muscle through to a re-election victory, raises the question of whether he might skip headlong toward reconstruction. This possibility is itself potent testimony to secular changes in the foundations of presidential power. But Trump's ambitions raise other questions as well, questions about the evolving relationship between political and secular time. These center around what might be call the Obama rule. It posits that as the nation has grown more inclusive and interdependent in its interests, leadership in the Jackson mode becomes more irrational. Trump has put that thesis to test. He has taken Ronald Reagan one better, taking the anti-government sentiment of the conservative revolution beyond mere rhetoric and deploying it ruthlessly in an attack on the "deep state." His presidency has become a frontal assault on the managerial norms that built the modern presidency. It has turned "policy central" on its head.

The gradually growing tensions between the mobilizing energy of the presidency and its managerial responsibilities have been expressed in this administration in the near-complete marginalization of the latter. Talk of the "deep state" conspiracy to defraud the people and hobble their rightful ruler has targeted as illegitimate the dense network of institutions, interests, and policy experts that anchor modern American government. If Obama's insight was that modern American government is incompatible with a Jackson-style reconstruction, Trump's was that a Jackson-style reconstruction is incompatible with modern American government. His wager was that the latter is expendable, that he could cut to the operational core of the modern state and still produce something durable.

That wager has gotten him bogged down in impeachment proceedings. Impeachment is not something we would expect of either a late regime affiliate or a reconstructive leader. Hitherto, the former have been deposed electorally, and the latter have wielded such commanding authority that they sideline their opposition. Interestingly, however, impeachment has been associated historically with preemptive leadership. It is hard to imagine two leaders more different than Barack Obama and Donald Trump, but if there is a common theme to be drawn from their political leadership, it might be convergence on the preemptive type. In both cases, secular time and political time combined to produce unresolved transformations. Each in its own way suggests a future like that, with leaders driven to deliver something categorically new but remaining, in effect, in the preemptive mode.

Notes

1. Stephen Skowronek, *The Politics Presidents Make: Leadership from John Adams to Bill Clinton* (Cambridge, MA: Belknap Press, 1993), 11, and *Presidential Leadership in Political Time: Reprise and Reappraisal* (Lawrence: University Press of Kansas, 2nd ed. 2011), 14–21, 167 *et seq.*
2. E. J. Dionne, Jr., "Clinton Swipes the GOP's Lyrics," *The Washington Post*, July 21, 1996. Available at: https://www.washington post.com/archive/opinions/1996/07/21/clinton-swipes-the-gops-lyrics/9c725e88-b5a7-46a5-bb74-8bc12b22795b/?utm_term=.32693f73c8dc (accessed August 2018).
3. Theodore Roosevelt, *An Autobiography* (New York: Macmillan, 1913), 379, 479.
4. Henry Jones Ford, *The Rise and Growth of American Politics: A Sketch of Constitutional Development* (New York: Macmillan, 1898), 357.
5. "In Their Own Words: Obama on Reagan," *The New York Times.* Available at: https://archive.nytimes.com/www.nytimes.com/ref/us/politics/21seelye-text.html; "Barack Obama's Inaugural Address," *The New York Times*, January 20, 2009. Available at: https://www.nytimes.com/2009/01/20/us/politics/20text-obama.html; David Weigel, "Fundamentally Transforming the United States of America," *Slate*, October 18, 2011, quoting Obama campaign rally (Columbia, MO: October 30, 2008); "Illinois Sen. Barack Obama's Announcement Speech," *The Washington Post*, February 10, 2007. Available at: http://www.washingtonpost.com/wp-dyn/content/article/2007/02/10/AR2007021000879.html; "Barack Obama's Acceptance Speech," Democratic National Convention, *The New York Times*, August 28, 2008. Available at: https://www.nytimes.com/2008/08/28/us/politics/28text-obama.html. All references accessed August 2018.
6. See, e.g., Helene Cooper, "Obama Rolls Out Midterm Metaphor," *The New York Times*, August 17, 2010. Available at: https://www.nytimes

.com/2010/08/18/us/politics/18obama.html; "Economic Report of the President," Council of Economic Advisors (Washington: U.S. Government Printing Office, 2010), 111. Accessed August 2018.

7. Franklin D. Roosevelt, "Acceptance Speech Before the Democratic National Convention," July 2, 1932, in *Franklin D. Roosevelt: Public Papers and Addresses*, vol. 1 (New York: Random House, 1939), 649.

8. *National Labor Relations Board v. Noel Canning*, 573 U.S. ____ (2014); *United States v. Texas*, 579 U.S. ____ (2016).

9. David Leonhardt, "After the Great Recession: An Interview with President Obama," *The New York Times*, April 28, 2009. Available at: https://archive.nytimes.com/www.nytimes.com/2009/05/03/magazine/03Obama-t.html (Obama describing his search for "a ruthless pragmatism"); accessed August 2018. See also James T. Kloppenberg, *Reading Obama: Dreams, Hope, and the American Political Tradition* (Princeton, NJ: Princeton University Press, 2011), 79.

10. "President Obama's Inaugural Address," *The New York Times*, January 21, 2013. Available at: http://archive.nytimes.com/www.nytimes.com/interactive/2013/01/22/us/politics/22obama-inaugural-speech-annotated.html (accessed August 2018).

11. See, e.g., "President Obama farewell address: full text," *CNN*, January 11, 2017. Available at: https://www.cnn.com/2017/01/10/politics/president-obama-farewell-speech/index.html (accessed August 2018).

12. "Remarks by the President in a Press Conference," *White House: Office of the Press Secretary*, November 5, 2014. Available at: https://obamawhitehouse.archives.gov/the-press-office/2014/11/05/remarks-president-press-conference ("the most important thing I can do is just get stuff done, and help Congress get some things done"); "Remarks by the President Before Cabinet Meeting," *White House: Office of the Press Secretary*, January 14, 2014. Available at: https://obamawhitehouse.archives.gov/the-press-office/2014/01/14/remarks-president-cabinet-meeting ("I've got a pen and I've got a phone – and I can use that pen to sign executive orders and take executive actions and administrative actions that move the ball forward"). Both accessed August 2018.

13. "Remarks of the President on the Supreme Court Decision in U.S. Versus Texas," *White House: Office of the Press Secretary*, June 23, 2016. Available at: https://obamawhitehouse.archives.gov/the-press-office/2016/06/23/remarks-president-supreme-court-decision-us-versus-texas (accessed August 2018).

14. Richard Wolf, "Obama Uses Executive Powers to Get Past Congress," *USA Today*, October 27, 2011.
15. See Sidney M. Milkis and John Warren York (2017), "Barack Obama, Organizing for Action, and Executive-Centered Partisanship," *Studies in American Political Development*, 31, 1: 1–23.
16. Paul Krugman, "Why Hillary Wins," *The New York Times*, October 21, 2016. Available at: https://www.nytimes.com/2016/10/21/opinion/why-hillary-wins.html (accessed August 2018).
17. "Donald Trump's Presidential Announcement Speech," *Time*, June 16, 2015. Available at: http://time.com/3923128/donald-trump-announcement-speech ("We have people that are morally corrupt. We have people that are selling this country down the drain."); Trevor Hughes, "Trump calls to 'drain the swamp' of Washington," *USA Today*, October 18, 2016. Available at: https://www.usatoday.com/story/news/politics/elections/2016/2016/10/18/donald-trump-rally-colorado-springs-ethics-lobbying-limitations/92377656 ("Either we win this election or we lose this country."); "Full transcript: Donald Trump's jobs speech," *Politico*, June 28, 2016. Available at: https://www.politico.com/story/2016/06/full-transcript-trump-job-plan-speech-224891 ("[Globalism] is a direct affront to our Founding Fathers, who wanted America to be strong, independent and free."); "Full transcript: Donald Trump NYC speech on stakes of the election," *Politico*, June 22, 2016. Available at: https://www.politico.com/story/2016/06/transcript-trump-speech-on-the-stakes-of-the-election-224654 ("Come this November, we can bring America back – bigger and better, and stronger than ever."). All accessed August 2018.
18. See "Donald Trump's Presidential Announcement Speech" ("We need a leader that wrote 'The Art of the Deal'."); Donald J. Trump, Tony Schwartz, *Trump: The Art of the Deal* (New York: Ballantine Books, 1987).
19. "Full text: Donald Trump 2016 RNC draft speech transcript," *Politico*, July 21, 2016. Available at: https://www.politico.com/story/2016/07/full-transcript-donald-trump-nomination-acceptance-speech-at-rnc-225974 (accessed August 2018).

2

Obama and the administrative presidency: Finding new meanings in old laws

Andrew Rudalevige

In early 2014 President Barack Obama pledged that he would utilize his "pen and phone" during a "year of action." As the president declared, "I can use that pen to sign executive orders and take executive actions and administrative actions that move the ball forward."[1] This was met by fervent denunciations from Republicans complaining of an "aggressive unilateralism," of an "imperial presidency," even of "dictatorship."[2]

Yet viewers could be forgiven for thinking they had seen that movie many times before. Indeed, in 1975, former presidential staffer Richard P. Nathan published a provocative book entitled *The Plot That Failed*. It described President Richard Nixon's efforts to implement what Nathan dubbed the "administrative presidency"; Nixon's managerial efforts to gain control of the bureaucratic outputs of the government. Over the course of his truncated presidency, Nixon sought to centralize policy-making resources in the Executive Office of the Presidency (EOP), to more closely direct bureaucratic policy-making choices, and to politicize the wider executive branch by appointing loyalists deep in the departments and agencies.[3] It helped inspire, of course, the original *Imperial Presidency*.[4]

While Nixon's plot may have failed – or was, at least, a collateral casualty of his other and rather more criminal plots – his successors continued to utilize the tools he had bequeathed to craft remakes. Nathan concluded his discussion by noting that "it is possible that a president with a coherent program could organize his administration to navigate a course similar to Nixon's . . . emphasis on administrative accomplishment," even if Watergate's "aftertaste" might make that problematic in the short term.[5] In the event, any bad taste faded quickly, and while Ronald Reagan may have been the "Great Communicator," the administrative presidency was at the heart of the Reagan Revolution; in a transition memo to the incoming president, long-time public administrator Dwight Ink opined that "the ability of the Reagan Administration to act will be no better than the capacity of the departments and agencies to manage."[6] By 1983, Nathan had churned out an updated edition of his book, reflecting Reagan's early wins in utilizing appointments and an effective White House bureaucratic oversight effort (helped by a newly strengthened process of centralized regulatory review) to achieve his policy ends.[7]

Reagan's successors took notice. If under Reagan the plot thickened, under Bush and Clinton it succeeded; Elena Kagan, a White House aide in the 1990s, observed in 2001 that "by the close of Clinton's presidency, a fundamental . . . transformation had occurred in the institutional relationship between the administrative agencies and the Executive Office of the President." The result was basically a bipartisan endorsement and near-codification of the efforts described by Nathan, using a variety of executive management tools to enhance presidential control of the bureaucracy. Flipping Nathan's phrase, Kagan called it "presidential administration."[8] Kagan wrote that Clinton acted to expand executive management of the bureaucracy because he was "faced for most of his time in office with a hostile Congress but eager to show progress on domestic issues."[9]

That motivation rang equally true and perhaps even louder for the Obama administration, given increased levels of partisan polarization and its resultant gridlock. Republican gains in Congress in 2010 and 2014 empowered a new majority's reflexive obstructionism to Obama's programmatic proposals.[10] In early 2011 Senate Republican leader Mitch McConnell actually defined bipartisanship as "see[ing] if [Obama] actually wants to work with us to accomplish things that we're already for."[11] Mostly, Obama did not, leading to a new iteration of the administrative presidency.

The taxonomy of the "orders and actions" developed therein was quite extensive. But one crucial commonality was a reliance on legalism, on aggressive statutory interpretation that could guide the implementation of policy to suit presidential preferences. Public administration scholar Martha Derthick could have been speaking of the Obama years when she observed (about the 1990s) that "[m]uch of the activity of American policymaking consists of attempts not to pass new laws but to invest old ones with new meanings."[12] Under Obama, executive orders, regulation, guidance documents, and prosecutorial discretion all shaped policies in key areas such as healthcare, environmental protection, and immigration.

The actions that the Obama team's interpretations justified were frequently contested, during the rule-making process and then in court. The president was largely able to outflank a polarized Congress during his term – only to see his initiatives find an uneven reception in the federal courts to which opponents inevitably appealed. Further, statutory interpretation, by its nature, can be changed by future interpreters. Some of Obama's actions became insulated from his successor's fervent efforts to deregulate; some were easily reversed. The Republicans who continued to hold congressional majorities during Trump's first years in office proved far less rankled by unilateralism when it was exercised by a Republican president.

That polarity may well reverse again after 2020, showing the potential fragility of unilateralism. However, Obama's aggressive use of the same basic tool of statutory interpretation in foreign policy – claiming an expansive scope for the 2001 Authorization for the Use of Military Force (AUMF) and a contrastingly narrow application of the 1973 War Powers Resolution – was given far more leeway, even by his partisan opponents. That self-inflicted blow to the powers and duties of Congress may leave a more permanent legacy.

From the grand bargain to presidential administration

None of this seemed of immediate concern as Obama entered office in January 2009. From the White House to the House of Representatives, Democrats had swept the 2008 elections. It was not surprising, then, that the administration's major stimulus proposal, the US$787 billion American Reinvestment and Recovery Act, became law less than a month after the president took office. By the end of 2010, the most comprehensive changes to Wall Street regulation since the Great Depression and an ambitious extension of healthcare coverage to thirty million uninsured Americans – inevitably termed "Obamacare" – had also become law. During the 2009–2010 legislative sessions Barack Obama had the highest rating for success on roll call votes ever recorded by *Congressional Quarterly*.[13]

But in the 2010 midterm elections Republicans regained a majority in the House of Representatives, netting a stunning sixty-three seats. The GOP also trimmed six votes from the Democratic margin in the Senate. The anti-government "Tea Party" wing of the party would have important sway over both new and returning members of both chambers, who showed few signs of compromising their putative mandate. Much of 2011 was wasted on failed attempts to strike a "grand bargain," an umbrella package of fiscal responsibility which would have pulled off a three-way trade involving entitlement reform, revenue enhancement, and spending cuts. Legislators claimed to want a lower deficit, but only in the abstract; given the paucity of lawmakers willing to put their votes where their rhetoric was, the president declared that "we can't wait" for "an increasingly dysfunctional Congress to do its job."[14]

This impatient rallying cry gave its name to a "we can't wait" section of the White House website touting a broad collection of executive actions. By the summer of 2012 this included forty-plus unilateral initiatives, ranging from cutting lending fees on government-backed mortgages to the creation of a new national park in Virginia. And that was only the start; faced with additional legislative intransigence that brought the United States perilously close to defaulting on its national debt in the fall of 2013, unilateralism would remain a cornerstone of Obama's agenda to the end of his administration. Key arenas for action included healthcare, labor law, and environmental protection, as well as exercises of prosecutorial discretion that ranged from the administration's decision not to defend the Defense of Marriage Act (DOMA) against legal challenges in advance of the *Obergefell* decision regarding same-sex marriage, to the wide use of his commutation power to shorten jail terms for those convicted of non-violent drug crimes. Obama's most sweeping and most controversial action, perhaps, discussed in greater depth later in this chapter, dealt with immigration and deportation via the Deferred Action for Parents of Americans initiative, announced by the president in the fall of 2014 and almost immediately denounced in court.

It's worth stressing that this brand of "presidential administration" was based on many different tools. Studies have tracked more than two dozen types of unilateral directives, including not only the well-known variants of executive orders and presidential proclamations but also various formal findings, designations, letters, guidance documents, memoranda (that might prod the production of regulations by departments and agencies), and a wide range of national security orders.[15] Executive orders got most of the press, but many actions that were not executive orders were often wrongly identified as such. When Obama announced a package of gun control measures in February 2016, for instance, former Florida governor Jeb Bush (then a candidate for president) tweeted that "I'll repeal his executive orders and protect 2nd amend[ment]." But the package did not contain a single executive order. Likewise in July 2014 then-Speaker of the House John Boehner (R-OH) observed that "every president issues executive orders," but "most of them . . . do so within the law" – specifically charging Obama with exceeding his authority as regarded educational waivers, environmental regulations, and a Taliban prisoner exchange involving a US serviceman as Obama examples to the contrary. Yet none of these was achieved by executive order but by other sorts of administrative documents and directives.[16] (As noted below, this might matter when it comes to their durability.)

What Obama's executive actions did have in common was their goal of executing the law according to the Obama administration's preferences regarding its execution. He had both motive and opportunity to do so. As Obama political aide David Axelrod noted in late 2010, "The next phase is . . . less about legislative action than it is about managing the change that we've brought about" – implementing enormous, complex statutes passed in 2009–2010, including the Affordable Care Act and the Dodd-Frank financial sector reforms.[17] But the idea of "managing change" developed to include longer-standing laws, especially when newer ones could not be passed – for example, when large-scale legislation acting to forestall climate change or comprehensive immigration reform stalled.

This is possible because "faithful" execution of the law is hardly black and white. We often think of "statutory interpretation" as a judicial function, and certainly it is a common one.[18] Courts, drenched in the (home-brewed) perfume of *Marbury v. Madison*, claim it is their job to say "what the law is." But Congress and the executive branch have a role to play here as well. Questions over presidents' interpretations of the Constitution date back to the Washington administration.[19] If nothing else, presidents have many laws to choose between – some of them contradicting others, and still more sitting in the statute books awaiting rediscovery. Given the difficulty of passing laws and the multiplicity of circumstances to which they must apply, it rarely makes sense to try to anticipate every possible outcome in legislative language. Thus, executive departments and agencies are routinely delegated power to promulgate regulations specifying how a given law will work in practice. Further, complex substantive debates tend to generate complex statutes: the Affordable Care Act ran to more than 900 pages, containing vague provisions, multiple drafting errors, and any number of unintended consequences. Even in the best circumstances, maneuvering a bill through Congress requires ambiguous statutory language, the better to allow all sides to point to the same language as supporting their ideals. Statutes also frequently grant waiver authority, allowing presidents or departmental secretaries to suspend provisions of the law under certain conditions. Such authority aggregates with the US Code itself.

Journalist Charlie Savage's analysis of national security questions under Obama hinges on this question too.[20] In contrast with the George W. Bush administration – partly, indeed, to make that contrast clear – Obama did not want to justify his directives by making broad claims of presidential prerogative. Rather, he wanted to ground each action in written law: "acting like Bush meant a president overriding statutory constraints," as Savage puts it, while "lawyerliness suffused the Obama administration . . . Legal ways of analyzing problems disciplined deliberations."[21] In short, "Obama's governance . . . cannot be seen clearly without looking at it through a legal lens."[22] Obama himself put it this way: he would act "with an abiding confidence in the rule of law and due process; in checks and balances and accountability."[23]

But the rule of law depends on what the law says. And the president's lawyers, of course, work for the president. "Creative lawyers can find lots of lawful ways for a determined president to advance a decision," Bush official John Graham once noted; more cynically, law professor Bruce Ackerman argues that a "steady stream of authoritative-looking opinions is produced under conditions that allow short-term presidential imperatives to overwhelm sober legal judgments."[24] Reagan aide Ed Meese put it this way in a White House meeting over aid to the Nicaraguan Contras in 1984: "It's important to tell the Department of Justice that we want them to find the legal basis [to give the aid] . . . You have to give lawyers guidance when asking them a question."[25]

Better yet, answers to such questions serve to undergird future claims – a self-justifying process much like the reflexive citation of *Marbury*. Savage traces a 2011 Justice Department memo effectively nullifying a law that constrained certain presidential staff from dealing with Chinese officials.[26] Justice's Office of Legal Counsel (OLC) held that "ample precedent" existed to show the Constitution intended the president to have "absolute discretion" over the people chosen for diplomatic tasks. The original source of that claim, however, was a 1990 opinion by George H. W. Bush's legal team. Repeated frequently enough over the years, that single memo became "ample precedent."

Statutory interpretation in practice

Thus, the specifics of policy implementation are often up for grabs, resulting from interpretations of the law that justify presidential preferences. To see this at work in the Obama years, this section traces four contentious domestic policy areas where Obama made aggressive claims about his abilities under statutory authority: healthcare; labor; the environment; and immigration. Results on the ground – and on the Hill – were decidedly mixed, with those

initiatives the administration was able to embed in formal regulation finding much firmer purchase than those implemented simply by presidential directive. The last part of the chapter, though,
turns to foreign policy and the war powers, where Congress and
the courts have been far more deferential.

HEALTHCARE

"This administration's lawlessness has been most widely noticed
with President Obama's implementation of Obamacare," complained Rep. Diane Black (R-TN) in a 2014 House testimony.[27]
Much of that implementation involved the Treasury's issuance of
tax regulations (since the individual mandate was enforced via the
tax code) or interpretations of the law's text within their ongoing
statutory authority under the Internal Revenue code – as, in Assistant Secretary Mark Mazur's framing in July 2013, "an exercise
of the Treasury Department's longstanding administrative authority to grant transition relief when implementing new legislation."
Others, such as an additional package of rules changes in March
2014, were announced by an administrative bulletin through the
Centers for Medicaid and Medicare Services.

Rep. Black's direct reference was to a series of delays to
Affordable Care Act requirements beginning in February 2013.
The administration put off the employer mandate portion of the
bill for twelve months in July 2013 and extended the deadline
further in February 2014 for medium-sized companies (those with
more than fifty, but fewer than 100, employees). Other adjustments included a smaller shift in the deadline for the individual
mandate, adjustments to the online marketplace for small businesses and, with the website HealthCare.gov then still in tatters,
extension of the general deadline for enrollment online. When
insurance companies (quite properly) began to cancel plans that
did not meet the ACA's minimum requirements, undermining the
president's pledge that "if you like your plan, you can keep it,"
Obama extended insurers the discretion to extend such plans for
an additional year. He did so again in early 2014 to push such can-
celations safely past the 2016 elections. It was not clear whether
these changes were in fact lawful – but since those affected could

hardly claim to have suffered "harm" in a legal sense (indeed, they welcomed the delays) there were no court challenges.

That was not the case, though, when the Internal Revenue Service announced that it would read the ACA to include individuals enrolled via the federal insurance "exchange" as well as state-run exchanges as eligible for tax credits to subsidize their policies. What became the Supreme Court case *King v. Burwell* centered on this question, since one section of the law seemed to state that subsidies could be given only to those purchasing coverage from an exchange run by one of the states. It didn't help that the ACA, thanks in part to the tortuous legislative process leading to its passage, at best suffered from (as the *Burwell* majority opinion gently put it) "inartful drafting." Some, including the IRS, argued the section in question was simply an elaborate typographical error.[28] But it became a crucial issue when two dozen or so states refused to set up their own exchanges, forcing the federal government to do the work.

Thus, unlike its first judicial audition in *NFIB v. Sebelius* (2010), where a split Court upheld the ACA's individual mandate as within Congress's power to tax, *King v. Burwell* dealt not with interpreting the Constitution but about interpreting the ACA's text.

In the 1984 *Chevron* case, the Supreme Court had preached judicial deference to an executive branch department or agency's reading of a vague law, assuming that reading rests on reasonable grounds. Following this logic, the Fourth Circuit Court of Appeals ruled in favor of the government. That is, the court decided that the section was ambiguous, that the agency (here, the IRS) had come up with a reasonable interpretation, and that, therefore, the tax credits for users of federal exchanges could remain. But following the same process, the D.C. Circuit Court of Appeals came up with the opposite result. It decided instead that the law was unambiguous – "so obvious there would hardly be a need for the Supreme Court to hear a case about it," according to Justice Antonin Scalia's later opinion – that the IRS could therefore not have reached the conclusion it did – and that the tax credits were therefore invalid.

To the surprise of most observers, the Supreme Court itself discarded the *Chevron* framework and decided to do the interpreting of the law itself. "Had Congress wished to assign that question to an agency, it surely would have done so expressly," Chief Justice John Roberts wrote for the majority. And the IRS could not in any case be expected to be expert in health insurance and its workings, the usual reason for deference. "This is not a case for the IRS," Roberts argued. "It is instead our task to determine the correct reading of Section 36B." Having done so, the Court found the notion of an exchange "established by the State" was indeed ambiguous when taken in the context of the law as a whole. Otherwise, the health-care marketplace governed by the law, and really the point of the law, would collapse in a "death spiral" – something Congress could not have meant to do. Thus, while a close call, the key section "can fairly be read consistent with what we see as Congress's plan, and that is the reading we adopt." This allowed subsidies to flow to federal exchanges.

Others, of course, were unimpressed with this line of reasoning. Justice Scalia's instantly famous dissent in *King* accused his colleagues of judicial malpractice, plain stupidity, and even something called "jiggery-pokery." But the law lived to fight another day – to battle against yet another court effort, for example, where opponents charged that Obama was spending money on provisions of the ACA without that money having been specifically appropriated by Congress. That case, which continued into the Trump administration, was made moot when Trump decided to stop making the payments in question – claiming the lawsuit as his rationale. Others argued the move was in keeping with an array of new administrative moves that were designed to undermine the ACA by increasing premium costs to those seeking coverage under the law and provide an array of new insurance options that were cheaper but that did not provide the range of coverage mandated for ACA plans. (Indeed, Trump himself bragged via Twitter that "The Democrats [sic] ObamaCare is imploding. Massive subsidy payments to their pet insurance companies has stopped. Dems should call me to fix!"[29] Trump's phone, however, did not ring.)

LABOR

Executive orders (EOs) constituted a relatively small proportion of Obama's executive actions generally. However, EOs did play an important role in shaping the administration's approach toward the American workforce.

Recall that EOs affect the private sector only indirectly: they are directed to government officials and agencies. Thus, Obama could not issue an order implementing a desire to raise the federal minimum wage. He could, however, require that contracts negotiated with private sector companies seeking to do business with the federal government mandate a higher minimum wage. Since the US government buys over US$500 billion worth of contracted products and services every year, requiring that the businesses receiving those contracts meet certain basic conditions can have an important impact on the wider economy. (John F. Kennedy's 1962 order barring racial discrimination in federally funded housing is an earlier example of this phenomenon.)[30]

Obama, then, sought to rework the relationship between the federal government and the private contractors it relies on. His orders limited government procurement to providers who agreed to pay a higher minimum wage (EO 13658, February 2014), ban discrimination on the basis of sexual orientation or identity (EO 13672, July 2014), comply fully with laws mandating "integrity and business ethics" so as to ensure "fair pay and safe workplaces" (EO 13673, July 2014), and provide paid sick leave (EO 13706, September 2015). The Department of Labor then developed regulations to implement the law. For example, the rules governing EO 13706 were issued in final form in early September, to take effect on January 1, 2017. The rules gave the orders more stability than orders themselves can claim. An EO, after all, can be reversed by a subsequent EO by a new president. Indeed, the Fair Pay and Safe Workplaces order was rescinded by President Trump in early 2017. Even before that, in late October 2016, a district court judge in Texas had issued an injunction holding up that order subject to a lawsuit brought by trade associations representing builders and security guard companies.[31]

Other Obama efforts to boost workers' rights were also held up in court as the administration wound to a close. In March 2014, Obama issued a presidential memorandum directing the Department of Labor to update its interpretation of the 1938 Fair Labor Standards Act so as to expand the number of full-time white-collar workers eligible for increased overtime pay when they worked more than forty hours per week. At the time, only non-managers who earned US$23,660 or less per year were eligible for overtime pay (a figure set in 2004, but not seriously examined since the 1960s. In 1975, more than 60 percent of full-time workers could receive overtime, but this number had dropped to only 7 percent by 2015.)

The Labor Department issued a proposed regulation in July 2015, greatly expanding overtime pay. After a public comment period, the final regulation was issued in May 2016; it rolled back the requirements slightly, but the department still estimated the new threshold of US$47,676 would benefit 4.2 million workers.

Businesses, which had provided most of the 270,000 public comments received by the Department, were not happy. Nor were some state governments. In September 2016, the US Chamber of Commerce sued (in, of course, a Texas courtroom), as did public officials in twenty-one states (including, of course, Texas). The complainants argued that "once again, President Obama is trying to unilaterally rewrite the law," which in their view did not permit the department to raise the threshold so dramatically nor to index it to inflation – since the latter could be interpreted as new regulation without the advance notice and ability to comment required by federal law.[32]

On November 22, 2016 the district court issued a national stay, preventing the rule from going into effect on December 1 as planned. The judge agreed with the plaintiffs that the Department had gone beyond its statutory authority, especially in creating the "automatic updating mechanism."[33] The Labor Department quickly appealed – but when the case returned to court in 2017, the Trump administration switched sides and promised to work with business to develop a less burdensome version of the rule.

ENVIRONMENTAL PROTECTION

The Obama administration had more, but hardly universal, success in the environmental arena. Here, its administrative tactics were clear substitutes for the failure of Congress to pass a carbon "cap and trade" bill combating global warming. Such a measure passed the House in June 2009, but never received a Senate vote.

In May 2010, Obama sent a memorandum to four agency heads, directing them to tighten greenhouse gas and fuel efficiency standards such that "coordinated steps . . . produce a new generation of clean vehicles."[34] One result came in March 2014, when the EPA announced new rules that would reduce sulfur in gasoline and drive changes in both automotive and oil refinery technology. After some hiccups – and some White House stalling designed to make sure controversial rules were not issued in time to become an issue in the 2012 election – the rule-writing project also resulted in draft rules aiming to extend Clean Air Act (CAA) authority to existing power plants, especially those fueled by coal, and to limit greenhouse gases produced by new development. Even agency attorneys suggested that EPA's interpretation of the CAA was aggressive, even "challenging."[35] It was not surprising, then, that a series of lawsuits soon questioned that interpretation.

The first case that wound up before the Supreme Court in 2014 was *Utility Air Regulatory Group (UARG)* v. *EPA*. This dealt with EPA regulation of larger industrial plants emitting greenhouse gases. The Court wound up largely upholding the EPA's substantive position, noting that "Congress's profligate use of [the phrase] 'air pollutant' is not conducive to clarity." Vague legal language led to administrative discretion.

However, in its regulations, the EPA had also sought to change the threshold for regulating carbon emissions produced by new (as opposed to existing) developments. The CAA states that regulation should kick in when a facility generates more than 250 tons of a given pollutant – but while that is a lot of mercury, it is a tiny amount of greenhouse gas. So the EPA's new rule raised the limit for carbon pollutants to 75,000 tons per year. That was better for industry, in fact, but it came as a result of disregarding language in the law that was *not* vague and the court did not allow it to stand. In oral argument, Justice Kagan – erstwhile proponent of "presidential administration" – mused disapprovingly that "the solution that EPA came up with actually seems to give it complete discretion to do whatever it wants, whenever it wants." As Justice Scalia later put the point in the decision, "An agency may not rewrite clear statutory terms to suit its own sense of how the statute should operate."[36]

Kagan and Scalia did not agree for long about the letter of the law. In *Michigan* v. *Environmental Protection Agency* (2015), for instance, Scalia went back to the *Chevron* case noted above, which (as he put it) "directs courts to accept an agency's reasonable resolution of an ambiguity in a statute that the agency administers." Yet Scalia (and four others) and Kagan (and three others) disagreed entirely on what constituted a "reasonable" interpretation of the CAA when it came to regulating the specific power plants under review in the case. Scalia accused the agency of "interpretive gerrymanders" that "keep parts of statutory context it likes while throwing away parts it does not." Kagan and the dissenters complained instead of judicial "micromanagement" by the Court that "ignores everything but one thing EPA did" in justifying its actions.

As detailed below, *Michigan* was a larger loss for the administration in theory than in practice. But the third round of litigation to reach the Court was more uniformly problematic for Obama's efforts to combat climate change. Just a few days before Justice Scalia's unexpected death in February 2016, he cast the deciding vote forcing a stay of the administration's Clean Power Plan (CPP) regulations.[37] The Supreme Court's intervention at that early stage of the proceedings was unprecedented – the appeals process had not played itself out yet – but so, some argued, was the CPP's, which used a very broad reading of the CAA to impose carbon pollution emission guidelines on existing electric utility plants.[38] The administration's legal case faced several problems, beginning with yet another typographical error. This one had resulted when Congress managed to revise the same section of the CAA twice in contradictory ways when it amended the law in 1990. The version that wound up printed in the law books would seem to prevent enactment of the CPP. So, as legal scholar Jonathan Adler explained, the EPA had to argue that

> either a) the wrong language was put in the US Code, b) the 1990 revisions, read properly, actually allow such regulation or c) the conflicting statutory language creates an ambiguity that the EPA has resolved by interpreting the language to allow for such regulation. This is an aggressive argument, and if the courts reject it, there is no CPP.[39]

Other questions included the procedural – whether the changes made to the regulations during the process of developing them from their original draft were so extensive as to basically create a new rule (which would then need to be published for comment again) – and also the "reasonable," again in the *Chevron* sense traced above. In this case, since the aim was to reduce reliance on coal-fired electricity generation, standards drawn from renewable energy sources were used as the goal for reducing emissions. But was this comparison allowed under the CAA?

Reflecting the importance of the case, a ten- (rather than three-) judge panel of the D.C. Circuit Court of Appeals heard an astonishing seven hours of arguments in September 2016.[40] When Trump became president, the new EPA leadership asked the Circuit Court to defer its decision until a new, less stringent rule could be drafted. But a Trump replacement rule did not emerge until the summer of 2018, with a lengthy period of public comment still before it.[41] With the Clean Power Plan still on hold, the regulatory framework defaulted to the pre-Obama status quo. This made the timing of the Supreme Court intervention in February 2016 important. In the *Michigan* case, the regulations that were ultimately overturned had already been in effect, pushing industry toward compliance by shaping business decisions about what kind of plants to build or expand. Those decisions involved high sunk costs (one estimate was US$10 billion) and were unlikely to be reversed even after the Court's ruling. By contrast, the CPP was not as solidly embedded in private-sector decision making.

Still, with the cost of coal far higher than the cost of natural gas or even wind power, in late November 2016 the CEO of Michigan's largest utility announced that all eight of the state's coal-fired plants were on the road to retirement even if the CPP was shelved. "I don't know anybody in the country who would build another coal plant," he said.[42]

IMMIGRATION

In June 2012, with the election approaching, the president announced a program of Deferred Action for Childhood Arrivals (DACA). DACA aimed to protect from deportation about

1.2 million people who were in the US illegally. This group consisted of young people who had been brought to the United States before they were sixteen and who were high-school students or graduates or had served in the armed forces, and had no criminal record. DACA was criticized as a unilateral implementation of the so-called DREAM Act, which had failed to pass Congress in 2010. But its beneficiaries were a sympathetic group and also one that, for legal purposes, was clearly defined and thus seemed well within the discretion granted by the Immigration and Nationality Act (INA) first passed in the 1950s.

After Obama's re-election, most observers thought action on immigration would move to the legislative arena, given that even key Republicans blamed their losses in 2012 on the party's militant refusal to appeal to minority voters. But a Senate bill passed in June 2013 was pronounced "dead on arrival" in the House. The 2014 midterms in which Democrats lost their Senate majority made new proposals dead there too.

In response, on November 20, 2014, Obama took to the national airwaves to announce he was acting to greatly expand his earlier initiative. Saying that he wanted to deport "felons, not families," the president announced that he would extend and expand the DACA program, while creating another, larger variant called Deferred Action for Parents of Americans (DAPA).[43] As with DACA, the upshot was that in certain circumstances the government would defer the deportation of as many as 4 million parents of US citizens. In the meantime, they would be able to work legally in the United States.

While Obama issued two presidential memoranda on the subject, these were largely tangential to the task.[44] The burden of the change fell on the enforcement of the INA by the Department of Homeland Security – the Department of Justice memo advising the action was legal was addressed to DHS rather than to the president. The Secretary of Homeland Security, in turn, issued guidance to law enforcement officials, reshaping their "removal priorities." The Justice Department's analysis focused on the INA's emphasis on keeping families together.

Even so, did the INA allow so much prosecutorial discretion? Obama's directives did not change the law, per se; rather, they set forth who was to be prosecuted (in this case deported) first, or rather last. The numbers were big, but then so was the chasm between the written requirements of the law and the resources actually available to enforce it. The administration also took solace in Justice William Rehnquist's claim in the 1985 case *Heckler* v. *Chaney*: "an agency's decision not to prosecute or enforce, whether through civil or criminal process, is a decision generally committed to an agency's absolute discretion." And as applied to immigration cases, discretion had a strong juris-prudential pedigree – as recently as 2012, in *Arizona* v. *US*, the Court had held that "[a] principal feature of the removal system is the broad discretion exercised by immigration officials" in order to deal with "immediate human concerns" as well as "policy choices that bear on this Nation's international relations" and "other realities."

Congress could, of course, limit the president's freedom of action. But since the polarized 114th Congress was not able to agree on a response to Obama's move, or much of anything else, opponents of the president's agenda again turned to the judiciary. This time the attack was from below, as Texas brought suit on behalf of some two dozen states and state officials. They argued that the "brazen lawlessness" of the president's administrative actions actually changed the substance of the law – that he had not made individual exceptions within the realm of prosecutorial discretion, but was instead affirmatively bestowing new rights on large groups of people.[45] In February 2015, a district court judge in Texas imposed an injunction blocking the DAPA program, an injunction upheld in May by a three-judge panel of the Fifth Circuit Court of Appeals.

Though the Circuit Court held that "the United States has not made a strong showing that [the president's action] is likely to succeed on the merits," neither decision directly addressed the merits of the question. Rather they centered on procedural concerns. It was unclear, for instance, whether the states even had the right ("standing") to sue over this policy (had they been harmed by it?). In January 2016, shortly before Justice Scalia's death, the Supreme Court agreed to hear the administration's appeal of the case and asked the parties to answer both the procedural questions and the substantive ones.

The standing question centered around costs – Texas argued, for example, that it would incur costs in issuing drivers' licenses to the newly non-deported, while the administration noted that states didn't *have* to subsidize licenses and the like but could change their laws to recover the costs. In any case, said the administration, immigration is a power reserved exclusively to the federal government by the Constitution. To allow states into court over incidental costs in such a case would undermine the supremacy clause. In oral argument at the Supreme Court, the justices split on this point. "Isn't losing money the classic case for standing?" asked Chief Justice John Roberts. Justice Sonia Sotomayor asked the states, however, "Can we give you standing just on the basis of you saying, 'I'm going to do this when it makes no sense?'" (She also argued that Texas could choose to avoid new costs by not hiring new licensing personnel, since customer service is so terrible at most motor vehicles departments that no one would notice if the DAPA population just got in the existing lines.)[46]

The substance of the question, again, was about whether the administration had properly interpreted the INA. Did that law allow these new rules? The administration argued that it had no choice but to set priorities: Congress's annual appropriation for dealing with "removable aliens" amounted to 3.5 percent of the amount needed to actually remove them. Given that fact, the president's lawyers said both that many presidents have acted in similar ways and, as noted above, that courts have given presidents wide deference in such cases. But Justice Anthony Kennedy worried about "upside down" arguments that emphasized congressional acquiescence to past executive decisions. "What we're doing," he noted, "is defining the limits of discretion. And it seems to me that that is a legislative, not an executive act." And the attorney representing Texas argued that perhaps "[DHS] could do forbearance from removal, but what they can't do is grant authorization to be in the country" if that meant also providing positive benefits like the right to work legally.[47]

In the end, the Court – with only eight members, given Senate Republicans' refusal to consider Obama's nominee for the seat vacated by Scalia's death – could not reach a decision. The holding, issued on June 23, 2016, was just one sentence long: "The judgment is affirmed by an equally divided Court." This meant the injunction issued by the district court, and upheld by the Fifth Circuit, remained in place. The merits of the case remained undecided as of election day. A Clinton victory would have forced the issue back through the system again, starting in Texas; but the Trump victory ended the case.

Indeed, in the fall of 2017, Trump also sought to rescind the DACA program. He cited advice from Attorney General Jeff Sessions which provided a completely new reading of the INA that argued Obama had surpassed his authority under the law.

But a year later, DACA was still in effect. Half a dozen federal courts blocked implementation of the effort to cancel the program, noting the need for thoughtful evaluation of the competing interpretations of the INA. Even the judge who had blocked DAPA refused to uphold Trump's order. By then, he noted, DACA had been implemented for six years: "here," he wrote, "the egg has been scrambled. To try to put it back in its shell ... does not make sense nor serve the best interests of this country." It remained bad policy, he argued. But it needed legislative attention, not judicial fiat.[48]

Foreign policy and the war powers

As noted, the Obama administration emphasized that its actions in foreign policy and national security would not rely on broad claims of inherent presidential power or prerogative. Instead, the president said he would act only when he had specific statutory or constitutional authority to do so.

Still, as already discussed in the domestic context, laws can be vague – and the administration had many resources for interpreting past statute in the way it preferred. Its foreign policy lawyers made up a large and acronym-laden population. In a 2010 speech listing just a subset of his interagency colleagues, State Department legal adviser Harold Koh tallied lawyers in the State Department; in the White House; at the National Security Council, the Central Intelligence Agency, and the office of the Director of National Intelligence; in the Department of Defense (from its general counsel to the Judge Advocate General's – JAG – corps); in five different divisions of the Department of Justice; at the Department of

Homeland Security; and even in the office of the US Trade Representative.

These lawyers found more sympathetic ears on the bench than their domestic policy counterparts. Certainly the Supreme Court seemed happy to give ground on executive power in the realm of foreign policy. In one important case dealing with the "recognition" power, in fact, it carved off one Article II power from congressional review entirely.

THE RECOGNITION POWER

Article II, Section 3, specifies that the president "shall receive Ambassadors and other public Ministers," language implying executive authority over diplomatic matters. But in 2002, Congress passed a law allowing Americans born in Jerusalem to state on their passports that they were born in "Israel" (rather than "Jerusalem").

President George W. Bush objected in a signing statement that this provision bound the executive branch to a diplomatic position it did not hold and should be under no obligation to assert. President Obama affirmed that position. In turn, Menachem Zivotofsky (or his parents, given that he was born in 2002) sued to uphold the plain text of the statute. The basic question, as the case *Zivotofsky* v. *Rice* became *Zivotofsky* v. *Clinton*, and finally *Zivotofsky* v. *Kerry*, remained as Justice Anthony Kennedy put it: "whether the President has the exclusive power to grant formal recognition to a foreign sovereign" and whether Congress can force the president to use that power in a certain way.

Presidents cling to the "sole organ" doctrine springing from the 1936 *Curtiss-Wright* case to argue that they have unimpeded power in foreign relations.[49] Yet as Justice Scalia pointed out, "Our cases say repeatedly that the president is the sole instrument of the United States for the *conduct* of foreign policy, but it doesn't necessarily mean that the president determines everything in foreign policy."[50] That is, in some areas Congress can and should call the tune that the presidential organ must play.

The passport case, according to the Court, did not fall into that category. The majority agreed with the Solicitor General, Donald Verrilli, who argued for the Obama administration that recognition "is an exclusive power with the President. Recognition is not lawmaking. It is an executive function."[51] As Justice Kennedy concluded, receiving an ambassador is "tantamount to recognizing the sovereignty of the sending state," and since "the Nation must have a single policy regarding which governments are legitimate in the eyes of the United States and which are not ... [t]he formal act of recognition is an executive power that Congress may not qualify."[52] Requiring the president to recognize Jerusalem as part of Israel was thus disallowed. (President Trump, of course, would do so of his own accord in 2017.)

The Court's decision seemed to place the recognition power somewhere near the pardon power as an unchecked and perhaps uncheckable presidential power. Even so, the majority opinion emphasized that despite the "sole organ" language of *Curtiss-Wright*, that case "did not hold that the President is free from Congress' lawmaking power in the field of international relations." Indeed, "the Executive is not free from the ordinary controls and checks of Congress merely because foreign affairs are at issue." The Court even signaled ways Congress could undermine in practice a president's recognition of a given nation through the budget power – a hint to legislators, perhaps, regarding the Obama administration's initiatives toward reestablishing diplomatic and economic ties with Cuba.

War powers

If the recognition power could be contested, the power to initiate war seems rather more clear: it is specifically granted to Congress by Article I of the Constitution, and *not* to the president. Yet over time, presidents have garnered a good deal of autonomy in this area as well, abetted both by Congressional inaction and the vagaries of past laws' delegations of power.[53] Thus, here too interesting questions of statutory interpretation arise.

The statutes of most interest for present purposes are the 1973 War Powers Resolution (WPR) and the 2001 Authorization for the Use of Military Force (AUMF). Other issues that have arisen – the use of drones as weapons, for example, especially where these have targeted American citizens – flow largely from the prior question of whether the United States is at war, with whom, and where. That decision in turn can be taken to activate a wider range of presidential authority.

The 2011 US intervention in Libya, in collaboration with its NATO allies, has received sustained attention, so its operational details do not need much elaboration here.[54] But recall that as Arab Spring uprisings threatened the regime of Muammar al-Qaddafi, the aging dictator threatened a "bloodbath" in retaliation. A UN Security Council resolution was sought to prevent a humanitarian disaster, a mission which soon enough expanded to provide military support for rebel forces that successfully overthrew Qaddafi's government and summarily executed Qaddafi himself.

Many strands wove into the decision to support military action in Libya, but none of them ran through Congress – even though the WPR envisions explicit congressional authorization for any American involvement in "hostilities, or into situations where imminent involvement in hostilities is clearly indicated by the circumstances." To be sure, the WPR was never a triumph of careful legal drafting, and its vague language has proved problematic in enforcing it.[55] Even so it clearly prohibits unauthorized involvement after a sixty- (sometimes ninety-) day clock has expired. As the Libya operation approached those markers, the Obama administration needed to decide its course of action.

Libya serves as a reminder that statutory interpretation is a product available through an intra-administrative market for legal advice. Obama's large but loose array of "lawfare" attorneys had diverging views on the legality of using the American military in Libya after the "clock" ran out. Most (including the Justice Department's Office of Legal Counsel and the Pentagon) seemed to think that, at the very least, the "operational tempo" would have to be reduced. In this scenario the United States would provide logistical support for NATO attacks but not carry out those attacks itself. However, White House Counsel Robert Bauer, along with Harold Koh at the State Department, developed "a very aggressive interpretation" of the War Powers Resolution.[56] They argued that the Libya operation did not constitute "hostilities" under the terms of the WPR and thus that the law simply did not apply. As Obama himself later put it at a press conference, "hostilities" only occurred in wars on the scale of Vietnam.[57] Though legislative (and legal) critics were not impressed with this logic, Congress as a whole was too divided on the merits of the policy to take firm action regarding its legality. No definitive votes were taken.

The use of American force in Syria and Iraq against the so-called Islamic State (ISIS) met with another creative exegesis of statute but even less little political opposition. Though the extensive use of airstrikes and more limited use of ground forces again certainly seemed to constitute hostilities under the WPR, the emotional resonance of ISIS's brutal tactics and efforts well beyond the Levant smothered efforts to revive the war powers debate. Obama, in an August 2014 letter to Congress, said he was notifying legislators about his decisions, "consistent with" the WPR but not "pursuant to" it.[58]

What legal authority governed the operation? Obama, unlike some of his predecessors, did not argue the WPR was unconstitutional – hence the administration's legal gymnastics regarding Libya. But the law was an awkward fit for the ISIS case.

In the WPR, presidents are given authority to use force under three circumstances: when there is (1) a declaration of war; (2) a specific statutory authorization; or (3) "a national emergency created by attack upon the United States, its territories or possessions, or its armed forces." Options (1) and (2) are self-explanatory. But they did not apply to ISIS.

Presidential uses of force without those authorizations have tended to fall into one or both of two categories: cases of self-defense (sometimes imaginatively defined), and/or cases with wide multilateral support. Self-defense links to the third option available under the WPR; examples include the failed rescue attempt of the American hostages in Iran in 1980 or the 1998 missile strikes after the African embassy bombings. Sometimes presidents are quite generous in their interpretation of the WPR's phrasing. The 1989 invasion of Panama was the reverse of an "attack upon the United States," but was explained by President Bush as a response to "reckless threats and attacks upon Americans in Panama [that] created an imminent danger to the 35,000 American citizens" there.[59]

Other cases appeal to a cause of action endorsed by the international community, normally with a humanitarian component.

In the 1983 Grenada operation, President Reagan combined arguments for the safety of American students there with the fact the United States had been invited to respond, that it was doing so in concert with other nations in the region, and that "this collective action has been forced on us by events that have no precedent in the eastern Caribbean and no place in any civilized society."[60] In Somalia (1992), Kosovo (1999), and in the Libya case just described, one could cite both humanitarian concerns and treaty obligations – normally to the United Nations or to NATO. While the WPR specifically rules out inferring authority to use force from treaties, those treaties are the law of the land too, and such an argument can at least muddy the waters and sway public opinion.

Obama's early arguments regarding ISIS feinted toward both self-defense and international obligation but, in the end, did not try very hard to establish the facts of a "national emergency." The president said the mission focused on the Mosul Dam, whose breach "could threaten the lives of large numbers of civilians, endanger US personnel and facilities, including the US Embassy in Baghdad, and prevent the Iraqi government from providing critical services to the Iraqi populace."[61] But his general argument at the time was a grab-bag: that "these actions . . . are in the national security and foreign policy interests of the United States, pursuant to my constitutional authority to conduct US foreign relations and as Commander in Chief and Chief Executive. These actions are being undertaken in coordination with the Iraqi government."[62]

A month later, in September 2014, Obama clarified that he did not need congressional authorization to expand air attacks on the Islamic State in Iraq, nor even to extend them to Syria. "I'm confident that I have the authorization that I need to protect the American people," he told a television interviewer.[63] *The Washington Post* reported that "the White House's belief that it has authority to act is based on the reports Obama has filed with Congress under the War Powers Act (sic) and the earlier congressional authorization for the war in Iraq."[64]

But neither rationale was very convincing. As noted above, the Obama administration had not actually filed any reports directly "under" the WPR, only a series of letters intended to keep Congress "fully informed." In each letter Obama claimed to be acting "pursuant to my constitutional authority to conduct US foreign relations and as Commander in Chief and Chief Executive."[65]

Likewise, the authorization to use force in Iraq passed in 2002 stated that the president could "defend the national security of the United States against the continuing threat posed by Iraq" and enforce all relevant United Nations Security Council resolutions regarding Iraq. It therefore authorized the use of force *against* (the state of) Iraq, rather than *in* Iraq. The Security Council resolutions referred to dealt with weapons of mass destruction, with Iraq's "repression of its civilian population," and with the Hussein regime's threats against its neighbors. ISIS was doing some of those things, to be sure, but Iraq itself was not; indeed, the threat to the United States from Iraq's government seemed to be from the latter's incompetence in dealing with ISIS. Potential attacks within Syria's borders seemed even more removed from the 2002 authorization's intent.

Recognizing this, the Obama administration soon argued instead that its authority to conduct the ISIS war lay in neither the WPR nor the Iraq resolution but a different source altogether: the 2001 AUMF passed just after the September 11 terror attacks. As White House press secretary Josh Earnest later framed it, "The answer simply is that Congress, in 2001, did give the executive branch authorization to take this action, and there's no debating that."[66]

The AUMF, passed just three days after 9/11, says that,

> the President is authorized to use all necessary and appropriate force against those nations, organizations, or persons he determines planned, authorized, committed, or aided the terrorist attacks that occurred on September 11, 2001, or harbored such organizations or persons, in order to prevent any future acts of international terrorism against the United States by such nations, organizations or persons.

This is very broad language: it allows the president to determine not only what counts as "necessary and appropriate force" but also whom to use it on – including anyone who might have "aided" the 9/11 attackers – with the goal of preventing *any* future terrorist attacks. Even so, it is linked explicitly to the 9/11 attacks, and thus to al-Qaeda. Al-Qaeda, in turn, is not ISIS.

Or is it? The administration argued that the connection was good enough for government work. Press Secretary Earnest briefed:

> So it is the view of the . . . Obama administration that the 2001 AUMF continues to apply to [ISIS] because of their decade-long relationship with Al Qaida, their continuing ties to Al Qaida; because of their—they have continued to employ the kind of heinous tactics that they previously employed when their name was Al Qaida in Iraq. And finally, because they continue to have the same kind of . . . aspiration that they articulated under their previous name."[67]

Stephen Preston, the Pentagon's General Counsel, said in April 2015 that "the name may have changed, but the group . . . has been an enemy of the United States within the scope of the 2001 AUMF continuously since at least 2004."[68]

This legal interpretation did not receive stellar external reviews; Jack Goldsmith, who headed the OLC for part of the Bush 43 administration, called it "presidential unilateralism masquerading as implausible statutory interpretation."[69] That ISIS used consistently "heinous tactics" was true – it did not, unfortunately, make them particularly distinctive in the modern world of warfare. The clearest critique of the chosen rationale was that ISIS was not in itself associated with the 9/11 attacks since it did not exist in 2001. Since then, in fact, it had broken rather firmly with al-Qaeda, which had repudiated its even more evil twin. How, then, could it be an "associated force," even under the administration's earlier definition of that term? As national security analyst Benjamin Wittes put it, "'associated' does not mean 'not associated' or 'repudiated by' or 'broken with' or even 'used to be associated with.'"[70] Another legal scholar asked, "If a *past* nexus is now all that is required . . . [w]ill we later hear of the AUMF applying to associated forces of this successor force?"[71] Would splinter groups from ISIS count? What about groups that splinter from the splinter groups?

There is, in short, a "six degrees of separation" problem with the rationale. Using the logic of the game that requires players to link Kevin Bacon to every other actor in the world, one could probably discover al-Qaeda connections to most current and future actors with evil intent against the United States. Indeed, in March 2016 the administration argued that airstrikes killing about 150 al-Shabab militants in Somalia were also authorized by the same law. A June 2016 "supplemental consolidated report" to Congress listed operations in Afghanistan, Iraq, Syria, Yemen, Somalia, Djibouti, and Libya as part of the AUMF umbrella – and in November, the administration announced a legal opinion assigning not just al-Shabab leaders but the entire group to those culpable for the September 11, 2001, attacks.[72] It is perhaps worth pointing out that the group did not exist until 2007.

Yet as the Obama administration wound down, Congress showed little inclination to get involved. The ISIS attacks in Paris in November 2015 and in Brussels in March 2016 – and the alleged allegiance of American murderers in California and Florida to the group – prompted both bellicose rhetoric and the use of special forces as "advisers" on the ground in Syria and Iraq. They did not prompt Congress, however, to deliberate matters of war and peace.

In February 2015 President Obama did send Congress a new draft AUMF to cover the ISIS war. Obama's version would have repealed the 2002 Iraq authorization AUMF while keeping the 2001 version in place. It provided for a three-year window in which the president was authorized "to use the Armed Forces of the United States as the President determines to be necessary and appropriate against ISIS or associated persons or forces," though it did not allow for the use of American troops in "enduring offensive ground combat operations" and expired after three years.

Congressional doves thought this too strong, while hawks thought it too restrictive. The draft itself received no serious legislative consideration. Neither did other versions, though Rep. Jim McGovern (D-MA) did manage to force a roll call on the blunt question of removing troops from Syria and Iraq altogether; this was rejected, with 288 members voting against withdrawal. In general, legislators seemed to agree with Senate Foreign Relations committee chair Bob Corker (R-TN) that "the administration has the authorities to do what they're doing against ISIS." Senate minority leader Harry Reid (D-NV) expanded this to a more faith-based approach: "I don't believe in AUMFs."[73]

Into this vacuum of existential doubt, the American military commitment across the Middle East, Africa, Pakistan, and Afghanistan kept ramping up. In 2016, the internal rules Obama had imposed governing drone strikes – dealing with zones of self-declared "active hostilities" and elsewhere – were loosened when US allies asked for support. The administration promised to avoid "boots on the ground" – but despite their apparently inadequate footwear, American special operations advisers numbered several hundred by the spring of 2016 and were very much on the front lines again in the Middle East. As the Obama administration drew to a close, at least sixteen Americans had been killed in anti-ISIS operations in Iraq, and one in Syria.[74]

This brought the story back to a familiar place: the courtroom. In May 2016, Army Captain Nathan Smith filed a lawsuit asking a US District Court to declare that "President Obama's war against ISIS is illegal because Congress has not authorized it."[75] He argued that the WPR's requirements had been ignored, and that as far back as the 1804 case *Little* v. *Barreme* the judiciary has required that presidential orders be "strictly warranted by law."

In August, responding to the government's effort to dismiss the case, Smith's attorney argued that "this is a garden variety statutory construction case," not a political question that the courts should or could avoid. Neither the 2001 nor the 2002 AUMF justify the war with ISIS, he argued; this was "precisely the kind of 'undeclared war' that the [War Powers] Resolution aimed to avoid."[76] Even so, in November the district court sided with the administration, holding that Smith had no standing to bring suit against the government.[77] By the time his appeal was heard, Smith had left the Army, and thus the case was dismissed again, as moot. Thus, no court reached a substantive conclusion about the broader argument concerning the WPR. This enabled additional expansion of the war against ISIS under the Trump administration.[78]

Statutory interpretation and presidential legacy

In casting his vote against John Roberts's nomination to the Supreme Court, Senator Barack Obama noted that in "truly difficult" cases, "adherence to precedent and rules of construction and interpretation will only get you through the 25th mile of the marathon. That last mile can only be determined on the basis of one's deepest values, one core concerns, one's broader perspectives on how the world works, and the depth and breadth of one's empathy."[79]

As president, Obama needed that last mile to detour around congressional gridlock. Since Congress refused to pass new laws (at least after 2010), the Obama administration looked to wring new authority from old ones. In the *King* v. *Burwell* oral arguments, the Solicitor General was asked why legislators couldn't simply fix the problem if it stemmed from a simple drafting error. He replied, to knowing laughter, "*this* Congress?"[80] Obama himself, in his November 2014 immigration address, almost taunted "those members of Congress who question my authority . . . or question the wisdom of me acting . . . I have one answer: pass a bill."[81] In the absence of legislative action, Obama pushed executive action generally, and statutory interpretation specifically, as a means of establishing a substantive legacy.

That legacy will produce mixed results. In some areas, Obama's changes will have real staying power. Indeed, where Congress has been most irresponsible in carrying out its constitutional duties, in the war powers, Obama was able to change facts both in legal textbooks and on the ground. Even as the Trump administration conducted missile strikes against the Syrian government itself (after the Assad regime's use of chemical weapons), a use of force surely not contemplated in response to the September 11 attacks, Congress failed to revisit the language of the 2001 AUMF.[82]

Likewise, where Obama's new understandings of old legal language made its way into formal regulation, that very process protected it. To repeal regulations, as President Trump promised to do, requires a lengthy exercise justifying the change and incorporating public comment. As of the fall of 2019, the Institute for Policy Integrity at New York University found the administration had prevailed in only four of fifty-seven court cases challenging its efforts to set aside Obama-era rules. This included matters of environmental protection, agriculture, land use, and transportation.[83] Further, even proposed regulations sometimes shaped private action in ways that made subsequent reversal expensive to industry, and thus hard to change – as with coal-powered electric plants.

But administrative action is inherently fragile compared to legislative change. Executive actions can be reversed simply by future chief executives, and President Trump was eager to do just that. As long-time chronicler of the presidency Peter Baker observed in June of 2017, "Whether out of personal animus, political calculation, philosophical disagreement or a conviction that the last president damaged the country, Mr. Trump has made it clear that if it has Mr. Obama's name on it, he would just as soon erase it from the national hard drive."[84] Some of those efforts are detailed above. More broadly, Trump issued numerous directives rescinding Obama's initiatives in areas ranging from workers' rights to the services required under the Affordable Care Act to the conservation of large swathes of public land as a "national monument." For the last, the Trump Interior Department decided to read the 1906 Antiquities Act as allowing not just the creation but the cancellation of declared monuments, a clear case of a new meaning given an old law.

So-called "guidance documents" issued by departments were particularly vulnerable. For instance, the Obama Education and Justice departments had read the civil rights statute known as Title IX to include protections for transgender students (for instance, to allow them to use the toilet facilities of their choice.) On the other hand, Obama's Department of Health and Human Services rejected "conscience protections" based on religious beliefs proffered by healthcare providers who did not want to offer certain services, such as contraceptive care. The Trump administration reversed both positions. Where Obama's policies rested in interpretation of the law, rather than in the letter of the law, so could his successor's.

Thus, given legislative intransigence, a strategy grounded in administrative action may have been necessary – but it was not sufficient in itself to cement permanent change. To be sure, part of Obama's legacy is substantive and consequential. But another portion of that legacy may be to highlight the brittle nature of unilateral change in a system that demands consensus and coalition building to achieve permanent reform.

Notes

1. "Remarks by the President Before Cabinet Meeting," 14 January 2014, available at https://obamawhitehouse.archives.gov/the-press-office/2014/01/14/remarks-president-cabinet-meeting (last accessed October 30, 2019).

2. See, *inter alia*, Speaker John Boehner to House Colleagues, "That the Laws be Faithfully Executed . . ." memo of June 25, 2014, available at http://www.scribd.com/doc/231315267/Boehner-memo-to-House-members (last accessed October 30, 2019); Office of House Majority Leader Eric Cantor, *The Imperial Presidency: An Update* (2014); Eugene Scott, "Maine Gov. Paul LePage: Barack Obama is a Dictator," CNN.com (October 12, 2016), available at http://www.cnn.com/2016/10/12/politics/paul-lepage-donald-trump-obama-dictator/ (last accessed October 30, 2019).

3. Richard P. Nathan, *The Plot that Failed: Nixon and the Administrative Presidency* (New York: Wiley, 1975); Terry M. Moe "The Politicized Presidency," in *New Directions in American Politics*, ed. John Chubb and Paul E. Peterson (Washington, DC: Brookings Institution Press, 1985); Andrew Rudalevige and David E. Lewis, "Parsing the Politicized Presidency: Centralization and Politicization as Presidential Strategies for Bureaucratic Control," paper presented at the 2005 Annual Meeting of the American Political Science Association, Washington, DC, 2005.

4. Arthur Schlesinger, Jr., *The Imperial Presidency* (Boston, MA: Houghton Mifflin, 1973); and see Andrew Rudalevige, *The New Imperial Presidency* (Ann Arbor: University of Michigan Press, 2005).

5. Nathan, *The Plot That Failed*, p. 93.

6. Dwight Ink, "Executive Branch Reorganization," December 2, 1980, NARA-II, RG 51, Deputy Director's Subject Files: Ed Harper, 1981–82 (FRC 51-82-50), Box 3 [Reorganization].

7. Reagan's White House counselor and Attorney General, Edwin Meese, for example, bemoaned "the legislative opportunism" of the era, arguing that "Congress had used [Watergate] to expand its power in various ways vis-à-vis the executive branch" and create a "major threat to constitutional government." See Edwin Meese, III, *With Reagan: The Inside Story* (Washington, DC: Regnery, 1992), p. 322; Richard P. Nathan, *The Administrative Presidency* (New York: Macmillan, 1983).

8. Elena Kagan, "Presidential Administration," *Harvard Law Review*, 114, June 2001: 2385.
9. Kagan, "Presidential Administration," 2248. Clinton was also aggressive in his use of unilateral tools in foreign policy; see, for a detailed account, Ryan Hendrickson, *The Clinton Wars: The Constitution, Congress, and War Powers* (Nashville, TN: Vanderbilt University Press, 2002).
10. The second-term 113th and 114th Congresses, spanning four years from 2013 to 2016, passed a total of only 540 public laws, a figure that was just over half the number passed in two years in 1947–1948 by a body considered so unproductive it was insultingly nicknamed the "Do Nothing" Congress.
11. Jeff Winkler, "McConnell Skeptical of Obama's Centrist Rhetoric Ahead of State of the Union," *The Daily Caller*, January 25, 2011, available at http://dailycaller.com/2011/01/25/mcconnell-skeptical-about-obamas-centrist-rhetoric-ahead-of-state-of-the-union/ (last accessed 9 October 2018).
12. Martha Derthick, *Up in Smoke* (Washington, DC: CQ Press, 3rd rev. ed., 2011), p. 56; see also Andrew Rudalevige, "The Obama Administrative Presidency: Some Late-Term Patterns," *Presidential Studies Quarterly*, 46, December 2016: 868–890, from which some of the examples herein are derived.
13. Andrew Rudalevige, "'A Majority is the Best Repartee': Barack Obama and Congress, 2009–12," *Social Science Quarterly*, 93, December 2012: 1272–1294.
14. Obama, "Remarks in Las Vegas," October 24, 2011, available via the online American Presidency Project housed at the University of California, Santa Barbara, at https://www.presidency.ucsb.edu/node/297388 (last accessed October 30, 2019).
15. See Harold C. Relyea, *Presidential Directives: Background and Overview* (Washington, DC: Congressional Research Service, 2008); Graham G. Dodds, *Take Up Your Pen: Unilateral Presidential Directives in American Politics* (Philadelphia: University of Pennsylvania Press, 2013), p. 6.
16. The quotes above are from Rudalevige, "The Obama Administrative Presidency," which also classifies these and other actions by the administrative tool or directive that actually enabled them.
17. Quoted in Peter Nicholas and Christi Parsons, "Rebuilding Staff, Obama Charts New Course," *Philadelphia Inquirer*, October 10, 2010.

18. R. Shep Melnick, *Between the Lines* (Washington, DC: Brookings Institution, 1994).
19. Harold H. Bruff, *Untrodden Ground: How Presidents Interpret the Constitution* (Chicago: University of Chicago Press, 2015); Keith E. Whittington, *Constitutional Construction: Divided Powers and Constitutional Meaning* (Cambridge, MA: Harvard University Press, 2001).
20. Charlie Savage, *Power Wars: Inside Obama's Post-9/11 Presidency* (Boston, MA: Little Brown, 2015).
21. Savage, *Power Wars*, pp. 52, 63, 65.
22. Savage, *Power Wars*, p. 67.
23. Obama, "Remarks by the President," May 21, 2009, available at https://www.presidency.ucsb.edu/node/286247 (last accessed October 30, 2019).
24. Graham quoted in Rebecca Adams, "Lame Duck or Leapfrog?" *CQ Weekly* (February 12, 2007), p. 450; Bruce Ackerman, *The Decline and Fall of the American Republic* (Cambridge, MA: Harvard University Press, 2010), p. 88. See also Chris Edelson, "In Service to Power: Legal Scholars as Executive Branch Lawyers in the Obama Administration," *Presidential Studies Quarterly*, 43, September 2013: 618–640.
25. Minutes available at http://nsarchive.gwu.edu/NSAEBB/NSAEBB 210/2-NSPG%20minutes%206-25-84%20(IC%2000463).pdf (last accessed October 30, 2019).
26. Savage, *Power Wars*, pp. 677–681.
27. Hearing of the Committee on the Judiciary, US House of Representatives, "Enforcing the President's Constitutional Duty to Faithfully Execute the Laws," February 26, 2014. Available at http://judiciary.house.gov/index.cfm/2014/2/enforcing-the-president-s-constitutional-duty-to-faithfully-execute-the-laws (last accessed October 9, 2018).
28. Robert Pear, "Four Words Imperil Health Law; All a Mistake, Its Writers Say," *The New York Times*, May 26, 2015, p. A1.
29. Tweet of October 13, 2017, available at https://twitter.com/realdonaldtrump/status/918772522983874561 (last accessed October 30, 2019).
30. Daniel P. Gitterman, *Calling the Shots: The President, Executive Orders, and Public Policy* (Washington, DC: Brookings Institution Press, 2017).
31. Texas was a highly favored site for "venue shoppers" filing suit against Obama administration actions, since it had many judges unsympathetic to aggressive regulatory behavior – because it moved fast – and because the Fifth Circuit Court of Appeals that covers Texas was

also dominated by Republican appointees. As one reporter noted, "Another day, another Obama administration regulation blocked nationwide by a federal court in Texas." (See Josh Gerstein, "Judge Blocks Obama Contracting Rules Nationwide," *Politico*, October 25, 2016), available at http://www.politico.com/blogs/under-the-radar/2016/10/obama-government-contractors-regulation-blocked-texas-court-230295 (last accessed October 30, 2019).

32. Daniel Wiessner, "States, Interest Groups Sue US Government on Overtime Pay Rule," Reuters.com (September 20, 2016), available at http://www.reuters.com/article/us-overtime-lawsuit-idUSKCN11Q2E2 (last accessed October 30, 2019).

33. Melanie Trottman, "Federal Judge Issues Nationwide Injunction," *The Wall Street Journal* (November 23, 2016).

34. Barack Obama, "Presidential Memorandum Regarding Fuel Efficiency Standards," Office of the White House Press Secretary (May 22, 2010), available at https://obamawhitehouse.archives.gov/the-press-office/presidential-memorandum-regarding-fuel-efficiency-standards (last accessed October 30, 2019).

35. Coral Davenport, "E.P.A. Staff Struggling to Create Pollution Rule," *The New York Times* (February 4, 2014), available at https://www.nytimes.com/2014/02/05/us/epa-staff-struggling-to-create-rule-limiting-carbon-emissions.html (last accessed October 30, 2019); Coral Davenport and Gardiner Harris, "Obama to Unveil Tougher Environmental Plan with His Legacy in Mind," *The New York Times* (August 2, 2015), available at https://www.nytimes.com/2015/08/02/us/obama-to-unveil-tougher-climate-plan-with-his-legacy-in-mind.html (last accessed October 30, 2019).

36. Kagan remarks from oral arguments for *Utility Air Regulatory Group* v. *Environmental Protection Agency*, February 24, 2014, available at https://www.supremecourt.gov/oral_arguments/argument_transcripts/2013/12-1146_8n6a.pdf (last accessed October 30, 2019). See more generally the opinion of the Court: *UARG* v. *EPA*, 573 U.S. 302 (2014).

37. Jonathan H. Adler, "Supreme Court Puts the Brakes on the EPA's Clean Power Plan," Volokh Conspiracy blog, *The Washington Post* (February 9, 2016), available at https://www.washingtonpost.com/news/volokh-conspiracy/wp/2016/02/09/supreme-court-puts-the-brakes-on-the-epas-clean-power-plan/?utm_term=.4a359fb75e87 (last accessed October 27, 2018).

38. Jonathan H. Adler, "Placing Obama's Clean Power Plan in Context," Volokh Conspiracy blog, *The Washington Post* (February 10, 2016),

available at https://www.washingtonpost.com/news/volokh-conspir-acy/wp/2016/02/10/placing-the-clean-power-plan-in-context/?utm_term=.bc1435759a3f (last accessed October 30, 2019).

39. Adler, "Placing Obama's Clean Power Plan in Context." See also Coral Davenport, "Obama Climate Plan, Now in Court, May Hinge on Error in 1990 Law," *The New York Times* (September 25, 2016), available at https://www.nytimes.com/2016/09/26/us/politics/obama-court-clean-power-plan.html (last accessed October 30, 2019).

40. Jonathan H. Adler, "The En Banc D.C. Circuit Meets the Clean Power Plan," Volokh Conspiracy blog, *The Washington Post* (September 28, 2016), available at https://www.washingtonpost.com/news/volokh-conspiracy/wp/2016/09/28/the-en-banc-d-c-circuit-meets-the-clean-power-plan/?utm_term=.8a76b4c05c12 (last accessed October 30, 2019).

41. Lisa Friedman and Brad Plumer, "E.P.A. Drafts Rule on Coal Plants to Replace Clean Power Plan," *The New York Times*, July 5, 2018, available at https://www.nytimes.com/2018/07/05/climate/clean-power-plan-replacement.html (last accessed October 30, 2019).

42. Brad Plumer, "Want to Know Why Trump Will Struggle to Save the Coal Industry? Look at Michigan," Vox.com (November 28, 2016), available at http://www.vox.com/energy-and-environment/2016/11/28/13763728/trump-coal-industry-michigan (last accessed October 30, 2019).

43. Barack Obama, "Address to the Nation on Immigration Reform," November 20, 2014, available at https://www.presidency.ucsb.edu/node/308498 (last accessed October 30, 2019).

44. Though DAPA is often described as having been created "by execu-tive order," in fact no executive orders were issued. The memoranda created a White House Task Force on New Americans and urged a creation of a better visa system (rules on the latter were prepared for issuance in late 2016).

45. See the suing states' "Complaint for Declaratory and Injunctive Relief," December 2014, available at https://www.clearinghouse.net/detail.php?id=14308 (last accessed October 30, 2019).

46. See the oral arguments in *United States v. Texas*, April 18, 2016, available at https://www.supremecourt.gov/oral_arguments/argu-ment_transcripts/2015/15-674_b97d.pdf (last accessed October 30, 2019).

47. Ibid.

48. The decision came in *Texas et al. v. United States*, No. 18-00068 (S.D. Tex. May 1, 2018). On the various DACA cases, see the National

Immigration Law Center, "Status of Current DACA Litigation," available at https://www.nilc.org/issues/daca/status-current-daca-litigation/ (last accessed October 30, 2019).

49. For an accurately unsympathetic history of these claims, see Louis Fisher, "Presidential Inherent Power: The 'Sole Organ' Doctrine," *Presidential Studies Quarterly*, 37, March 2007: 139–152.

50. Emphasis added. This was in *Zivotofsky* v. *Clinton* (2011), an earlier iteration of the case hinging on whether this was a "political question" that the courts could not answer. The Supreme Court ruled 8–1 that it was not. So the case returned to the D.C. Circuit for decision on the merits, whence it returned to the Supreme Court as *Zivotofsky* v. *Kerry* in 2015.

51. From the oral arguments for *Zivotofsky* v. *Kerry*, November 3, 2014, available at https://www.supremecourt.gov/oral_arguments/ argument_transcripts/2014/13-628_dk8c.pdf (last accessed October 30, 2019).

52. *Zivotofsky* v. *Kerry*, 576 US 1059 (2015).

53. See, for example, Rudalevige, *The New Imperial Presidency*.

54. Jo Becker and Scott Shane, "Clinton, 'Smart Power,' and a Dictator's Fall," *The New York Times* (February 28, 2016), available at https://www.nytimes.com/2016/02/28/us/politics/hillary-clinton-libya.html (last accessed October 30, 2019), A1; Chris Edelson, *Emergency Presidential Power* (Madison: University of Wisconsin Press, 2013); Louis Fisher, "Military Operations in Libya: No War? No Hostilities?" *Presidential Studies Quarterly*, 42, March 2012: 176–189.

55. Louis Fisher and David Gray Adler, "The War Powers Resolution: Time to Say Goodbye," *Political Science Quarterly*, 113, spring 1998: 1–20.

56. Savage, *Power Wars*, 645.

57. "Press Conference by the President," June 29, 2011, available at https://obamawhitehouse.archives.gov/the-press-office/2011/06/29/ press-conference-president (last accessed October 30, 2019).

58. Barack Obama, "Letter from the President: War Powers Resolution Regarding Iraq," available at https://obamawhitehouse.archives. gov/the-press-office/2014/08/08/letter-president-war-powers-resolution-regarding-iraq (last accessed October 30, 2019).

59. George H. W. Bush, "Address to the Nation Announcing United States Military Action in Panama," December 20, 1989, available at https://www.presidency.ucsb.edu/node/264344 (last accessed October 30, 2019).

60. Ronald Reagan, "Remarks of the President and Prime Minister Eugenia Charles of Dominica Announcing the Deployment of United States Forces in Grenada," October 25, 1983, available at https://www.presidency.ucsb.edu/node/261906 (last accessed October 30, 2019).

61. Barack Obama, "Letter from the President – War Powers Resolution Regarding Iraq," August 17, 2014, available at https://obamawhite-house.archives.gov/the-press-office/2014/08/17/letter-president-war-powers-resolution-regarding-iraq (last accessed October 30, 2019).

62. Ibid.

63. "Meet the Press Transcript," NBC News (September 7, 2014), available at http://www.nbcnews.com/meet-the-press/meet-press-transcript-september-7-2014-n197866 (last accessed October 30, 2019).

64. Juliet Eilperin and David Nakamura, "Obama Ready to Strike at Islamic State militants in Syria, He Tells Policy Experts," *The Washington Post* (September 9, 2014), available at https://www.washingtonpost.com/politics/obama-prepared-to-order-airstrikes-in-syria-as-part-of-strategy-against-islamic-state/2014/09/09/058199e2-3834-11e4-bdfb-de4104544a37_story.html (last accessed October 30, 2019).

65. Obama, "Letter from the President" of August 8, 2014 and August 17, 2014.

66. Daily Press Briefing by the White House Press Secretary, October 31, 2015. Available at https://obamawhitehouse.archives.gov/the-press-office/2015/10/30/daily-press-briefing-press-secretary-josh-earnest-103015 (last accessed October 30, 2019).

67. Quoted in Steven T. Dennis, "Here's Obama's Legal Justification for ISIS War," *Roll Call* (September 11, 2014), http://www.rollcall.com/news/home/heres-the-administrations-legal-justification-for-isis-isil-war (last accessed October 30, 2019).

68. "The Legal Framework for the United States' Use of Military Force Since 9/11," speech delivered to the Annual Meeting of the American Society of International Law, Washington, DC, April 10, 2015, available at http://www.defense.gov/News/Speeches/Speech-View/Article/606662 (last accessed October 30, 2019).

69. Jack Goldsmith, "Obama's Breathtaking Expansion of the President's Power to Make War," *Time*, September 11, 2014, available at http://time.com/3326689/obama-isis-war-powers-bush/ (last accessed October 30, 2019).

70. Benjamin Wittes, "AUMF: Scope and Reach: Not Asking the Girl to Dance," *Lawfare*, September 10, 2014, available at https://www.lawfareblog.com/not-asking-girl-dance (last accessed October 30, 2019).

71. Robert Chesney, "The 2001 AUMF: From Associated Forces to (Disassociated) Successor Forces," *Lawfare*, September 10, 2014, available at https://www.lawfareblog.com/2001-aumf-associated-forces-disassociated-successor-forces (last accessed October 30, 2019).

72. Charlie Savage, Eric Schmitt, and Mark Mazzetti, "Obama Expands War with Al-Qaeda to Include al-Shabab in Somalia," *The New York Times*, November 28, 2016, available at https://www.nytimes.com/2016/11/27/us/politics/obama-expands-war-with-al-qaeda-to-include-shabab-in-somalia.html (last accessed October 30, 2019).

73. Burgess Everett, "New War Authorization Left for Dead," *Politico*, September 11, 2015, available at http://www.politico.com/story/2015/11/syria-corker-veterans-day-war-authorization-215702 (last accessed October 30, 2019).

74. Brendan McGarry, "1st US Service Member Killed Fighting ISIS in Syria," Military.com, November 25, 2016, available at http://www.military.com/daily-news/2016/11/25/2-us-servicemembers-killed-in-syria-iraq.html (last accessed October 30, 2019).

75. Charlie Savage, "An Army Captain Takes Obama to Court Over ISIS War Policy," *The New York Times*, May 4, 2016), available at https://www.nytimes.com/2016/05/05/us/islamic-state-war-powers-lawsuit-obama.html (last accessed October 30, 2019).

76. Bruce Ackerman, "Is Obama Enabling the Next President to Launch Illegal Wars?" *The Atlantic*, August 24, 2016, available at http://www.theatlantic.com/politics/archive/2016/08/obama-illegal-wars/497159/ (last accessed October 30, 2019).

77. Marty Lederman, "Judge Kollar-Ketelly Dismisses Captain Smith's Suit," JustSecurity.org, November 22, 2016, available at https://www.justsecurity.org/34778/judge-kollar-kotelly-dismisses-captain-smiths-suit/ (last accessed October 30, 2019).

78. See, e.g., Daniel J. Rosenthal and Loren DeJone Schulman, "Trump's Secret War on Terror," *The Atlantic*, August 10, 2018, available at https://www.theatlantic.com/international/archive/2018/08/trump-war-terror-drones/567218/ (last accessed October 30, 2019).

79. Quoted in Jeffrey Toobin, *The Oath: The Obama White House and the Supreme Court* (New York: Anchor, 2013), p. 36.

80. From the oral arguments for *King* v. *Burwell*, March 4, 2015, available at https://www.supremecourt.gov/oral_arguments/argument_transcripts/2014/14-114_1bo2.pdf (last accessed October 30, 2019).

81. Obama, "Remarks by the President in Address to the Nation on Immigration."

82. See Andrew Rudalevige, "Attacking Syria Wasn't Legal a Year Ago; It's Still Not," Monkey Cage blog, *The Washington Post* (April 13, 2018), available at https://www.washingtonpost.com/news/monkey-cage/wp/2018/04/13/attacking-syria-wasnt-legal-a-year-ago-its-still-not/?utm_term=.c5a74014c925 (last accessed October 30, 2019).

83. See the figures calculated by the Institute for Policy Integrity at the New York University School of Law, "Roundup: Trump-Era Agency Policy in the Courts," updated as of October 15, 2019, available at https://policyintegrity.org/deregulation-roundup (last accessed October 30, 2019). See also Conor Raso, "Trump's Deregulatory Efforts Keep Losing in Court," *Brookings Institution*, October 25, 2018, available at https://www.brookings.edu/research/trumps-deregulatory-efforts-keep-losing-in-court-and-the-losses-could-make-it-harder-for-future-administrations-to-deregulate/ (last accessed October 30, 2019).

84. Peter Baker, "The Anti-Legacy," *The New York Times*, June 25, 2017, p. SR1, available at https://www.nytimes.com/2017/06/23/sunday-review/donald-trump-barack-obama.html (last accessed October 30, 2019).

3

Congressional gridlock reconsidered: The emergence of a "conducive coalition"?

Alix Meyer

When the Republican Party took back control of the House of Representatives following the midterm elections of 2010, the United States found itself once again under divided government. In an apparent contradiction to David Mayhew's classic conclusions about the relative productivity of Congress when the other party controls the White House,[1] most observers[2] have insisted on the unprecedented level of gridlock brought by a determined GOP opposition to the Obama administration. The Democratic Party candidate of 2008 had built his whole career on the idea that he could bridge the partisan divide. He came to national attention by giving a remarkable keynote at the 2004 Democratic convention. In that speech, he was adamant that the depth of partisan polarization should be nuanced.[3] Meanwhile, the leader of the Republican Party in the Senate was just as famously saying that "the single most important thing we want to achieve is for the president to be a one-term president."[4] To achieve that goal, Republican congressional leaders proved determined to reject most presidential overtures and policy concessions, before and after Republicans returned to majority status on Capitol Hill.

According to most accounts of the period, between 2011 and 2017 legislative productivity fell to historical lows, and in 2013 the government shutdown for two weeks and the country came close to defaulting on its debt when House Republicans unsuccessfully tried to use their power of the purse to force president Obama to accede to major concessions. The effort largely failed to achieve the policy goals set forth as the president stood firm and the temporary dip in the polling for Republican lawmakers convinced them to fold.[5] Following that episode, the two elected branches of the government have seemed content with keeping cooperation to the bare minimum. During president Obama's second term, as the hopes for a potential "grand bargain" eventually faded away, attention quickly turned toward the next presidential contest as the only potential way out of this legislative gridlock.

In an attempt to provide a counterpoint to this narrative, this chapter focuses on the record of congressional accomplishment in that period. The 113th Congress (2013–2015) and the 114th Congress (2015–2017) saw some areas of cooperation between Democrats and Republicans which led notably to the adoption of a major budget deal (Ryan-Murray),[6] a consequential reform of entitlements with the reform of the Medicare "doc-fix,"[7] and an overhaul of the controversial education program No Child Left Behind with the adoption of the Every Student Succeeds Act.[8] Without denying the extent of the obstruction, it seems worthwhile to take a look at the laws that were actually passed. To be clear, the intent is not to deny the weight of evidence and prove that, contrary to what most people think and what data shows, Congress in Obama's second term was productive. Indeed, it was not. Still, the very lack of overall productivity makes it a worthwhile endeavor to investigate what led to the adoption of the few laws that did pass.

This approach is somewhat comparable to that adopted by Lawrence Rothenberg[9] in his study of the adoption of the Toxic Substance Control Act of 2016 or Lautenberg act in the same period. He tried to explain how an environmental reform law decades in the making would finally be adopted by a Republican majority in Barack Obama's second term. According to him, this unlikely outcome was caused by

> a confluence of circumstances such that the costs of gridlock were so great that the bough broke. As political forces external to the national political scene changed the existing status quos in ways beyond effective administrative management, the relevant players preferred an alternative approach. Industry support for new legislation allowed legislators, their party leaders, and their group allies to coordinate and to overcome the numerous and time-consuming obstacles to change.[10]

Under Rotheneberg's framework, two main factors could therefore be highlighted: external forces making the status quo untenable and industry buy-in. We will see to what extent they apply to our own set of case studies.

The manner in which legislating took place in the 113th and 114th Congresses is particularly interesting. Indeed, because of the resolute and blanket opposition of a group of forty or so hardline conservative Republicans organized in the Freedom Caucus, most of the major laws adopted by Congress in Obama's second term could only be adopted with the support of House Democrats. In the roll-call data over the past four years, we can therefore discern in the shadows, sometimes out of reach for the C-SPAN cameras, a bipartisan group of representatives willing to vote together if only to allow the institution to function. They may be said to form a "conducive coalition" in that they were conducive to that modicum of efficient lawmaking that took place. In an era of partisan polarization,[11] it is intriguing to witness the remnants of a bipartisan voting pattern that was so standard in decades past.

To further our understanding of what Congress can achieve in periods of divided government, it is thus necessary to look at the make-up of this coalition and the issues on which Democrats and Republicans were able to work together. I will first return to the literature on congressional gridlock before focusing on a small sample of case studies of successful legislation in Obama's second term and what they can teach us about lawmaking in a polarized era.

Gridlock reconsidered

If we are to reconsider whether the situation on Capitol Hill during Obama's second term truly was one of legislative gridlock, it is necessary to consider first what we mean by gridlock.

The most conventional way to determine legislative productivity is to simply tally the number of laws that were passed during the two-year period of a specific Congress and compare the said number to the legislative output of previous Congresses. This data, easily accessible and historically consistent, often serves as the source for newspaper stories about Congress.

If we rely only on this crude measure of legislative productivity, it is obvious that relatively few laws were passed in the 113th and 114th Congresses. According to data compiled by Brookings,[12] 296 bills were enacted into laws in the 113th Congress (2013–2014) and 329 in the 114th (2015–2016). For context, the average for the first decade of the twenty-first century was 463 bills enacted into laws by Congress. It is worth keeping in mind that until the 2014 midterms, the Republican Party had a majority in the House of Representatives but not in the Senate. We could therefore be tempted to see the slight uptick in the number of laws voted in the 114th Congress as a sign of the impact of unified Republican control in Congress. Indeed, a closer look at the data reveals that more bills were introduced and passed in the House after the GOP gained control of the Senate. In the 113th Congress, House members had introduced 6,030 bills and passed 682; in the 114th Congress, the respective numbers were 6,634 and 896. Obviously, the expectation that House Republican bills would be systematically ignored by a Senate under Democratic control could be a factor. On the other side of the Capitol, senators in the 114th Congress introduced more bills (3,589) but fewer of them (427) were actually passed than in the previous congress when 618 bills had been adopted out of the 3,038 that had been introduced. Given the limited range in the variations, it would still be quite premature to draw any conclusion.

Ultimately, the number of laws adopted or even introduced by Congress is rightly seen as insufficient for a rigorous analysis. First, it is premised on the idea that more laws are inherently good. That idea is of course at odds with the ideology of a large group of lawmakers, libertarians, or conservatives who purport to aim at reducing the size of the government. Others have actually praised the numerous obstacles that stand in the way of legislative achievement as a necessary and constitutionally intended check on the impulses of the people's representatives and the parties.[13] As such, for some, a lack of legislative productivity would not be inherently negative. The other glaring flaw of this simple accounting is that lumping every public law together makes it impossible to distinguish between a minor piece of legislation – the ever popular example being bills renaming a post office – and a landmark reform like the

2010 Patient Protection and Affordable Care Act (better known as Obamacare) that dramatically overhauls public policy with clear consequences for millions of Americans.

In his seminal study, David Mayhew attempted to solve that problem by creating a taxonomy of the various levels of legislation.[14] He tried to determine the actual number of important laws whether they be considered as such by media (Sweep 1) and by policy experts looking back (Sweep 2). The database he built led him to conclude that, contrary to common wisdom, the effect of divided government on legislative productivity was null. His methodology was criticized[15] and spawned alternative measures of legislative productivity. In *Stalemate*, Sarah Binder[16] built on Mayhew's work but added an important element by creating a measure of the overall number of issues that were to be addressed by each specific Congress. The idea was to compute a denominator by which the crude number of laws could be refined to determine how many laws were actually passed in the context of the perceived ongoing issues that had to be tackled. Using that metric, she did find that divided government was less productive than unified government and added that intraparty conflict was a very important factor. In a more recent work,[17] Mayhew added the number of presidents' requests as a denominator. This time, in keeping with common wisdom, he found that unified government actually means that presidents get slightly more of their agenda enacted into law.

Whatever the metric used, it should therefore not be surprising to see fewer laws being adopted between the years 2013 and 2017 as President Obama struggles to convince a reluctant Republican Party to join him in passing various pieces of legislation. A lot of ink was spilled describing the conflictual relationship between congressional Republicans and President Obama.[18] What has also been clear is the extent of intraparty opposition inside the Republican Party. Within the House Republican conference, a group of about forty lawmakers started to organize in early 2015 as the Freedom Caucus.[19] Their ambition was to ensure that Speaker Boehner would toe to their particular version of conservative orthodoxy according to which the only strategy that was worth considering with President Obama was refusing to fund the government as long as he did not simply accede to their demands. The group led by Representatives Mark Meadows, Mick Mulvaney, and Raùl Labrador set their sights on John Boehner, whom they saw as unsufficiently committed to the cause and too willing to compromise. Their efforts quickly bore fruit since they obtained his forced resignation in September of 2015.[20] This was a somewhat ironic fall for a Speaker who had risen up in the House GOP by being part of the group of "bombthrowers" who coalesced around Newt Gingrich to orchestrate the hostile takeover of a Republican conference they saw as too complacent and cozy with the Democrats.[21]

These interbranch and intrabranch dynamics provide a useful background to the legislative gridlock that occurred during President Obama's second term. As expected by most models, under such conditions, gridlock indeed came, and yet a few pieces of legislation did manage to sneak through and were enacted into laws. It is to these unrepresentative examples that this chapter now turns.

The laws that did pass

It is not my purpose to amend or add to the existing database of significant and legislative achievement nor to offer an extensive quantitative treatment of same. In an attempt to explain how laws came to be adopted under the inauspicious circumstances stated above, I have selected a handful of specific pieces of legislation and one procedural motion in the House of Representatives. Looking at the winning coalition for these votes will allow me to describe the different dynamics at play. By design, this methodology cannot claim to offer a systematic view of the voting patterns in the 113th and 114th Congresses. I am well aware of the selection bias embedded in an approach centered on case studies. Still, inspired by the pioneering work of the late Barbara Sinclair,[22] I do believe that the stories from these votes offer illustrative examples for some of the sometimes surprising or counterintuitive logic that was created by what others have described as an asymmetric polarization[23] in a divided government setting.

BUDGET AGREEMENTS

Article 1, Section 9 of the US Constitution entrusted Congress with the power of the purse by providing that "No Money shall be drawn from the Treasury, but in Consequence of Appropriations made by Law." This has evolved into the annual appropriations process that, at least on paper, forces Congress to adopt at the very least this piece of legislation for the US government to be able to make payments and continue to function. This is one area where Congressional inaction is not a viable option. Because bills must be presented to the president for his signature, some inter-branch cooperation is quite obviously required.

Better known as the Ryan-Murray bill, the Bipartisan Budget Act of 2013 became Public Law 113–67 with President Obama's signature on December 26, 2013. Negotiated by the House Republican Budget Committee Chairman Paul Ryan and his Senate Democrat counterpart Patty Murray, it capped two years of ongoing debate and negotiation around the Budget Control Act of 2011 (Public Law 112–25) and its attending mechanism of sequestration that both sides had intended as a deterrent to force them into real action and negotiation on the deficit.[24] What followed was of course an impasse which culminated in the government shutdown of October 2013 and its attendant fear of debt default. What Patty Murray and Paul Ryan negotiated over was how to extricate Congress out of this self-inflicted wound. The deal itself mostly canceled some of the spending cuts mandated by sequestration. It restored funding to military programs that were popular with Republicans while also restoring funding for domestic programs that Democrats wanted to preserve. The content of the deal itself was less surprising than the fact that it could be reached. After years of multiple failures, few people had hoped that Ryan and Murray would actually deliver against the odds.[25] According to Jill Lawrence, the reason for their success was to be found in the way they interacted with each other, the leeway they were given by their leaders, as well as the parameters of a negotiation where a lack of agreement would lead to severe pain for all involved. Indeed, absent a deal, more across-the-board cuts would have been triggered by sequester. To return to Rothenberg's framework we thus had an unsustainable (or undesirable) status quo. There was also some form of industry buy-in since most business leaders were quite vocal in support of a deal as they seemed to truly fear yet more fiscal brinksmanship. While this helped nudge Patty Murray and Paul Ryan toward a deal, it did not ensure its adoption in Congress.

To assuage the critics within his party, Paul Ryan defended the agreement on the House floor by acknowledging its limits. He reminded them that, "In a divided government, you don't get everything you want, but I think this bill is a firm step in the right direction. It is not perfect. It is a start. That is how it works in divided government."[26] After that speech, the bill was indeed passed just before the House recessed on December 12, 2013. Yet, on that vote, only 169 Republicans were in favor (Roll Call 640) – far from the requisite 218 votes for majority adoption in a 435-member legislature. For the agreement to be adopted by the House, it thus took the overwhelming support of the Democratic caucus whose members cast 163 Yeas. The opposition to Murray-Ryan was thus made up of 62 Republicans and 32 Democrats. On the Senate side, the vote on December 18, 2013 was 64 Yeas to 36 Nays (Vote number 281). All the Nays came from Republican Senators while the Democratic majority found support from nine Republican colleagues.

The Ryan-Murray agreement was then prolonged by Speaker Boehner before he left the speakership in December of 2015. It took the form of the Omnibus Bill of December 2015 (Public Law 114–113) which was adopted by the House thanks to a comparable coalition of only 150 Republicans joined by 166 Democrats (Roll Call 705). This time there were thus more Democrats than Republicans voting in favor of a bill pushed by the Republican leadership which theoretically controlled the majority of the House. In the Senate, the situation was also surprising with 65 Yea votes coming from only 27 Republicans and 38 Democrats (Vote 339) even though, since the 2014 midterms, Republicans made up a majority of the Senate.

On these two major budget agreements which set the fiscal trajectory in Obama's second term, it is therefore clear that Republican majorities in the House and then in the Senate only reluctantly consented to sign off on the compromise that their leaders had negotiated. Given the special nature of budget legislation, known as a must-pass in congressional lingo, there was a strong incentive for congressional Democrats to fund the US government headed by the Obama administration. It should thus come as no surprise that Republicans would be reluctant even with the additional military spending as a sweetener. Budget deals usually make for strange bedfellows but the number of Republican defections remains puzzling. In addition, by refusing to vote in favor of their own leadership's bills, congressional Republicans allowed the minority party to bargain for more than what their institutional position would theoretically warrant. That development was not lost on some House Republicans. A former member of the Freedom Caucus voiced his concern that they "unwittingly become Nancy Pelosi's tactical ally."[27]

MEDICARE ACCESS AND CHIP REAUTHORIZATION ACT

In this instance, again, Congress was confronted with an unsustainable status quo resulting from a predictable, self-inflicted, and recurring problem. This piece of legislation reformed the way physicians get paid by Medicare, the government-run health insurance program for seniors and the disabled. Contrary to the budget, Congress was not legally bound to reform Medicare payments but it had forced its own hands by constantly delaying the application of cuts to doctors and hospitals as mandated under the normal application of the SGR (Sustainable Growth Rate). Since the creation of this mechanism by the Balanced Budget Act of 1997, the SGR was supposed to ensure that Medicare payments to doctors could not grow much faster than the rest of the economy. It was effective as long as the economy was growing. When in 2002 a recession hit, applying the SGR would have meant that physicians would have seen growingly drastic cuts in the amounts Medicare paid them. This would have led many of them to stop taking Medicare patients and would have been politically untenable. More generally, these increasingly severe cuts to doctors' payments were found to be politically unpalatable as doctors and their Medicare patients make up a very vocal and critical constituency. To avoid this problem, every year or so since 2002, Congress has adopted a so-called "Doc-Fix" to delay the implementation of the SGR for another year and therefore keep doctors' payments steady.

There was a bipartisan consensus that the formula set up in 1997 was not adequate but it nevertheless took two decades to reform it. The main reason for this delay was that getting rid of the

101

SGR would mean higher spending by Medicare. It would therefore necessarily be scored by the Congressional Budget Office (CBO) as adding to the deficit. As lawmakers often profess a strong dislike of additional new deficit spending, it was assumed that any reform of the Medicare SGR would have to be coupled with a "pay-for": a commensurate spending cut or tax hike. Unsurprisingly, that always proved to be the hardest part. To resolve the impasse between lawmakers who refused to cut other programs or raise taxes to pay for higher doctors payments and the same lawmakers who refused to allow those cuts to go into effect, the solution Congress found was to decide that it didn't need a pay-for and would simply add US$140 billion dollars to the deficit over the next ten years.

After two decades of temporary fixes, the Medicare Access and CHIP Reauthorization Act (Public Law 114-10), or MACRA, finally terminated the SGR mechanism. It passed the House of Representatives on March 26, 2015 with a broad bipartisan majority of 392 Yea votes, as 212 Republicans and 180 Democrats voted in favor of the reform. The Republican majority was still a few votes shy from a simple majority but, given the overwhelming support from the Democrats, the 33 Republican Nays could well afford to signal their opposition without causing any danger to doctors' payments and their Medicare beneficiaries. On the Senate side, the final vote on April 14, 2015 was also an overwhelming 92 to 8 (Record Vote 144) but the crucial vote was actually taken earlier on a motion to waive budgetary discipline. On that vote, the margin was relatively closer with 71 Yeas to 29 Nays, all coming from Republican senators (Record Vote 143). Policy agreement on the merits of the reform, a shared incentive to deflect a cut to a politically potent constituency, and the convenient abandonment of a heretofore required equivalent pay-for eventually led to a bipartisan reckoning for the SGR.

REFORMING NO CHILD LEFT BEHIND

In 1965, President Johnson signed into law the Elementary and Secondary Education Act (Public Law 89-10). To mark this adoption of what he called "a major new commitment of the Federal

Government to quality and equality in the schooling that we offer our young people," Lyndon Johnson traveled to his Texas hometown and had his own school teacher by his side for a historic photo-op. The law was rightly understood to be a dramatic expansion of federal involvement into what was until then a preserved state prerogative. LBJ saw it as a central part of its declared "war on poverty" since as he liked to remind his audience: "As a son of a tenant farmer, I know that education is the only valid passport from poverty."[28]

Since 1965, the law had been reauthorized every five years. In 2001, George W. Bush had negotiated with the legendary liberal "lion of the Senate," Democratic Senator from Massachusetts Ted Kennedy, to achieve a bipartisan overhaul of the way the federal government contributed to the financing of public education. That law was entitled No Child Left Behind. It was supposed to be renewed after ten years but in the Obama years it proved controversial enough to lead to delays. Democrats and some of their supporters among teachers unions decried the fact that the law put in place a funding formula that overemphasized results on standardized tests at the expense of struggling school districts and educational facilities.[29] On the other end of the political spectrum, conservative Republicans were still decrying an overreach of the Bush administration in what should be a state and local policy.[30] Unexpectedly, Republican majorities in the House and the Senate nevertheless found a compromise that President Obama was willing to sign.

In very orthodox but now fairly rare legislative fashion, the Every Student Succeeds Act (Public Law 114–95) was enacted following a Conference Report drafted by House and Senate members.[31] It passed the House on December 2, 2015 by a bipartisan vote of 354 to 64. Once again, there were more Democratic than Republican Yeas since 181 Democrats voted for the bill to 178 Republicans. In the Senate, the vote was also bipartisan with only 12 Nay votes all coming from Republicans (Record Vote 334). Upon signing the legislation, President Obama joked that this was "an early Christmas present. After more than 10 years, Members of Congress from both parties have come together to revise our national education law. A Christmas miracle: a bipartisan bill signing right here."[32] White House support for the bill again helped convince Democrats to join a portion of the Republican majority who wanted to support a reform that returned a lot of education policy discretion to the states while maintaining strong financial support and coordination from Washington, DC. It is worth pointing out that, once again, opposition to the final compromise came almost solely from Republicans whose party was in control of both houses of Congress.

A conducive coalition?

It should be clear by now that these votes revealed a fracture within the Republican party in Congress. A significant number of members of the majority party came to represent the opposition to proposals that their own leadership supported and whipped for.

While the Republican Party had a theoretical majority they were consumed with factional disputes, as was shown by the ascendance of the Tea Party-inspired Freedom Caucus within their midst. The Freedom Caucus came to represent around forty members[33] in the 114th Congress and, more often than not, they came to represent the lone No votes in overwhelming bipartisan votes. As an example, among the lone 64 Noes in the House vote on the Every Student Succeeds Act, we find thirty members of the thirty-six House Freedom Caucus members identified by the Pew Research Center.[34] Among them, we see notably their chairman Representative Jim Jordan of Ohio's 4th congressional district as well as other self-appointed spokespersons such as Mark Meadows of North Carolina's 11th district, Raùl Labrador of Idaho, or Dave Brat of Virginia's 7th congressional district. The members of the House Freedom Caucus were often cast by the press as radical right-wing extremists. Their extremist nature is borne out by the data at our disposal. Using the spatial voting methodology put forward by Keith T. Poole and Howard Rosenthal,[35] as made available on Voteview.com, with a DW-NOMINATE score of 0.691 on the first dimension,[36] the median member of the House Freedom Caucus does sit relatively to the far right of the ideological spectrum. The leaders of the House Freedom Caucus do appear to be among the most conservative House members. Their chairman Jim Jordan has a DW-NOMINATE score of 0.71 which identifies him as more conservative than 94 percent of Republicans in the 114th Congress. Representative Meadows's 0.621 DW-NOMINATE score on the first dimension makes him more conservative than 80 percent of his colleagues. With 0.736, his colleague Raùl Labrador is even further to the right, only to be bested by Dave Brat who, according to this data, was simply the most conservative member of the House in the 114th Congress with a DW-NOMINATE score of 0.823 on the first dimension.

Because of this intraparty opposition, House leadership found themselves forced to negotiate with the Democratic minority to get the bulk of the Democratic party's vote before then turning around to ask for the support of a reliable group of their own supporters. These Republicans and Democrats who heeded the calls of their leaders and supported the bipartisan pieces of legislation highlighted make up what I tentatively called a "conducive coalition." Democrats and Republicans voting together to keep the government open and sign off on a limited number of reforms if only to ward off what they saw as the unacceptable consequences of their inaction in those specific instances.

In an attempt to learn more about this coalition, it is worth identifying those House Republican members who voted in favor of the three bills highlighted to see if they share some common traits. By design, we chose to focus mostly on Republican members since they were the majority party and, as such, the supposed locus of decision making. Likewise, I chose to devote my attention solely to the House votes. First, because the GOP did not have the majority in the Senate until 2014 and it was thus impossible to have comparable data between the 113th and 114th Congress. Second, because of the non-majoritarian rules of the Senate. In the Senate, the party that is in the minority can rely on the use of the filibuster and related parliamentary tools to thwart the will of the majority party. As every senator and every observer of the Senate knows, it usually takes sixty votes – the threshold to achieve cloture, i.e. to end debate on a proposal – to achieve most of anything in the 100-member Senate.

Table 3.1 at the end of this chapter lists the 121 House Republicans who voted in favor of the Murray-Ryan budget agreement, the Medicare Access and CHIP Reauthorization Act, and the

Every Student Succeeds Act. They form a fairly heterogeneous group in terms of regional and ideological make-up but some generalizations can still be put forward.

First of all, as a group, the House Republicans who voted in favor of these laws represent the more moderate side of the GOP conference. Indeed, the median DW-NOMINATE group for this cohort is 0.407. With a DW-NOMINATE score of 0.407 himself, Representative Randy Forbes of Virginia's 4th congressional district can thus be seen as sitting right at the center of this group and yet his score marks him as more liberal than 65 percent of House Republicans. If one looks at the extremes within the group, the most liberal would be Representative Christopher Henry Smith of New Jersey with a DW-NOMINATE score of 0.161 which actually makes him the most liberal member of the House Republican conference. The most conservative member of our cohort is Representative Jeb Hensarling of Texas whose DW-NOMINATE score of 0.703 puts him on almost equal footing with his colleague from Ohio Jim Jordan and the House Freedom Caucus chairman. The presence of such a staunch conservative as Jeb Hensarling helps shed light on an important point. While the Republicans who participated in this conducive coalition were overall less conservative than the House Freedom Caucus, they should not be seen as ideologically close to the Democrats. The simple reason which helps explain that the very conservative Hensarling could vote with Nancy Pelosi's Democrats is that their vote should be seen as a show of support for their own leadership. Hensarling himself is part of the House GOP leadership team[37] and, as such, he is simply bound to vote with them.

On the Republican side of the conducive coalition, we can identify a group of moderate conservative Republicans who tried to counterbalance the influence of the Freedom Caucus. They organized themselves as the Main Street Partnership.[38] Among the 121 House Republicans who voted in favor of the three bills highlighted, 41 are identified as members of the Main Street Partnership. On their website (https://republicanmainstreet.org/), they cast themselves as "the governing wing of the Republican Party" and vowed to "uphold the Republican tradition of responsible, results-oriented government." One of their leaders is Charlie Dent of Pennsylvania's 15th congressional district. With a DW-NOMINATE score of

0.244 on the first dimension, Representative Dent's voting record made him more liberal than 94 percent of House Republicans in the 114th Congress. The most conservative member of the Main Street Partnership in our cohort is Lynn Jenkins from Kansas, whose DW-NOMINATE score of 0.523 makes her more conservative than 57 percent of House Republicans in the 114th Congress.

As can be seen clearly in Table 3.1, the membership of the Main Street Partnership mostly overlapped with the more informal Tuesday Group, a weekly meeting of like-minded moderates who first gathered in 1995.[39] The Tuesday Group does not list its members, but in 2007 it set up a Political Action Committee (Tuesday Group PAC) to give more visibility and efficacy to their joint efforts by directing political donations to the members who supported their goals.[40] As a Political Action Committee, the Tuesday Group PAC is bound to disclose to the Federal Election Commission the sums it received and distributed. This data is used in Table 3.1 to identify the thirty-one members of the coalition who received campaign contributions from the Tuesday PAC Group. The most liberal member of that subgroup is Representative Frank A. LoBiondo of New Jersey with a DW-NOMINATE score of 0.211.

While generally supportive of leadership, Charlie Dent led a rebellion of some of these moderate House Republicans in the fall of 2015. Controlling the agenda is one of the prominent tools of the Speaker of the House. The Speaker controls the all-important Rules Committee that can keep bills bottled up in committees and off the House floor. One way to remove this obstacle is to force debate on a bill by the use of a discharge petition. A simple majority of the House – 218 votes – can sign a discharge petition to release a bill from committee and open debate. Because this undermines the power of the Speaker that the majority party elected, it is seen as an act of rebellion for any member of the House majority to sign a discharge petition. And yet, on October 9, 2015 a group of forty-two Republican House members agreed to sign a Discharge Petition put forward by the Democratic minority to reinstate funding for the Export-Import Bank. Among them were twelve members of the Main Street Partnership. The mostly moderate House Republicans who joined that discharge petition explained that they were forced to take a stand against the excessive sway that they thought the more radically conservative Freedom Caucus had on the majority.[41]

As they joined with Democrats to try to restore funding to the Export-Import Bank, members of the Tuesday Group seemed to give credence to Keith Krehbiel's model of pivotal politics.[42] An overly schematic reading of Krehbiel's theory would indeed predict that, never mind their party affiliation, a majority of 218 members of the House can and will make their will known and overwhelm partisan constraints. On the other hand, House Republican leaders liked to insist on their respect for the so-called "Hastert Rule" according to which House leadership would only put on the floor bills that have the support of a majority of the majority. In the 114th Congress, that meant 120 House Republicans had to support a bill. We have seen that there were 121 Republicans in what I called the "conducive coalition." This simple arithmetic fact seems to offer countervailing evidence of the strength of party control[43] despite strident factional opposition. While the Freedom Caucus seems to have mostly punched above its weight in terms of its numbers, the more numerous group of more moderate Republicans prevailed at least in the instances under scrutiny. Their usually less abrasive manners ensured they received less media attention while their ideological heterogeneity made it difficult for them to act or communicate in a coherent fashion. As a matter of course, they followed the directives from their leaders, even when that meant voting with the other party.

The 113th and 114th Congresses were dominated by Republican majorities in the House and then in the Senate. They had to contend with the Democratic administration of President Barack Obama, a situation commonly described as divided government. This constitutionally provided arrangement is considered to be made more dysfunctional in a context of partisan polarization where the two parties find it ever harder to cooperate. During that period, gridlock was indeed the default position on Capitol Hill.

Nevertheless, there were a few legislative successes scattered among the numerous failed efforts. This chapter focused on three particular bills which were passed by both houses of Congress and signed by the president to investigate how lawmakers and the White House managed to overcome their differences and achieve some rare legislative victories. How could lawmakers adopt a bipartisan budget deal, an overhaul of Medicare payments to doctors, and a revamping of federal educational policies? I argued that the answer to that question was held by the members of what I called a "conducive coalition" of Democrats and Republicans who came together to push the bills over the majority threshold in spite of vocal opposition from within the majority party itself. A closer look at the members who made up this unlikely coalition revealed that, among House Republicans, there was still a large group of relatively moderate or simply disciplined conservatives who proved willing to follow their leaders.

Eventually, the decision on each vote was made by the largest share of the caucus that navigated between the two poles of the Freedom Caucus and the Tuesday Group. As we've seen, Representative Randy Forbes of Virginia's 4th district was the median member of the group of House Republicans who made up the GOP's share of the "conducive coalition." His DW-NOMINATE score marked him as a conservative Republican. He was not a member of the House Freedom Caucus, nor a member of the Main Street Partnership, nor a part of the leadership team. First elected in 2000, he lost his re-election bid in 2016 when he was defeated in the Republican primary that year. His record in Congress is unlikely to find him a place in history beyond an obscure footnote on congressional voting pattern in the early twenty-first century. Yet, his fate is somewhat illustrative of the difficulties of maintaining a level understanding of Congress in a polarized era fueled by a hyper-partisan media. As Richard Fenno had shown,[44] a Congressmember's motivation to vote for or against bills ought to be traced back to their vision of their constituents' wishes. Despite the numerous polls, focus groups, direct contact through e-mails, petitions, or town-hall meetings, the view that elected officials have of their own constituents, and the view of the constituents themselves, is necessarily tainted by the treatment of the issues by the media.[45] In a sense, lawmakers are sharing the pen with media organizations as they ghostwrite their own constituents' aspirations.[46] At the center of the political landscape, they only see a black hole[47] and thus act accordingly. Cross-pressured between partisan discipline and ideological purity, most House Republicans in our study eventually chose the former. It is somewhat noteworthy that this behavior itself has become noteworthy. Ideology has become an ever more predictive factor in the votes of members of Congress but the lack of partisan cohesion – inherent in most forms of bipartisanship – displayed in the votes highlighted evokes a manner of legislating that dominated in previous eras. Given the experience of the Trump years, these efforts now appear more anachronistic than ever.

Table 3.1

Name	DW-NOMINATE SCORE (1st dimension)	Main Street Partnership member (1 = yes; 0 = no)	Tuesday Group PAC recipient
Robert Aderholt (LA)	0.361	0	0
Mark E. Amodei (NV)	0.375	0	0
Lou Barletta (PA)	0.278	0	0
Garland H. Barr (KY)	0.485	0	0
Dan Benishek (MI)	0.491	1	0
Gus Bilirakis (FL)	0.404	0	0
Diane Black (TN)	0.58	0	0
Charles W. Boustany (LA)	0.392	0	0
Kevin Patrick Brady (TX)	0.518	0	0
Susan Brooks (IN)	0.376	1	1
Vernon G. Buchanan (FL)	0.359	0	0
Larry Bucshon (IN)	0.39	1	0
Kevin Calvert (CA)	0.348	1	0
John R. Carter (TX)	0.466	0	0
Tom Cole (OK)	0.335	0	0
Chris Collins (NY)	0.366	1	1
Doug Collins (GA)	0.624	0	0
Michael Conaway (TX)	0.59	0	0
Paul Cook (CA)	0.39	1	1
Ander Crenshaw (FL)	0.333	0	0
Rodney Davis (IL)	0.296	1	1
Jeff Denham (CA)	0.306	1	1
Charles W. Dent (PA)	0.244	1	1
Mario Diaz-Balart (FL)	0.276	1	1

Name	DW-NOMINATE SCORE (1st dimension)	Main Street Partnership member (1 = yes; 0 = no)	Tuesday Group PAC recipient
Sean Duffy (WI)	0.507	1	1
Renee Elmers (NC)	0.406	1	1
Stephen Lee Fincher (TN)	0.526	0	0
Michael G. Fitzpatrick (PA)	0.202	1	0
Chuck Fleischmann (TN)	0.471	0	0
Bill Flores (TX)	0.605	0	0
Randy J. Forbes (VA)	0.407	0	0
Jeff Fortenberry (NE)	0.299	1	1
Virgina Ann Foxx (NC)	0.642	0	0
Rodney P. Frelinghuysen (NJ)	0.292	1	1
Bob Gibbs (OH)	0.46	0	0
Christopher Gibson (NY)	0.203	1	0
Robert William Goodlatte (VA)	0.496	0	0
Kay Granger (TX)	0.392	0	0
Samuel Graves (MO	0.432	0	0
Bret Guthrie (KY)	0.413	0	0
Richard Hanna (NY)	0.215	1	1
Gregg Harper (MS)	0.384	0	0
Vicky Hartzler (MO)	0.496	0	0
Jeb Hensarling (TX)	0.703	0	0
Jaime Herrera Beutler (WA)	0.38	1	1
Richard Hudson (NC)	0.676	0	0
Bill Huizenga (MI)	0.632	0	0
Duncan Duane Hunter (CA)	0.512	0	0
Robert Hurt (VA)	0.568	0	0
Lynn Jenkins (KS)	0.523	1	1
Bill Johnson (OH)	0.428	1	1
David Joyce (OH)	0.253	1	1
Mike Kelly (PA)	0.319	0	0
Peter King (NY)	0.26	1	0
Adam Kinzinger (IL)	0.27	1	1
John Kline (MN)	0.49	0	0
Leonard Lance (NJ)	0.319	1	1
Robert E. Latta (OH)	0.52	0	0

Name	DW-NOMINATE SCORE (1st dimension)	Main Street Partnership member (1 = yes; 0 = no)	Tuesday Group PAC recipient
Billy Long (MO)	0.552	0	0
Franck Lucas (OK)	0.363	0	0
Blaine Luetkemeyer (MO)	0.446	0	0
Doug LaMalfa (CA)	0.549	0	0
Frank A. LoBiondo (NJ)	0.211	1	1
Thomas A. Marino (PA)	0.351	0	0
Kevin McCarthy (CA)	0.462	0	0
Patrick Meehan (PA)	0.22	0	0
Luke Messer (IN)	0.564	0	0
John L. Mica (FL)	0.453	0	0
Candice Miller (MI)	0.343	0	0
Timothy Murphy (PA)	0.258	0	0
Michael McCaul (TX)	0.45	0	0
Patrick T. McHenry (NC)	0.578	0	0
Cathy McMorris Rodgers (WA)	0.43	1	1
Kristi Noem (SD)	0.398	0	0
Devin Nunes (CA)	0.447	0	0
Erik Paulsen (MN)	0.403	1	1
Robert Pittenger (NC)	0.561	0	0
Joseph Pitts (PA)	0.538	0	0
Tom Price (GA)	0.644	0	0
Thomas W. Reed II (NY)	0.294	1	1
David G. Reichert (WA)	0.224	1	1
Jim Renacci (OH)	0.387	1	1
Reid Ribble (Wi)	0.603	0	0
Tom Rice (SC)	0.577	0	0
Scott E. Rigell (VA)	0.401	1	0
Martha Roby (AL)	0.367	0	0
David P. Roe (TN)	0.493	0	0
Hal Rogers (KY)	0.333	0	0
Tod Rokita (IN)	0.6	0	0
Thomas J. Rooney (FL)	0.458	0	0
Ileana Ros-Lehtinen (FL)	0.244	1	1
Peter Roskam (IL)	0.429	0	0

Name	DW-NOMINATE SCORE (1st dimension)	Main Street Partnership member (1 = yes; 0 = no)	Tuesday Group PAC recipient
Dennis Ross (FL)	0.531	0	0
Edward Randall Royce (CA)	0.658	0	0
Austin Scott (GA)	0.571	0	0
Pete Sessions (TX)	0.585	0	0
John M. Shikmus (IL)	0.371	0	0
Bill Shuster (PA)	0.374	1	0
Michael K. Simpson (ID)	0.293	1	0
Christopher Henry Smith (NJ)	0.161	0	0
Lamar Smith (TX)	0.425	0	0
Steve Stivers (OH)	0.299	1	1
Glenn Thompson (PA)	0.307	0	0
William Thornberry (TX)	0.527	0	0
Pat Tiberi (OH)	0.386	1	1
Scott Tipton (CO)	0.454	0	0
Michael Turner (OH)	0.266	1	1
Fred Upton (MI)	0.339	1	1
David Valadao (CA)	0.254	1	1
Ann Wagner (MO)	0.477	0	0
Greg Walden (OR)	0.339	1	1
Jackie Walorski (IN)	0.446	0	0
Lynn Westmoreland (GA)	0.672	0	0
Wayne Whitfield (KY)	0.303	0	0
Addison Wilson (SC)	0.545	0	0
Robert Wittman (VA)	0.425	0	0
Steve Womack (AZ)	0.347	0	0
Rob Woodall (GA)	0.645	0	0
Donald Young (AK)	0.279	0	0
Todd Young (IN)	0.481	1	0
Total	121	41	31
Average DW-NOMINATE score	0.422	N/A	N/A
Median DW-NOMINATE score	0.407	N/A	N/A

Source: data compiled from Lewis, Jeffrey B., Keith Poole, Howard Rosenthal, Adam Boche, Aaron Rudkin, and Luke Sonnet (2020). *Voteview: Congressional Roll-Call Votes Database*. https://voteview.com

Notes

1. Mayhew, David R. (2005). *Divided we govern: party control, lawmaking and investigations, 1946–2002.* New Haven, CT: Yale University Press.
2. Thurber, James A. and Antoine Yoshinaka, ed. (2016). *American gridlock: the sources, character, and impact of political polarization.* New York: Cambridge University Press.
3. In his own words: "The pundits, the pundits like to slice-and-dice our country into red states and blue states; red states for Republicans, blue states for Democrats. But I've got news for them, too. We worship an awesome God in the blue states, and we don't like federal agents poking around in our libraries in the red states. We coach Little League in the blue states and yes, we've got some gay friends in the red states. There are patriots who opposed the war in Iraq and there are patriots who supported the war in Iraq. We are one people, all of us pledging allegiance to the stars and stripes, all of us defending the United States of America." Barack Obama, 2004 Democratic National Convention Keynote Address, delivered July 27, 2004. https://www.americanrhetoric.com/barackobamaspeeches.htm (last accessed December 18, 2018).
4. Kessler, Gary. (2012). "When did McConnell say he wanted to make Obama a 'one-term president'?". *The Washington Post*, September 25, 2019.
5. Weisman, Jonathan. (2013). "Republicans back down, ending crisis over shutdown and debt limit". *The New York Times*, October 16, 2013.
6. 113th Congress, HJ res 59, Bill title: Making Continuing Appropriations for Fiscal Year 2014, and For Other Purposes. Became Public Law 113–73.
7. 114th Congress, HR 2, Bill title: Medicare Access and CHIP Reauthorization Act of 2015. Became Public Law 114-10.
8. 114th Congress, S1177, Bill title: To Reauthorize the Elementary and Secondary Education Act of 1965 to Ensure that Every Child Achieves. Became Public Law 114–85.
9. Rothenberg, Lawrence S. (2018). "Policy success in an age of gridlock." *Elements in American Politics*, June. https://doi.org/10.1017/9781108628044 (last accessed December 15, 2018).
10. Ibid., 75.
11. McCarty, Nolan M., Keith T. Poole, and Howard Rosenthal. (2006). *Polarized America: the dance of ideology and unequal riches.* The Walras-Pareto lectures. Cambridge, MA: MIT Press.

12. Reynolds, Molly E. (2018). "Vital statistics on Congress." Brookings. https://www.brookings.edu/multi-chapter-report/vital-statistics-on-congress/ (last accessed December 15, 2018).
13. Rawls, Lee W. (2009). *In praise of deadlock: how partisan struggle makes better laws*. Washington, DC: Woodrow Wilson Center Press.
14. Mayhew, David R. (2005). *Divided we govern: party control, lawmaking and investigations, 1946–2002*. New Haven, CT: Yale University Press.
15. Howell, William, Scott Adler, Charles Cameron, and Charles Rieman. (2000). "Divided government and the legislative productivity of Congress, 1945–94." *Legislative Studies Quarterly*, 25 (2): 285–312.
16. Binder, Sarah A. (2003). *Stalemate: causes and consequences of legislative gridlock*. Washington, DC: Brookings Institution Press.
17. Mayhew, David. (2011). *Partisan balance : why political parties don't kill the U.S. Constitutional system*. Princeton, NJ: Princeton University Press.
18. Corn, David. (2012). *Showdown: the inside story of how Obama fought back against Boehner, Cantor, and the Tea Party*. 1st ed. New York: William Morrow.
19. Lizza, Ryan. (2015). "A House divided". *The New Yorker*, December 14, 2015. https://www.newyorker.com/magazine/2015/12/14/a-house-divided (last accessed July 6, 2020).
20. Steinhauer, Jennifer. (2015). "John Boehner, House Speaker, will resign from Congress." *The New York Times*, September 26, 2015.
21. Zelizer, Julien E. (2004). *On Capitol Hill: the struggle to reform Congress and its consequences, 1948–2000*. Cambridge: Cambridge University Press.
22. Sinclair, Barbara. (2007). *Unorthodox lawmaking: new legislative processes in the U.S. Congress*. 3rd ed. Washington, DC: CQ Press.
23. Grossman, Matt and David A. Hopkins. (2015). "Ideological Republicans and group interest Democrats: the asymmetry of American party politics." *Perspectives on Politics*, 13 (1): 119–139.
24. Spar, Karen. 2013. "Budget 'sequestration' and selected program exemptions and special rules." R42050. Washington, DC: Congressional Research Service.
25. Lawrence, Jill. (2015). "Profiles in negotiation: the Murray-Ryan budget deal." Center for Effective Public Management at Brookings. February 2015. https://www.brookings.edu/wp-content/uploads/2016/06/BrookingsMurrayRyanv421315.pdf (last accessed December 15, 2018).
26. Rep. Ryan (WI). 2013. *Congressional Record – Daily Digest* 159 (176): H8053.

27. Lizza, Ryan. (2015). "What House moderates can learn from the Freedom Caucus." *The New Yorker*, December 9, 2015. https://www.newyorker.com/news/news-desk/what-house-moderates-can-learn-from-the-freedom-caucus (last accessed December 15, 2018).

28. Johnson, Lyndon B. 1965. "Remarks in Johnson City, Tex., upon signing the Elementary and Secondary Education Bill." Online by Gerhard Peters and John T. Woolley. *The American Presidency Project.* https://www.presidency.ucsb.edu/node/241886 (last accessed December 21, 2018).

29. Rhodes, Jesse Hessler. (2011). "Progressive policy making in a conservative age? Civil rights and the politics of federal education standards, testing, and accountability." *Perspectives on Politics*, 9 (03): 519–544. https://doi.org/10.1017/S1537592711002738 (last accessed December 21, 2018).

30. Uzzell, Lawrence A. (2005). "No Child Left Behind: the dangers of centralized education policy." Policy Analysis 544. Cato Institute. https://www.cato.org/publications/policy-analysis/no-child-left-behind-dangers-centralized-education-policy (last accessed December 21, 2018).

31. Wolfensberger, Donald R. (2008). "Have House-Senate Conferences gone the way of the dodo?". *Roll Call*, April 28, 2008. A Conference Report is the compromise put forward by a conference committee. This committee is made up of House members and senators tasked with resolving the differences in legislative language between a bill passed in the House and its companion measure in the Senate. While this is a traditional way of resolving House and Senate differences, congressional leaders now prefer to use other means to achieve the same goal.

32. Obama, Barack. (2015). "Remarks on signing the Every Student Succeeds Act." Online by Gerhard Peters and John T. Woolley. *The American Presidency Project.* https://www.presidency.ucsb.edu/node/311392 (last accessed December 21, 2018).

33. The exact number of members of the House Freedom Caucus is difficult to ascertain as it varied over time and, more importantly, as the group does not advertise its membership. The closest thing we have to an accurate count comes from the Pew Research Center which, on October 20, 2015, ascertained that, thanks to their reporting, they could confirm the identities of thirty-six House Freedom Caucus members. Desilver, Drew. (2015). "What is the House Freedom Caucus, and who's in it?" Pew Research Center. October 20, 2015. http://www.pewresearch.org/fact-tank/2015/10/20/house-freedom-caucus-what-is-it-and-whos-in-it/ (last accessed December 20, 2018).

34. Ibid.
35. Poole, Keith T. and Howard Rosenthal. (1997). *Congress: a political-economic history of roll call voting*. New York: Oxford University Press.
36. DW-NOMINATE scores in the first dimension range for -1 for the most liberal and +1 for the most conservative. A score of 0.0 therefore places a lawmaker in the theoretical absolute center.
37. He was the chairman of the House Republican Conference in the 112th Congress before becoming Chair of the coveted Committee on Financial Services.
38. Conveniently for our purpose, the Main Street Partnership's website <https://republicanmainstreet.org/> (last accessed December 21, 2018) has a list of its members. The Tuesday Group is a more informal organization that does not list its members but is estimated to gather between forty and fifty House Republicans. Zwick, Jesse. (2011). "Tuesday mourning." *The New Republic*, January 29, 2011. https://newrepublic.com/article/82420/tuesday-group-gop (last accessed December 21, 2018).
39. Ibid.
40. Bolton, Alexander. (2007). "Centrist House Republicans establish Tuesday Group PAC." *The Hill*, July 11, 2007. https://thehill.com/homenews/news/12509-centrist-house-republicans-establish-tuesday-group-pac (last accessed December 20, 2018).
41. Lizza, Ryan. (2015). "What House moderates can learn from the Freedom Caucus." *The New Yorker*, December 9, 2015. Art. cit.
42. Krehbiel, Keith. (1998). *Pivotal politics: a theory of U.S. lawmaking*. Chicago: University of Chicago Press.
43. Cox, Gary W. and Mathew D. McCubbins. (2005). *Setting the agenda: responsible party government in the U.S. House of Representatives*. Illustrated ed. New York: Cambridge University Press.
44. Fenno, Richard F. (1978). *Home style: House members in their districts*. Boston, MA: Little, Brown.
45. Zaller, John R. (1992). *The nature and origins of mass opinion*. New York: Cambridge University Press.
46. Lippmann, Walter. (1925). *The phantom public*. New York: Harcourt, Brace.
47. Abramowitz, Alan I. (2010). *The disappearing center: engaged citizens, polarization, and American democracy*. New Haven, CT: Yale University Press.

4

Federalism: Barack Obama's accidental devolution revolution

Thad Kousser

Though it was a consequence that was far from intended, a significant legacy of the Obama administration is that it reshaped the contours of American federalism.[1] At the same time that he was moving policy sharply left on the ideological spectrum in his first term, President Obama also brought a dramatic shift in the balance of power from states to the federal government. Like a latter-day federalist, he leveraged Washington, DC's implied powers to create a national bank of new programs. To achieve his policy goals, he pushed for strict national mandates and standards in the spheres of healthcare, the environment, and education. This initially moved all states – whether they liked it or not – along in his ideological direction.

Predictably, this reignited the eternal debate of American politics – raging from the Articles of Confederation through Philadelphia's Constitutional Convention through the Civil War and the civil rights movement – about states' rights versus federal authority. When should states operate as "laboratories of democracy," in the words of Justice Louis Brandeis (*New State Ice Co. v. Liebmann*, 1932), and when should their powers be trumped by a federal government that makes, in the declaration of the Constitution's Article VI, the "supreme Law of the Land"? This has been a constant field of conflict in American politics,[2] with its outcome never fully resolved. Though Obama most likely did not begin his political career with deeply held views on federalism, his presidential policy agenda required him to act for strong federal powers.

But a funny thing happened on the way to federal supremacy. Through a series of intertwined policy victories, political defeats, and judicial decisions, the path toward uniform federal standards was blocked. State governments, which became ever more polarized along partisan lines during the Obama era, were freed to move in whatever ideological direction they preferred in some policy realms. In other spheres, state attorneys general sued for or governors seized the autonomy to resist what they saw as overreaching mandates from Washington, DC.

By the end of the Obama presidency, states were more powerful than they were when it began. This chapter tells the story of the accidental "devolution revolution" that empowered states. After an initial burst of federal policies in which Washington dictated state actions, forcing all fifty to move in lockstep, the Obama administration set in place the conditions for a massive counter-reaction. Now that this counter-reaction has taken full effect during the Trump administration, states have taken hold of more power, and become more varied in the patchwork of policies that they present their residents, than they were in 2008. While it was by no means intentional, this devolution revolution is nonetheless part of the Obama legacy.

The story begins with a brief history of past devolutions of programmatic authority and policy-making power to the states, noting which ones led to wider variations across states and which, counterintuitively, made states more uniform. Then I cover President Obama's federalist impulses. This designation harkens back to America's first political party, which favored a muscular national government that rose above the authority of the states. Through the mandated Medicaid expansion contained in the Affordable Care Act, the promotion of the Common Core educational standards, and the ambitious environmental goals of the Clean Power Plan, Obama pushed for uniform standards in three of the most critical policy areas.

Yet these leftward pushes, and especially the passage of his signature policy of Obamacare, led to political counter-reactions in the 2010 and 2014 midterm elections. Republicans won major gains both in Washington, DC and in state houses, with both venues becoming ever more polarized. Red states became redder and blue states bluer, setting in place the conditions for the states to move in divergent directions if they were freed to do so. That freedom came through court decisions and costly political choices, with the next section of this chapter showing how states have regained their autonomy in healthcare, education, and the environment. President Trump has sought to reverse all of the policy gains won by Obama, often advocating for state-level control in order to advance this agenda. As the final section shows, one of Obama's signature policies has been undone by Trump while the other has survived him. Yet regardless of the permanence of his policy record, an enduring feature of Barack Obama's legacy is that, whether intentional or not, his presidency devolved power away from Washington, DC and toward the states.

A brief history of devolutions

Throughout America's history, and especially over the past century, governing authority has ebbed and flowed between the federal and state governments, often in tandem with the funding required to put policies into practice. The solidification of America's welfare state from the 1930s to the 1960s brought a nationalization of power.[3] Franklin Roosevelt's New Deal instituted a federally designed and funded welfare system in Aid to Families with Dependent Children. It replaced the existing state and local programs which provided assistance to indigent families[4] and forced states to create them where they didn't exist, thus bringing much uniformity to a policy realm that had been deeply uneven across the states. Lyndon Johnson's Great Society program set in place a similar system to provide healthcare for the poor, aged, blind, and disabled. The federal government set criteria for who would receive it and what services they would get, while allowing the states the discretion only to move beyond a baseline level breadth of coverage and level of care. Washington, DC provided most of the funding for each program.[5] The result of these two moves was both a wider welfare safety net that brought increasing state and federal costs[6] and a nationalization of authority that delivered more uniform policies.

In reaction to both trends, Republican presidents Nixon and Reagan called for a "new federalism" that gave power back to state and local governments.[7] Of course, their support for the decentralization of social policy was as much about their opposition to big government as it was about their support for states' rights.[8] Giving power back to the states would mean freeing them to provide welfare or healthcare services that fell below the federal baseline, or not provide them at all, thus saving federal taxpayer dollars. Nixon's and Reagan's push for a new federalism was only partly successful,[9] creating some grant programs but often being thwarted by the Democrats who controlled Congress. When Newt Gingrich led the Republican takeover of the House in 1994, the political conditions were finally in place for what became known as the "devolution revolution."[10]

The primary victory in this revolution for those favoring state power came through the abolition of the Aid to Families with Dependent Children program, signed under political pressure by Bill Clinton just as his 1996 re-election campaign ramped up. AFDC was replaced by the Temporary Aid to Needy Families (TANF) program, a change that went far deeper than a new acronym. At first glance, the new federal program looked tougher on the poor, bringing the "end to welfare as we have come to know it" that Bill Clinton had promised on the campaign trail. The new program set forth a five-year lifetime limit on receiving welfare benefits and required recipients to go back to work after two years on the rolls.[11] Yet a closer look showed how much freedom states were granted: they could set their lifetime limits either longer or shorter than the federal guidelines, they were allowed to determine how many hours per week recipients had to work, and they could create other new limits on or extensions of services. Most importantly, states were given a specific "block grant" of funding for the program, meaning that they could keep every dollar of spending that they trimmed from their programs. Not surprisingly, state leaders shaped welfare policies to their liking, and without as much federal largesse, the growth in welfare spending stagnated over the following decade.[12]

The other major thrust of the devolution revolution came in 1997, when a resurgent Clinton and a grudging Gingrich negotiated a deal to create the Children's Health Insurance Program (CHIP). Like TANF, this new program to provide health coverage for the children of the working poor gave states great flexibility in how to design their systems and deliver services, in the bounds of federal benchmarks.[13] Unlike with welfare reform, though, the federal government provided nearly all of the funding for the program, leading it to grow steeply in the ensuing two decades. It grew unevenly, with the most liberal states expanding their services most aggressively.

With these two new programs, states now exert significant control over the healthcare and welfare safety nets. And as other federal policies have evolved, states have managed to claw back devolved authority. At the time of its passage in 1973, the Endangered Species Act seemed to set hard and fast rules for how species would be protected once federal scientists designated them as "endangered." Yet a series of mechanisms such as Habitat Conservation Plans and Safe Harbor Agreements have been put in place, which allow states and property owners to bargain with Washington, DC to obtain leniency in enforcement of the Act.[14]

Are these devolutions of power to the state good or bad for American federalism? The fiscal federalism literature in economics has long argued that states can better tailor policies to local needs and demands. "In our 'ideal' model," wrote Wallace Oates, "the central government provides the efficient out-put of the national public good, while numerous local governments offer individuals a wide variety of output of the local public good."[15] Yet in fitting policies to local needs, state official clearly bring in their political and ideological leanings. National leaders can anticipate which direction policy will move if it is either nationalized or devolved. Thus, fights over whether the states or Washington, DC should govern an area are often proxies for ideological battles. As Robertson observes, "political opponents have fought about federalism because it affects who wins and who loses a particular fight."[16]

Obama the federalist

Barack Obama certainly intuited the policy stakes of federalism after he won election in 2008 and began working with Democrats in Congress to enact his liberal policy program. Moving key points of his agenda forward necessitated shifting power from the states back to the federal government, which the president did not hesitate to do. Working with a Democratic Congress in 2009 and 2010 to pass his signature policy accomplishment, the Affordable Care Act, Obama dramatically expanded federal mandates in the size and scope of state Medicaid programs. Throughout his administration, the president used federal grant-making powers to create strong fiscal incentives for states to adopt the Common Core in their schools. Toward the end of his second term, Obama attempted to exercise his unilateral powers to enact what he termed the "single most important step that America has ever made in the fight against global climate change,"[17] by forcing states to adopt plans to limit carbon emissions. While each of these moves came through different policy-making paths and had divergent levels of eventual success, what they all had in common is that they aimed to shift policy-making discretion and thus political power from the states to the federal government.

The first of these, the Affordable Care Act, approached the goal of moving the United States toward universal health through two routes: an individual mandate requiring that every American carry health insurance, and a state mandate requiring that every state dramatically expand its Medicaid program. The individual mandate was set in place to prevent healthy, young, or risk-acceptant Americans from foregoing coverage until they got sick or injured, effectively free-riding on the social safety net paid for by others and leaving the insurance risk pool filled only with expensive patients. The Medicaid mandate was designed to leverage the existing state social service program in order to make insurance free (or very inexpensive) for those who could not otherwise afford it. State Medicaid programs had already covered Americans with low incomes or tremendously high medical bills, but at the time of Obamacare's passage, there was dramatic variation across the fifty programs in exactly who they covered and what services they provided, beyond a baseline set of federal requirements. Obama, along with the slim Democratic majority in Congress that passed the Affordable Care Act, wanted to end this variation.

Democrats aimed the new policy specifically at boosting coverage for the working poor, who often had jobs at businesses that did not provide healthcare for their employees. They mandated that every state Medicaid program cover families making up to 138 percent of the federal poverty line.[18] The Act also allocated all of the funds for this expansion, at least initially. From 2014 though 2016, the federal government would provide 100 percent of the funding for this expansion, with the funding rate then phasing down to 90 percent by 2020 and remaining at that level thereafter.[19] Thus, states could expand their programs for free initially, and in the long run could still provide this critical coverage for their residents while only paying a dime for every dollar's worth of services. In Washington, DC, liberal policy-makers saw this as a boon to all states and their most vulnerable constituents. While many state leaders welcomed the funded mandate, others worried about the precedent it set for expanding federal power over a program that accounted for such a large part of their budgets. Reacting against Obamacare's expansion of federal power, twenty-five states joined Florida's lawsuit arguing that this was an impermissible enlargement of federal authority over state programs.[20]

Also quickly controversial was the Obama administration's embrace of the Common Core educational standards. This set of national testing standards was actually generated by the states themselves: in 2009, the National Governors Association worked with a council of school superintendents to fund the development of a set of clear standards designed to guide schools toward the skills that colleges and employers demanded. In a press release announcing the program, Virginia governor Tim Kaine (who would later serve as Hillary Clinton's vice-presidential nominee) made the argument that "Today, we live in a world without borders. It not only matters how Virginia students compare to those in surrounding states – it matters how we compete with countries across the world."[21]

Within five years, however, these state-initiated standards designed to help Americans compete in a worldwide workforce became a battleground for ideological battles and a fight between states' rights and federal power. Obama's Department of Education strongly supported the standards. Lacking the power to compel states to adopt them, the administration created a US$4.35 billion grant program, entitled "Race to the Top," that gave states a much better chance of winning funding if they joined the Common

Core's learning goals.[22] This was a clear example of the classic federal strategy of tying funding for state programs to the adoption of national standards. Governors on both sides of the political spectrum objected. New York's Andrew Cuomo, a Democrat, called for a delay in the standards' implementation, arguing that they focused too much on testing. But on the right, the rebellion against the Common Core became a central platform of Tea Party governors and of those opposed to Obama's assertions of national authority. Indiana governor Mike Pence, who would become Donald Trump's vice-president, announced that his state planned to create its own standards. "They will be written by Hoosiers, for Hoosiers, and will be among the best in the nation," declared the Hoosier state governor.[23] Louisiana's Bobby Jindal, who had been an initial supporter of the standards, charged that "the federal government has hijacked and destroyed the Common Core initiative. Common Core is the latest effort by big government disciples to strip away states' rights and put Washington, D.C. in control of everything."[24]

The same arguments were made, in the press, in Congress, and in the courts, against President Obama's Clean Power Plan, a federal mandate for state environmental action. Announced from the Rose Garden on April 3, 2015, the Plan was a regulation issued by the Environmental Protection Agency. Obama used the regulatory process to bypass a Congress that by then was firmly in Republican hands and had refused to act to reduce greenhouse gas admissions. Citing the public health and economic advantages that would come from weaning the nation off coal and toward renewable energy sources, Obama's regulation set an ambitious national goal of reducing carbon emissions by a third over the next fourteen years. Standing with the head of the EPA and the Surgeon General, the President declared that the Plan would prevent up to 3,600 premature deaths and save billions of dollars, at least in the long term.[25]

In order to reach these goals, the Clean Power Plan set emissions reductions targets for each state, allowing them to devise their own plans to meet the targets but ensuring that they were, indeed, met. Because greenhouse gas emissions from one state can affect air quality in neighboring states and climate patterns worldwide, Obama's argument was that a national standard was crucial to ensuring that national goals could be met and no state could free-ride on the environmental efforts of the others. Only a mandate could bring the hoped-for national and global benefits, while ensuring that the costs of transitioning away from coal would be borne by all states. Of course, some states would be harmed more than others by this transition, with leading coal producers West Virginia and Kentucky most staunchly opposed. As the Obama administration was developing the Plan, leaders from these states created a coalition that eventually grew to include twenty-nine states, bound together by their objections to a uniform standard that overrode what they saw as states' rights. Just as President Obama was announcing the Clean Power Plan, West Virginia Attorney General Patrick Morrisey was decrying it as a policy that "blatantly disregards the rule of law and will severely harm West Virginia and the U.S. economy."[26]

Do these three major policy moves show that Barack Obama was a hard-and-fast supporter of federal power, devoted to pressing for national standards over state flexibility everywhere and always? An exception in another policy realm proves that Obama did not consistently follow this rule. Federal law prohibits the use, whether recreational or medical, of marijuana. National policy has not shifted, but many states have changed their laws to allow for the use, cultivation, and sale of medical marijuana or, most recently, of recreational use of the drug. A federalist response would have been to heighten federal enforcement efforts, but President Obama's Attorney General, Eric Holder, explicitly moved in the other direction in 2013. He released an August 29, 2013 memorandum addressing the recreational marijuana laws passed by voters in Colorado and Washington. "Based on assurances that those states will impose an appropriately strict regulatory system," the memorandum reported, "the Department has informed the governors of both states that it is deferring its right to challenge their legalization laws at this time."[27] In other words, when it came to marijuana legalization, the Obama Administration took a states' rights approach. This underscores the point that few political leaders maintain consistent views on the correct balance between state and federal authority: if delegating power to states helps them advance their policy agenda, they will do so, following the path of the Jeffersonians. If consolidating power in the federal government serves their policy aims, they follow that approach, acting as a latter-day Hamilton.

The anti-federalist reaction

To accomplish either goal, of course, presidents greatly benefit when they can count on the support of Congress. As other chapters in this book recount, the path of the Obama presidency took a sharp turn when he lost any hope of that support after the 2010 midterm elections. At the federal level, these contests were an unqualified disaster for Obama. His Democratic Party lost sixty-three seats in the House, the largest midterm loss for a president's party since 1938. In Obama's own words, this was a "shellacking." Analyses of the causes of these losses point to multiple determinants. Republican voters, especially those who affiliated with the Tea Party, were energized by opposition to the Affordable Care Act, suggesting that Obama's policy victory on healthcare in March 2010 sowed the seeds of his political losses in November 2010. Exit polling from the election points to a more nuanced story: public opinion on the ACA was split at the time, while it was the president's handling of the still-struggling economy and the unpopular economic stimulus bill that caused a majority of independent voters to turn away from him and kept his party's base disillusioned and at home.[28]

Whatever the cause, the Democratic losses at the national level carried even more deeply into the states. Adding up the victories and losses across all state legislatures, the Republican Party gained a net of 680 state legislative seats. This easily set the record for the largest seat gain in the modern era, surpassing the size of Republican gains in the Gingrich Revolution of 1994 or the post-Watergate Democratic wave in 1974.[29] The GOP took over control of fourteen new state legislative chambers, giving the party unified control of legislatures in twenty-six states. Republicans also finished the election cycle with control of a majority of the governors' chairs across the nation.

During the 2012 presidential contest, the pendulum in the states swung back in the other direction. Barack Obama's coattails allowed Democrats to gain seats and capture unified control of four more legislatures, bringing their total of unified state legislatures to nineteen.[30] Yet another midterm drubbing for Obama in 2014 again brought huge Democratic losses at the state level.

According to the post-election analysis by the National Conference of State Legislatures,[31]

> Republicans ran the table, taking the majority in 11 legislative chambers previously held by Democrats ... It appears that Republicans will have a net gain of between 300 and 350 seats and control over 4,100 of the nation's 7,383 legislative seats. That is their highest number of legislators since 1920. Republicans gained seats in every region of the country and in all but about a dozen legislative chambers that were up this year.

Republican also gained a net of three governors' chairs, to control a total of thirty-one.[32]

What these historic swings added up to were political conditions that were ripe for legislative gridlock in Washington DC, and for a rightward swing in the statehouses. Looking ahead after his 2010 midterm losses, Obama vowed to reach out to congressional Republican leaders to find common ground, but he recognized the difficulty of this task. "I'm not suggesting this will be easy," Obama admitted. "I won't pretend that we'll be able to bridge every difference or solve every disagreement."[33] He knew that these shifts were occurring in the context of dramatic partisan polarization that had reached historic highs at the national level.[34] In many states, the ideological gulf between the two parties was even broader than in Congress.[35] What this meant was that passing major policy initiatives through the legislative process would become nearly impossible in Washington, DC and Obama's fierce political opponents in the states would look for every opportunity to halt his agenda. This combination would serve to shift the balance of power between the federal and state governments throughout the remainder of the Obama administration.

The unintended devolution revolution

The first major shift came in the centerpiece of Obama's early accomplishments, the Affordable Care Act. Soon after its passage, the ACA faced a series of legal challenges, including the one led by Florida and twenty-five other states charging that the federal mandate that states expand their Medicaid program overstepped the bounds of federal authority. The 2012 Supreme Court case that resolved the legality of the ACA, *National Federation of Independent Business* v. *Sebelius*, was a victory for most provisions of Obamacare but a resounding defeat for federal power overall.[36] First, the individual mandate to purchase health insurance was upheld as a permissible exercise of federal power only on very narrow grounds. A majority of Justices on the Court held that it could not be justified through Article I, Section 8 of the Constitution, also known as the "elastic clause," which gives Congress the authority to "make all Laws which shall be necessary and proper for carrying into Execution the foregoing Powers." Nor did they find support for it through the Constitution's grant of power to Congress to regulate interstate commerce. Instead, the mandate was upheld as a proper exercise of Congress's taxation powers, because the penalty for failing to sign up for health insurance was a US$300 tax payment (*NFIB* v. *Sebelius*, pp 3950). Relying on these narrow grounds demonstrated that the federal government did not possess broad powers to regulate state health insurance markets. The individual mandate and penalty for not following it survived the legal challenge, but on grounds that limited what Congress and the president could do in realms like healthcare in the future.

Second, and with more immediate consequences for the policy implementation, the Court held that the Medicaid expansion provisions of Obamacare were unconstitutionally coercive. The penalty for states that refused the expansion was the loss of all of their existing Medicaid funding, a sum in the billions of dollars annually for many states. Saying that this provision put a "gun to the head" of states, the majority opinion held that "the States must have a genuine choice whether to accept the offer," and gave them this choice in the future.[37] This legal precedent clearly shifted power to the states.

At first glance, it appeared that the massive subsidies for Medicaid expansion – with the federal government paying the full cost of the expansion until 2016 – would still tempt states to expand their coverage. Yet with the Republican takeover of so many statehouses in 2010, and under the highly polarized conditions of American politics, ideological battles intervened.

Many Republican governors, especially those allied with the Tea Party, refused to expand Medicaid in their states, even with the free federal dollars. Between 2012 and 2016, thirty-one of the states followed the recommended expansion, but nineteen states refused. All but two of those states were led by Republican governors.[38] The map of which states expanded and which did not closely parallel the Electoral College map of which states voted for Barack Obama and which states supported Mitt Romney, who ran strongly against the ACA, in the 2012 presidential contest. This left an estimated 4 million Americans, in states such as Texas, Florida, North Carolina, and Georgia, without health insurance.[39] An unintended but nonetheless important legacy of the implementation of Obamacare was that its provisions, along with the new flexibility granted to states by the Supreme Court, created a patchwork of policy across the states. In the vitally important policy realm of healthcare, blue states and red states moved farther apart from each other in what they provided to their residents, with coverage provision closely following state political patterns.

A second area of conflict came in education, with the reaction – that again polarized along partisan lines – against the Common Core standards. The Obama administration had issued no formal mandate that states adopt the standards, since this would have clearly overstepped the bounds of federal authority. Yet Obama's Department of Education clearly supported them and used the carrot of grants to states to incentivize adoption. The combination of this attempted imposition of de facto federal control, along with the partisan identity of its source (President Obama), polarized the seemingly nonpartisan issue and led many states to reject the standards. Texas Governor Rick Perry vowed that, "Texas is on the right path toward improved education, and we would be foolish and irresponsible to place our children's future in the hands of unelected bureaucrats and special interest groups thousands of miles away in Washington."[40]

In 2014, state lawmakers authored more than 100 bills aimed at halting or delaying the adoption of the Common Core in their states' schools. Four states – Texas, Virginia, Nebraska, and Alaska – never adopted the Common Core standards, while twelve states repealed, rewrote, or only partially adopted them.[41] Much as with the adoption of Medicaid expansion, the patterns in Common Core adoption followed electoral trends, with Republican states, especially those in the South, taking the lead in attacking the federal standards. Again, state-to-state variation in a fundamental policy realm increased in response to an Obama initiative, displaying the power of state leaders to set their constituents on divergent paths.

A third realm in which power was devolved to the states was in environmental policy. Because Republican control of Congress blocked his route to action on climate change from 2010 onward, President Obama turned to the regulatory process in an attempt to shift toward lower greenhouse gas emissions. The regulation that his administration promulgated, the Clean Power Plan, sought to achieve his national goals by compelling state action. It quickly became the most heavily litigated federal environmental regulation in US history, facing a suit by twenty-nine states, joined by business groups and the coal industry. This time, the states had a federal ally in Congress, which has seen its policy-making authority bypassed when Obama took the regulatory route. The Republican-led Congress held hearings on the issue, giving a platform to those who called for states' rights to determine what type of energy they could produce and consume. The Supreme Court responded aggressively, again striking a blow against Obama's assertion of federal and in this case regulatory power. In a 5–4 decision, on February 9, 2016 the Court temporarily halted the plan, the first time ever that the Supreme Court acted to stop a regulation before it had been reviewed by a federal appeals court.[42]

By issuing this stay, the conservative majority on the Court signaled that its members were sympathetic to the contention by states that the Clean Power Plan was a "power grab" under which "the federal environmental regulator seeks to reorganize the energy grids in nearly every state in the nation."[43] The Plan was then sent back to a lower court for expedited review, with many expecting that it would soon return to the Supreme Court. Yet all expectations about the future of the case and the Court were soon upended by the death, just four days later, of Justice

Antonin Scalia, who had voted with the majority. When President Obama nominated Merrick Garland to succeed Scalia, it seemed likely that he would shift the court majority toward support of the Clean Power Plan.

When the Republican-led Senate refused to hold hearings on the Garland nomination, this threw the Plan, and all of climate policy, into limbo. Without a push toward a uniform set of emissions reduction goals, states were left to move in the directions preferred by their own political leaders. In the eighteen states that had lined up in support of the legal defense of the Clean Power Plan, this meant more moves toward renewable energy sources. The twenty-nine states that opposed it, especially coal producing states such as West Virginia and Kentucky, were freed to move in any way that their leaders desired. Again, the policy distance between the states – often driven by the ideological gulf between the parties – was widened as a result of an Obama initiative.

It is important to note that not every court decision favored the states over the federal government or went against President Obama. In 2010, the state of Arizona passed into law one of the most far-reaching and controversial pieces of immigration legislation of the modern era, Senate Bill 1070. It made it a state misdemeanor to be an "unauthorized immigrant" in Arizona without documents and forbade anyone not authorized to work in the United States from seeking employment. The legislation was immediately held up in federal courts, and in the 2012 *Arizona* v. *United States* case, a 5–3 majority struck down key provisions of the law. Justice Anthony Kennedy opined that "The National Government has significant power to regulate immigration. Arizona may have understandable frustrations with the problems caused by illegal immigration while that process continues, but the State may not pursue policies that undermine federal law."[44] Still, one important provision of the law, permitting state law enforcement officials to verify a person's immigration status while they were enforcing other laws, was upheld by the court. And despite this partial victory for the president and for federal power, the overall trend from 2010 was toward more state authority and increasing policy divergence across the states throughout the remainder of the Obama administration.

Trump's victory continues the revolution

Like Barack Obama before him, Donald Trump likely did not come to the presidency with deeply held beliefs about the proper balance of power between the federal and state governments. Yet following the path of his predecessor, he has pushed for shifts in that balance in order to achieve the policy aims dictated by his ideology. While President Trump has used the rhetoric of states' rights when it served those aims, he has not been a consistent proponent of that approach. Sometimes he has pushed for national power, sometimes he has advocated state flexibility. In some realms, Trump has been successful, while in others he has so far been thwarted. On balance, though, the broad movement toward devolution of power that began under Obama has continued so far in the Trump administration.

Healthcare stands out as the clearest example of a policy realm in which President Trump has so far been unable to fulfill his campaign goals. Even with GOP control of both the House and Senate, assembling a coalition in favor of repealing and replacing the Affordable Care Act turned out to be a surprisingly difficult task. The various versions of President Trump's proposals to do so would all have devolved even more power to the states. In spring 2017, his budget proposed to strike at one of the key provisions of the ACA, the expansion of Medicaid, by shifting the financing of the program from federal matches of state expenditures to a single block grant given to each state. This was the same shift in fiscal federalism that was made to state welfare programs through the Clinton-Gingrich welfare reform plan of 1996. It would have brought a fundamental change to constraints faced by states and the incentives presented to them. Instead of being incentivized to expand Medicaid through a federal match that provided at least 90 percent of the funds for any expansion, they would have a fixed budget. Spending more state dollars would not bring in more federal money, and states would be able to keep all of the budget savings from cuts. Instead of pushing states to expand their healthcare safety net, this would have incentivized contractions. Indeed, the Congressional Budget Office estimated that the president's budget plan would have led to 14 million Americans losing Medicaid coverage by 2026.[45] This figure became one the most-quoted CBO estimates ever, playing a critical rule in turning public opinion against Trump's proposal. The president was forced to abandon his calls for block granting Medicaid, just as his plan to overhaul the other provisions of the ACA failed later in the year. Obama's centerpiece policy survived the first wave of attacks on it. Of course, due to the changes that the Supreme Court had mandated in *NFIB* v. *Sebelius* (2012), Obamacare only survived in the modified form that allowed states to determine whether they wanted to expand Medicaid or not, a significant devolution in itself.

In education, the Trump administration has made an explicit states' rights argument and has encouraged states to move away from the uniform standards of the Common Core that were pushed so strongly by the Obama administration. When she spoke to the American Enterprise Institute, a conservative think-tank, in January of 2018, Secretary of Education Betsy DeVos recounted that, "The Obama administration dangled billions of dollars through the 'Race to the Top' competition, and the grant-making process not so subtly encouraged states to adopt the Common Core State Standards . . . Then, rightly, came the public backlash to federally imposed tests and the Common Core," argued DeVos. "I agree – and have always agreed – with President Trump on this: 'Common Core is a disaster.' And at the U.S. Department of Education, Common Core is dead."[46] Of course, this statement did nothing to kill the Common Core standards in the thirty-six states that have adopted them. Yet it sent the strongest possible signal to the states that had moved away from the uniform standards, or any state considering doing so, that state flexibility in this area would be supported by the federal Department of Education.

In the realm of energy policy, President Trump delivered a strong and personal guarantee that states would have the authority to set their own goals and standards. Trump staunchly criticized the Clean Power Plan, left in legal limbo by the Supreme Court's February 2016 decision to halt the regulation and set it for further review, throughout the campaign. When he signed an executive order to overhaul it in the spring of 2017, though, this did not automatically scrap the rule, which had moved through the full regulatory process under Obama. The Trump administration's most formal blow to the regulation was struck by someone who had earlier pushed for states' rights on energy policy, EPA chief Scott Pruitt. When he served as Attorney General of Oklahoma, Pruitt had been part of the legal challenge to Obama's Clean Power Plan. As a member of Trump's cabinet, he was able to sign the rule that scrapped it, while delivering a critique of federal power run amok. The Plan, Pruitt charges, "ignored states' concerns and eroded long-standing and important partnerships that are a necessary part of achieving positive environmental outcomes."[47] While the Trump administration's order to end the Clean Power Plan will likely face just as many legal challenges as the original plan itself, the action clearly puts the federal government on the side of devolving power over energy policy to the states.

Of course, President Trump has not always pushed for states' rights. On his signature issue of immigration, he has battled with state and local governments throughout his presidency. Seeking to compel state and local governments to cooperate with federal authorities to enforce immigration laws, Trump took on "sanctuary cities" and states. Sanctuary cities – joined by the entire state of California in 2017 – prevented their law enforcement officers from working with the federal government on immigration enforcement. In his first week in office, Trump signed an executive order to cut off federal funding to sanctuary cities, in the attempt to compel them to cooperate fully with federal immigration agents. Chicago and a number of other cities filed suit against what they saw as an overreach of federal power, and they have so far been successful. After California passed legislation that effectively made itself a sanctuary state, Attorney General Jeff Sessions travelled to Sacramento to deliver a speech attacking the "radical extremists" who passed "irrational, unfair, and unconstitutional policies." Governor Jerry Brown ramped up the rhetoric even further, criticizing the federal "reign of terror" and portraying it as "basically going to war against the state of California."[48] In the realm of immigration, President Trump's policy goals outweighed any commitment to states' rights, since they could be pursued only by expanding federal power. Yet so far, he has not won, allowing blue cities and states to resist his approach to immigration enforcement.

The starkest and perhaps most consequential devolution of power to the states during the Trump administration could come through the changing make-up of the Supreme Court. Trump's successful nomination of Neil Gorsuch in 2017 as a replacement to Justice Antonin Scalia preserved the prior ideological balance of the court. The retirement of Anthony Kennedy in 2018 opened the strong possibility that the court would swing decisively to the right. Before the confirmation of Trump's nominee, Brett Kavanaugh, some Court observers viewed it as a near certainty that at least some portions of *Roe v. Wade* would be struck down.[49] A decision in this direction would grant the states much more latitude to craft policies on reproductive rights. By allowing states the ability to impose restrictions on abortion that had been prohibited since the 1973 *Roe* decision, such a move would dramatically devolve power to the states. It could also create a patchwork of laws in the most private and contentious of policy domains.

Conclusion

The Obama presidency has profoundly affected and has been affected by the states. This has happened through policy mechanisms – with the Affordable Care Act putting a major political decision and an implementation challenge before states, and the states putting issues like Arizona's SB1070 on the national agenda. The Common Core originated as a curriculum developed by the National Governors Association and was then embraced as a national set of standards by Obama's Department of Education. The Clean Power Plan mandated that states craft renewable energy policies in order to support a national emissions reduction goal that was key to international efforts to fight climate change.

But political trends have also reverberated back and forth from Washington, DC to statehouses, with Obama's coat-tails bringing Democratic gains in presidential years but especially sharp backlashes against him in the 2010 and 2014 midterms. These electoral swings put in power partisan enemies of the president in legislatures and in governors' chairs, ensuring intense fights whenever moving a Democratic agenda in the federal government required cooperation by the states. The Obama legacy of federalism has also been shaped by the courts, with key Supreme Court decisions on Obama's healthcare and environmental policies reshaping the jurisprudence on federalism at the same time that they set obstacles in the path of leftward policy moves.

President Obama took as his starting point a set of liberal policy aims, then used the lever of heightened federal power over states to achieve them. One of those policies, Obamacare, was among the causes that triggered a political reversal at the national level in 2010, which sent hundreds more Republicans into statehouses under ever more polarized conditions. Decisions by the federal courts and the political will exerted by GOP-led states then led to an accidental devolution of power over healthcare, education, and the environment.

That shift in power toward the states continued under Donald Trump, whose appointees often use the language of states' rights to advance a conservative policy agenda. President Trump has so far been unable to repeal the signature accomplishment of the Affordable Care Act, but has been undoing the most fragile parts of Obama's policy legacy in the environment and in education by moving to end the Clean Power Plan and by declaring the Common Core dead. With his successful second Supreme Court nomination, states may gain full power to legislate abortion restrictions for the first time since the *Roe* v. *Wade* decision of 1973.

In the early years of the Obama presidency, it looked as if states would come closer together in the design of their healthcare safety nets, in their approaches to the pressing issue of climate change, and even in what they taught in their schoolhouses. By 2019, our politically polarized states are much further apart on policy grounds they were a decade before, when the Obama era began.

Notes

1. While no scholarly consensus has yet emerged about the relationship between federalism and the Obama administration, Metzger recognizes the complex interplay between states and Washington under his

presidency (Metzger, Gillian E., "Federalism Under Obama," *William & Mary Law Review*, 2011, 53: 567–619). Greenblatt notes that this presidency was marked both by strong federal action in domestic policy realms and by bold state moves where Washington has deadlocked (Greenblatt, Alan, "Federalism in the Age of Obama," *State Legislatures Magazine*, July/August 2010). Vock's account emphasizes the adversarial nature of the relationship between state and federal governments that grew over the course of the Obama presidency (Vock, Daniel C., "How Obama Changed the Relationship Between Washington, the States and the Cities," *Governing the States and Localities*, June 2016).

2. See Kernell, Sam, Gary Jacobson, Thad Kousser, and Lynn Vavreck, *The Logic of American Politics*, 9th ed. (Washington, DC: Congressional Quarterly Press, 2019).

3. See Ibid., pp. 82–120.

4. See Skocpol, Theda, *Protecting Soldiers and Mothers: The Political Origins of Social Policy in the United States* (Cambridge, MA: The Belknap Press of Harvard University Press, 1992) and Johnson, Kimberly S., *Governing the American State: Congress and the New Federalism, 1877–1929* (Princeton, NJ: Princeton University Press, 2007).

5. See Congressional Research Service, *Medicaid Source Book: Background Data and Analysis* (Washington, DC: Congressional Research Service, 1993) and Coughlin, T. A., L. Ku, and J. Holahan, *Medicaid Since 1980: Costs, Coverage, and the Shifting Alliance Between the Federal Government and the States* (Washington, DC: The Urban Institute Press, 1994).

6. See Weissert, Carol S., "Medicaid in the 1990s: Trends, Innovations, and the Future of the 'PAC-Man' of State Budgets," *Publius*, 1992, 22: 93–109.

7. See Nathan, Richard P., "There Will Always Be a New Federalism," *Journal of Public Administration Research and Theory*, 2006, 16(4): 499–510.

8. See Béland, Daniel and François Vergniolle de Chantal, "Fighting 'Big Government': Frames, Federalism, and Social Policy Reform in the United States," *Canadian Journal of Sociology*, 2004, 29(2): 241–264.

9. See Timothy Conlan, *New Federalism: Intergovernmental Reform from Nixon to Reagan* (Washington, DC: Brookings Institution, 1988).

10. See Kousser, Thad, "La Dévolution: Une reformulation du fédéralisme américain," *Revue Française de Science Politique*, 2014, 64(2): 265–287.
11. See CNN All Politics, "Clinton Signs Welfare Reform Bill, Angers Liberals," *CNN All Politics*, August 22, 1996.
12. See Kousser, Thad, "La dévolution," *Revue Française de Science Politique*, 2014.
13. See Health Care Financing Administration, *The Children's Health Insurance Program* (CHIP). Health Care Financing Administration Press Release, July 17, 1998.
14. See Kerosky, Sara, "Relaxing Federal Rules: Political Determinants of Targeted Leniency," Dissertation, University of California, San Diego, 2018.
15. Quoted p. 48 in Oates, Wallace E., "The Theory of Public Finance in a Federal System," *The Canadian Journal of Economics*, 1968, 1(1): 37–54.
16. See p. 8 of Robertson, David Brian, *Federalism and the Making of America* (New York and London: Routledge, 2012).
17. Quoted in Perkins, Lucy and Bill Chappell, "President Obama Unveils New Power Plant Rules in 'Clean Power Plan'," NPR.org, April 3, 2015.
18. See RAND Corporation, "Should States Expand Medicaid Under the ACA?" Rand.org, September 2018.
19. See Rudowitz, Robin, "Understanding How States Access the ACA Enhanced Medicaid Match Rates," Henry J. Kaiser Family Foundation, September 29, 2014.
20. See RAND, "Should States Expand Medicaid," 2018.
21. Quoted in National Governors Association, "Forty-Nine States and Territories Join Common Core Standards Initiative," Press Release, June 1, 2009.
22. See Bidwell, Allie, "The Politics of the Common Core," *U.S. News and World Report*, March 6, 2014.
23. Quoted in ibid.
24. Quoted in "Gov. Bobby Jindal to Sue Feds over Common Core," *Associated Press*, August 27, 2014.
25. Perkins and Chappell, *art. cit.*
26. Quoted in Davenport, Coral and Julie Hirschfeld Davis, "Move to Fight Obama's Climate Plan Started Early," *The New York Times*, August 3, 2015.

27. Quote from Department of Justice, "Justice Department Announces Update to Marijuana Enforcement Policy," Department of Justice Press Release, August 29, 2013.
28. See Best, Samuel, "Why Democrats Lost the House to Republicans," *CBS News*, November 3, 2010.
29. See Jacobs, Jeremy P., "Devastation: GOP Picks up 680 State Leg. Seats," *National Journal*, November 4, 2010.
30. See National Conference of State Legislatures, "History Holds True in 2012 Legislative Elections," NCSL.org, November 7, 2012.
31. See National Conference of State Legislatures, "Statevote 2014: Election Results," NCSL.org, November 19, 2014.
32. Ibid.
33. Quoted in Brannigan, William, "Obama Reflects on 'Shellacking' in Midterm Elections," *The Washington Post*, November 3, 2010.
34. See Fiorina, Morris P., *Culture War? The Myth of a Polarized America* (New York: Pearson-Longman, 2005) and McCarty, Nolan, Keith T. Poole, and Howard Rosenthal, *Polarized America: The Dance or Ideology and Unequal Riches* (Cambridge, MA: MIT Press, 2006).
35. See Shor, Boris and Nolan McCarty, "The Ideological Mapping of American Legislatures," *American Political Science Review*, 2011, 105(3): 530–551.
36. See Liptak, Adam, "Supreme Court Upholds Health Care Law, 5–4, in Victory for Obama," *The New York Times*, June 28, 2012.
37. Quoted in Prokop, Andrew, "The Battle Over Medicaid Expansion in 2013 and 2014, Explained," *Vox.com*, May 12, 2015.
38. See Kernell et al., *op. cit.*, 2019.
39. See Prokop, *art. cit.*
40. Quoted in Bidwell, *art. cit.*
41. See Education Week, "Map: Tracking the Common Core Standards," Edweek.org, 2018.
42. Liptak, Adam and Coral Davenport, "Supreme Court Deals Blow to Obama's Efforts to Regulate Coal Emissions," *The New York Times*, February 9, 2016.
43. Quoted in ibid.
44. Quoted in Cohen, Tom, and Bill Mears, "Supreme Court Mostly Rejects Arizona Immigration Law; Gov Says 'Heart' Remains," CNN.com, June 25, 2012.
45. See Jacobs, Harrison, "Trump's Proposed Trillion-Dollar Cuts to Medicaid Include a 'Fundamental Change' in How the Program Would Operate," *Business Insider*, May 24, 2017.

46. Quoted in Abamu, Jenny, "Betsy DeVos Touts Personalized Learning, Slams Common Core and Reform Efforts," EdSurge.com, January 16, 2018.
47. Quoted in Eilperin, Juliet, "Pruitt Signs Rule Undoing Clean Power Plan," *The Washington Post*, October 10, 2017.
48. Quoted in Ulloa, Jazmine and Liam Dillon, "Sessions, State Officials at 'War' Over Immigration,", *Los Angeles Times*, March 8, 2018, p. A1.
49. See Stern, Mark Joseph, "How Brett Kavanaugh Will Gut *Roe v. Wade*," Slate.com, July 9, 2018.

Part 2

POLICIES

5

"Our immigration system is broken": Barack Obama and the challenge of comprehensive immigration reform

Isabelle Vagnoux[1]

"The system just isn't working and we need to change it"[2] was candidate Barack Obama's observation and promise during the 2008 campaign, just like his Republican predecessor in 1999 and 2000. The issue became one of the priorities of the incoming presidency, after Senators McCain and Kennedy and the Bush administration came close to an historic overhaul in 2006 but ultimately failed.[3] The acknowledgement of the inadequacy between US immigration legislation and the reality of migration flows is not a new phenomenon and has been at the origin of all migration legislation since the beginning of the Cold War. Reforming migration legislation involves so many conflictual interests and parties that, since the end of the Cold War, only the 1965 Hart–Celler Act overhauled the decaying system inherited from the 1920s immigration laws. In the more than fifty years since this law, only piecemeal laws have been passed that never thoroughly overhauled the legislative frame of immigration to the United States. Candidate and then President Obama's assertion is inscribed in this historical trend, where presidents and Congress either fight or collaborate to try to update legislation to conform more fully with the actual practice and the "national interest" or the values of the country. The son of an immigrant himself,[4] a unique occurrence in the history of American presidents, Barack Obama could be seen as naturally more willing to establish a fair and efficient system. This came at a time of high immigration flows, reaching annual levels comparable to the early years of the twentieth century. The number of foreign-born residents in the United States (43.7 million) reached its highest level in US history in 2016 and as a proportion of the US population (13.5 percent) they approached the levels of 1910 (14.8 percent).[5] As nearly 47 percent of all immigrants to the United States come from Latin America and the Caribbean, far ahead of the second group, South and East Asians, with nearly 27 percent,[6] the issue is often seen as affecting primarily Latin Americans and the US Hispanic minority. Because all immigration debates are intimately tied to the nation's identity and values, the issue severely polarized the country and the political class, reminiscent of the culture wars of the late 1960s.

This chapter will analyze the many obstacles faced by President Obama in his efforts to pass an immigration reform: the tug of war with Congress, the tension between security and the American tradition of welcoming immigrants, Obama's endeavour to find a creative solution to break the stalemate, as well as the intermestic dimension of the migration issue.

Fatal hesitations

Comprehensive immigration reform, which several of his predecessors had failed to obtain, was one of candidate Obama's first ten domestic priorities, but not a top one. In an October 31, 2008 interview with CNN anchor, Wolf Blitzer, he made it clear that his top five priorities would be the stabilization of the financial system, energy independence, healthcare reform, a broader tax reform effort that would include tax cuts for the middle class, and a reform of the education system.[7] The introduction of a comprehensive immigration bill in the first year of the new administration ranked only ninth in the list of the candidate's domestic policy priorities. And with good reason: the great recession of 2007–2009 was still in full swing. A nationwide consensus prevailed: the top priority was to fix and revitalize the economic and financial system of the country. A May 30, 2008 Gallup poll showed that only 6 percent of respondents chose immigration as a policy priority, far behind the economy (43 percent), the situation in Iraq (35 percent), and oil prices and the energy crisis

(28 percent).[8] An analysis of Pew Research polls by Roberto Suro added that while 11 percent of respondents had rated immigration as a top priority in 2006, only 4 percent made this choice in 2008 and 1 percent in February 2009.[9] An interesting interactive compilation of Gallup polls by *The New York Times* perfectly highlights the low levels of interest in immigration among respondents.[10] In addition, several polls showed that economic improvements and education and healthcare reform were just as important to Hispanics as they were to the rest of the population. Two Pew Hispanic polls, conducted in December 2008 and August/September 2010 respectively, concluded that only 31 percent of the Latino respondents (registered voters only in the second poll) rated immigration as an "extremely important" issue, both times placing it near the bottom of the list of policy priorities, way behind the economy, education, and healthcare.[11] A similar poll conducted in 2014 returned similar results.[12]

Yet, particularly in ceremonies involving Latinos, or in Latino media, the president continued to state that the current immigration system was "broken," and time and again he confirmed his commitment to start working on the issue as early as spring and summer 2009,[13] but without offering a precise timeline. The Obama team had early on outlined its principles for comprehensive immigration reform, with a net emphasis on enforcement, which hardly made it different from Senator McCain's policy positions:

> Create Secure Borders: Protect the integrity of our borders. Support additional personnel, infrastructure and technology on the border and at our ports of entry. Improve Our Immigration System: Fix the dysfunctional immigration bureaucracy and increase the number of legal immigrants to keep families together and meet the demand for jobs that employers cannot fill. Remove Incentives to Enter Illegally: Remove incentives to enter the country illegally by cracking down on employers who hire undocumented immigrants. Bring People Out of the Shadows: Support a system that allows undocumented immigrants who are in good standing to pay a fine, learn English, and go to the back of the line for the opportunity to become citizens. Work with Mexico: Promote economic development in Mexico to decrease illegal immigration.[14]

The main difference on immigration between Senators Obama and McCain in the 2008 campaign had been that Obama would not require the borders to be secured *before* unauthorized immigrants could seek a path to legal residence, while McCain probably pushed a tough stance because his party called for the immediate round-up and deportation of the estimated 2 million unauthorized immigrants with criminal backgrounds. Both had voted for the Secure Fence Act in 2006 and both had co-sponsored the DREAM (Development, Relief, and Education for Alien Minors) Act.[15]

"An economic imperative"

One of the arguments President Obama emphasized time and again to gather wide support for immigration reform was the decades-old economic argument, adjusted to the twenty-first century. A comprehensive reform would suppress the "massive underground economy that exploits a cheap source of labor while depressing wages for everybody else" and as such has to be seen as an "economic imperative."[16] Reform would also "help to make America more competitive in the global economy" by allowing the thousands of students trained in the United States to stay and enrich the country instead of training "them to create jobs for our competition."[17] It would be "a driving force in our economy that creates jobs and prosperity for all of our citizens."[18] It would boost the economy through the growth of new companies and a steady supply of labor and tax revenues. Even the path to citizenship proposed in the 2013 Senate plan would have a positive impact on the budget as it entailed paying fines and back taxes. Although "ascertaining the effects of immigration policies on the economy and the federal budget is complicated and highly uncertain," a 2013 study by the Congressional Budget Office (CBO) concurred that a comprehensive immigration reform would boost economic output and shrink the federal budget deficit, although "average wages for the entire labor force would be 0.1 percent lower in 2023 and 0.5 percent higher in 2033 than under current law."[19] The business community also supported comprehensive reform because immigrants "create more jobs through entrepreneurship, economic activity and tax revenues," in the words of US Chamber of Commerce President, Tom Donahue.[20]

It actually takes three to tango

Congressional hearings on the immigration issue had started right at the beginning of the 111th Congress and seemed to offer a bipartisanship that augured well.[21] In Senator Schumer's words (D-NY, Chairman of the Subcommittee): "We are off to a great start because he [Senator Cornyn (R-TX), Ranking member of the Subcommittee] agrees with 90 percent of my statement and I agree with 90 percent of his statement."[22] Senator Cornyn recalled that this new round of hearings did not start in terra incognita as Senators had "already spent 36 business days on the floor of the US Senate grappling with this issue" in 2005–2007 and that they would be well inspired to take the Cornyn-Kyl plan of 2005 and the McCain-Kennedy Plan of 2006 into account and to proceed from there as "the status quo is not acceptable to anyone."[23] One dissenting note, however, perfectly seized the hesitations of the administration: if Senator Cornyn welcomed the "President's announcement that he considers immigration reform to be an important subject," he was "a little discouraged that he seems now to be talking about establishing working groups to develop a framework for legislation rather than tackling this head on . . . I hope he will tell us, the Congress, who must work on this legislation, what his plan is."[24] Yet, it is usual for Congress to take the lead on immigration legislation because it has to be bipartisan. Passing the buck constantly between Congress and the administration highlighted how embarrassing the debates were for both parties. The President met with Senators Schumer (D-NY) and Graham (R-SC) and members of both parties in June 2009. Schumer assured that comprehensive immigration reform legislation could be taken up later in 2009, but only if the first priority was a crackdown on illegal immigration.[25] Things seemed to move forward slightly in August 2009 when Senator Schumer tapped Senator Graham, a long-time ally and supporter of John McCain, who worked well with Democrats, to be his partner in crafting bipartisan reform legislation. Although a few hearings had been held in the spring, two Senate hearings on Comprehensive Immigration Reform and its economic consequences were canceled or postponed in the second part of 2009, which never happens when a bill is about to materialize.

The presidential determination to put full political weight into the battle was increasingly questioned as nothing seemed to materialize on the administration side except the most restrictive aspects of enforcement. The January 2010 State of the Union Address was particularly disappointing to the advocates of immigration reform as only two lines were devoted to the issue, and as a mere passing remark that emphasized more enforcement than reform: "And we should continue the work of fixing our broken immigration system, to secure our borders and enforce our laws and ensure that everyone who plays by the rules can contribute to our economy and enrich our Nation."[26] Yet, time was pressing, as the political rationale signaled that any reform had to be introduced early 2010 at the latest. Later in the year would be too politically dangerous because of the upcoming congressional primaries in the spring and the midterm elections in November. The issue would then be postponed to the next term.

In January, Senator Graham urged the Senate to take on the reform but added that it was necessary to secure the border first. In March 2010, the process seemed to take off when the two senators met with the president and published their blueprint, "The right way to mend immigration," in *The Washington Post*. In essence, their plan borrowed much from the 2006 McCain-Kennedy plan and focused on enforcement first:

> requiring biometric Social Security cards to ensure that illegal workers cannot get jobs; fulfilling and strengthening our commitments on border security and interior enforcement; creating a process for admitting temporary workers; and implementing a tough but fair path to legalization for those already here.[27]

Alas, the next day, Senator Graham criticized the president for not making a real effort in advancing the immigration reform and warned that "the first casualty of the Democratic health care bill will be immigration reform. If the health care bill goes through this weekend, that will, in my view, pretty much kill any chance of immigration reform passing the Senate this year."[28] Pressing the White House to move forward, Senator Graham blamed the president for his failure to put forward a bill of his own. Senator Schumer publicly begged him to continue working on the issue. By the end of April, Senator Graham had left the boat and the Democrats went ahead with their own plan, Real Enforcement with Practical Answers for Immigration Reform (REPAIR). Even though it fully assumed the Republican mantra to "secure the border first before any action can be taken to adjust the status of people in the United States illegally,"[29] the plan was doomed if not supported by Republicans. Why did Senator Graham turn around so rapidly? Some of the reasons include increasing GOP pressure to be tough after Arizona's anti-immigration legislation,[30] a difficult race facing his old friend Senator McCain in Arizona, but also the GOP's sour feelings at the end of the healthcare reform debates. The immigration reform was the collateral victim of all these elements and, in Graham's words, "there is just not the appetite – on either side of the aisle – for this issue right now. Until we secure the border, that dynamic is unlikely to change."[31]

Obama proved he was no Lyndon B. Johnson, keeping aloof from his former fellow senators and never managing to build a strong bond that would have helped steer the bill through Congress. Accused by the McCain team of having contributed to killing the bipartisan immigration bill of 2006,[32] Obama had a hard time getting his crucial support for his own reform. When, following the midterm elections of November 2010, Republicans regained control of the House of Representatives and Democrats retained only a small majority in the Senate, in a deeply polarized atmosphere the task of passing a comprehensive immigration reform became even more difficult for the administration.

Executive tensions

While Secretary Janet Napolitano, a Westerner raised in New Mexico and living in Arizona, particularly aware of border and migration issues, was put in charge of the reform, with a strong emphasis on enforcement, various influences and advice clashed within the White House. Chief of staff Rahm Emanuel was not

convinced the Democrats had much to win in pushing an immigration reform so early in the term. He was not convinced there
would be enough Republican votes to pass such legislation, and
bipartisanship had always been crucial to any immigration legislation. A few years before, while Chairman of the House Democratic Caucus, he had allegedly called immigration the "third
rail" in politics, dangerous to those who touched it,[33] and had
clashed with members of the Congressional Hispanic Caucus
on the issue. At the other end of the spectrum, Cecilia Muñoz,
a Latina pro-immigration and civil rights activist appointed
as White House Director of Governmental Affairs, strongly
pushed in favor of making good on the campaign promise and
committing rapidly to a comprehensive reform.[34] One of the
few Hispanics nominated by President Obama, Cecilia Muñoz
also echoed the expectations and growing disappointment of
the Hispanic/Latino community, the first ethnic minority in the
United States and a key element in electoral maths. Although
they usually tend to vote for the Democratic Party, George W.
Bush had managed to win more than 40 percent of Latino voters in 2004, an unprecedented high for the Republican party. In
terms of strategy, the two options were all about votes: whether
the comprehensive immigration reform was popular enough
in the socio-economic context of 2009–2010 to pass through
Congress, whether the emotional debates that accompany
every immigration bill – and particularly the hot unauthorized
immigration issue – would be detrimental to the president's top
domestic priority, healthcare reform, and whether the Democrats could lose the Latino minority vote in the midterm elections if no concrete action was taken.

At the end of the day, President Obama chose a holistic
approach: economic and healthcare measures would also impact
Latinos favorably. Why risk endangering healthcare reform in
Congress for an issue that was not rated as extremely important by those who were most concerned? It was a realpolitik
choice but also one forced by circumstances. According to Doris
Meissner, Commissioner of the Immigration and Naturalization
Service during the Clinton administration and one of the most
renowned experts on immigration issues,

if you want to do something on migration, you have to do it quickly, early in the Administration. But Obama chose health care first. Should health care have come first? It was a debate within the Administration. But Obama identified himself personally more with health care. And the health care reform took much longer than anybody had planned. More and more opposition developed and the Administration was not able to fight back. It was a lost opportunity, one year was lost.[35]

Enforcement first: "deporter in chief"?[36]

Ever since the 1980s, the main bone of contention in any debate on immigration has always been unauthorized immigration, not the number or the type of visas. The president had to walk a very fine line, working in both directions at the same time, infuriating both anti-immigration Republicans who accused him of being soft on unauthorized immigrants, and immigrants' rights groups who accused him of privileging an enforcement-only and often inhumane policy. Even while publicly committing to a comprehensive immigration reform, President Obama always insisted that if the United States was a nation of immigrants, it was also "a nation of laws," an assertion bound to meet with wide support in a law-abiding culture.

> The American people believe in immigration, but they also believe that we can't tolerate a situation where people come to the United States in violation of the law, nor can we tolerate employers who exploit undocumented workers in order to drive down wages. That's why we're taking steps to strengthen border security, and we must build on those efforts. We must also clarify the status of millions who are here illegally, many who have put down roots.[37]

In this, he very much followed the line presented by Senators Kennedy and McCain in 2006: a path to citizenship for unauthorized immigrants under strict conditions, while increasing enforcement measures and making it more difficult to cross the border illegally. Over the past three decades, and increasingly after the 9/11 attacks that catapulted security as an absolute top priority, moderate Republicans and many Democrats alike have felt it necessary to secure the border first, to deter unauthorized immigration, before engaging in a softer program. "Democrats always have the perceived need to show toughness" said Doris Meissner, and, given the robust Republican opposition, Obama felt that toughness on enforcement and the rule of law would be key to getting a future comprehensive reform in Congress. "He tried to compromise in order to get something in return, but he didn't get anything in return from the opposition. He should have acted earlier," adds Joy Olson, former Executive Director of the Washington Office on Latin America.[38]

President Obama inherited a robust immigration machinery. As early as 1996, under the aegis of a Republican Congress, a series of laws established new grounds for deportation, penalties for illegal entry or re-entry, mandates for detention of deportable noncitizens, as well as a framework for better cooperation between the federal government and state and local law enforcement agencies. Many of these enforcement tools were not fully resourced until the aftermath of the September 11, 2001 terrorist attacks. By the end of the Bush administration, some seventy agreements allowing state and local law enforcement officials to perform certain immigration enforcement tasks had been signed. Starting in 2005, formal removal proceedings became increasingly common, as opposed to the practice of allowing unauthorized entrants to return to Mexico voluntarily that had prevailed thus far. The Obama administration only increased these enforcement tendencies.[39]

By the fall of 2010, on the eve of the midterm elections and probably spurred by the Arizona legislation, the administration proudly announced a record-high number of both removals and penalties on employers hiring unauthorized immigrants,[40] as well as a border law (August 2010) adding some US$600 million to the staffing of the border. This was to no political avail, as the elections returned a vocal and confrontational Republican majority to the US House of Representatives as well as a stronger Republican minority in the Senate, while Republican opposition in many state governorships increased.

The Department of Homeland Security also increasingly prioritized border removals – before unauthorized immigrants became integrated into US communities and built families – over interior removals (often the consequences of worksite raids). Border removals had prevailed until 2005 when they still accounted for about 60 percent of all removals. Following the implementation of the Secure Border Initiative in 2005 and the interior enforcement surge after the breakdown of congressional negotiations on immigration reform in 2006 and 2007, removals increased quickly. Interior removals accounted for the lion's share of this growth, doubling between fiscal year (FY) 2006 and FY 2008 and accounting for 43 percent of all removals in FY 2008. The beginning of the Obama administration marked another turning point in 2009. Border, interior, and overall removals all reached historically high levels during its first three years. Following the announcement of the DHS's enforcement priorities in 2010, total removals reached all-time high levels in both FY 2012 and FY 2013. Border removals accounted for about 60 percent of all removals in FY 2012, 70 percent in FY 2013, and nearly 73 percent in FY 2016.[41]

At the federal level, enforcement was implemented through an increased number of Border Patrol Agents, of border apprehensions, removals, and returns. The number of Border Patrol Agents had increased from 12,346 in FY 2006 to 20,119 in FY 2009, a consequence of the Secure Fence Act passed in 2006, and the number continued to rise during the first Obama administration, reaching an all-time high of 21,444 in FY 2011, a far cry from the meagre 4,028 agents stationed on the borders in FY 1993. It regularly declined during the rest of Obama's administration, to reach 19,437 in FY 2017. Eighty-five percent of these agents were stationed in the Southwest Border sector, slightly down from 87 percent in FY 2013.[42]

Initiated in 2008, the Secure Communities program (Immigration and Customs Enforcement 2018) was part of this enforcement arsenal, allowing DHS officers to use FBI information – mainly biometric information – to remove individuals presenting significant threats to public safety as well as those who violated immigration laws. The program was gradually implemented. It became operational in all state prisons and local jails by January 2013 and was suspended on November 20, 2014 when it was replaced by the Priority Enforcement Program before it was resumed under

Table 5.1 Apprehensions, removals, and returns of unauthorized immigrants (1993–2016)

Year	Total apprehensions	US–Mexico border apprehensions	Removals	Returns
1993	1,327,261	1,212,886	42,542	1,243,410
1994	1,094,719	979,101	45,674	1,029,107
1995	1,394,554	1,271,390	50,924	1,313,764
1996	1,649,986	1,507,020	69,680	1,573,428
1997	1,536,520	1,368,707	114,432	1,440,684
1998	1,679,439	1,516,680	174,813	1,570,127
1999	1,714,035	1,537,000	183,114	1,574,863
2000	1,814,729	1,643,679	188,467	1,675,876
Totals for Clinton administration	12,211,234	11,036,463	869,646	11,421,259
2001	1,387,486	1,235,718	189,026	1,349,371
2002	1,062,270	929,809	165,168	1,012,112
2003	1,046,422	905,065	211,098	945,294
2004	1,264,232	1,160,395	240,665	1,166,576
2005	1,291,065	1,189,031	246,431	1,096,920
2006	1,206,408	1,071,972	280,974	1,043,381
2007	960,673	858,638	319,382	891,390
2008	1,043,759	705,005	359,795	811,263
Totals for Bush administration	9,262,315	8,055,633	2,012,539	8,316,311
2009	889,212	540,865	391,341	582,596
2010	796,587	447,731	381,738	474,195
2011	678,606	327,577	386,020	322,098
2012	671,327	356,873	416,324	230,360
2013	662,483	414,397	434,015	178,691
2014	679,996	479,371	407,075	163,245
2015	462,388	331,333	333,341	129,122
2016	530,250	408,870	340,056	106,167
Totals for Obama administration	5,370,849	3,307,017	3,089,910	2,186,474

Source: Department of Homeland Security, *Yearbook of Immigration Statistics 2016*; Chishti, Pierce, and Bolter (2017).

the Trump administration in January 2017. The Obama administration expanded this program to better target removable aliens,
emphasizing those with a criminal record who posed a threat to
the security of US citizens, rather than those who merely lived illegally in the United States. During the last two years of the Obama
administration, a minimum of three misdemeanors was necessary
to risk deportation, which meant roughly 87 percent of the unauthorized population was protected from deportation.[43] According
to the US Immigration and Customs Enforcement (ICE), during
the last year of the administration, 94 percent of removals and
returns were classified within a Priority 1 category, which included
national security threats, individuals apprehended at the border
while attempting to enter unlawfully, and the most serious categories of convicted criminals as well as gang members; 5 percent
were classified within a Priority 2 category (serious and repeat mis-
demeanants, individuals who unlawfully entered the United States
on or after January 1, 2014, and significant abusers of the visa system or visa waiver program), and 1 percent were classified within
a Priority 3 category (individuals issued a final order of removal on
or after January 1, 2014). Less than 0.1 percent of removals and
returns involved individuals classified as other federal interests,
and less than 0.3 percent had unknown priority classifications.[44]

Worksite enforcement

The other side of the increased enforcement policy focused on making it more difficult, if not impossible, for unauthorized immigrants
to find work. Consequently, it targeted employers. The argument
was not new. As early as 1953, a Mexican official argued that

> as long as Mexican workers know that by crossing the Rio Grande
> or getting over border barbed wire, they will easily find jobs, even
> in violation of the law, they will never learn to discipline themselves
> and wait until they get a legal visa, and no surveillance will ever be
> enough to prevent this process.[45]

After two failed attempts, in 1952 and during the Carter administration, this rationale led Congress for the first time ever, in 1986,

to include penalties for employers who "knowingly" employ unauthorized workers (Immigration Reform and Control Act, IRCA, Public Law 99–603). However, the difficulty of determining whether workers had been hired "knowingly," as well as pressure from many local economic interests, prompted the end of controls on employers by 1999. But employers still had to verify their new workers' identity and work eligibility and complete verification forms known as I-9 forms.

Worksite raids, which multiplied after 2007, particularly in industries known for employing large numbers of immigrants (e.g. construction, hotels, restaurants, meat-packaging) had resulted in interior removals, but these were seen as largely inefficient (in 2008 only 1.76 percent of removals originated in worksite raids) and highly traumatic for consequently disrupted families. The authorities relied on the very fear of such controls to deter unauthorized immigrants from applying for jobs and even from entering the country in the first place. The employer sanctions dimension of IRCA was resurrected with modern technological means. Here, also, the Obama administration changed the rationale, trying to create a culture of compliance to immigration and labor laws and expanding surveillance of employers by significantly increasing administrative audits between 2009 and 2013. Despite these increased efforts, however, the number of penalties remained very low relative to the number of US employers. Less than .02 percent of US employers were sanctioned. The number of audits, as well as the amount of financial sanctions, dropped steeply in the last three years of the administration.[46]

The Employment Eligibility Verification program is another worksite enforcement instrument. It was initially created as a voluntary internet-based pilot program by the Illegal Immigration Reform and Immigrant Responsibility Act of 1996 (IIRIRA) to help employers verify the work authorization of their newly hired employees. The program is administered by the DHS in partnership with the Social Security administration but it relies heavily on the states. Congress extended its use to all voluntary states in 2003. It is, however, mandatory for employers with federal contracts or those in states that mandate the use of the system. The program was renamed E-verify in 2007, and it thus predates the

Obama administration which only tried to make it more efficient. The system remains vulnerable to identity theft and employer fraud and varies significantly from one state to another.[47] Only nine states – Alabama, Arizona, Georgia, Louisiana, Mississippi, North Carolina, South Carolina, Tennessee, and Utah – require E-verify for all employers. Thirteen more require its use for some public and/or private employers. The remaining states do not require its use. California, Illinois, and Rhode Island have even passed legislation preventing E-verify from being a *requirement* for any organization, and permit employers to use it or not on a voluntary basis.[48]

States step in

Frustrated with the absence of new federal legislation, some states, generally headed by Republican governors, also played a significant role in deterring potential candidates for unauthorized immigration and in opposing the administration by adopting anti-immigrant legislation. On this issue the federal and state governments share concurrent powers: the federal government is in charge of legislation affecting migration flows and visas, while the states are in charge of immigrants. But any anti-immigrant law is bound to have an impact on subsequent flows. The best-known example is Arizona, which in April 2010 passed Senate Bill 1070, the Support Our Law Enforcement and Safe Neighborhoods Act, which allowed state law officers to determine immigration status during any lawful stop if there was "reasonable suspicion of immigrant status." It required aliens to carry registration documents, it prohibited unauthorized immigrants from applying for work, and it also allowed warrantless arrests if there was probable cause that the offense would make the person removable from the United States.[49]

Although each provision stipulates "that law enforcement cannot consider race, color, or national origin in the enforcement when implementing the provision, except as permitted by the US or Arizona Constitution," SB 1070 potentially paved the way for racial profiling and arbitrary arrests. The law infuriated immigration activists, business leaders, and the governments of more liberal cities in the Southwest (Los Angeles, for instance), and also the Obama administration which believed it would "end up polarizing the situation instead of solving the problem"[50] and sued Arizona. A series of questions were raised about the constitutionality of the law, including due process, equal protection under the 14th Amendment, and the prohibition on unreasonable search and seizure under the 4th Amendment. In a 5-to-3 ruling in 2012,[51] the Supreme Court struck down part of the law that would have allowed the police to arrest those suspected of being in the country illegally, without a warrant. But the court ruled in favor of a key provision enabling the state to require that police officers check the immigration status of people they detain, a mixed decision that highlights the ambiguity of all immigration-related cases. Under a settlement reached in September 2016, the so-called "show your papers" or "papers, please" provision was suspended. Police officers are still authorized to inquire about immigration status but are no longer required to.[52]

In the wake of the Arizona law, several states with Republican governors also crafted similar legislation in 2011: Alabama, Georgia, Indiana, South Carolina, and Utah. All of them required law enforcement to attempt to inquire about the immigration status of a person involved in a lawful stop, allowed state residents to sue state and local agencies for non-compliance with immigration enforcement, required E-verify, and made the failure to carry an alien registration document a state violation. Alabama's law required schools to verify students' immigration status. As in Arizona, most laws were subsequently stripped of their most contentious contents and were barely enforced.

This state-led movement emphasizes the political and ideological gap between some governors (generally Republican) and the Democratic White House. It also highlights the role of the states and local government in migration issues and the multi-layered structure of immigration decision making. It also speaks volumes about US citizens' position toward unauthorized migrants and predated Donald Trump's success.

At the same time, other states were making life easier for the unauthorized. For instance, some twelve states, including Maryland and Connecticut, permitted unauthorized immigrant students to be eligible for in-state tuition. Some cities also tried to "roll out the welcome mat."[53] In the absence of new and consistent federal legislation, the concurrent powers held by the federal, state, and local governments in the migration issue were fully used by the lower levels, leading to a highly atomized and contradictory landscape.

The tribulations of the DREAM Act

The Development, Relief, and Education for Alien Minors (DREAM) Act was intended to give alien minors the opportunity to earn "conditional permanent residency" provided they earned a university degree or served in the armed forces and met other requirements. It intended to give minors who had come to the United States fraudulently with their parents a chance to become legal residents and stay in the country where they had spent most of their lives. The narrative insisted on the innocence of these young people and the capital they represented for the United States. The first version of the federal DREAM Act was introduced in the Senate in 2001. After several aborted attempts, the House finally passed the Act on December 8, 2010 (216–198, with 208 Democrats and eight Republicans approving)[54] with full presidential support. But it failed in the Senate a few days later, "in an incredibly disappointing vote,"[55] falling short by just five votes from the sixty necessary for passage. Proponents tried to reintroduce it in the Senate in May 2011, to no avail. Worse still, even those who had initially supported the bill in the 2000s now turned hostile, viewing it as a kind of amnesty, and stuck to the "border security first" mantra. John McCain, who co-sponsored the 2003 and 2005 versions of the bill, was one of them.[56] A local version of the DREAM Act was passed in California in 2011, giving unauthorized immigrant students the right to apply for loans, state-financed scholarships, and aid at state universities. Other states followed suit.

In addition to the purely political or electoral dimension, an exterior element contributed to this security-first orientation. Between 2008 and 2012, the Mexican border states were plagued by extreme narcoviolence, first in Baja California and then in Nuevo León, adjacent to Texas. Republican congressmen quickly spread the fear of the "spillover" effect on the US side, underscoring the danger of migration from the south and the need for strict enforcement of security at the border,[57] in addition to the then decade-old rampant fear of Hezbollah activities near the border.

After the failure to materialize a reform proposal through Congress before the midterms, the resounding failure of the DREAM Act at the very end of the Democratic Congress was a severe blow for the President. At this juncture, Obama's early procrastination and tactics could be seen as a failure. Not only had he disappointed all those who had believed in the prospect of immigration reform in his first two years, but he was dubbed "deporter in chief" by the very immigrants' rights activists who had supported him in 2008, and he had failed to sway enough Republicans to his side on the immigration issue. The Dreamer generation was becoming a pivotal force and the lack of legislation by the Democratic administration deeply disappointed them. The risk that some of their US relatives would turn to the Republican party was real; as Senator Marco Rubio had declared, he wanted to introduce DREAM legislation. Moreover, many Democratic constituents, especially in California, a Democratic stronghold, were also increasingly critical of the administration.[58] Action was necessary if the president wanted to fare better in the presidential election. Facing additional pressure from the young Dreamers,[59] President Obama resorted to one of the very few instruments that the Executive can use to act without congressional approval: executive orders.

DACA

Facing Congress's procrastination and deep divisions on the issue, President Obama decided to bypass the legislative circuit and issued an executive order (valid for two years but renewable) in June 2012 – in the middle of the presidential campaign, which predictably was seen by his critics as an electoral strategy to rally those US citizens who had such young people among their relatives. The Deferral Act, or Deferred Action for Childhood Arrivals (DACA), which is about deferring deportation, provides a path to legalization for eligible unauthorized youth and young adults, who can apply for legal permanent status resident if they are under the age of thirty-five, if they arrived in the United States before the age of sixteen, if they have been resident in the United States for at least five years and have obtained a high school diploma or equivalent. DACA is renewable. Out of 1.6 million potentially eligible, 750,000 unauthorized young adults applied. Among the reasons for such a gap between eligible young people and actual number of applications were: delays, lack of outreach and information, the US$465 application fee, and also the fear of disclosing their parents' unauthorized status.

Restrictionists promptly argued that these young people who arrived illegally as children were taking jobs from US citizens and that too much public funding was invested in the program, at the expense of American taxpayers. One of the most vocal opponents of DACA is the Center for Immigration Studies, headed by Mark Krikorian.[60] Conversely, Migration Policy Institute analyses have showed that DACA opened doors to higher education or skilled jobs for many[61] and that many employers would suffer from the loss of these young people.[62] Politically speaking, while DACA infuriated Republicans it certainly contributed to keeping immigrant voters and pro-immigrant groups within the Democratic Party. To what extent it played a part in President Obama's re-election is more difficult to ascertain.

Chronicle of a failure foretold

Prompted to action by the emergency of the migration situation in early 2013, a bipartisan group of eight senators – the so-called Gang of Eight: Michael Bennet, D-CO; Richard J. Durbin, D-IL; Jeff Flake, R-AZ; Lindsay Graham, R-SC; John McCain, R-AZ; Bob Menendez, D-NY; Marco Rubio, R-FL; Chuck Schumer, D-NY – initiated a reform bill that would attempt to combine the irreconcilable aspects of the immigration issue. They wrote the first draft of the Border Security, Economic Opportunity, and Immigration Modernization Act of 2013, with Rubio arguing that Americans would be more willing to support immigration reform if border security was beefed up first, and if the law was fully enforced. At the same time, another key figure of the Republican party, former governor of Florida Jeb Bush, also advocated a reform that would offer solutions for unauthorized immigrants.[63]

Even Senator Graham optimistically believed that "2013 presents us the best chance to pass immigration reform in many years. The time is right and the way forward."[64]

A major overhaul of US immigration laws, the bill (S. 744) was passed by 68–32 in the Senate on June 27, 2013, with fourteen Republicans[65] joining Democrats in a favorable vote after weeks of debates and months of private negotiations by the members of the Gang of Eight.[66] While the top priority was set on securing the border, a path to legalization under strict conditions was made possible for non-criminal undocumented immigrants. The bill also confirmed the DACA provisions if all the criteria were met.

Despite significant Republican figures pleading in favor of similar action in the House, things rapidly bogged down in the lower chamber. The Gang of Eight's failure seemed to stem from divisions among Democrats over strategy and policy, the reluctance of many Republicans to appear in any way as "soft on immigration" to their growing anti-immigration, Tea Party electorate – Senator Rubio himself even backed off from his own bill later in 2013 – as well as Speaker Boehner's refusal to put his weight behind the bill and help steer it through the House.[67]

Seeking GOP help on the bill, the White House reached out to certain Republican members of the House, conservative CEOs, and former George W. Bush officials (Michael Chertoff, Carlos Gutierrez) – all in vain. What came out of the White House meetings was the feeling that there was no clear agenda; the White House did not know to whom they should talk and the conservative participants did not really know what they were supposed to do. It also seemed that the White House reached out for help from conservative congressmen who were too close to the Tea Party, like Michael McCaul of Texas, while other immigration-friendly Republicans such as Jeff Denham, David Valadao, or Mario Díaz-Balart were not invited to the initial meetings.[68] At the same time, the president tried to play the Latino card and gave several interviews to the Spanish-language press to remind the GOP that the issue was important for the first minority of the United States. Political circumstances were not favorable, however, in the middle of a government shutdown, with a Republican Party more than irritated by healthcare reform and the executive order on DACA

that "far exceeded" the president's authority,[69] and afraid of losing the support of the Tea Party voters in the 2014 midterm elections. In this very tense and highly polarized climate, the bill ran
into severe opposition in the House, which never even voted on
it. There was no discussion in conference committee and no intention of discussing the Senate bill at all. For the second time in the
twenty-first century, the US Congress failed to pass a much-needed
comprehensive immigration reform that would be consistent with
the needs and values of US society and the US economy. Instead,
the House preferred to act on a set of immigration bills dealing
with some aspects of the issue, such as border security, interior
enforcement, or agricultural guest workers, among others.

Executive initiative again

Following this new congressional failure and in the wake of the
Republican electoral victories in the two chambers of Congress in
November 2014, President Obama realized that the prospects for
passing comprehensive immigration reform in the remainder of his
administration had waned. For the second time he chose to act by
executive initiative,[70] insisting on "cracking down on illegal immigration at the Border," "deporting felons, not families," and offering some unauthorized immigrants the chance to come out of the
shadows and a path to legal residence while paying their dues to
US society. Because nearly one-third of undocumented immigrants
are the parents of US-born children or legal permanent residents,
he announced in November 2014 that he would expand DACA
to more young people as well as to some adults (DAPA: Deferred
Action for Parents of Americans and Lawful Permanent Residents,
or Deferred Action for Parental Accountability), deferring deportation for the undocumented parents of American citizens or lawful
permanent residents and allowing them to work legally for three
years.[71] The two measures combined offered a path to legalization
for some four to five million people. Although it was in keeping with
the majority opinion in the country,[72] the executive action caused
considerable uproar and contributed to increasing the polarization
of the country between anti-immigration hardliners and champions
of action to break the stalemate. However, even pro-reform voices

argued that the president had overstepped his immigration powers by doing what Congress had refused to do. Starting from there, the House leadership adamantly refused to act on immigration, accusing the president of having "poisoned the well" with his executive orders and concluding that it was now "almost impossible to do immigration reform."[73] Never enforced, the executive decision was blocked by a lower federal court in 2015 and again in June 2016 by the Supreme Court in *United States* v. *Texas* (4–4), after twenty-six states sued to prevent further enforcement of the executive order. Although presidents frequently resort to executive orders, Justice Kennedy, often the court's swing voter, argued that the president overstepped his executive authority in granting deferred deportation to nearly five million immigrants and that Obama's actions seemed more like a legislative act than an executive one. "It's as if the president is setting the policy and the Congress is executing it," he said. "That's just upside down."[74] "Today's decision is frustrating to those who seek to grow our economy and bring a rationality to our immigration system," President Obama said about the ruling. "It is heartbreaking for the millions of immigrants who have made their lives here."[75]

In addition to blunt partisan opposition – Republican governors versus a Democratic president – and an unusual move by the House of Representatives to file an amicus brief which allowed House Republicans to have their arguments presented before the court – the states argued that the executive decision entailed too much expenditure for them in public services like healthcare, law enforcement, and education, and the issuance of large numbers of drivers' licenses (Texas). Although tied, the Supreme Court decision was a blow to presidential power as well as to Obama's legacy on the migration issue. Predictably it killed further action toward a comprehensive reform.

An intermestic issue

Although the migration issue is not limited to the Western Hemisphere, because the majority of immigrants, both legal and unauthorized, come from the Americas, diplomatic talks with Mexico, Central America and the Caribbean countries are prioritized. A comprehensive reform was also expected by the governments of Mexico, El Salvador, and Guatemala, the prime sources of immigrants to the United States with a total of approximately 15 million persons.

A HOLISTIC APPROACH

The Mexican government, in particular, had long championed the idea that a free trade agreement should include freedom of movement, just as in the European Union. Mexico never came so close to a significant opening of the border as in the summer of 2001.[76] The 9/11 terrorist attacks annihilated this dream and brought the two NAFTA partners back to the usual contentious discussions on the issue. But immigration is never an isolated phenomenon. It is intimately linked to serious problems at home: poverty, lack of jobs, underemployment or low wages, violence, insecurity. When he met with President Calderón of Mexico in the very first months of 2009, President Obama adopted a holistic approach: Mexican immigration to the United States, involving a large proportion of undocumented migrants, would also be solved by working together to improve security and economic conditions in Mexico,[77] a determination that was reiterated in 2015 with President Peña Nieto.[78] This is why, in 2011, the Obama administration expanded the 2007 Mérida Initiative – a binational (with Mexico) counterdrug and anti-crime program – and provided for a long-term approach to improve socio-economic conditions in the areas controlled by the drug cartels. It was the fourth pillar of the Mérida Initiative, "Building Strong and Resilient Communities."[79] Of course, these very long-term efforts first had to fight against drug trafficking, and they could not result in immediate changes to local living conditions nor, even indirectly, affect subsequent migration flows. Many analysts doubt that the initiative will have any effect at all. Yet, a coincidence of factors – slower demographic growth, combined with improved economic conditions and job creation in Mexico, as well as a deterioration in conditions in the United States due to the Great Recession of 2007–2009 – did result in a slackening of Mexican immigration. However, even if the Mexican migration flows did recede, the number of immigrants remained robust, and in the absence of a comprehensive reform the Mexican and Central American governments welcomed DACA in 2012 and supported DAPA in 2014 before its implementation was barred by legal challenges.

The Central American tragedy

At the same time, increasing violence and natural disaster-related poverty pushed more Central Americans from El Salvador, Honduras, and Guatemala to the north, through Mexico, leading to an unprecedented humanitarian crisis of unaccompanied minors at the US border, sent north to flee poverty and violence and reunite with their parents or close relatives. Nearly 52,000 were apprehended in FY 2014, as opposed to approximately 21,000 in 2013 and a mere 3,300 in 2009.[80]

The diplomatic response of the United States was organized in several directions. As early as mid-2005, the Millenium Challenge Corporation (MCC) had injected economic aid into the region, and the programs were increased in 2014. The State Department and USAID increased aid for the region in FY 2015, 2016, and 2017. The US administration also engaged in public diplomacy, running public awareness campaigns in the region and in the United States to warn against the dangers of taking the migration path (with questionable impact), sent top officials as envoys to the region (Vice-President Biden, "a point person to Central America,"[81] or Secretary of State John Kerry, among others), and worked closely with the governments of these countries to coordonate efforts. It increased anti-human smuggling operations and established an in-country refugee processing program for minors.[82] In Washington DC, the administration adopted a holistic approach and introduced a comprehensive US Strategy for Engagement in Central America in March 2015 because "the security and prosperity of Central America are inextricably linked with our own."[83] This bill requested one billion dollars from Congress to implement the new strategy and address the root causes of the exodus. On December 18, 2015, the Consolidated Appropriations Act was signed into law, providing "up to" US$750 million out of the one billion requested. Between FY 2012 and the requested FY 2017 budget, aid was multiplied by nearly three times for El Salvador (from US$29 million to US$87.9 million), and by approximately 80 percent for both Honduras (from US$57 million to US$105.6 million) and Guatemala (from US$84.4 million to US$145 million). The USAID Central America Regional budget also increased by over 60 percent (from US$32 million to US$53.4 million.) It turns out that only US$650 million was appropriated[84] – and not totally spent yet as final, exact figures are not absolutely clear – suggesting at least a 35 percent decrease from the initial billion-dollar request. But the Obama administration nonetheless managed to ensure significantly increased assistance for the region. It also improved collaboration with Mexico to turn back unauthorized Central American migrants at Mexico's southern borders with Guatemala and Belize (Southern Border Plan) and used some US$130 million of Mérida Initiative assistance for border security in Mexico. At the same time, ICE deported a high of 1,379 children in FY 2014 and 1,141 children in FY 2015, which raised the question of how those weak home countries could safely reintegrate them.

Although it was not directly related to the humanitarian crisis at the US border but participated in alleviating the burden of reintegrating their nationals, El Salvador and Honduras also made diplomatic efforts to renew their Temporary Protected Status, a US measure that allows for a deferral of deportation for unauthorized nationals in the United States for eighteen months due to severe conditions in their home countries. The TPS was granted to El Salvador during its civil war, and to Honduras and Nicaragua in 1999 after the devastation wrought by Hurricane Mitch. El Salvador became eligible again in 2001 following a series of earthquakes. The remittances sent by their nationals living in the United States are a significant source of income for these countries (10 percent of El Salvador's GDP, for example). At the end of every eighteen-month period, diplomats actively negotiate with the US administration and Congress to extend their TPS and to legalize the status of their nationals, individually, with their own national arguments, rather than as a unified group of Central American countries. For instance, after 2003, El Salvador discreetly reminded US officials that it agreed to partipate in the Iraq War. The Obama administration took into account the impact of refusing TPS extension. For example, what would happen to those deported? Would they try to come back illegally? Would they fall prey to narcotraffickers? What would be the impact on the respective governments' cooperation with the United States on security and drug trafficking?[85] The humanitarian crisis of unaccompanied children and the renewal of TPS have to be seen as one geostrategic issue involving a region on the verge of becoming a powder keg, in the very "backyard" of the United States. As a consequence, and arguing that those countries "remain unable, temporarily, to handle adequately the return of [their] nationals,"[86] the Department of Homeland Security again accepted their extension requests, thus allowing deportable nationals to stay in the United States as part of a holistic policy in the Central American security challenge. In a drastically different approach to the issue, the Trump administration put an abrupt end to this policy in September 2017, announcing the termination of TPS for El Salvador, Honduras, and Nicaragua (as well as Haiti, Nepal, and Sudan). Several lawsuits have been filed challenging these decisions, in particular the *Ramos* v. *Nielsen* court order in October 2018, suspending TPS termination for Sudan, Nicaragua, Haiti, and El Salvador pending a legal decision.[87]

END OF THE CUBAN EXCEPTION

The diplomatic scene of migration decisions includes Cuba, which, ever since the early years of the Revolution, has remained an exception in US migration legislation. From the Cuban Refugee Program of 1961 and the Cuban Adjustment Act of 1966, which automatically granted Cuban immigrants the status of refugees as well as access to welfare assistance, to the Clinton administration's "wet foot/dry foot" policy, which returned to Cuba migrants caught at sea while accepting those who managed to set foot on US soil, even without proper documents, Cuban immigrants have been an exception deeply resented by the other national groups. What was widely accepted during the Cold War as evidence that "refugees from communism" elected for the United States, became increasingly difficult to maintain.

The acrimonious debate about immigrants which marred the Obama years was bound to impact Cubans as well. Ironically, it was the historic decision to normalise relations and to renew diplomatic relations with Cuba which triggered a significant migration policy change. On January 12, 2017, after months of negotiations, the administration announced the end of both the "wet foot/dry foot" policy and specific provisions that applied exclusively to Cubans.[88] "By taking this step, we are treating Cuban migrants the same way we treat migrants from other countries," President Obama explained. It was the end of the Cuban exception, a decision supported even by Cuban American Florida legislators, and not overturned by President Trump.[89]

Conclusion

Executive orders and initiatives – the main Obama achievement on immigration – are by definition easy to repeal at a stroke of the pen. Thus, Obama's decisions, which triggered deep anger in parts of the country, were predictably the first to be questioned by President Trump.[90] The Obama years will be remembered as years of missed opportunities in spite of presidential efforts to be creative in the face of political adversity. They will be remembered as years of political mistakes on the part of both the White House and Congress, and as highly ideological, with politicians instrumentalizing immigration issues for electoral purposes. They also illustrate the difficulty of drafting a nationwide immigration policy in a federal country, when various strata of government enjoy concurrent immigration powers. In 2013, Senator Graham predicted that "if for some reason we fail in our efforts to pass comprehensive immigration reform, I do believe it will be many years before anyone is willing to try and solve this problem."[91] Many times, President Obama – as well as Republicans and Democrats in Congress – repeated the mantra that the US "immigration system was broken." Broken it was in 2009 and broken it still is today – with little enlightened perspective for the near future.

Notes

1. I would like to express my gratitude to my research center, *Laboratoire d'Etude et de Recherche sur le Monde Anglophone*, LERMA, E.A. 853, Aix-Marseille Université for making my research stay in Washington, DC in 2018 possible, and to all those who, in DC, kindly shared their time and their valuable insights with me, and to Dr. Carol Kaplan for her careful editorial help.
2. Barack Obama, "Obama's Remarks to the National Council of La Raza, San Diego, CA," July 13, 2009, http://www.ontheissues.org/2008/Barack_Obama_Immigration.htm (last accessed July 24, 2018).
3. David L. Leal provides a good summary of the ups and downs of the 2005–2007 immigration reform negotiations in "Stalemate: United States Immigration Reform Efforts, 2005–2007," *People and Place*, 17, 3, 2009: 3–6.
4. Barack Obama, "Floor Statement of Senator Barack Obama Immigration Reform," April 3, 2006, http://obamaspeeches.com/061-Immigration-Reform-Obama-Speech.htm (last accessed July 24, 2018).
5. Congressional Research Service, *US Immigration Policy: Chart Book of Key Trends*, CRS Report R42988, March 14, 2016, 4; Jie Zong, Jeanne Batalova, and Jeffrey Hallock, *Frequently Requested Statistics on Immigrants and Immigration to the United States*, February 8, 2018, https://www.migrationpolicy.org/article/frequently-requested-statistics-immigrants-and-immigration-united-states#Numbers (last accessed June 18, 2018).
6. Gustavo Lopez, Kristen Bialik, and Jynnah Radford, *Key Findings about U.S. Immigrants*, September 14, 2018, http://www.pewresearch.org/fact-tank/2018/09/14/key-findings-about-u-s-immigrants/ (last accessed September 27, 2018).
7. CNN, "Economy Tops Obama's list of '09 Priorities," October 31, 2008, http://edition.cnn.com/2008/POLITICS/10/31/obama.blitzer/index.html (last accessed July 24, 2018).
8. Jeffrey M. Jones, *The People's Priorities*, Gallup Poll, May 30, 2008, https://news.gallup.com/poll/107605/Peoples-Priorities-Economy-Iraq-Gas-Prices.aspx?g_source=link_NEWSV9&g_medium=tile_6&g_campaign=item_108748&g_content=The%2520People%25E2%258 0%2599s%2520Priorities%3a%2520Economy%2c%2520Iraq%2c %2520Gas%2520Prices (last accessed June 21, 2018).

9. Roberto Suro, *America's Views of Immigration: The Evidence from Public Opinion Surveys*, Migration Policy Institute, 2009, https://www.migrationpolicy.org/pubs/TCM-USPublicOpinion.pdf (last accessed August 12, 2018).
10. Grego Aisch and Alicia Parlapiano, "What Do You Think Is the Most Important Problem Facing This Country Today?", *The New York Times*, February 27, 2017, https://www.nytimes.com/interactive/2017/02/27/us/politics/most-important-problem-gallup-polling-question.html (last accessed July 4, 2018).
11. Mark Hugo Lopez and Gretchen Livingston, "Hispanics' Priorities for the New Administration," Pew Hispanic Center, Washington, DC, January 15, 2009, http://assets.pewresearch.org/wp-content/uploads/sites/7/reports/101.pdf (last accessed June 10, 2018); Mark Hugo Lopez, "Latinos and the 2010 Elections: Strong Support for Democrats; Weak Voter Motivation," Pew Hispanic Center, Washington, DC, October 5, 2010, http://assets.pewresearch.org/wp-content/uploads/sites/7/2010/10/127.pdf (accessed June 10, 2018).
12. Jens Manuel Krogstad, "Top Issue for Hispanics? Hint: It's not Immigration," Pew Research Center, June 2, 2014, http://www.pewresearch.org/fact-tank/2014/06/02/top-issue-for-hispanics-hint-its-not-immigration/ (last accessed June 10, 2018).
13. Julia Preston, "Obama to Push Immigration Bill as One Priority," *The New York Times*, April 8, 2009, https://www.nytimes.com/2009/04/09/us/politics/09immig.html (last accessed August 12, 2018); Barack Obama, "Remarks at the National Hispanic Prayer Breakfast," June 19, 2009, online by Gerhard Peters and John T. Woolley, *The American Presidency Project*, http://www.presidency.ucsb.edu/ws/?pid=86311 (last accessed July 24, 2018).
14. Barack Obama and Joe Biden (2008), *Blueprint for Change. Obama and Biden's Plan for America*, https://archive.org/stream/346512-obamablueprintforchange/346512-obamablueprintforchange_djvu.txt (last accessed September 28, 2018); Congressional Research Service, *Immigration Reform Issues in the 111th Congress*, CRS Report R40501, October 29, 2010, 10–11.
15. *National Journal*, "Where They Stand," August 29, 2008.
16. Barack Obama, "Remarks by the President on Comprehensive Immigration Reform in El Paso, Texas," May 10, 2011, https://obamawhitehouse.archives.gov/the-press-office/2011/05/. . . marks-president-comprehensive-immigration-reform-el-paso-texas (last accessed July 24, 2018).

17. Obama, "Remarks by the President."
18. Barack Obama, "Remarks on Immigration Reform," June 11, 2013, online by Gerhard Peters and John T. Woolley, *The American Presidency Project*, http://www.presidency.ucsb.edu/ws/?pid=103763 (last accessed July 24, 2018).
19. Congressional Budget Office, *The Economic Impact of S. 744, the Border Security, Economic Opportunity, and Immigration Modernization Act*, June 20, 2013, https://www.cbo.gov/sites/default/files/113th-congress-2013-2014/reports/44346-immigration.pdf (last accessed September 27, 2018).
20. Tom Donahue, "The Reason To Not Give Up On Immigration Reform," *The Washington Times*, November 18, 2014, https://www.washingtontimes.com/news/2014/nov/18/the-reason-to-not-give-up-on-immigration-reform/ (last accessed September 20, 2018).
21. US Senate, *Comprehensive Immigration Reform in 2009: Can We Do It and How?* Hearing before the Subcommittee on Immigration, Refugees and Border Security, Committee on the Judiciary, 111th Congress, 1st session, April 30, 2009 (Washington, DC: GPO), 2–5.
22. US Senate, 5.
23. US Senate, 4.
24. US Senate, 5.
25. Charles E. Schumer, "Schumer Announces Principles for Comprehensive Immigration Reform Bill in Works in Senate," press release, June 24, 2009, http://schumer.senate.gov/new_website/record.cfm?id=314990 (last accessed August 12, 2018).
26. Barack Obama, "Address Before a Joint Session of the Congress on the State of the Union," January 27, 2010, online by Gerhard Peters and John T. Woolley, *The American Presidency Project*, http://www.presidency.ucsb.edu/ws/?pid=87433 (last accessed July 24, 2018).
27. Charles E. Schumer and Lindsey O. Graham, "The Right Way to Mend Immigration," *The Washington Post*, March 19, 2010, http://www.washingtonpost.com/wp-dyn/content/article/2010/03/17/AR2010031703115_pf.html (last accessed August 12, 2018).
28. Lindsey O. Graham, "Graham on Health Care and Immigration Reform," March 19, 2010, https://www.lgraham.senate.gov/public/index.cfm/2010/3/post-7823d135-802a-23ad-42b4-96ff4630f8c5 (last accessed September 29, 2018).
29. The Real Enforcement with Practical Answers for Immigration Reform (REPAIR) Proposal, April 29, 2010, p. 1. Available at:

https://www.aila.org/infonet/practical-answers-for-immigration-reform-proposal (last accessed November 26, 2019).

30. His move came just one day after Obama called on both parties to pass immigration reform at the federal level, in response to a new law in Arizona that allowed local police officers to stop individuals suspected of being unauthorized immigrants.

31. Lindsey O. Graham, "Bipartisan Support for Border Security," May 5, 2010, https://www.lgraham.senate.gov/public/index.cfm/2010/5/post-6a2c94f9-802a-23ad-45e9-e0dfbceea6a4 (last accessed September 29, 2018).

32. John McCain, "Press Release – Barack Obama – A 'Poison Pill' To Immigration Reform," June 28, 2008, online by Gerhard Peters and John T. Woolley, *The American Presidency Project*, http://www.presidency.ucsb.edu/ws/?pid=94079 (last accessed June 28, 2018).

33. Ruben Navarette, "Rahm Emanuel no Friend on Immigration," CNN, September 30, 2010, http://edition.cnn.com/2010/OPIN-ION/09/30/navarrette.rahm.emanuel.immigration/index.html (last accessed June 10, 2018); Peter Nicholas, "Democrats Point the Finger at Obama's Chief of Staff for Immigration Reform's Poor Progress," May 21, 2010, *Chicago Tribune*, available at http://articles.latimes.com/2010/may/21/nation/la-na-immigration-20100521 (last accessed June 10, 2018); Jonathan Weisman, "GOP Finds Hot Button in Illegal Immigration," *The Washington Post*, October 23, 2007, http://www.washingtonpost.com/wp-dyn/content/article/2007/10/22/AR2007102201717_pf.html (last accessed June 18, 2018).

34. Cecilia Muñoz, "Worth It," in Gautam Raghavan, ed., *West Wingers: Stories from the Dream Chasers, Change Makers, and Hope Creators Inside the Obama White House* (New York: Penguin Books, 2018), 95–111.

35. Interview with author, Washington, DC, March 1, 2018.

36. The phrase was reportedly coined by the National Council of La Raza.

37. Barack Obama, «Remarks at the National Hispanic.»

38. Interview with author, Washington, DC, February 28, 2018.

39. Muzaffar Chishti, Sarah Pierce, and Jessica Bolter, "The Obama Record on Deportations: Deporter in Chief or Not?", *Migration Policy Institute*, January 26, 2017, https://www.migrationpolicy.org/article/obama-record-deportations-deporter-chief-or-not (last accessed August 10, 2018).

40. Department of Homeland Security, "Secretary Napolitano Announces Record-Breaking Immigration Enforcement Statistics Achieved under the Obama Administration," October 6, 2010, https://www.dhs.gov/news/2010/10/06/secretary-napolitano-announces-record-breaking-immigration-enforcement-statistics (last accessed November 24, 2019).

41. Marc R. Rosenblum and Kristen McCabe, "Deportation and Discretion: Reviewing the Record and Options for Change," MPI, October 2014, https://www.migrationpolicy.org/research/deportation-and-discretion-reviewing-record-and-options-change (last accessed November 24, 2019); Department of Homeland Security, "DHS Releases End of Year Fiscal Year 2016 Statistics," December 30, 2016, https://www.dhs.gov/news/2016/12/30/dhs-releases-end-year-fiscal-year-2016-statistics (last accessed November 24, 2019).

42. Customs and Border Patrol, *BP Staffing FY 1992–FY 2017*, https://www.cbp.gov/sites/default/files/assets/documents/2017-Dec/BP%20Staffing%20FY1992-FY2017.pdf (last accessed September 28, 2018).

43. Interview with Doris Meissner, Washington, DC, March 1, 2018.

44. Immigration and Customs Enforcement (ICE), *DHS Releases End of Fiscal Year 2016 Statistics*, https://www.ice.gov/removal-statistics/2016 (last accessed August 24, 2019).

45. Miguel Calderón, *Memorandum preparado por el Canciller de Relaciones exteriores*, 26 de enero 1953, T15-2, SRE, Ciudad de Mexico, Archivo de concentraciones.

46. Jessica M. Vaughan, "ICE Records Reveal Steep Drop in Worksite Enforcement Since 2013," *Center for Immigration Studies*, June 2015, https://cis.org/sites/default/files/vaughan-WSE.pdf (last accessed September 27, 2018).

47. Government Accountability Office, *Employment Verification: Agencies Have Improved E-Verify, but Significant Challenges Remain*, April 14, 2011, < https://www.gao.gov/products/GAO-11-522T > (last accessed August 27, 2018).

48. National Conference of State Legislatures, *State E-Verify Action*, August 19, 2015, http://www.ncsl.org/research/immigration/state-e-verify-action.aspx; National Immigration Forum, *Fact Sheet E-Verify*, August 14, 2018, https://immigrationforum.org/article/fact-sheet-e-verify/ (last accessed November 23, 2019).

49. National Conference of State Legislatures, *Arizona's Immigration Enforcement Laws*, July 28, 2011, http://www.ncsl.org/research/immigration/analysis-of-arizonas-immigration-law.aspx (last accessed September 27, 2018).

50. Barack Obama, "Remarks to the White House Press Pool and an Exchange with Reporters," April 28, 2010, online by Gerhard Peters and John T. Woolley, *The American Presidency Project*, http://www .presidency.ucsb.edu/ws/?pid=87815 (last accessed July 24, 2018).
51. Supreme Court of the United States Blog, *S.B. 1070: in Plain English*, https://www.scotusblog.com/2012/06/s-b-1070-in-plain-english/ (last accessed November 23, 2019).
52. Sophia J. Wallace, "Papers Please: State-Level Anti-Immigrant Legislation in the Wake of Arizona's SB 1070," *Political Science Quarterly*, 129, 2, 2014: 261–291; Luige del Puerto, "A Timeline—the tumultuous legal life of Arizona's SB 1070," October 3, 2016, https://azcapitoltimes.com/news/2016/10/03/a-timeline-the-tumultuous-legal-life-of-arizonas-sb1070/ (last accessed November 23, 2019).
53. Els De Grauw, "Rolling Out the Welcome Mat: State and City Immigrant Affairs Offices in the US," *IdeAs, Idées d'Amérique*, 2015, https://journals.openedition.org/ideas/1293 (last accessed September 7, 2018).
54. Propublica, "House Vote 625 Approves Dream Act," https://projects.propublica.org/represent/votes/111/house/2/625 (last accessed November 23, 2019).
55. Barack Obama, "Statement on Senate Action on Legislation Providing Citizenship Opportunities for Alien Minors," December 18, 2010, online by Gerhard Peters and John T. Woolley, *The American Presidency Project*, http://www.presidency.ucsb.edu/ws/?pid=88845 (last accessed July 24, 2018).
56. John Mc Cain, "Statement by Senator John McCain on the DREAM Act," December 18, 2010, https://www.mccain.senate. gov/public/index.cfm/press-releases?ID=fa569b87-be5a-a559-5a1f-8b3f0d770421 (last accessed July 24, 2018); Mariela Olivares, "Renewing the Dream: Dream Act Redux and Immigration Reform," *Harvard Latino Law Review*, 16, 79, 2013: 79–125, 85–90.
57. US Congress, *The US Homeland Security Role in the Mexican War against Drug Cartels*, Hearing before the Subcommittee on Oversight, Investigations, and Management of the Committee on Homeland, House of Representatives, 112th Congress, 1st session, March 31, 2011 (Washington, DC: US Government Printing office), https://www.gpo.gov/fdsys/pkg/CHRG-112hhrg72224/pdf/CHRG-112hhrg72224.pdf (last accessed August 12, 2018).
58. Interview with Doris Meissner, Washington, DC, March 1, 2018.

59. Muñoz, «Worth It," p. 100–104; Sidney M. Milkis and Daniel J. Tichenor, *Rivalry and Reform, Social Movements, and the Transformation of American Politics* (Chicago: University of Chicago Press, 2019), 294–295.

60. Mark Krikorian, "Mark Krikorian on America's Immigration DREAM," *The Washington Times*, August 17, 2012, https://cis.org/Mark-Krikorian-Americas-immigration-DREAM (last accessed September, 20 2018).

61. Julia Gelatt, Julia, "All Eyes Turn to Congres, Following Trump Decision to Terminate DACA Program," September 2017, Migration Policy Institute, http://www.migrationpolicy.org/news/all-eyes-turn-congress-following-trump-decision-terminate-daca-program (last accessed September 30, 2018).

62. Randy Capps, Michael Fix, and Jie Zong, *The Education and Work Profiles of the DACA Population*, August 2017, Washington, DC, Migration Policy Institute, http://migrationpolicy.org/research/education-and-work-profiles-daca-population (last accessed September 30, 2018).

63. Jeb Bush and Clint Bolick, "Solving the Immigration Puzzle," January 24, 2013, *The Wall Street Journal*, https://www.wsj.com/articles/SB10001424127887323482504578229660442099732 (last accessed July 10, 2018).

64. Lindsey O. Graham, "Statement on Immigration Reform," January 28, 2013, https://www.lgraham.senate.gov/public/index.cfm/2013/1/post-82caa771-c9e4-b92b-b5c1-b31da60de8d7 (last accessed September 29, 2018).

65. Lamar Alexander of Tennessee; Kelly Ayotte of New Hampshire; Jeff Chiesa of New Jersey; Susan Collins of Maine; Bob Corker of Tennessee; Jeff Flake of Arizona; Lindsey Graham of South Carolina; Orrin Hatch of Utah; Dean Heller of Nevada; John Hoeven of North Dakota; Mark Kirk of Illinois; John McCain of Arizona; Lisa Murkowski of Alaska; Marco Rubio of Florida.

66. US Congress, *Border Security, Economic Opportunity, and Immigration Modernization Act*, S. 744, June 27, 2013, https://www.congress.gov/bill/113th-congress/senate-bill/744 (last accessed August 12, 2018).

67. Russell Berman, "How Immigration Died," *The Hill*, November 12–13, 2013, http://thehill.com/homenews/senate/189917-how-immigration-died——part-1 and http://thehill.com/homenews/house/190060-how-immigration-died-part-2-boehner-bails (last accessed August 12, 2018).

68. Reid J. Epstein and Seung Min Kim, "W.H. seeks GOP Immigration Help," *Politico*, November 10, 2013, https://www.politico.com/story/2013/11/white-house-seeks-gop-immigration-help-099640 (last accessed July 19, 2018).

69. Jim Boehner, "Immigration Reform is 'Almost Impossible'," CBS, *Face the Nation*, July 12, 2015, https://www.youtube.com/watch?v=FRz8xWWwCN8 (last accessed August 27, 2018).

70. Although it is frequently stated that DAPA was an executive order, Louis Fisher argues that technically it was an executive initiative. See Louis Fisher, *President Obama. Constitutional Aspirations and Executive Actions* (Lawrence: University of Kansas Press, 2018), 136.

71. White House, Office of the Press Secretary, *Fact Sheet: Immigration Accountability Executive Action*, November 20, 2014, https://obamawhitehouse.archives.gov/the-press-office/2014/11/20/fact-sheet-immigration-accountability-executive-action (last accessed August 10, 2018).

72. Pew Research Center, "Broad Public Support for Legal Status for Undocumented Immigrants," June 4, 2015, http://www.people-press.org/2015/06/04/broad-public-support-for-legal-status-for-undocumented-immigrants/ (last accessed October 3, 2018).

73. Boehner, "Immigration Reform."

74. Lydia Wheeler, "Court Appears Divided, Signaling Trouble for Obama on Immigration," *The Hill*, April 18, 2016.

75. Barack Obama, "Remarks by the President on the Supreme Court Decision on US Versus Texas," June 23, 2016, https://obamawhitehouse.archives.gov/the-press-office/2016/06/23/remarks-president-supreme-court-decision-us-versus-texas (last accessed August 12, 2018).

76. Jorge G. Castañeda, *Ex Mex. From Migrants to Immigrants* (New York: The New Press, 2007).

77. Barack Obama, "The President's News Conference with President Felipe de Jesús Calderón Hinojosa of Mexico in Mexico City," April 16, 2009, online by Gerhard Peters and John T. Woolley, *The American Presidency Project*, http://www.presidency.ucsb.edu/ws/?pid=86014 (last accessed July 24, 2018).

78. Barack Obama, "Remarks Following a Meeting with President Enrique Peña Nieto of Mexico," January 6, 2015, online by Gerhard Peters and John T. Woolley, *The American Presidency Project*, http://www.presidency.ucsb.edu/ws/?pid=108256 (last accessed September 30, 2018).

79. Congressional Research Service, *U.S.-Mexican Security Cooperation: The Mérida Initiative and Beyond*, CRS Report R41349, June 12, 2013.
80. Congressional Research Service, *Unaccompanied Children from Central America: Foreign Policy Considerations*, CRS Report R43702, April 11, 2016, 1.
81. Joy Olson, interview with author, Washington, DC, February 28, 2018.
82. Congressional Research Service, *Unaccompanied Children*, 6.
83. Joe Biden, "Joe Biden: A Plan for Central America," *The New York Times*, January 29, 2015.
84. Congressional Research Service, *US Foreign Assistance to Latin America and the Caribbean. Trends and FY 2017 Appropriations*, CRS Report R44647, February 8, 2017, 9–12.
85. Joy Olson, interview with author, Washington, DC, February 28, 2018.
86. *Federal Register*, "Extension of the Designation of Honduras for Temporary Status," October 16, 2014, 79 FR 62170; *Federal Register*, "Extension of the Designation of El Salvador for Temporary Status," January 7, 2015, 80 FR 893.
87. US Citizenship and Immigration Services, "Update on *Ramos v. Nielsen*," November 18, 2019, https://www.uscis.gov/update-ramos-v-nielsen (last accessed November 26, 2019).
88. Congressional Research Service, *Rescission of the Wet Foot/Dry Foot Policy as to Aliens from Cuba Raises Legal Questions*, January 18, 2017, https://fas.org/sgp/crs/row/wetfoot.pdf (last accessed September 28, 2018).
89. Ted Piccone, "US-Cuba Normalization: US Constituencies for Change," in Isabelle Vagnoux and Janette Habel, *Etats-Unis/Cuba: une nouvelle donne? IdeAs, Idées d'Amérique*, décembre 2017, https://journals.openedition.org/ideas/2107 (last accessed September 30, 2018).
90. As of November 2019, the US Supreme Court considered President Trump's 2017 decision to end the DACA program. Its final decision is expected in the spring of 2020.
91. Graham, "Statement on Immigration Reform."

6

War and peace in cyberspace: Obama's multifaceted legacy

Frédérick Douzet and Aude Géry

Cyberspace is probably the foreign policy domain where Obama's legacy will turn out to be the most important. It is by far the area which has witnessed the most rapid and striking new developments. Under Obama's watch, this new environment, born out of the global interconnection of information and communication systems, has become a new military domain and a strategic priority for the United States – and many other countries in the world – along with a critical issue in diplomatic relations. More than any other issue, cyber policy-making revealed the multifaceted nature of Obama's approach to global strategic and security challenge.[1]

This chapter examines the dual dynamic of war and peace pushed by the Obama administration with regards to cyberspace. Obama's two terms have been marked by a proliferation of cyber-attacks and a cascade of revelations about the offensive cyber operations conducted by the US administration, including an attack on a critical infrastructure in Iran that has been regarded as the first-known – and to this day unique – cyber-attack that could qualify as an act of war. Edward Snowden, a former employee of the National Security Agency, revealed the massive scale of the intrusions and surveillance operated by the US government, including against its own allies. The rapid growth and greater sophistication of cyber-attacks led to a cyber-arms race among great powers, while these attacks became increasingly creative and targeted, creating a succession of strategic surprises. In the meantime, the proliferation of tools of cyber offense started to backfire, raising awareness about the country's own vulnerabilities and the systemic risk that could result from cyber instability. In search of a deterrence strategy, the Obama administration resorted to a "naming and shaming" policy that both exacerbated tensions and called for responses. Hence, tensions over cyber-espionage dangerously escalated with China, raising concerns about a new "cool war".[2]

Faced with growing transnational threats, the Obama administration – while still developing its own cyber arsenal – took a radical approach on norms building and international cooperation. After years of systematic diplomatic obstruction[3] on the issues of information and telecommunications in the context of international security, the Obama administration radically shifted its position and became proactive. This shift was first expressed in the US official doctrine as soon as 2011. Two years after Obama took office, the White House published the *International Strategy for Cyberspace* which identified three mechanisms – international regulation, confidence and security building measures, and capacity building – to protect seven priority fields: economy, networks security, law enforcement, military, internet governance, international developments, and internet freedom. International law but also norms of responsible behavior for states were therefore identified as key mechanisms to ensure security and stability in cyberspace. These changes were later materialized in Obama's diplomacy through international agreements, both at the bilateral and multilateral levels, based on these norms and principles.

Obama, the cyber warrior

Conflictuality in cyberspace has literally exploded during Obama's two terms. The military strategists in the United States had understood early on the strategic advantage they could gain from the use of cyberspace, mainly to collect intelligence or enable military operations.[4] The Obama administration built the doctrinal and operational capabilities to exploit such opportunities but also conducted operations that eventually contributed to the instability of this new environment. In the meantime, many state and non-state actors (such as individuals, political groups, terrorists, etc.) took advantage of the low cost and wide availability of the technology to conduct their own offensive operations, leading to a series of strategic surprises that unsettled the administration.

The 2007 attack against Estonia which paralyzed most of the public services, banks, and media websites came as a wake-up call for many states. They realized how ill-prepared they were to face such a threat. For the first time, what was believed to be a state-sponsored operation[5] became public with direct consequences for non-state actors. The following year, cyber-attacks against Georgia disrupted its servers just before the Russian military assault. It was the first time a publicly known cyber-attack came in support of a military operation.

When Obama took office the following year, the decision had been made to separate the informational sphere from the digital space, which were initially combined, in the context of the Revolution in Military Affairs (RMA), as the strategic concept of information warfare. In the 2000s, cyberspace was increasingly perceived as a new military domain which required specific technical skills to protect critical infrastructures and conduct offensive operations. Obama launched a new organizational structure to bring together the skills and resources scattered across agencies within the Department of Defense into a new US Cyber Command in charge of the protection of the DoD networks and critical infrastructures, but also to conduct offensive cyber operations in support of military operations. The first commander, Keith Alexander, was appointed in 2010 and also served as the head of the National Security Agency, the agency that developed mass surveillance programs at a global scale and conducted cyber-intelligence operations. Both agencies are located at Fort Meade, Maryland. This so-called dual-hat relationship was initially meant to be temporary and it stirred hot debates.[6] Many senior officials at the end of Obama's presidency advocated for a split, and options are still being discussed.

If the first cyber operations were initiated before Obama's first term, they clearly intensified under his presidency and directly contributed to the militarization of cyberspace. The exploitation of resources and capabilities translated into actions likely to prompt instability. In 2012, *The New York Times*[7] revealed that Obama had secretly ordered increasingly sophisticated attacks against Iranian nuclear facilities. The operation, code-named *Olympic Games*, was initiated by the Bush administration yet Obama, from his first months in office, decided to accelerate the attacks in a joint effort with Israel to undermine Iran's nuclear program. The virus accidentally became public and was named by cybersecurity experts Stuxnet. This operation constituted the first, and to this day the only, cyber operation that, according to legal experts, could qualify as an armed attack.[8] For many, this incident opened the Pandora box by setting a precedent, creating a serious risk of instability. It also raised concerns about the fact that cyber-weapons could be analyzed, copied, reengineered, and reused; indeed Iran may have learned from Stuxnet.[9]

In addition, the NSA and US Cyber Command have maximized their technical and financial resources to collect and exploit a large number of vulnerabilities, contributing to the gray market of zero-days[10] and undermining the overall cybersecurity of the networks. The revelations of Edward Snowden in 2013 have demonstrated the extent of these operations and have opened a debate about the need to notify vulnerabilities to the industry in order to have them create a patch.

Furthermore, the agencies have built an arsenal of tools exploiting these vulnerabilities. In 2016, some of these tools were released online by the hackers group Shadow Brokers, and exploited in two devastating attacks that demonstrated the risk of cyber-arms proliferation: WannaCry in May 2017 and NotPetya in June 2017. The rapid, dramatic, and uncontrolled propagation of these attacks caused severe damage to companies and public services across the world and triggered a blame game among actors, pointing also to the responsibility of the NSA for not securing its offensive tools.[11]

The NSA engaged in other adventurous operations such as the program PRISM/US-984XN, conceived for counter-terrorism purposes and which led to a massive collection of data through the coercion of US global companies to secretly cooperate with them. This led to a major backlash when the program was revealed by Snowden, as major companies such as Apple developed strong end-to-end encryption and refused to further cooperate with the government, including for law enforcement purposes.

The proliferation and wide availability of offensive tools benefits a whole range of state and non-state actors, who seized the technology to advance their own agenda, creating a series of strategic surprises for the Obama administration.

The cyber-arms race backfires

During the Obama years, the cyber-threats became more sophisticated, more diverse, and more complex both in their operational modes and in their targets. In 2012, the attack against Saudi Aramco, by hackers who called themselves the "Cutting Sword of Justice," demonstrated that other actors could create severe damage to a strategic target. The virus Shamoon destroyed 30,000 computers at once, forcing the oil company to shut down its internal network. It was perceived by the US administration as Iran's response to the Stuxnet attack. The US became fully focused on an attack against critical infrastructures, coined by Leon Panetta as a "cyber Pearl Harbor."[12]

The administration was therefore taken completely by surprise with the major cyber-attack against Sony Pictures in 2014. The attack, which was attributed by the US to North Korea, was politically motivated – Sony Pictures was about to release a movie caricaturizing Kim Jong-un – but the target was a private entertainment company – hardly a critical infrastructure – and yet caused major damage, disruption, and media resonance. The following year TV5 Monde in France was targeted by another attack, confirming how unpredictable political targets had become.

Operational modes kept evolving, too, with the first large-scale DDoS attack mobilizing connected objects (surveillance cameras, TV sets) against Dyn in 2016. Dozens of websites including Twitter, e-Bay, Netflix, and Paypal remained inaccessible for about ten hours. The greatest surprise, however, came from informational attacks, for which the administration was largely unprepared. Fighting ISIS's online propaganda raised complex problems considering the defiance of platforms toward the government and the many legal loopholes, but also the cryptographic and anonymization tools the jihadis were able to exploit. That said, the enemy was clearly identified and fought against on the ground as well. The Russian meddling with the 2016 presidential election, however, came as a true shock. The great focus on technical threats had distracted the cybersecurity strategists from the risk of information manipulations and the potential disruption of democratic processes through combined cyber- and informational operations. The rapid evolution of conflictuality and its increasingly public consequences prompted a need for a response and a deterrence strategy, which could also induce instability.

In search of a deterrence strategy

Deterrence is not easy in cyberspace due to the specific nature of the environment.[13] Yet, and however tempting it may sound, applying the principles of nuclear dissuasion to cyberspace doesn't work.[14] One of the main obstacles is attribution, which remains technically difficult – some say impossible – and particularly resource-intensive. Ultimately, it ends up being a political decision. Considering the low barrier of entry and the multiple ways to cover up traces, the ratio cost/benefits is often in favor of the attacker.

Despite serious limitations, the Obama administration has attempted – and struggled – to find ways to impose costs on the attackers likely to dissuade them from taking actions. The Obama administration's cyber-deterrence efforts have mainly taken the form of strong policy statements, "naming and shaming" tactics, and most likely covert operations.

The *International Strategy for Cyberspace* published by the White House in 2011[15] clearly states that the US will not tolerate a major cyber-attack: "We reserve the right to use all necessary means – diplomatic, informational, military, and economic – as appropriate and consistent with applicable international law, in order to defend our Nation, our allies, our partners, and our interests." In the following years, the administration has constantly insisted on the need to deter attacks both through access denial and the threat of a response, and has adopted a "naming and shaming" tactic that has provided mixed results. According to the administration, the attacks did not stop, leading to conflict escalation with China over cyber-espionage (see below).

Part of the political message delivered by this tactic was about the administration's ability to attribute cyber-attacks. Its position progressively evolved from emphasizing the difficulty of attributing an attack to displaying great confidence in identifying attackers.[16] For example, in 2012, Leon Panetta stated that the DOD "has made significant advances in solving a problem that makes deterring cyber adversaries more complex: the difficulty of identifying the origins of an attack [. . .] Potential aggressors should be aware that the United States has the capacity to locate them and to hold them accountable for their actions that may try to harm America."[17]

Despite the uncertainties of technical attribution, the administration has multiplied direct public accusations against individuals, organizations, hackers linked to governments, but also governmental agencies, along with indirect accusations through highly publicized cybersecurity companies' statements. For example, in 2014, the US was the first state to publicly attribute a cyber-attack to another state. Tensions escalated with China over accusations of cyber-espionage, leading to the indictment of five People's Liberation Army officers in 2015 – who are unlikely ever to see an American court – and a cyber pact between China and the US was signed few months later (see below). The indictments of alleged hackers have become a tool for the US to attribute cyber-attacks and to reveal evidence, thus becoming a new form a retorsion in reaction to state-sponsored cyber operations. But the conversation was complicated by the distinction the US administration made between strategic espionage (legitimate) and economic espionage (forbidden), while regarding Chinese cyber-espionage as a strategic threat for the US. And when the administration discovered that the Office of Personnel Management's data had been breached, it pointed to state-sponsored attackers working for the Chinese government. The justice department arrested a Chinese national but has been silent about the hacker since his arrest. The public blame was primarily put on the agency itself for security negligence.

In addition to strong statements, the Obama administration increasingly but not explicitly relied on international principles of law to shape its response to major attacks. The attack on Sony Pictures is the first example. After a few days of confusion, President Obama publicly attributed the attack to North Korea and warned that the US would respond proportionally, "in a place and time and manner that we choose."[18] Following his statement, the internet went down in North Korea for more than nine hours. Obama did not qualify the attack against Sony Pictures, but the terms he used to describe the response refer to measures of retorsion or countermeasures, which are unilateral, extrajudicial self-help responses organized through international law.

There are risks associated with strong statements and with going public on attribution and responses to cyber-attacks. They do create a public demand for action even when it is not the most appropriate response or they can create a sense of powerlessness when the response is complicated to articulate or is not immediate. Misattribution can also lead to conflict escalation.

The proliferation of cyber-attacks, the awareness about systemic risks, along with the need for response and the risk of conflict escalation have led to a shift in the position of the US on the international regulation of cyberspace. The Obama administration chose to push regulations within the framework of international law in order to achieve its strategic goals: to be able to continue conducting cyber operations, to legitimately respond to cyber-attacks for deterrence and defense purposes, and to restrain other states' behaviors.

Obama the cyber-peacemaker? International regulation as one of the pillars of the US diplomatic strategy

The evolution of conflictuality in cyberspace led the Obama administration to reconsider its approach of international cyber-stability. The 2011 *International Strategy for Cyberspace* acknowledges the need for international regulation and cooperation to protect American interests and security: "the growth of these networks brings with it new challenges for our national and economic security and that of the global community" and "[c]ybersecurity threats can even endanger international peace and security more broadly, as traditional forms of conflict are extended into cyberspace."[19] The goal was therefore to have "an open, interoperable, secure and reliable cyberspace," and in order to achieve it the US sought to "build and sustain an environment in which norms of responsible behavior guide states' actions, sustain partnerships, and support the rule of law in cyberspace."[20] For the first time in a national strategy, there were lengthy developments in international regulation to maintain security and stability in cyberspace. These developments were twofold. On the one hand, the *International Strategy for Cyberspace* affirmed that international law applied to cyberspace. On the other hand, it called for the adoption of norms promoting responsible behaviors to guide the states' conduct in cyberspace in order to fill in the gaps left by international law.

THE APPLICABILITY OF INTERNATIONAL LAW IN CYBERSPACE

International law was developed to regulate the states' behaviors, notably to limit the use of force as an option in managing their relationships in order to maintain international peace and security. International law mainly regulates the conduct of states, although today it also regulates the conduct of international organizations as well as that of other actors. The cornerstone of the collective security system is the Charter of the United Nations which defines rights and obligations to ensure the pacific coexistence of states. As cyberspace was becoming a new battlefield, the question of the applicability of international law started arising. This question was profoundly linked to the representation of cyberspace as a space – like the earth, the seas, the air, and the extra-atmospheric space – that had to be conquered.[21] In the *International Strategy for Cyberspace*, the US affirmed that international law applies to the states' conduct in cyberspace and that cyberspace does not "render existing international norms obsolete."[22] They also explicitly recognized that a cyber operation could amount to an armed attack, thus triggering the right of self-defense.[23] More implicit was the reference to the states' international responsibility for international wrongful acts and its applicability to cyberspace. It therefore recognized the right for the US to adopt measures of retorsion, countermeasures, and the right of self-defense depending on the legal qualification of the cyber operations targeting its territory and the political motives underpinning the response to the operation. A year later, Harold H. Koh, legal adviser of the State Department, went further. Building on what was written in the document, he explained in a speech delivered to the USCYBERCOM Inter-Agency Legal Conference at Fort Meade on September 18, 2012 how the US interpreted international law when applied to the states' conduct in cyberspace. For the first time, a state was publicly exposing its views on the applicability of international law in cyberspace. This speech is of particular relevance considering that due to cyberspace's characteristics (speed, ubiquity, anonymity, etc.), the implementation of international law faces serious challenges. For example, in order to engage states' international responsibility it must first be attributed to a state, which could prove to be difficult because of anonymity. Another example is identifying cyber operations' effects that meet the traditional thresholds in international law of the violation of the principle of non-intervention or the use of force, or of an armed attack, etc.[24] These specificities challenge the application of international law but do not render it useless. The flexibility of international law provides a capacity to adapt to many situations but there is a need for states to clarify how they interpret these rules in the context of cyber operations in order to identify wrongful conducts and ensure the stability and security of cyberspace. Most of Harold H. Koh's speech focused on international humanitarian law, on the use of force and self-defense, two issues that were the most debated at the time among international lawyers. But there were two questions which were of particular relevance for the following years: sovereignty and attribution.

Harold H. Koh claimed that

[t]he physical infrastructure that supports the Internet and cyber activities is generally located in sovereign territory and subject to the jurisdiction of the territorial state. Because of the interconnected, interoperable nature of cyberspace, operations targeting networked information infrastructures in one country may create effects in another country. Whenever a state contemplates conducting activities in cyberspace, the sovereignty of other states needs to be considered.[25]

This assertion is important as it implies that a state's jurisdiction applies to infrastructures located on its territory and thus that these infrastructures are subjected to the laws and regulations of that country. It also means that whenever a cyber operation targets an infrastructure located on a territory, it might violate that state's sovereignty. As a consequence, if a cyber operation was to be attributed to a state, the attacking state might be held responsible under international law. Due to the interconnection of systems, the question of the need for a certain level of gravity for the violation of sovereignty to materialize arose quickly. If Koh's speech did not answer this question, that given by Brian J. Egan, Legal Adviser of the State Department in 2016, brought clarity on where the US stood regarding sovereignty. Brian J. Egan declared that

> remote cyber operations involving computers or other networked devices located on another State's territory does not constitute a per se violation of international law. In other words, there is no absolute prohibition on such operation as a matter of international law. This is perhaps most clear where such activities in another State's territory have no effects or de minimis effects.[26]

The American interpretation, which has also been adopted by the Tallinn Manual[27] and later by the UK, serves as an excuse to legitimate intelligence gathering by the states but also to try to limit other states' ability to regulate content on their territory. This was clearly explained by Egan who asserted that intelligence collection did not violate international law per se but also that the principle of sovereignty should not be used as an excuse to limit the freedom of expression.

Legal attribution is another issue that exemplified the importance of public cyber diplomacy in the Obama administration. In his 2012 speech, Harold H. Koh affirmed that "States are legally responsible for activities undertaken through 'proxy actors', who act on the state's instructions or under its direction or control,"[28] referring to the International Law Commission's Articles on the Responsibility of States for Internationally Wrongful Acts endorsed by the United Nations General Assembly in 2001.[29]

2222

This assertion was confirmed by Brian J. Egan in 2016. He added that

> [t]he law of state responsibility does not set forth explicit burdens or standards of proof for making a determination about legal attribution. In this context, a State acts as its own judge of the facts and may make a unilateral determination with respect to attribution of a cyber operation to another State[.]

and that

> despite the suggestion by some States to the contrary, there is no international legal obligation to reveal evidence on which attribution is based prior to taking appropriate action. There may, of course, be political pressure to do so, and States may choose to reveal such evidence to convince other States to join them in condemnation, for example. But that is a policy choice – it is not compelled by international law.[30]

These two precisions are important as they constitute a direct answer to both the criticisms of the difficulties to attribute an attack and to a provision that had been defended by Russia and adopted by the UN Group of Governmental Experts (GGE) in 2015 on the necessity to bring evidences when attributing an attack.

These two examples illustrate the US strategy on international regulation under Obama for two reasons. First, it shows that, unlike Russia, which argues for new rules of international law, the US chose to demonstrate the ability of existing international law to regulate the states' conduct in cyberspace by exposing its own interpretation of the law. By doing so, the US reinforced its argument that new rules of international law were not needed to maintain security and stability in cyberspace. Second, by being one of the first countries to do so, it provided the US with leadership and influence to address the many uncertainties about how international law applies to cyberspace. The failure of the fifth GGE in June 2017 showed how central this question was and highlighted the major differences existing among states. Member states of the fifth GGE could not reach a consensus on how some of the rules of international law should apply to cyberspace and thus could not adopt a report, putting an end to international negotiations until they restarted two years later. Clarity on how international law applies to cyberspace is one of the keys to maintaining peace and stability in cyberspace. It is therefore essential for states to share their views in order to achieve consensus and decrease tensions in cyberspace. Understanding the unique characteristics of cyberspace, the Obama administration went further and promoted the adoption of norms of responsible behavior to better define what states should or should not do in cyberspace.

THE PUSH FOR STATES' ADOPTION OF NORMS OF RESPONSIBLE BEHAVIOR IN CYBERSPACE

The *International Strategy for Cyberspace* also called for the adoption of norms of responsible behavior and stated that the states' behaviors in cyberspace "have not been matched by clearly agreed-upon norms for acceptable behavior in cyberspace. To bridge the gap, we will work to build a consensus on what constitutes acceptable behavior."[31] The US proposed two sets of norms : norms that aimed at guiding the states in accordance with their international law obligations when acting in cyberspace, and norms that were more specific to cyberspace and aimed at "preserving global network functionality and improving cybersecurity"[32] such as global interoperability, network stability, reliable access, or multi-stakeholder governance.

The first set of norms is of particular importance to understand the US position on international regulations in cyberspace and what its strategy was. The *International Strategy for Cyberspace* gave quite a lot of details about the status of these norms. It did not qualify them as principles of international law, nor did it separate them from the international legal framework that had been in place for decades. On the contrary, it reminded everyone that norms have brought predictability to the conduct of the states and have helped prevent conflicts in other spheres of international relations, and that the "unique attributes of networked technology require additional work to clarify how these norms apply and what additional understandings might be necessary to supplement them."[33] The goal of the US, according to the *International Strategy for Cyberspace*, was thus not to reinvent customary international law but

193

to "work internationally to forge consensus regarding how norms of behavior apply to cyberspace, with the understanding that an important first step in such efforts is applying the broad expectations of peaceful and just interstate conduct to cyberspace."[34] These norms should thus be understood as norms based on international law and as an interpretation of existing international law principles, thus participating in the clarification about the application of international law to cyberspace. This can be explained by two factors. First, Russia and some other countries had pushed for the adoption of new international principles, arguing that positive international law was inadequate to regulate the states' conducts in cyberspace and thus that states' rights and obligations had to be redefined.[35] By anchoring their proposed norms in international law, the US admitted that new rules were necessary while reaffirming the applicability of current international norms to cyberspace. Second, by proposing new norms based on international legal obligations, the US did not simply keep distancing itself from Russia, it was also more likely to convince other like-minded states to support its position on these issues, thus taking the lead on the diplomatic scene.

But the American approach to norms evolved as states were increasingly reaching a consensus on international regulations. It moved from supporting norms of behavior anchored in international law to norms that were purely non-binding. Although Brian J. Egan acknowledged that "[t]hese voluntary, non-binding norms (. . .) may, in certain circumstances, overlap with standards of behavior that are required as a matter of international law," he insisted on differentiating these two sets of norms.

With these proposals, the US tried to define more precisely the legal framework applying to states' conduct in cyberspace, therefore directly influencing the clarification of international law and the definition of what states should or should not do in cyberspace

For the first time, a state was publicly exposing its strategy to maintain security and stability in cyberspace, procuring lengthy details about its approach to international regulation. Meanwhile, the US promoted its vision and increased cyber-stability both at the bilateral and multilateral levels.

US public diplomacy at the bilateral and multilateral levels

A lot has been done in terms of international agreements under the Obama administration. The US entered into many bilateral agreements with other states such as China and Russia but also played a greater role in reaching consensus at the OSCE or within the United Nations, enabling important progress in cyber diplomacy at the multilateral level. These international agreements are the direct translation of Obama's new diplomacy on cybersecurity issues.

BILATERAL AGREEMENTS WITH CHINA AND RUSSIA: A TOOL TO LIMIT CONFLICT ESCALATION

The first example of American cyber diplomacy at the bilateral level is the agreements signed with Russia in June 2011[36] and June 2013.[37] In 2011, for the first time, confidence-building measures in the field of Information and Communications Technologies (ICT) were put in place between Russia and the US. They focused mainly on information exchange between both nations' Computer Emergency Response Teams (CERTs) and the establishment of communication protocols between Moscow and Washington on cybersecurity issues in order to decrease existing and future crises. In June 2013, President Putin and President Obama signed three agreements on confidence-building measures in the field of ICT and signed a joint statement. The three agreements established a direct communication link between high-level officials in the White House and the Kremlin, authorized the use of communication links between the American and Russian Nuclear Risk Reduction Centers created in 1987 for nuclear matters, and, finally, furthered cooperation between the US and Russian CERTs. The final mechanism established under these agreements was the creation of a "working group under the auspices of the Bilateral Presidential Commission, dedicated to assessing emerging ICT threats and proposing concrete joint measures to address them."[38] These agreements, qualified as "a non-aggression pact for cyberspace"[39] by Andrey Krutskikh, led to concrete cooperation during the 2014 Winter Olympic Games but did not survive the Crimea crisis[40] nor, a few years later, the crisis following the alleged Russian interference in the American presidential election.

Another example is the cyber pact signed between President Xi and President Obama in September 2015. The cyber pact was signed as there were mounting tensions between the two countries over economic espionage accusations, and after a name and shame campaign. On April 1, 2015, President Obama signed Executive Order 13694 allowing the administration to adopt sanctions against any person or entity responsible or complicit in a cyber-enabled activity that could threaten national security.[41] The day before President Xi's visit to the US, President Obama declared "we will indicate to the Chinese that this is not just a matter of us being mildly upset, but is something that will put significant strains on the bilateral relationship if not resolved, and that we are prepared to some countervailing actions in order to get their attention."[42] The signing of the agreement, which was a surprise, contained not only norms and cooperation measures, but it also put in place a group of high-level experts to share views on measures and principles of international cooperation. Among the provisions signed by the two countries, they agreed that "timely responses should be provided to requests for information and assistance concerning malicious cyber activities," "neither country's government will conduct or knowingly support cyber-enabled theft of intellectual property, including trade secrets or other confidential business information, with the intent of providing competitive advantages to companies or commercial sectors," and that "[b]oth sides are committed to making common efforts to further identify and promote appropriate norms of state behavior in cyberspace within the international community."[43] The impact of the cyber pact on economic cyber espionage is hard to assess. But according to some experts,[44] there was a significant decrease in such activities after the cyber pact was signed by both countries.

These two bilateral agreements can be seen as part of a confidence-building process that aimed at decreasing conflicts in cyberspace. The US has also signed other such bilateral agreements with countries like Japan, Israel, the United Kingdom, and India that all aimed at reinforcing cooperation in the field of ICTs, with a particular focus on information exchange.

The role of the US at the UN Group of Governmental Experts (GGE)

Since the first General Assembly (UNGA) resolution on cyber-security in the context of international security in 1998, five groups of governmental experts (GGE) have convened to better understand the risks pertaining to cyberspace and the actions that could be taken to address them, leading to the adoption of three consensus reports.[45] The 2013 and the 2015 reports are of particular importance to account for Barack Obama's cyber diplomacy.

The 2013 consensus report is a landmark document upon which US influence was very important. The mandate of the GGE, established by paragraph 4 of the General Assembly Resolution 66/24, was, among other things, to study "cooperative measures to address [threats in the sphere of information security] including norms, rules or principles of responsible behaviour."[46] It affirmed, for the first time in a multilateral instrument, that "[I]nternational law, and in particular the Charter of the United Nations, is applicable and is essential to maintaining peace and stability and promoting an open, secure, peaceful and accessible ICT environment."[47] But the states' membership of the GGE went further than just stating the applicability of international law. They also recommended seven norms of responsible behavior to be respected by the states. The concept of norms, rules, and principles of responsible behavior was not defined in the report. However, the first paragraph anchored them in international law. It states that "[t]he application of norms derived from existing international law relevant to the use of ICTs by States is an essential measure to reduce risks to international peace, security and stability."[48] Russia and China had proposed new norms based on international law in 2011.[49] The GGE's approach can therefore be seen as a consensus between major cyber powers.

Seven norms were recommended by the GGE report. The study of these seven recommendations shows that four out of the five bases for norms stated in the *International Strategy for Cyberspace* are to be found in the GGE report, while one of the specific norms refers to a norm adopted by the GGE (see Table 6.1).

Table 6.1 Comparison between the norms proposed by the US and the norms adopted in 2013 at the UN level

Norms proposed by the US	2013 GGE norms
Upholding fundamental freedoms	State efforts to address the security of ICTs must go hand in hand with respect for human rights and fundamental freedoms set forth in the Universal Declaration of Human Rights and other international instruments (para. 21).
Respect for property	–
Valuing privacy	State efforts to address the security of ICTs must go hand in hand with respect for human rights and fundamental freedoms set forth in the Universal Declaration of Human Rights and other international instruments (para. 21).
Protection from crime	States should intensify cooperation against criminal or terrorist use of ICTs, harmonize legal approaches as appropriate, and strengthen practical collaboration between respective law enforcement and prosecutorial agencies (para. 22).
Right to self-defense	International law, and in particular the Charter of the United Nations, is applicable and is essential to maintaining peace and stability and promoting an open, secure, peaceful, and accessible ICT environment (para. 19).
Global interoperability	–
Network stability	–
Reliable access	State efforts to address the security of ICTs must go hand in hand with respect for human rights and fundamental freedoms set forth in the Universal Declaration of Human Rights and other international instruments (para. 21).
Multi-stakeholder governance	–
Cybersecurity due diligence	–

Source: compiled by the authors.

Conversely, the norms stated in the Code of Conduct for Information Security proposed by Member States of the Shanghai Cooperation Organization gained little success and were not, mostly, adopted by the GGE.

The US influence was very important in the 2013 report. However, the report adopted by the fourth GGE in 2015 shows a decline in its influence and should be seen as a more consensual report between different approaches to international regulation. International events, and especially the Snowden revelations on American programs of mass surveillance and cyber operations, have undoubtedly impacted the negotiations taking place at the UN and have undermined American credibility and its influence. The study of the 2015 report gives several examples of its consensual character.

The first example concerns the content of the norms and international law provisions stated in the report. Most of the provisions focus on peacetime norms and not wartime norms. Peacetime norms are applicable to states' behavior that does not, in its effects, reach the threshold of the use of force nor take place during an armed conflict. It is about the legal context where they apply and not about the content of the norms. Unlike Russia and China, the US wanted the GGE to focus more on norms applicable during armed conflicts. The GGE chose to limit the scope of the norms of responsible behavior and norms of international law to norms applying in times of peace.

Yet US influence can still be seen in the mention of the four core principles of international humanitarian law (para. 28 d) and in the implicit mention of states' right to self-defense (para. 28 c). But even in these two provisions, there was a consensus on the wording used. For example, provision (28 c) states

> [u]nderscoring the aspirations of the international community to the peaceful use of ICTs for the common good of mankind, and recalling that the Charter applies in its entirety, the Group noted the inherent right of States to take measures consistent with international law and as recognized in the Charter. The Group recognized the need for further study on this matter.

Again, the wording used illustrates a consensus between the US, Russia, and China. Although states' right of self-defense is not explicitly mentioned, the right to take measures consistent with international law remains, and as recognized in the Charter. This has been recognized by all states, including Russia.[50] But Russia and China did not want this principle to be clearly written in the report, so diplomats agreed to a work-around in the language. As James Lewis, rapporteur of the GGE, explained: "[t]here's language in there that makes it clear that the right of self defense applies and you have to observe principles of [the Law of Armed Conflict] in doing it. Some of this was thinking of ways to say Article 51 without saying it."[51] The question of when a cyber operation amounts to an armed attack has been largely debated among scholars but still lacks state practice.[52] The opposition between the US and other countries mainly deals with the fact that the US doesn't recognize the two thresholds when it comes to the use of force (use of force according to Article 2(4) of the UN Charter and armed attack according to Article 51 of the UN Charter). This was recalled by Harold H. Koh in his 2012 speech.[53] Another illustration of this consensus is the mention of the use of "ICT for the common good of mankind." It aims at recalling that states must respect international law when using cyber capabilities and that the use of unilateral and extrajudicial measures can only remain the exception.

The second example of the increased influence of the Russians and Chinese is the issue of proof in the GGE report. Provision (28 f) states "[t]he Group noted that the accusations of organizing and implementing wrongful acts brought against States should be substantiated." This provision recognizes the applicability of the law of the state's responsibility to cyber operations conducted or attributed to states. But it also gives indications on how to attribute an attack. It states that technical attribution might not be sufficient to attribute an attack, and that evidences should be brought when attributing an attack. Interestingly, the US had started to publicly attribute attacks. The document does not explicitly mention public attribution but it can be seen as a way to limit public attribution by some states or at least constrain states making those accusations to provide evidence. The US has stated its opposition to this provision, affirming it was not a new international obligation.[54] Conversely, when accused, Russia recalls the GGE report provision.[55]

The GGE negotiations were marked by an important speech entitled "An Open and Secure Internet: We Must Have Both" delivered by John Kerry, Secretary of State, in May 2015 in Seoul. In his remarks, he promoted the adoption of five norms by the GGE.[56] First, no country should conduct or knowingly support online activity that intentionally damages or impedes the use of another country's critical infrastructure. Second, no country should seek either to prevent emergency teams from responding to a cybersecurity incident or allow its own teams to cause harm. Third, no country should conduct or support cyber-enabled theft of intellectual property, trade secrets, or other confidential business information for commercial gain. Fourth, every country should mitigate malicious cyber activity emanating from its soil, and they should do so in a transparent, accountable, and cooperative way. And, fifth, every country should do what it can to help states that are victimized by a cyber-attack.

The US was again publicly exposing its views on international regulation and cyber-stability. Four out of the five norms promoted by John Kerry have been adopted by the GGE. The one that wasn't was nevertheless adopted by the G20 in its final declaration at the Antalya Summit in November 2015, a few months after the GGE produced its report. The remarks delivered by John Kerry illustrated the US priorities for international regulation: the protection of the free flow of information and the fight against cyber-attacks that could threaten its economy.[57] This speech can nevertheless be seen as a means for the US to regain diplomatic influence after the Shanghai Cooperation Organization proposed a new *International Code of Conduct for Information Security*[58] to the United Nations at the beginning of 2015. Although the language adopted in the *International Code of Conduct* was more in line with the GGE's, it still contained provisions that were unacceptable for the US and its allies.[59]

Despite these examples the US influence remains very important, and no consensus report could have been adopted without the will of the US to make progress on the regulation of cyberspace. The US strategy on international regulation was also a means to develop both legal and political ground for responses in case of a cyber operation targeting its territory or citizens.[60]

201

Conclusion

Under Obama's presidency, cyberspace clearly became a battle-field, even though most of the attacks occurred in peacetime. Cyber-attacks have proliferated, diversified, and become increasingly creative and complex, creating a series of strategic surprises that posed serious challenges to state security and raised awareness about cyber threats. These attacks are both the result and the driver of a cyber-arms race that led over thirty states to develop offensive cyber capabilities, according to US intelligence. Devastating attacks such as WannaCry and NotPetya have demonstrated that some of these attacks could get out of control and threaten the security and stability of cyberspace, with a dramatic impact on societies.

Obama's legacy in the cyber domain is both major and mutlifaceted. The Obama administration played a leading role in this arms race and launched actions likely to prompt instability. The administration set a dangerous precedent with audacious attacks against Iran's nuclear facilities and contributed to the proliferation of offensive tools to conduct mass surveillance and targeted operations. In search of a deterrence strategy, President Obama also provided strong statements and retaliatory measures that have exacerbated tensions.

At the same time, the administration realized the need for international regulation and cooperation to limit cyber threats, avoid conflict escalation, and mitigate systemic risks. Obama's administration was also a leader in the norms building process and the development of international law for cyberspace. It also engaged in bilateral and multilateral treaties to restrain state behavior in cyberspace and increase cooperation. The consensus between states about the applicability of international law to cyberspace and a number of principles, norms of responsible behavior, and confidence building measures can be regarded as a major achievement for collective security.

This legacy, however, is threatened. Under Donald Trump's presidency, multilateral institutions have been undermined and the last GGE discussions failed in a context of heightened tensions between the US and Russia. The ongoing negotiations at the UN level are taking place in two different tracks, one initiated by the US (GGE) and the other by Russia (OEWG), and raise concerns about the ability to achieve consensus.[61] The cyber strategy published in 2018 by the White House mentions the possibility of preemptive cyber attacks for deterrence purpose. The White House has multiplied public attributions of cyber-attacks, indictments of alleged hackers involved in state-sponsored cyber operations, threats of reprisals, and intention to pursue cyber warfare. In this context, private global companies – namely Microsoft – and multi-stakeholder groups such as the Global Commission on the Stability of Cyberspace have stepped in to promote peace, security, and stability in cyberspace, and have proposed new norms that later may be adopted by states to guide both states' and non-state actors' conduct in cyberspace.

Notes

1. See, for instance: Joseph S. Nye Jr., *Cyber Power* (Harvard Kennedy School, Belfer Center for Science and International Affairs, 2010); Kim Zetter, *Countdown to Zero Day: Stuxnet and the Launch of the World's First Digital Weapon* (New York: Crown, 2014); Solange Ghernaouti, *Cyberpower: Crime, Conflict, and Security in Cyberspace* (Lausanne: Presses polytechniques romandes, 2013); Tim Maurer, *Cyber Mercenaries, The States, Hackers and Power* (Cambridge: Cambridge University Press, 2018); Stéphane Taillat and Frédérick Douzet, "Collective Security and Strategic Instability in the Digital Domain," *Contemporary Security Policy*, 40, 3, 2019: 362–367; Martin Libicki, *Cyber Deterrence and Cyber War* (Washington DC: RAND, 2009).
2. David Rothkopf, "The Cool War," *Foreign Policy*, 20, 2013.
3. Tim Maurer, *Cyber Norm Emergence at the United Nations – An Analysis of the Activities at the UN Regarding Cyber-Security*, (Belfer Center for Science and International Affairs, Harvard Kennedy School, September 2011).
4. Frédérick Douzet and Stéphane Taillat, "L'affirmation du leadership américain," pp. 111–122, in Stéphane Taillat, Amaël Cattaruzza, Didier Danet (eds.), *La cyberdéfense. Politique de l'espace numérique* (Paris: Armand Colin, 2018).
5. The attack took place in the wake of protests against the relocation of the Bronze Soldier of Tallinn, a Soviet World War II war

memorial. Estonia blamed Russia, which denied any involvement. A group of Russian patriot hackers claimed responsibility for organizing the attack.

6. Michael Sulmeyer, "Much ado bout nothing? Cyber Command and the NSA," *War on the Rocks*, June 19, 2017, https://warontherocks.com/2017/07/much-ado-about-nothing-cyber-command-and-the-nsa/ (accessed November 26, 2019).

7. David E. Sanger, "Obama Order Sped Up Wave of Cyberattacks Against Iran," *The New York Times*, June 1, 2012, https://www.nytimes.com/2012/06/01/world/middleeast/obama-ordered-wave-of-cyberattacks-against-iran.html?_r=1%27amp;pagewanted=all (accessed February 9, 2019).

8. Kim Zetter, "Legal Experts: Stuxnet Attack on Iran was Illegal 'Act of Force,'" *Wired*, March 25, 2013, https://www.wired.com/2013/03/stuxnet-act-of-force/ (accessed February 9, 2019).

9. Glenn Greenwald, "NSA Claims Iran Learned from Western Cyberattacks," *The Intercept*, February 10, 2015, https://theintercept.com/2015/02/10/nsa-iran-developing-sophisticated-cyber-attacks-learning-attacks/ (accessed February 9, 2019).

10. Exploitable vulnerabilities unknown from the software vendor and for which no patch has been developed.

11. Bruce E. Cain and Frédérick Douzet, "Cyber Insecurity. Arms Race to the Bottom," *The American Interest*, June 27, 2018, https://www.the-american-interest.com/v/frederick-douzet/ (accessed February 9, 2019).

12. Elisabeth Bumiller and Thom Shanker, "Panetta Warns of Dire Threat of Cyberattack on U.S.," The *New York Times*, October 11, 2012, https://www.nytimes.com/2012/10/12/world/panetta-warns-of-dire-threat-of-cyberattack.html?pagewanted=all (accessed February 9, 2019).

13. Martin Libicki, *Cyber Deterrence and Cyber War* (Washington, DC: RAND, 2009).

14. Andrew F. Krepinevich, "Cyber Warfare: A 'Nuclear Option'?" CSBA, August 24, 2012, http://www.csbaonline.org/publications/2012/08/cyber-warfare-a-nuclear-option (accessed February 9, 2019).

15. White House, *International Strategy for Cyberspace. Prosperity, Security and Openness in a Networked World*, May 2011, https://obamawhitehouse.archives.gov/sites/default/files/rss_viewer/international_strategy_for_cyberspace.pdf (accessed February 9, 2019).

16. Herbert Lin, *Attribution of Malicious Cyber Incidents. From Soup to Nuts* (Hoover Institution, Aegis Paper Series No. 1607, 2016).

17. Leon Panetta, "Defending the Nation from Cyber Attack," Remarks on Cybersecurity to the Business Executives for National Security, New York City, October 11, 2012, http://archive.defense.gov/speeches/speech.aspx?speechid=1728 (accessed February 9, 2019).
18. Barack Obama, 2014, https://obamawhitehouse.archives.gov/the-press-office/2014/12/19/remarks-president-year-end-press-conference (accessed February 9, 2019).
19. White House, *International Strategy for Cyberspace*, p. 4.
20. White House, *International Strategy for Cyberspace*, p. 8.
21. Alix Desforges and Frédérick Douzet, "Du cyberspace à la datasphère. Le nouveau front pionnier de la géographie," *NETCOM*, 32, 1–2, 2018: 87–109.
22. White House, *International Strategy for Cyberspace*, p. 9.
23. White House, *International Strategy for Cyberspace*, p. 14.
24. Mathias Forteau, "Les seuils de gravité d'une cyberattaque," pp. 23–44, in Maryline Grange and Anne-Thida Norodom (eds.), *Cyberattaques et droit international. Problèmes choisis* (Paris: Pedone, 2019).
25. Harold H. Koh, H, "International Law in Cyberspace," *Harvard International Law Journal*, 54, December 2012.
26. Brian J. Egan, "Remarks on International Law and Stability in Cyberspace," Berkeley Law School, California, November 10, 2016.
27. The Tallinn Manuel is one of the most comprehensive academic works on how international law applies to cyber operations. If the first edition only focused on the law of war, the second edition goes beyond that and includes developments on the law of state responsibility and other branches of international law that apply outside of an armed conflict. It was written by a group of international experts gathered under the auspice of the NATO Cooperative Cyber Defence Centre of Excellence.
28. Harold H. Koh, "International Law in Cyberspace."
29. General Assembly of the United Nations, Resolution 56/83 "Responsibility of States for Internationally Wrongful Acts", December 12, 2001, A/RES/56/83, Annex "Responsibility of States for Internationally Wrongful Acts."
30. Brian J. Egan, "Remarks on International Law and Stability in Cyberspace."
31. White House, *International Strategy for Cyberspace*, p. 9.
32. White House, *International Strategy for Cyberspace*, p.10.
33. White House, *International Strategy for Cyberspace*, p. 9.
34. White House, *International Strategy for Cyberspace*, p. 9.

35. General Assembly of the United Nations, Developments in the Field of Information and Telecommunications in the Context of International Security, Report of the Secretary-General, August 10, 1999, A/54/313; General Assembly of the United Nations, Developments in the Field of Information and Telecommunications in the Context of International Security, Report of the Secretary-General, August 10, 1999, A/55/140.
36. "Joint Statement by Cybersecurity Coordinator Schmidt and Deputy Secretary Klimashin, U.S. and Russian Delegations Meet to Discuss Confidence-Building Measures in Cyberspace," June 21, 2011, https://obamawhitehouse.archives.gov/sites/default/files/uploads/2011_klimashin_schmidt_cyber_joint_statement.pdf
37. "Fact Sheet: U.S.-Russian Cooperation on Information and Communications Technology Security," June 17, 2013, https://obamawhitehouse.archives.gov/the-press-office/2013/06/17/fact-sheet-us-russian-cooperation-information-and-communications-technol
38. "Fact Sheet: U.S.-Russian Cooperation on Information and Communications Technology Security."
39. "We Stand for the Internationalization of the Internet Governance" (in Russian), *Kommersant*, June 16, 2014, http://www.kommersant.ru/doc/2492013
40. Oleg Demidov, "U.S.-Russian CBMs in the Use of ICTs: A Breakthrough with an Unclear Future," *Security Index: A Russian Journal on International Security*, 20, 3–4, 2014: 77.
41. Executive Order 13694, April 1, 2015, https://www.govinfo.gov/content/pkg/FR-2015-04-02/pdf/2015-07788.pdf
42. White House, "Remarks by the President to the Business Roundtable," Washington, DC, September 16, 2015, https://obamawhitehouse.archives.gov/the-press-office/2015/09/16/remarks-president-business-roundtable
43. White House, "Fact Sheet: President Xi Jinping's State Visit to the United States," September 25, 2015, https://obamawhitehouse.archives.gov/the-press-office/2015/09/25/fact-sheet-president-xi-jinpings-state-visit-united-states
44. FireEye, *Redline Drawn: China Recalculates its Use of Cyber Espionage*, June 2016, p. 15, https://www.fireeye.com/content/dam/fireeye-www/current-threats/pdfs/rpt-china-espionage.pdf; Adam Segal, "The U.S.-China Cyber Espionage Deal One Year Later," *Council on Foreign Relations*, September 28, 2016, https://www.cfr.org/blog/us-china-cyber-espionage-deal-one-year-later

45. General Assembly of the United Nations, Group of Governmental Experts on Developments in the Field of Information and Telecommunications in the Context of International Security, July 30, 2010, A/65/201; General Assembly of the United Nations, Group of Governmental Experts on Developments in the Field of Information and Telecommunications in the Context of International Security, June 24, 2013, A/68/98; General Assembly of the United Nations, Group of Governmental Experts on Developments in the Field of Information and Telecommunications in the Context of International Security, July 22, 2015, A/70/174.

46. General Assembly of the United Nations, Resolution 66/24 "Developments in the Field of Information and Telecommunications in the Context of International Security," A/RES/66/24, para. 4.

47. General Assembly of the United Nations, Group of Governmental Experts on Developments in the Field of Information and Telecommunications in the Context of International Security, June 24, 2013, A/68/98, para. 19.

48. General Assembly of the United Nations, Group of Governmental Experts on Developments in the Field of Information and Telecommunications in the Context of International Security, para. 16.

49. General Assembly of the United Nations, *Letter Dated 12 September 2011 from the Permanent Representatives of China, the Russian Federation, Tadjikistan and Uzbekistan to the United Nations addressed to the Secretary General*, September 14, 2011, A/66/359, Annex, "International Code of Conduct for Information Security."

50. "UN Cybersecurity Report Compromises on Self-Defense Issue – Russian Official," *Sputnik*, 17 August 2015, https://sputniknews.com/politics/201508171025819426-UN-cybersecurity-report-compromises-on-self-defence/

51. "U.N. Body Agrees to U.S. Norms in Cyberspace," *Politico*, 9 July 2015, https://www.politico.com/story/2015/07/un-body-agrees-to-us-norms-in-cyberspace-119900

52. See for instance: Marco Roscini, *Cyber Operations and the Use of Force in International Law*, (Oxford: Oxford University Press, 2016); Michael N. Schmitt, , Liis Vihul (dir.), *Tallinn Manual 2.0 on the International Law Applicable to Cyber Operations*, (Cambridge:, Cambridge University Press, 2017).

53. Harold H. Koh, "International Law in Cyberspace. Remarks as Prepared for Delivery by Harold Hongju Koh to the USCYBERCOM Inter-Agency Legal Conference Ft. Meade, MD, Sept. 18 2012," *Harvard International Law Journal*, 54, December, 2012: 7.

54. Brian J. Egan, "Remarks on International Law and Stability in Cyberspace."
55. "UN Cybersecurity Report Compromises on Self-Defense Issue – Russian Official," *Sputnik*.
56. Jason Healey and Tim Maurer, "What it'll Take to Force Peace in Cyberspace," *CSMonitor*, March 20, 2017, https://www.csmonitor. com/World/Passcode/Passcode-Voices/2017/0320/What-it-ll-take-to-forge-peace-in-cyberspace
57. Brian J. Egan, "Remarks on International Law and Stability in Cyberspace."
58. General Assembly of the United Nations, *Letter Dated 9 January 2015 from the Permanent Representatives of China, Kazakhstan, Kyrgystan, the Russian Federation, Tadjikistan and Uzbekistan to the United Nations addressed to the Secretary General*, January 13, 2015, A/69/723, Annex, "International Code of Conduct for Information Security."
59. François Delerue and Aude Géry, *Etat des lieux et perspective sur les normes de comportement responsable des Etats et mesures de confiance dans le domaine du numérique*, Paris, CEIS, Les notes stratégiques, janvier 2017.
60. Brian J. Egan, "Remarks on International Law and Stability in Cyberspace."
61. Digital Watch Observatory, https://dig.watch/processes/un-gge (last accessed December 2019).

7

A decent-sized foundation: Obama's urban policy

Thomas J. Sugrue

For a time in 2009, it looked like urban policy would move to the center of the national agenda for the first time in decades, finally rescued from the not-so-benign neglect that cities had suffered from the White House since the 1970s. Not even a month after Barack Obama was inaugurated, he signed an executive order creating a cabinet-level Office of Urban Affairs to implement "a comprehensive approach to urban development." He described the office in visionary terms: Obama's new urban team would reflect his "belief that our cities need more than just a partner; they need a partner who knows that the old ways of looking at our cities just won't do." For many urban analysts, the Obama presidency was a moment of extraordinary promise.[1]

Obama, the first urban born and raised president in decades, came into office at a transitional moment for American cities. Many observers celebrated the fact that "cities were back," pointing to new corporate headquarters rising in many downtowns, the gentrification of long-declining neighborhoods, and the expansion of an urban "creative class," which converted industrial lofts into tech incubators and art studios, and gritty storefronts into hip coffeehouses and brewpubs. Nearly all of the nation's ten largest cities had gained population between 1990 and 2010 after four decades of steady decline. Perhaps the most striking indicator of urban health was the dramatic drop in crime rates, which peaked at the height of the crack epidemic in the late 1980s and, by 2010, had fallen to pre-1960s levels.[2]

The visibility of empty nesters and hipsters reclaiming down-towns, however, obscured deep patterns of inequality that profoundly shaped the geography of metropolitan America. For all of the hype about the uptick in big-city population, urban growth was small in scale compared to suburban and exurban sprawl. Most Americans commuted suburb to suburb, because the majority of jobs in metropolitan America were outside central cities. Rates of black–white segregation fell modestly between 1990 and 2010, but nearly all of the nation's major metros remained highly segregated by race. More than half of African Americans lived in what sociologist Douglas Massey identified as "hypersegregated" neighborhoods, where more than 75 percent of their neighbors were black. Urban Latinos faced lower levels of segregation, but rates rose in the largest immigrant-receiving metropolitan areas, most notably Los Angeles, and East Coast cities with large Afro-Caribbean populations.[3]

Two other parlous long-term trends affected big cities. The first was the concentration of African Americans and Latinos in struggling school districts, with concentrated poverty, high teacher turnover, and decrepit facilities. In the late 1960s and 1970s, public schools had slowly desegregated, but by the 1990s they began to resegregate by race and grow more stratified by class.[4] The second was the dramatic increase in the population of urban minorities entangled in the criminal justice system, the result of the strict enforcement of anti-drug laws, the prevalence of stop-and-frisk police action, and especially the dramatic expansion of the incarcerated population.[5]

Whatever gains cities had made were imperiled by the Great Recession and, by nearly every measure, urban inequalities worsened in the aftermath of the crash. Millions of homeowners, disproportionately African-American and Latino urbanites, held subprime mortgages, unable to pay the ballooning adjustable rate mortgages that banks had peddled to eager homebuyers. In the year before Obama took office, lenders foreclosed on more than 3.5 million homes, devastating neighborhoods and leaving families to fend for themselves, with bad credit ratings, in expensive rental markets.[6]

Finally, urban areas bore the brunt of federal and state austerity measures. Since the 1970s, big cities had suffered a steady decline of federal expenditures, including cuts in federal aid to housing (beginning in the 1970s), in infrastructure funding (beginning in the 1980s), and welfare (beginning with the bipartisan welfare reform act of 1996). As the federal government devolved spending to the states through block grant programs, and left discretion on spending priorities to state agencies and state legislators, cities took big hits. Since the middle of the twentieth century, once powerful cities had lost their clout in Washington and in state capitals as suburban and rural districts gained population and representation. Big cities had long struggled with fiscal constraints, aging infrastructures, huge criminal justice expenditures, impoverished populations, and massive pension and debt obligations. To make ends meet, nearly every major city cut municipal workforces and trimmed public services to the bone, and relied increasingly on revenue-generation gimmicks like increased service fees, fines, and (in many cities), casino gambling. Some, including Stockton and Vallejo, California, and, most infamously, Detroit, declared bankruptcy in the aftermath of the 2008 financial crisis.[7]

Who better to address the challenges of American cities than a president who had spent his formative years in Jakarta and Honolulu, attended college in Los Angeles and New York, and lived nearly his entire adult life in Chicago? Who better to shift attention to cities than the man who spent three years as community organizer on Chicago's South Side, working with displaced steel workers and mobilizing the residents of a rundown public housing project to demand better living conditions? Who better to bring urban issues to the White House than a president who had launched his political career as a state senator representing a big-city district that included the University of Chicago and a large swath of surrounding, mostly African-American poor and working-class neighborhoods, and after the 2000 redistricting, much of Chicago's wealthy Gold Coast? Who better to grapple with the challenges of urban inequality than a policy intellectual who counted among his influences the prominent urban sociologist William Julius Wilson, and who drew his policy prescriptions

211

from the Brookings Institution's highly regarded Metropolitan Policy Program?[8]

No place influenced Obama more than Chicago, a city that embodied, in high relief, the tensions and contradictions of contemporary American urbanism. Chicago was a case study in urban deindustrialization and intense racial segregation. The nation's third largest metropolitan area, it had sprawled galactically nearly sixty miles to the north, west, and south. It was also a city that underwent substantial gentrification in the 1990s, as wealthy whites colonized formerly white working-class and lower middle-class neighborhoods on the city's North Side. And in the fifteen years before Obama ran for the presidency, Chicago was a hotbed of experimentation for downtown redevelopment, affordable housing policy, and education reform, all overseen by liberal policy-makers who embraced market-based solutions to urban problems over costly public investments.[9]

Many of Obama's closest advisors came out of the rough-and-tumble world of Chicago politics. David Axelrod launched his political career as an operative for Mayor Harold Washington and then as a chief of staff for Mayor Richard M. Daley, whose father had presided over Chicago's infamous political machine. During his twenty-two years as mayor, the younger Daley recast himself as the city's "CEO," built close alliances with Chicago's business elite, and worked to recast the city as a global economic center. Drawing from the market-based solutions that had migrated from Republican circles via the centrist Democratic Leadership Council, various think-tanks, and the Clinton administration into the heart of liberal policy-making, Daley worked to create a business- and tourist-friendly urban environment. He also launched influential experiments in the expansion of public–private partnerships to beautify city neighborhoods and redevelop blighted commercial districts. And most consequentially, he reorganized the Chicago's Housing Authority and Chicago Public Schools around the principles of privatization, competition, and innovation.[10]

Arne Duncan, Obama's first secretary of education, was Daley's appointee to run Chicago's public schools from 2001 to 2009. Valerie Jarrett, one of Obama's closest advisors, had been Daley's chief of staff. Obama's own first chief of staff, the abrasive Rahm Emanuel, had led Daley's fundraising efforts during his 1992 campaign and, with Daley's support, was elected to Congress, representing part of Chicago's North Side. Daley's brother William, a lawyer and investment banker who had served in the Clinton administration, replaced Emanuel as Obama's chief of staff. Even the First Lady, Michelle Obama, who grew up on Chicago's South Side, the daughter of a city employee, had spent two years early in her career working as a planner in the Daley administration. Chicago imprinted nearly every aspect of Obama's urban policy.[11]

During the long presidential campaign of 2007–2008, Obama mostly distanced himself from his Chicago roots for good reason. For all of the celebration of Chicago's reinvention, the Windy City could not escape its tawdry political past. When Obama's campaign assembled an urban advisory team early in 2008, it included academics, urban policy analysts, community organizers, and staffers at urban nonprofits and foundations, who mostly communicated through an unwieldy listserv, occasionally providing advice but mostly staging local events and helping with voter mobilization efforts.[12] On the stump, Obama seldom discussed urban policy, saving the issue for just a handful of rallies with substantial African-American audiences, a meeting of the National Council of Mayors, and a brief mention at the Democratic National Convention.

Obama's reluctance to discuss urban issues was carefully calculated. A crucial part of his electoral strategy was fashioning a "post-racial" identity that signaled to white voters that he was not beholden to black constituents (in popular discourse, the terms "urban" and "black" were often used interchangeably). Obama learned on the campaign trail that his mere mention of race could generate days or even weeks of controversy and headlines. He downplayed what many voters saw as distinctively "urban" issues like poverty and racial segregation. And his campaign team was careful to be sure that when he mentioned cities, he also highlighted programs that targeted entire metropolitan areas or even regions.[13]

What Obama offered was a hodge-podge of programs that appealed to the Democratic Party's base, including increased federal funding for urban infrastructure, public education, community policing, and job training.[14] But he also nodded toward market-based solutions to urban problems. Taking a leaf from Arne Duncan's school reform initiatives in Chicago, he pledged his support for charter schools and used education reform buzzwords like "innovation," "standards and accountability," and "competition." Inspired by urban reinvestment experiments in Chicago and other cities, he supported programs that provided incentives for corporations to locate their operations in central cities, including tax abatements and low-interest loans. Drawing from the work of Brookings Institution scholars, he supported "smart growth" strategies like investment and tax breaks for regional economic development. Urban policy advocates to 1960s-era poverty warriors to liberal hedge fund managers could all project their images of a future urban America onto the candidate.[15]

In the White House

For all of his reticence to discuss urban issues on the campaign trail, Obama sent out a strong signal that urban issues were near the top of his administration's priorities when he announced the creation of the new White House Office of Urban Affairs on February 19, 2009. Obama's announcement bore a striking resemblance to a long-forgotten urban initiative launched with great fanfare three decades earlier. In 1977, President Jimmy Carter created a high-level Urban Policy Research Group to advise him. Both presidents promised "comprehensive urban reform" and interagency cooperation. But Obama's office differed from Carter's group in one key dimension: his urban policy advisors did not consist of an ad hoc combination of domestic policy staffers and executive branch undersecretaries. Instead, Obama's appointees reported directly to him.[16]

Putting together a new executive branch office proved to be challenging. Attracting and retaining first-rate, experienced leadership was difficult because the office lacked the power and perquisites of a cabinet-level position. Many urban policy advocates were surprised by Obama's appointment of Bronx Borough President Adolfo Carrion as head and by his successor, Derek Douglas, a former aide to New York governor David Patterson. Both lasted about a year in their posts. Neither of them had substantial urban policy expertise nor were they political heavyweights. The third head, Xavier de Souza Briggs, a city planner on the faculty at MIT, was a highly regarded scholar, but he lacked political connections and policy-making experience. Under them was a revolving group of young aides, few of whom brought extensive on-the-ground experience or stellar academic credentials to the job, like their counterparts in more prestigious offices such as the Council of Economic Advisors or the Office of Management and Budget.[17]

Early on, the Office of Urban Affairs sponsored an "urban tour" to meet with local elected officials, planners, and policy-makers and a "national conversation" on cities and metropolitan areas. Most ambitiously, it created Urban Policy Working Groups to evaluate existing programs and eventually make recommendations to cabinet-level agencies on how to revitalize neighborhoods and spur regional growth. It also published an occasional newsletter on urban initiatives.[18] The Office of Urban Affairs met with skepticism across the board. Conservatives charged that it was an example of government overreach. "Cities improved dramatically in periods when the federal government backed off the most," argued Fred Siegel, a historian and former aide to New York mayor Rudolph Giuliani. Critics on the left were skeptical that the new agency had enough resources to make a difference. Brad Ladner, a specialist in community economic development, worried that "it's not clear that the office, as established, has the tools or resources to make a lot of headway."[19] By 2011, the Office of Urban Affairs was so invisible that the White House switchboard operator often could not find its phone extension.

When political scientists Theda Skocpol and Lawrence Jacobs gathered ten scholars to offer the first scholarly assessment of Obama's domestic policies, they left urban affairs out altogether.[20] Although the office remained in place through Obama's second term, seasoned observers dismissed the OUA as a lost opportunity. "The Office of Urban Affairs is [an] example of a grand idea that was implemented in a half-hearted way, and then lost its momentum over time," New York University sociologist Patrick Sharkey contended. The president, however, bore only some of the responsibility. Urban affairs had little congressional support: the Republican Party had long abandoned cities and, after its victory in the 2010 midterm elections, thwarted the administration's entire domestic agenda. Even congressional Democrats, especially from suburban districts, concerned about taxpayer backlash, were reluctant to support programs that did not obviously benefit their constituents.[21]

Obama may well have intended his creation of the Office of Urban Affairs to be a symbolic gesture. During his first two years in office, the action was elsewhere. When the House and Senate were under Democratic Party control, the president directed his domestic policy toward addressing the Great Recession and winning passage of sweeping health insurance reform. Both the 2009 American Reinvestment and Recovery Act (ARRA, also known as the stimulus package) and the 2010 Affordable Care Act were, in effect, massive urban investment initiatives. ARRA spending reached nearly every sector of the economy, and included substantial funds to rural areas, in part as a vain attempt to win the support of small-town Republicans. But many of its expenditures benefitted cities. The emphasis on "shovel-ready" projects favored big municipalities that had public works departments, a large backlog of infrastructural needs, and the equipment and personnel in place to move quickly. For example, US$27.5 billion went to port and rail infrastructure improvements, most in cities; another US$20 billion went to improving airports, largely under municipal control; and US$1.5 billion supplemented surface transportation improvement projects in both metropolitan and exurban areas. The stimulus also spent US$97.5 million on public education at a moment when states were axing school spending and local tax revenues had plummeted, leading to massive layoffs, especially in big-city school districts. Based on grantee reports, the administration estimated that about ARRA had saved or created between 275,000 and 300,000 education jobs between September 2009 and September 2010.[22]

Even seemingly minor stimulus expenditures sent federal dollars cascading into the coffers of financially strapped central cities. For example, ARRA funded energy-efficient streetlights and stoplights, a program that benefitted small towns and suburbs, but had the greatest impact in cities dense with streetlights and highly trafficked intersections. ARRA funds also went to programs that subsidized the weatherproofing of low-income residents' homes, which likewise benefitted cities, especially in the Northeast and Midwest, with older housing stock, neighborhoods with concentrated poverty, and municipal agencies and nonprofits that could easily identify needy homeowners and manage the program. White House advisor Van Jones argued that weatherization would "green the ghetto," while training urban workers for new environmentally friendly jobs retrofitting older homes.[23] One urban economic sector was particularly well poised to benefit from Obama's domestic programs: healthcare. By the time Obama entered office, healthcare employed more than eighteen million people nationwide. More people worked in healthcare than in manufacturing. Hospitals comprised the fifth largest labor market in the country. And most of those jobs were urban, many clustered in or near minority-dominated neighborhoods. As industry decentralized and manufacturing moved to low-wage markets at home and overseas, hospitals had for the most part stayed rooted in cities. While commerce moved from downtowns to suburban malls and corporate offices fled to suburban office parks and corporate campuses, medical centers were sticky. As a result, the healthcare sector was at the top or near the top of the list of largest employers in nearly every major city, and the top employment sector for African Americans as well. Hospitals, in particular, provided a wide range of jobs, employing orderlies and janitors, nurses and neurosurgeons. And a growing number of healthcare jobs did not directly involve patient care. Major medical centers relied on an army of workers to enter data, ensure compliance with federal regulations, administer insurance policies, manage complex budgets, and procure supplies. In big cities that had hemorrhaged jobs, hospitals stanched the flow. Obama's stimulus program provided US$155 billion for healthcare, including a US$86 billion expansion of Medicaid, US$25 billion to upgrade medical information technology systems, and US$2 billion to bolster federal community health centers (a struggling, underfunded survivor of the Great Society), most of which were located in African-American and Latino neighborhoods in central cities.[24] Even more consequential for the healthcare sector was the Affordable Care Act.

ACA substantially reduced the number of uninsured patients and it provided a predictable income stream for medical centers, including charitable hospitals and big-city research hospitals, which carried the burden of serving large numbers of uninsured patients. The impact on hospital employment was indirect but substantial: the healthcare sector grew at a faster rate than the economy. Obamacare was a de facto job creation program.[25]

The ARRA and ACA bolstered urban economies, at least temporarily. But the administration's efforts to deal with another dimension of the Great Recession – the collapse of the home finance market – were notably less successful. Between the late 1990s and 2008, banks, hedge funds, and insurance companies had profited immensely from the deregulation of financial markets and, in particular, the dramatic overextension of home credit through predatory lending and subprime financing. The home lending crisis affected a wide swath of American communities, but it hit hardest in cities and older suburbs, particularly those with large nonwhite populations. In 2006, more than half of subprime loans nationwide went to African Americans, who comprised only 13 percent of the population. And a recent study of data from the Home Mortgage Disclosure Act found that 32.1 percent of blacks, but only 10.5 percent of whites, got higher interest mortgages – that is, mortgages with an annual percentage rate three or more points higher than the rate of a Treasury security of the same length.[26] The federal government – under both President George W. Bush and President Obama – oversaw the Troubled Assets Relief Program (TARP), which provided hundreds of billions to bail out failing financial institutions. Many Democrats argued that if the government salvaged banks, it should also provide aid to the victims of predatory lending. On the campaign trail, Obama promised to allow homeowners to modify their mortgages to prevent foreclosures and, in January 2009, the incoming administration pledged to set aside up to US$100 billion in funds to help underwater households reduce their mortgage payments. In February 2009, the administration launched the Making Home Affordable Program (MHA), which oversaw the Home Affordable Modification Program (HAMP). President Obama pledged that HAMP would bail out at-risk homeowners, just as the White House had bailed out insolvent banks. But he oversold the program. HAMP provided incentives to banks and mortgage servicers to work with at-risk borrowers to modify mortgages by reducing interest rates and making other changes in the terms of their mortgages. But the application and qualification process was complicated and burdensome. Lenders retained control over the loan modification process and often arbitrarily turned down applicants. Government regulators provided little oversight over the program. Although the president promised that the program would protect as many as four million households from foreclosure, fewer than one million eventually benefited from HAMP.[27]

Between the onset of the Great Recession and the end of Obama's presidency, nearly nine million American households had suffered foreclosures, with devastating consequences. In many large cities and overbuilt suburbs, neighborhoods were pockmarked with abandoned houses. The foreclosure crisis fell particularly hard on people of color. The Obama years saw a dramatic decline in household wealth (which for most Americans consisted primarily of equity in real estate), particularly among African-American and Latino homeowners who were more likely to have been the victims of both predatory lending and foreclosures. By 2011, the household wealth of blacks and Latinos reached a record low of only one-twentieth that of white Americans. The gap barely narrowed by 2013, the last year for which data are available.[28]

Thinking big

In the two years when stimulus dollars were flowing to cities, Obama embarked on a mission to streamline urban planning initiatives through interagency cooperation. Getting federal agencies to collaborate has been the holy grail of good government reformers since the New Deal. Cabinet members often view their agencies as fiefdoms and have great discretion to set their own priorities. Pulling their staffs together to work even on small projects was usually a logistical nightmare. Because urban policy did not fall under the purview of any single executive branch agency, federal officials often worked at cross-purposes or created duplicative programs. In July 2009, Obama stated that

> I've directed the Office of Management and Budget, the Domestic Policy Council, the National Economic Council, and the Office of Urban Affairs to conduct the first comprehensive interagency review in 30 years of how the Federal Government approaches and funds urban and metropolitan areas so that we can start having a concentrated, focused, strategic approach to Federal efforts to revitalize our metropolitan areas.

Among journalists covering the event, Obama's statement surely drew a yawn: it went unmentioned in news accounts. But because Obama had appointed arguably the most competent cabinet in decades, achieving interagency cooperation was one of his noteworthy successes. For the next few years, the Department of Housing and Urban Development, the Department of Transportation, the Department of Education, and the Department of Labor collaborated to an unprecedented extent.[29]

Interagency cooperation was especially important because the Obama administration hoped to address economic development, job creation, and affordable housing at the regional level, rather than simply focusing on communities or neighborhoods. Since the 1950s, city planners had fairly consistently called for metropolitan-wide interventions to mitigate unemployment, improve infrastructure, and repair failing schools. And they just as consistently came up against huge obstacles. Most American metropolitan areas were hopelessly balkanized into dozens – sometimes hundreds – of municipalities and school districts that usually reinforced deep city–suburban political, economic, and racial divides. Suburbanites looked at the cities they left behind with a mix of horror and romance, unwilling to pay for public works, schools, or social services for "those people" whom they blamed for urban decline. Many urban politicians, especially African Americans and Latinos, feared that regional cooperation was a thinly disguised attempt to wrest away their hard-won political power. But while advocates of regionalism struggled to gain political traction, metropolitan areas were remade by economic shifts that respected no municipal boundaries.

To deal with urban sprawl and environmental degradation required collaboration across city and county lines. To deal with the gap between where low-wage workers lived (mostly central cities) and where low-wage jobs were expanding (mostly suburbs and exurbs) required the expansion of affordable housing on the periphery and the improvement of surface transportation.[30]

By the time Obama was elected, a chorus of urban planners pushed the agenda of regional cooperation with urgency. Former Albuquerque, New Mexico, mayor David Rusk argued that the healthiest metropolitan areas were those with regional governance. University of Minnesota law professor Myron Orfield conducted studies of metropolitan areas throughout the country, arguing that municipal fragmentation was costly, that racial and socio-economic segregation jeopardized urban labor markets, and that older cities and their nearby suburbs had many common political interests. Most influentially, a group of scholars at the Brookings Institution, led by former Clinton administration official, Bruce Katz, promoted a new metropolitan policy, and produced influential books and reports documenting urban competitiveness, labor markets, business location, shifting demographic patterns, and housing needs. Their data pointed directly toward coordinated regional solutions. They made the forceful argument that urban problems were metropolitan problems, and vice versa.[31] Obama listened. In his most detailed campaign speech on urban issues, Obama criticized "an outdated 'urban' agenda that focuses exclusively on the problems in our cities, and ignores our growing metro areas; an agenda that confuses anti-poverty policy with a metropolitan strategy, and ends up hurting both." He acknowledged the need to address urban poverty, but argued for "investing in the clusters of growth and innovation" in different metropolitan regions around the United States.[32]

By his first year in office, he grafted that policy onto a call for sustainable growth. "For too long," stated Obama, "federal policy has actually encouraged sprawl and congestion and pollution, rather than quality public transportation and smart, sustainable development. And we've been keeping communities isolated when we should have been bringing them together." To that end, Obama hoped to build on a pilot Clinton administration program called Moving to Opportunity (MTO), which provided vouchers to public-housing-eligible urban residents to live outside of declining "inner city neighborhoods," where they would find better jobs and better schools.[33] Obama pulled together Ray LaHood, his secretary of transportation and one of the few Republicans in his cabinet, Shaun Donovan, the secretary of Housing and Urban Development, and Lisa Jackson, the head of the Environmental Protection Agency, to create an interagency group on sustainable cities to

> make sure that when it comes to development – housing, transportation, energy efficiency – these things aren't mutually exclusive, they go hand in hand. And that means making sure that affordable housing exists in close proximity to jobs and transportation. That means encouraging shorter travel times and lower travel costs. It means safer, greener, more livable communities.

HUD had a stake in bridging the gap between workers and job; Transportation had an interest in getting people to and from their workplaces; the EPA hoped to reduce carbon emissions. Obama hoped to provide incentives for transit-oriented development, namely dense townhouse and apartment projects and retail districts adjoining transit hubs.[34]

The stimulus package had included rail and highway transportation programs, but the funds needed to be spent down quickly to jolt the economy toward recovery. The ARRA specified that the stimulus funds be fully used by 2011. The time frame simply did not allow cabinet agencies to fully coordinate their investment strategies. Obama's vision of metropolitan planning had a somewhat longer horizon. But his ambitious plans were unfulfilled, put on the backburner when the administration channeled its energy toward healthcare, and then decisively crushed because of the obstructionist tactics of congressional Republicans who swept Congress in the Tea Party wave of 2010. Obama's hopes for urban light rail and high-speed intercity transit fell to austerity budgets; his plans for green and sustainable cities and suburbs found no Republican support. By 2012, Republicans had turned Obama's urban policy ideas against him. Conservative author Stanley Kurtz argued the president hoped to "force Americans out of their cars and into high-density urban centers, squeezing the population into a collection of new Manhattans. Obama also aims to force suburbanites to redistribute tax money to nearby cities while effectively merging urban and suburban school districts to equalize their funding." It was a nightmare scenario for suburban and exurban Republicans which echoed through the right-wing news media and on conservative websites through the 2012 election season.[35]

Thinking small

With a major regional agenda in tatters, Obama turned to small-scale interventions. In fundamental respects, he revisited and reinvigorated community-oriented urban development strategies that dated back to the Nixon administration. Post-Great Society federal urban programs had several distinct features that reflected a turn away from "big government" and toward the market. They were small in scale; they devolved policy decisions to states and municipalities. They privileged public–private partnerships over direct federal spending. They deployed pro-business incentives, including tax cuts and deregulation to encourage urban investment. They demanded the reorganization of public-sector institutions so that they resembled private businesses. And they valued competition, individual initiative, and discipline. For all of Obama's rhetoric about change, his urban programs did not fundamentally deviate from these principles.

Obama, like all presidents, built on precedents, his options shaped and constrained by his predecessors' legacies. In particular, Obama offered an updated version of Enterprise Zones, an idea first hatched by British conservatives in the 1970s, imported to American think-tanks in the 1980s, and baked into federal urban policy during the George H. W. Bush administration. EZs were carved out of rundown, usually old industrial sections of cities, and offered special incentives, loans, tax breaks, and laxer regulations to firms that located there. In the 1990s, the Clinton administration rebranded the program as Empowerment Zones, adding a nominal community participation requirement, but otherwise changing little. Some states, like Pennsylvania, offered their own version of EZs, creating tax-free zones as honey pots to lure corporate headquarters to declining downtowns; and some municipalities offered lucrative tax abatements to attract investors to rehabilitate older homes or build new ones in central city neighborhoods. What all of these programs shared was the use of government to spur market activity where it might not otherwise happen. The record of EZs and related programs was mixed at best: many zones attracted few employers, and state and local tax abatement programs drained municipal tax coffers and transferred wealth to developers, corporations, and well-to-do homeowners, with few public benefits.[36]

Since his days as a community organizer, Obama had been attracted to community-based economic development initiatives and supported the principle of public–private partnerships and federal incentives behind the Enterprise and Empowerment Zones. But, befitting his emphasis on "comprehensive" urban programs, Obama grafted anti-poverty initiatives, housing, social services, and education onto the EZ model. He took as his inspiration the Harlem Children's Zone, a program launched in New York in the early 2000s by education reformer Geoffrey Canada. The Harlem Children's Zone combined education, social services, preschool and academic enrichment programs for students, and childrearing training programs for poor parents-to-be. Obama described it as "an all-encompassing, all-hands-on-deck effort that's turning around the lives of New York City's children, block by block." Whatever its positive benefits (and those were intensely debated), the Harlem Children's Zone was small in scale, expensive to administer, and shaped by the vision of a single, charismatic leader.[37]

Whether Canada's experiment could be replicated on a nationwide scale was a doubtful proposition. It depended on hundreds of millions of dollars in support from hedge fund managers, investment banks, and private foundations in New York that only funded a program that covered a few dozen blocks in one city. No other city in the United States had New York's depth of wealthy donors. To replicate the program elsewhere would require massive federal investment. But convinced that the model would work, Obama launched "Promise Neighborhoods," modeled on the Harlem Children's Zone, in the summer of 2009. The program would "make grants available for communities in other cities to jump-start their own neighborhood-level interventions that change the odds for our kids."[38] Promise Neighborhood grants (what he called a "community innovation fund") would provide seed money to nonprofits, but not sustained federal investment in disadvantaged communities. To assuage his critics – and attract private donors – Obama justified the program in market-friendly terms: its goal "was giving people the tools they need to pull themselves up." In method, rhetoric, and goals, Promise Neighborhoods were a far cry from the major interventions that the federal government had made in urban redevelopment and public education during the Great Society.[39]

Closely related to Promise Neighborhoods, but with a substantially larger financial commitment, was the Department of Education's support for the expansion of privately run, publically funded charter schools. Charter school experiments proliferated beginning in the 1990s, the result of a bipartisan push to bring "market discipline" to public education, by letting nonprofits, individual entrepreneurs, and educational corporations manage public schools. In most cities, like Chicago, where Obama's Secretary of Education Arne Duncan had run the public school system, charters were loosely regulated. Premised on the ideals of competition (parents were consumers with the right to choose the "best" school for their children), charters often skimmed higher-achieving students from neighborhood schools. Most charters did not provide special education services. Through strict disciplinary procedures, they regularly forced out troubled students. And charter school CEOs had authority to override teachers' collective bargaining agreements and food service and maintenance union work rules. In effect, many charters were de facto private schools that drained enrollment and funds away from neighborhood schools.

Adolfo Carrion, the first head of the Office of Urban Affairs, singled out one project as exemplary of the administration's place-based programs: the construction of a new charter school on 129th Street in Harlem. The project required coordination across cabinet-level agencies and relied on elaborate public–private partnerships. The US Department of Education provided US$60 million. The remainder came from big investors. The investment bank Goldman Sachs, looking to burnish its image after the Great Recession, donated US$20 million. Google added another US$6 million. The school's general contractor donated US$5 million of in-kind support. The Department of Housing and Urban Development oversaw the remapping of a city street through one of its housing projects there. It was a complicated venture, its small scope a reminder of the limits to the administration's efforts to reshape American cities.[40]

Like the Harlem Children's Zone, charter schools were a distinctive creature of the post-*Brown* v. *Board of Education* era. Rhetorically, Obama supported the principle of Brown that racially separate education could not be equal. But in practice, Brown was mostly a dead letter. In the aftermath of court decisions – from *Milliken* v. *Bradley* (1975) that rendered most metropolitan-wide school desegregation plans impermissible to Parents United (2007) that struck down even voluntary efforts to create racially balanced schools – most education policy took entrenched racial segregation as a given. The rationale behind charters was that if most minority and low-income children were to be concentrated in underperforming schools in troubled school districts, perhaps new forms of school administration or new curricula or loosened teacher hiring and firing procedures would solve the problem.[41]

Obama linked schooling, housing, and employment in his next place-based initiative, "Choice Neighborhoods," launched in 2011. Choice Neighborhoods built on HOPE VI, a federally funded program, which expanded rapidly in the Clinton years, to replace postwar urban public housing projects with mixed-income, low-rise developments, usually with detached or semi-detached houses designed to resemble their suburban counterparts, often with porches overlooking fenced yards and driveways. Obama watched as neighborhoods near his own state senate district were transformed as the gloomy modernist towers fell. Chicago's mayor Richard M. Daley aggressively deployed HOPE VI funds to demolish and redevelop the city's infamous Cabrini-Green, Robert Taylor, and State Street Homes. HOPE VI was riddled with problems: it did not come close to meeting the demand for new, decent, affordable housing and it displaced many public housing residents, while enriching politically connected developers and community development organizations. In some neighborhoods, like the gentrifying North Side neighborhood around Cabrini-Green, the destruction of the projects fueled a massive boom in new luxury housing, adding to the city's affordable housing crunch.[42]

Obama mended but did not end HOPE VI. Choice Neighborhoods would provide grants to link residents of new, federally underwritten HOPE VI-type developments to anchor institutions, including universities, medical centers, convention centers, and downtown districts. Many HOPE VI communities – like the public housing projects they replaced – were geographically isolated, cut off from good public transit, and distant from jobs. Choice Neighborhoods provided relatively small grants to cities and civic groups, with hopes of leveraging additional funds from businesses, nonprofits, and foundations to connect impoverished residents with jobs. Obama launched yet another place-based program, Promise Zones, in January 2014. A hybrid of Clinton's Empowerment Zones and the Promise Neighborhoods experiments, Promise Zones brought the federal government together in partnership with municipal economic development agencies, local nonprofits, and philanthropists to improve schools and incubate small businesses through grants and tax incentives, and to improve the delivery of municipal services. Using the language of small government and personal responsibility, Obama pledged that the federal government would support poor areas, "not with a handout but as partners with them every step of the way."[43]

Of the twenty-two Promise Zones, fourteen were located in impoverished urban areas (the remainder were rural communities and Indian reservations). Promise Zone grants were small, and so were the program's achievements. The administration used its website to highlight its modest successes: the opening of a community grocery store that employed forty workers in Sacramento, California; US$2.1 million in federal funding to launch a recycling program that would hire ex-convicts in East Indianapolis; and US$14.2 million in US Department of Education to seventeen schools in Los Angeles to prepare students for college by helping them develop "non-cognitive skills . . . such as confidence and resiliency." On Atlanta's West Side, federal grants would support the construction of a new football stadium, with hopes that it would "catalyze commercial activity."[44]

Obama came into office with a mandate for change. He drew deep support from urban voters who hoped that his presidency would reverse the drift of federal policy from "benign neglect," through devolution, to market-based solutions. But the scope and scale of his urban programs was minuscule compared to the magnitude of social, economic, and educational problems that metropolitan America faced. Obama attempted to rebuild, expand, or retool existing programs, and streamline the federal agencies responsible for coordinating transportation, labor, housing, and education policy. Obama bears some of the blame for the weakness of his urban policy. He was a product of the bipartisan neoliberalism of the late twentieth century, too enamored of market-based solutions and public–private partnerships to fight for a more vigorous public sector. He was too cautious when it came to pushing pro-integration policies, particularly in public education and housing, fearful of firing up racial animosities and alienating white suburban and exurban voters. But, even more so, Obama was a captive of a climate of fiscal austerity and, after 2010, of bitter congressional hostility to any significant domestic policy initiatives. Perhaps, when it came to responding to persistent urban inequality and joblessness, Choice Neighborhoods and Promise Zones were the best the Obama administration could do.

Under Obama's watch, government took third fiddle to private capital and philanthropy when it came to setting an urban agenda. In cities, the federal government had become, in effect, a decent-sized foundation, providing grants to support urban demonstration projects, offering a flicker of hope at least until the grants dried up and the local philanthropic and business "partners" moved on. In the meantime, American metropolitan areas remain, with a few exceptions, deeply divided socio-economically and still fragmented by race, still struggling with troubled schools. In Obama's last two years in office, American cities began to burn again, as protestors and the police clashed and as big cities like Baltimore, Milwaukee, and Ferguson, Missouri, exploded. Even the president's adopted hometown, Chicago, was rocked by tense protests, against the police, but also against charters and school closings, a process that began under Arne Duncan; against evictions and gentrification; and against a downtown-oriented mayor who left his office in the West Wing to move into Chicago's city hall just months later. American urban policy has only feebly responded to the ongoing crises.

Acknowledgments

This chapter was written with the support of the Carnegie Corporation of New York. Thanks to Andrew Diamond, Gary Gerstle, Nick Guyatt, Alice O'Connor, and Julian Zelizer for their comments on this chapter, and to participants in workshops at Princeton and Cambridge for their feedback.

Notes

1. Executive Order 13,503, 74 Federal Register 8139, February 19, 2009. For a mostly optimistic early assessment see "Obama's Urban Policy: A Symposium," *City and Community*, 9, 1 (March 2010): 3–60.
2. Richard Florida, *The Rise of the Creative Class and How It's Transforming Work, Leisure, and Everyday Life* (New York: Basic Books, 2002); Alan Berube, Bruce Katz, and Robert Lang, *Redefining Urban and Suburban America: Evidence from Census 2000* (Washington, DC: Brookings Institution, 2005); Edward Glaeser, *The Triumph of the City: How Our Greatest Invention Makes Us Richer, Smarter, Greener, Healthier, and Happier* (New York: Penguin, 2011); Alan Ehrenhalt, *The Great Inversion and the Future of the American City* (New York: Knopf, 2012).
3. Jacob Rugh and Douglas S. Massey, "Segregation in Post–Civil Rights America: Stalled Integration or End of the Segregated Century?" *Du Bois Review*, 11, 2, October 2014: 205–232; Patrick Sharkey, *Stuck in Place: Urban Neighborhoods and the End of Progress toward Racial Equality* (Chicago: University of Chicago Press, 2013); Gary Orfield, John Kucsera, and Genevieve Siegel-Hawley, *E Pluribus . . . Separation* (Los Angeles: UCLA Civil Rights Project/ Proyecto Derechos Civiles, September 2012).
4. Sean F. Reardon and John T. Yun, "Integrating Neighborhoods, Segregating Schools: The Retreat from School Desegregation in the South, 1990–2000," *North Carolina Law Review*, 81 (2003):

1563–1596; Gary Orfield, *Schools More Separate: Consequences of a Decade of Resegregation* (Cambridge, MA: Harvard University Civil Rights Project, 2001).

5. Heather Ann Thompson, "Why Mass Incarceration Matters: Rethinking Crisis, Decline, and Transformation in Postwar American History," *Journal of American History*, 97 (2010): 703–734.

6. In 2006, more than half of subprime loans went to African Americans, who comprised only 13 percent of the population. And a recent study of data from the Home Mortgage Disclosure Act found that 32.1 percent of blacks, but only 10.5 percent of whites, got higher priced mortgages – those with an interest rate three or more points higher than the rate of a Treasury security of the same length. See Debbie Gruenstein Bocian, Wei Li, Carolina Reid, and Roberto G. Quercia, *Lost Ground, 2011: Disparities in Mortgage Lending and Foreclosures* (Durham, NC: Center for Responsible Lending, 2011), http://www.responsiblelending.org/mortgage-lending/research-analysis/Lost-Ground-2011.pdf; Matthew Desmond, *Evicted: Poverty and Profit in the American City* (New York: Crown, 2016).

7. Roger Biles, *The Fate of Cities: Urban America and the Federal Government, 1945–2000* (Lawrence: University Press of Kansas, 2011); Michael B. Katz, *The Price of Citizenship: Redefining the American Welfare State* (Philadelphia: University of Pennsylvania Press, 2008); Jamie Peck, "Pushing Austerity: State Failure, Municipal Bankruptcy, and the Crises of Fiscal Federalism in the USA," *Cambridge Journal of Regions, Economics, and Society*, 7, 1 (2014): 17–44.

8. On Obama's background, see Thomas J. Sugrue, *Not Even Past: Barack Obama and the Burden of Race* (Princeton, NJ: Princeton University Press, 2010); David Remnick, *The Bridge: The Life and Rise of Barack Obama* (New York: Simon & Schuster, 2010); David Maraniss, *Barack Obama: The Story* (New York: Simon & Schuster, 2011). See also Obama's own memoir, *Dreams From My Father* (New York: Times Books, 1995).

9. Andrew J. Diamond, *Chicago on the Make: Power and Inequality in a Modern City* (Berkeley: University of California Press, 2017); Sugrue, *Not Even Past*, esp. chapter 1.

10. Costas Spirou and Dennis R. Judd, *Building the City of Spectacle: Mayor Richard M. Daley and the Remaking of Chicago* (Ithaca, NY: Cornell University Press, 2016).

11. Andrew J. Diamond, "Chicago: A City on the Brink," *Books and Ideas*, May 15, 2012, http://www.booksandideas.net/Chicago-A-City-on-the-Brink.html

12. I served as a mostly passive member of the campaign's Urban Advisory Committee; my comments are based on my reading of the hundreds of messages that came through the listserv.

13. Fredrick C. Harris, *The Price of the Ticket: Barack Obama and the Rise and Decline of Black Politics* (New York: Oxford University Press, 2012); Sugrue, *Not Even Past*, chapter 3.

14. For examples, see Barack H. Obama, "Remarks in Spartanburg, SC," June 15, 2007, http://www.presidency.ucsb.edu/ws/index.php?pid=77003; Barack H. Obama, "Remarks in Washington, DC: 'Changing the Odds for Urban America,'" July 18, 2007, http://www.presidency.ucsb.edu/ws/index.php?pid=77007; Barack, H. Obama, "Remarks to the U.S. Conference of Mayors," Miami Florida, June 21, 2008, http://www.presidency.ucsb.edu/ws/index.php?pid=77555&st=urban&st1=; and "Democratic Convention: Obama Promotes Plan for Urban Development," *Wall Street Journal*, August 25, 2008.

15. Barack H. Obama, "Remarks to the National Association of Education Annual Meeting in Philadelphia," July 5, 2007, http://www.presidency.ucsb.edu/ws/index.php?pid=77006; Obama, "Remarks to the U.S. Conference of Mayors;" Bruce Katz, "Obama's Metro Presidency," *City and Community*, 9, 1 (March 2010): 23–31.

16. Executive Order 13,503; Thomas J. Sugrue, "Carter's Urban Policy Crisis," in *The Carter Presidency*, ed. Gary Fink and Hugh Davis Graham (Lawrence: University Press of Kansas, 1997), 137–157.

17. For details on the staff, programs, and initiatives of the White House Office of Urban Affairs, see https://obamawhitehouse.archives.gov/urbanaffairs

18. "National Conversation of America's Cities and Metropolitan Areas," "Urban Tours," and "Urban Policy Working Groups," Office of Urban Affairs Initiatives, https://obamawhite house.archives.gov/administration/eop/oua/initiatives

19. Quoted in "New White House Office to Redefine What Urban Policy Encompasses: Agenda May Address Suburbs Too," *The Washington Post*, July 3, 2009.

20. "Obama to Cities, Drop Dead: The Life and Death of a Great American Urban Policy," *New York Observer*, February 15, 2012, http://observer.com/2012/02/obama-to-cities-drop-dead-the-life-and-death-of-a-great-american-urban-policy/. Theda Skocpol and Lawrence Jacobs, eds., *Reaching for a New Deal: Ambitious Governance, Economic Meltdown, and Polarized Politics in Obama's First Two Years* (New York: Russell Sage, 2011). It is also notable

that none of the essays in the book focused on civil rights, a topic that is, in many respects, closely related to urban policy.

21. "Obama's Urban Affairs Office Brings Hope but Not Much Change," *The Huffington Post*, July 26, 2013.

22. The American Recovery and Reinvestment Act of 2009 (Pub. L. 111–5); for an overview, see the White House information pages and blogs about ARRA: https://www.whitehouse.gov/recovery/about. On the impact of the stimulus on education employment, see ED Recovery Act Report, Summary of Programs and State-by-State Data, http://www2.ed.gov/policy/gen/leg/recovery/spending/index.html

23. For a general overview, see Michael Grunwald, *The New New Deal: The Hidden Story of Change in the Obama Era* (New York: Simon & Schuster, 2012), Van Jones quoted on p. 305. Hilary Silver, "Obama's Urban Policy: A Symposium," *City and Community*, 9, 1 (March 2010): 5, calls the ARRA a "stealth" urban program.

24. For details, see American Recovery and Reinvestment Act of 2009. Generally on the impact of healthcare spending on cities, see Daniel Gitterman, Joanne Spetz, and Matthew Fellowes, "The Other Side of the Ledger: Federal Health Spending in Metropolitan Economies," Discussion Paper, Brookings Institution Metropolitan Policy Program, September 2004, http:// www.brook.edu/metro/pubs/20040917_gitterman.htm; Margaret Pugh O'Mara, *Cities of Knowledge* (Princeton, NJ: Princeton University Press, 2005); Guian McKee, *Health-Care Policy as Urban Policy: Hospitals and Community Development in the Postindustrial City* (Charlottesville: University of Virginia, Miller Center for Public Affairs, 2010).

25. The Patient Protection and Affordable Care Act of 2010 (Pub. L. 148): https:// www.gpo.gov/fdsys/granule/PLAW-111publ148/PLAW-111publ148/content-detail.html. "Since Obamacare Was Passed Fifty Months Ago, Healthcare Has Gained One Million Jobs," *Forbes*, June 6, 2014; "Obamacare Is Creating More Jobs Now: Will There Be More Health Care Costs Later?" *Forbes*, July 2, 2015. The most substantial healthcare job growth occurred after the expansion of healthcare enrollment in 2014, and cannot be attributed entirely to the ACA. The population continued to age and the economy had been rebounding from recession since late 2009.

26. Gregory D. Squires and Derek S. Hyra, "Foreclosures – Yesterday, Today, and Tomorrow," *City & Community*, 9, 1 (March 2010): 50–60; Algernon Austin, "Subprime Mortgages Are Nearly Double for Hispanics and African Americans," Economic Policy Institute,

June 11, 2008, http://www.epi.org/economic_snapshots/entry/web-features_snapshots_20080611/; Andrew Jakabovics and Jeff Chapman, "Unequal Opportunity Lenders? Analyzing Racial Disparities in Big Banks' Higher Priced Lending," Center for American Progress, September 2009, http://www.americanprogress.org/issues/2009/09/pdf/tarp_report.pdf; Jennifer Wheary, Tatjana Meschede, and Thomas M. Shapiro, "The Downside before the Downturn: Declining Economic Security among Middle-Class African Americans and Latinos, 2000–2006," Brandeis University, Institute on Assets and Social Policy and Demos, n.d., http://www.demos.org/pubs/bat_5.pdf; Douglas S. Massey and Jacob S. Rugh, "Racial Segregation and the American Foreclosure Crisis," *American Sociological Review*, 75 (2010): 629–651.

27. Squires and Hyra, "Foreclosures." For the Department of Treasury's ongoing evaluation of MHA and HAMP, see https://www.treasury.gov/initiatives/financial-stability/TARP-Programs/housing/mha/Pages/Surveys.aspx. For critical overviews of the program, see David Dayen, "Obama Program That Hurt Homeowners and Helped Big Banks Is Ending," *The Intercept*, December 28, 2015, https://theintercept.com/2015/12/28/obama-program-hurt-home-owners-and-helped-big-banks-now-its-dead/ and "Obama Failed to Mitigate America's Foreclosure Crisis," *Atlantic*, December 14, 2016.

28. Rakesh Kochhar, Richard Fry, and Paul Taylor, *Twenty-to-One: Wealth Gaps Rise to Record Highs between Whites, Blacks and Hispanics* (Pew Research Center, Social and Demographic Trends, July 26, 2011), http://www.pewsocialtrends.org/2011/07/26/wealth-gaps-rise-to-record-highs-between-whites-blacks-hispanics/

29. Barack H. Obama, "Remarks in a Discussion on Urban and Metropolitan Policy," June 13, 2009, http://www.presidency.ucsb.edu/ws/?pid=86417. On the history of efforts at executive branch reorganization, see Brian Balogh, Joanna Grisinger, and Philip Zelikow, *Making Democracy Work: A Brief History of Twentieth Century Executive Reorganization* (Miller Center of Public Affairs, University of Virginia, Working Paper, July 2002). On Carter's effort to coordinate urban policy across federal agencies (which Obama alluded to in his 2009 speech), see Sugrue, "Carter's Urban Policy Crisis."

30. Margery Austin Turner, "New Life for US Housing and Urban Policy," *City and Community*, 9, 1 (March 2010): 35–36.

31. David Rusk, *Cities without Suburbs* (Baltimore, MD: Johns Hopkins University Press, 1993); Myron Orfield, *Metropolitics: A Regional*

Agenda for Community and Stability (Washington, DC: Brookings Institution, 1997); Bruce Katz, ed., *Reflections on Regionalism* (Washington, DC: Brookings Institution, 2000); Bruce Katz and Robert Puentes, *Taking the High Road: A Metropolitan Agenda for Transportation Reform* (Washington, DC: Brookings Institution, 2005); and especially Bruce Katz and Jennifer Bradley, *The Metropolitan Revolution: How Cities and Metros Are Fixing Our Broken Politics and Fragile Economy* (Washington, DC: Brookings Institution, 2013). For a comprehensive overview, including an archive of reports, see Brookings Metropolitan Policy Program, https://www.brookings.edu/program/metropolitan-policy-program/

32. See, especially, Obama, "Remarks to the U.S. Conference of Mayors."
33. Ibid.
34. Obama, "Remarks in a Discussion on Urban and Metropolitan Policy." U.S. Conference of Mayors, "DOT Secretary Ray LaHood, HUD Secretary Shaun Donovan, and EPA Administrator Lisa Jackson Announce Interagency Partnership for Sustainable Communities," July 13, 2009, http://www.usmayors.org/usmayornewspaper/documents/07_13_09/pg10_lahood.asp
35. Stanley Kurtz, *Spreading the Wealth. How Obama Is Robbing the Suburbs to Pay for the Cities* (New York: Sentinel, 2012); Ben Adler, "Urban Nation: How Stanley Kurtz Is Defending the Suburbs from His Own Doomsday Fantasy," *Next City*, August 22, 2012.
36. Timothy P. R. Weaver, *Blazing the Neoliberal Trail: Urban Political Development in the United States and the United Kingdom* (Philadelphia: University of Pennsylvania Press, 2016).
37. Obama, "Changing the Odds for Urban America." Few urban ventures appealed to Obama more than the Harlem Children's Zone. For an overview, see Paul Tough, *Whatever It Takes: Geoffrey Canada's Quest to Change Harlem and America* (Boston, MA: Houghton Mifflin, 2008). Obama was on a program with Canada in 2009, and favorably mentioned Canada and the Harlem Children's Zone in several speeches. Barack H. Obama, "Remarks on Community Service Programs," June 30, 2009, http://www.presidency.ucsb.edu/ws/index.php?pid=86358
38. Obama, "Remarks in a Discussion on Urban and Metropolitan Policy."
39. Barack H. Obama, "Remarks on the 20th Anniversary of the Points of Light Institute," College Station, Texas, October 16, 2009, http://www.presidency.ucsb.edu/ws/index.php?pid
40. "Obama to Cities, Drop Dead."

41. Thomas J. Sugrue, *Sweet Land of Liberty: The Forgotten Struggle for Civil Rights in the North* (New York: Random House, 2008), chapter 13; Davison M. Douglas, *Reading, Writing, and Race: The Desegregation of the Charlotte Schools* (Chapel Hill: University of North Carolina Press, 1995); Matthew Lassiter, "'Socioeconomic Integration' in the Suburbs: From Reactionary Populism to Class Fairness in Metropolitan Charlotte," in *The New Suburban History*, ed. Kevin M. Kruse and Thomas J. Sugrue (Chicago: University of Chicago Press, 2005), 140–143; *Milliken v. Bradley*, 418 U.S. 717 (1974); *Capacchione v. Charlotte-Mecklenburg Schools*, 57 F. Supp. 2d 228 (1999); *Parents Involved in Community Schools v. Seattle School District No. 1*, 551 U.S. 701 (2007).
42. Promise Neighborhoods Act of 2011 (H.R. 2098 and S. 1004); David Raskin, "Revisiting the Hope VI Public Housing Program's Legacy," *Governing* (May 2012), http://www.governing.com/topics/ health-human-services/housing/gov-revisiting-hope-public-housing-programs-legacy.html; "Fighting Poverty and Creating Opportunity: The Choice Neighborhoods Initiative," Department of Housing and Urban Development, *PD&R Edge Magazine*, https://www.huduser .gov/portal/pdredge/pdr_edge_frm_asst_sec_101911.html
43. Weaver, *Blazing the Neoliberal Trail*, 281; White House, Office of the Press Secretary, "Fact Sheet: President Obama's Promise Zone Initiative," https://obamawhitehouse.archives.gov/the-pressoffice/2014/01/08/fact-sheet-president-obama-s-promise-zones-initiative; Barack H. Obama, "Remarks on the Promise Zones Initiative," January 20, 2014, http://www.presidency.ucsb .edu/ws/index.php?pid=104576
44. White House, Office of the Press Secretary, "Obama Administration Releases Final Round of Promise Zone Designations," June 6, 2016, https://obamawhitehouse.archives.gov/the-press-office/2016/06/06/obama-administration-announces-final-round-promise-zone-designations

8

From Clinton to Obama to Trump: The politics and political economy of health insurance reform

Nelson Lichtenstein

Passage and implementation of the Patient Protection and Afford-able Care Act (ACA or Obamacare) was the most significant domestic accomplishment of the Obama administration, an expansion of the US welfare state unmatched since the era of the Great Society. Although an imperfect piece of social legislation, the ACA culminated nearly a century of progressive struggle on the health provision front, bringing to American society European levels of health insurance coverage. Obamacare, as both its detractors and supporters came to label it, was based on a taxation regime that was remarkably progressive, that bent the healthcare industry cost curve downward, while in the process reawakening the idea that the Democrats and other liberals might again inaugurate an era of New Deal-ish welfare state building.

And yet, the ACA was structured in a radically discordant fashion. Its origins lay in a self-contradictory corporatist compact, one which linked the ACA to a set of neoliberal, market-centric mechanisms that left intact many of the most dysfunctional tensions inherent in American politics and political economy. The ACA was forever forced to contend with market forces that it could not control and that at any time threatened to sabotage the law's capacity to deliver affordable health insurance. Moreover, the corporatism that gave birth to Obamacare deprived the health insurance law of a degree of democratic legitimacy, a debility that hyper-partisan Republican opponents leveraged against the law during every moment of its existence and despite its manifest success in reducing the proportion of American citizens still without health insurance.

This chapter makes three substantive points. First, the failure of the Clinton Health Care plan in 1993 and 1994 proved crucial to the shape and the eventual legislative passage of the ACA. Second, and despite all its limitations, the ACA had two outstanding successes. It was an extraordinarily progressive piece of legislation when it came to revenues and expenditures. It taxed the wealthy, the truly rich, and spent money on the poor and the lower middle class. But the third point is equally important: despite providing health insurance for 22 million uninsured Americans, which dropped the rate of the uninsured from a post-recession high of 18 percent to 11 percent in early 2016,[1] Obamacare never escaped the intense partisanship which almost destroyed it at birth. Unlike Social Security and Medicare, whose beneficiaries came to constitute a powerful bloc that sustained these expansions of the welfare state, the ACA proved a lightning rod for partisan conflict, even in states and regions where it radically improved not just health insurance coverage but medical provision itself and the health of hundreds of thousands of individuals. Ironically, the ACA's near-death encounter during the first year of the Trump administration proved a turning point, and thereafter its popularity with the general public finally achieved majoritarian support and political bite.

The Clinton legacy

To understand the ACA, both its success and failures, one must revisit the effort to pass comprehensive health insurance legislation in 1993 and 1994. President Clinton and his wife Hillary, who was initially in charge of the healthcare project, rejected a Canadian-style single-payer system. Although recognizing its economic efficiency and political popularity, they argued that healthcare reform had to be built on the existing system of employer-paid benefits and private insurance. By the early 1990s this had become the majority position among Democratic Party advocates of health insurance reform, despite much continuing support for a single-payer system. Instead, the Clinton plan put a tight "global" cap on insurance and hospital costs, thereby making it possible for the government to "mandate" that all large employers provide health insurance for all their employees. Those not so employed would join "alliances" where they could purchase subsidized health insurance from regulated companies. But unlike the Obama plan fifteen years later, the employer mandate stood at the contentious heart of the Clinton law. It represented a retreat by labor and liberals from the single-payer idea, as in Medicare, but it was thought more politically feasible because it built on the existing and long-standing tradition of employer provided health insurance in the United States.[2]

The Clintons counted on support from those high-wage business sectors that already provided health insurance: the new employer mandate would cost them nothing but instead spread insurance costs equally among all employers. American auto companies paid more for health insurance than for steel, but Walmart, Marriott, and thousands of other low-wage service sector firms shifted the healthcare costs of their employees to the state, to charity, or to other firms' payrolls. Walmart, which had nearly a million workers at the end of the twentieth century, provided a health insurance package that was so burdensome and inadequate that less than 50 percent of its employees subscribed. The Clinton plan would have mandated that all large employers provide affordable insurance. "Right now, big companies pay all of the health costs of small companies that are not providing insurance," argued one pro-reform businessman. "It's another form of tax."[3]

But the Clintons miscalculated. American capitalism had transformed itself dramatically since the last era of healthcare reform in the 1960s, and low-wage, low-benefit companies in the swollen service sector, especially restaurants and retailers, bitterly resisted employer mandates. In addition, almost all the smaller insurance companies, who sought the youngest and least risky clients, assailed the plan. A service sector revolt against the employer mandate generated something close to a coup within the Chamber of Commerce, which had initially favored Clintonite reform at the behest of many big, old-line manufacturing companies like Chrysler and Bethlehem Steel.[4] Likewise, a set of smaller insurance companies, who made money by "cherry picking" the most healthy and profitable clients, feared that the system of "managed competition" championed by the Clintons would put them at a disadvantage when it came to new regulations and a fight over market share with the big five insurance firms of that era, who were willing to turn themselves into something close to a utility in return for millions of new government mandated customers. Hence these smaller insurance companies, organized into the Health Insurance Association of America, sponsored the infamous but highly influential set of "Harry and Louise" TV advertisements of 1993 and 1994, which equated employer mandates and cost controls with a cumbersome and intrusive federal government.[5]

Indeed, the fate of the Clinton plan turned into a referendum on the capacity of the state to resolve social problems and advance a welfare state agenda. The Clinton reforms would have instituted a new layer of social citizenship, symbolized by a uniform health security card the government would issue to every American. But conservatives feared such an entitlement, less because of the expense than because of the legitimacy it conferred on governmental activism. Thus, during the months when the Chamber of Commerce was debating the degree to which it would support the Clinton plan, congressional Republicans demanded that the Chamber reject any compromise, while back in their districts and states these same Republicans urged their small business constituents to make their voices heard at the Chamber and other business associations. Note the irony: politicians lobbying the lobbyists to sabotage Clinton's corporatist compact.[6]

The ideological stakes in this fight were graphically highlighted in late 1993 when journalist and sometime Republican advisor Bill Kristol wrote a memo to GOP legislators and activists that remains perhaps the single most important document laying out the rational for wall-to-wall conservative opposition to healthcare reform, both in the early 1990s and in the years since 2009. Kristol was the son of Irving Kristol, arguably the most important theorist of neo-conservative ideology in the post-1968 era. The younger Kristol, who had abandoned any vestige of solicitude for the welfare state, once a neo-con trace element still detectable from their New Deal heritage, argued that any Republican compromise with Clinton would "likely make permanent an unprecedented federal intrusion into and disruption of the American economy." It would help the Democratic electoral prospects in forthcoming contests, but of even more ideological and cultural consequence, warned Kristol, a successful Clinton plan, "will revive the reputation of the party that spends and regulates, the Democrats, as the generous protector of middle-class interests." Republicans therefore had to "adopt an aggressive and uncompromising counter strategy" to "delegitimize" the Clinton plan and bring about its "unqualified political defeat."[7]

The Kristol strategy had a long afterlife. In subsequent years, Republicans would be willing to expand the welfare state – as with the subsidy for prescription drugs, Medicare Part D, passed during the administration of George W. Bush – but they sought to root such initiatives as much as possible in the private insurance market, not a benevolent state. Equally important, when they were willing to expand the welfare state it had to be under GOP leadership; otherwise they were unalterably opposed. Hence, in both the 1990s and throughout the era of the Obama administration, we find that in a world of extreme partisanship, Republicans – in the legislature, the states, and on the courts – often sought not only to block passage of most health insurance laws but to sabotage or politicize their implementation.

During the 2009 debate over the Obama health insurance reform, when some Republicans toyed with compromise and co-sponsorship, Senate Minority Leader Mitch McConnell made clear that a unified opposition was a ruthless but imperative political tactic. He later said, "It was absolutely critical that everybody be together because if the proponents of the bill were able to say it was bipartisan, it tended to convey to the public that this is O.K., they must have figured it out."[8] McConnell's hardball strategy worked. The idea that Obama and the Democrats steamrollered Congress and enacted a hyper-partisan, if not socialist, law proved decisively successful in stimulating conservative anger and Republican solidarity.

Democrats took Kristol to heart as well. If Republicans were so afraid of an expansion of the welfare state under Democratic Party auspices, seeing it as game-changing ideological repudiation of Reaganism, why then the Democrats would proceed full steam ahead, reasonably certain that once something approaching universal health insurance was in place, its roots would sink as deeply into the body politic as Social Security and Medicare. The settled existence of these programs naturalized both the taxes needed to pay for them and the benefits tens of millions of citizens enjoyed and expected. Political scientists have long made this point: an innovative public policy, no matter how initially divisive, creates its own mass constituency and therefore a "feedback loop" that in turn sustains the new public policy and the loyalty of the electorate that benefits from that governmental program. "New policies create a new politics" is the way some social scientists have put it.[9]

But this liberal conviction would not fully crystalize until the start of the Obama administration. By the late summer of 1994, when the Clinton health plan expired in Congress, even many Democrats had abandoned the ambitious effort to restructure one-seventh of the US economy. That failure proved an ideological victory for the likes of Bill Kristol and laid the basis for Republican capture of the House of Representatives for the first time since 1946. The era of ambitious Clinton reformism was over, even if some incremental expansions of the welfare state, including the 1997 Children's Health Insurance Plan and still later the 2003 expansion of Medicare drug benefits, a Bush administration project, were still possible. In the mid-1990s healthcare inflation did moderate, both because of the regulatory scare engendered by the Clinton plan and because of the rapid rise of health maintenance organizations (HMOs), which had eclipsed hospitals and individual physicians as the primary providers of medical services. But health insurance was still linked primarily to employment, which meant that when unemployment and healthcare inflation resumed their upward trajectory early in the twenty-first century, millions of additional citizens were left stranded without medical insurance.[10] By the time the next chance for a major overhaul of the American healthcare system arrived after Obama's 2008 victory, the Democrats shaped both their political strategy and the very structure of their plan in reaction to the failed Clinton initiative. They would do what Clinton did not do in 1993 and 1994.

Obama's opportunity

In some instances, the differences were those of circumstance, not conscious planning. Obama had a much bigger electoral mandate than Clinton and the Democrats fifteen years before. Equally important, his congressional majorities were much larger than those of Clinton and they were more ideologically united. Even conservative Democrats were on board. The so-called blue dog Democrats knew that failure spelled certain defeat, as it had for Democratic moderates and conservatives in 1994. So virtually all Democrats were ultimately in favor of reform, even if they were wont to insist that the law remain within carefully constrained parameters in return for their vote. Such party unanimity, especially in the Senate, was essential if the Democrats were to retain a filibuster-proof sixty-vote majority, even if only for a brief few months in the fall of 2009.[11]

Second, and despite the Great Recession, Obama put health insurance reform at the top of his agenda, right after passage of an emergency economic stimulus, but before the Democrats began a push for much needed regulation and reform of the banking industry. The stimulus passed quickly, in February 2009, which left the field clear for healthcare. In contrast, Bill Clinton had allowed a divisive debate over the North American Free Trade Agreement to precede a big push for health insurance reform, thereby sapping the energy and unity congressional Democrats would need to pass healthcare legislation.

Third, Obama let Congress do it. While the White House had a plan, Obama let Congress do most of the work in putting together the legislation, a decisive contrast to the legislation-writing task forces that the Clintons assembled in 1993 before they submitted an administration bill to Congress.[12] Obama felt that such a strategy was possible because, as we shall see, most Democrats agreed on the essential elements of any health insurance reform in 2009, a stark contrast to 1993.[13] The key Congressional Committee was Senate Finance, where Obama and Chairman Max Baucus hoped to get some Republicans on board, in particular Iowa's Charles Grassley who was on record favoring the individual mandate as a healthcare analogue to compulsory auto insurance.[14] This extended the negotiations for several additional months and ended in partisan failure, but the orientation toward Congress and the Republican demonstration of intransigence probably served to keep conservative and maverick Democrats like Joe Lieberman and Jim Webb on board, even if the price was elimination of a government funded "public option" among the health insurance plans from which the uninsured might choose.[15]

Fourth, Obama proved a more skillful corporatist than did Clinton. It was still crass and crude, but his team avoided the conflicts and betrayals that bedeviled Clinton as business and insurance support for his plan collapsed. There was nothing pretty about Obama's corporatist deal-making, and it is the thesis of this chapter, especially in light of the Trump victory, that such elite sausage making opened wide the door to partisan attack from the GOP and sharp criticism from liberals and leftists inside the Obama coalition. And from the perspective of the Tea Party grassroots, which surged to prominence in the summer of 2009, such corporatism seemed an elite conspiracy not dissimilar from the multi-billion dollar bailouts that had saved the big banks, brokers, and insurance companies just a few months before. Obama's team thought cutting deals with potential high-profile opponents was a necessary strategy for dampening and dividing opposition while a new framework for health insurance was put in place. Rahm Emanuel, Obama's chief of staff, and Senate Finance Committee Chair Max Baucus took the lead in developing this game plan. As *The New York Times* put it, they would "keep powerful groups at the table (and) . . . prevent them from allying against (Obama) as they did against Clinton." David Axelrod, who had orchestrated Obama's electoral victory in 2008, thought such accommodations with stakeholders was the price of "getting things done within the system as it is."[16]

The first and most important bargain struck by Obama was a quid pro quo with the insurance industry. In exchange for guaranteed issue – no insurance company could henceforth deny a policy to an individual because of a pre-existing condition – the government would mandate, under an escalating financial penalty, that all individuals, including the young and healthy, purchase medical insurance if they did not already have it through a government program or through their employer.[17] They would buy it through a set of insurance exchanges designed to be run by the states or, if these jurisdictions declined, by the federal government. The purchase of such insurance policies would be subsidized by the federal government, sometimes at a ratio of as much as eight or nine federal dollars for every dollar paid by an individual. The divisive employer mandate was not quite dropped, but it was made far less financially onerous, even to the low-wage, low-benefit service sector firms which had revolted against the Clinton plan.[18]

Originally, the individual mandate had been a Republican idea, put forward by some individuals associated with the Heritage Foundation in the early 1990s and then championed by GOP moderates such as John Chafee of Rhode Island. Its advocacy by elements of the Republican hard right in the early 1990s was almost certainly a cynical ploy to subvert the Clinton health insurance plan, but the Democrats thought that they could make it work fifteen years later with enough carrots – government financed insurance subsidies for moderate income people – and sufficient sticks, which in this instance entailed the threat to slash tax refunds for all those who failed to purchase health insurance. Combined with such a penalty, the individual mandate had worked in Massachusetts, where Mitt Romney, a moderate Republican governor, had proudly worked with a Democratic legislature to create a state-level insurance exchange that had boosted insurance coverage to the highest in the nation, and without much backlash against this mildly coercive government mandate.[19]

Although the insurance industry would make billions from the 20 million new policies they were expected to issue under the ACA, they were ambivalent about the overall scheme. In 2009 they worried about new competition from a "public option, run by the government," which might be enacted if the private policies on the exchanges proved too expensive or inadequate. More important, the insurance companies were not sure that in exchange for "guaranteed issue," a major concession on their part, enough healthy young customers would sign up through the exchanges. Indeed, it is telling that what ultimately prompted insurers to move into formal opposition to Obama and the bills developing in Congress was the September 2009 decision of the Senate Finance Committee – under pressure from Republicans – to weaken the planned penalties for Americans who, after 2014, did not obtain insurance. This weakening of the individual mandate worried private insurers because they feared that new reform regulations would force them to take all patients regardless of health conditions, whereas insignificant penalties for people choosing not to buy insurance would allow a lot of younger Americans to skip coverage. And in subsequent years the industry was proven largely right: even before a Republican Congress eliminated the individual mandate in 2017, millions of young singles chose to pay a penalty to the IRS rather than sign up for health insurance on an exchange. But the irony remains: despite ads and criticisms of Obamacare as representing too much government, insurers moved into opposition to the bill only when they came to believe the individual mandate penalties were too low, when too little government coercion was applied to those they hoped would constitute a new set of customers.[20]

A more successful deal was struck with the big drug companies in June 2009. Working with both Max Baucus, the moderate Democrat, and Ted Kennedy, the liberal lion of the Senate, the Obama White House struck an agreement with Big Pharma. The industry had been a bitter and effective opponent of the Clinton health insurance plan, but now the industry would offer US$80 billion over ten years in rebates, assessments, and contributions. In return it received a commitment from the administration and Baucus to resist measures opposed by the industry, such as permitting reimportation of drugs from outside the United States or downward Medicaid and Medicare price pressure on pharmaceutical products. The deal was immediately attacked by Republicans, who saw another conspiracy, and by liberals who wanted Canadian-style governmental buying pressure applied to the big drug companies. But the deal stuck: Big Pharma refrained from attacking the Obama plan, and in fact contributed some US$150 million in advertising to support the reform, including a new set of Harry and Louise commercials touting the ACA.[21]

A similar compact was reached with the hospital industry, which agreed to US$155 billion in Medicare and Medicaid payment reductions in return for the vast new number of paying patients they would reap from an expansion of health insurance under the ACA. The hospitals expected that once most people had some form of medical insurance, the ultra-expensive use of emergency rooms would sharply decline, likewise the cost of charity care for those who showed up at hospitals without adequate insurance.[22]

No formal compact was reached with the business community and most of the major business associations, including the
Chamber of Commerce and the National Retail Federation went
on record in opposition to the Obama health insurance program.
But their bark was much less than their bite in 2009 because
the absence of a tough employer mandate greatly moderated
the Clinton-style cost shifting between old line unionized manufacturing industries and the much larger low-cost retail/service
sector.[23] Under Obama the major cost of his healthcare plan would
be borne by wealthy individual taxpayers, not by the corporations
per se. All firms with more than fifty workers who did not offer at
least a minimum creditable coverage and whose workers – at least
one – secured subsidized coverage from an exchange were required
to pay a penalty, in some cases up to US$2,000 per employee. But
this was not a mandate, which would have cost much more, and,
as we shall see, the expansion and upgrading of Medicaid took
many low-wage workers out of the insurance market entirely and
therefore out of the hands of corporate benefit managers. For a
company like Walmart, whose own pre-Obama plan had been so
unattractive that barely 45 percent of its own employees signed
up, the ACA relieved the company of much responsibility and
embarrassment. It was a de facto subsidy to the company, which
is one reason that Walmart President H. Lee Scott could share a
podium with the SEIU's Andy Stern at a June 2009 press conference endorsing Obamacare's essential framework.[24]

All this corporatist deal-making reduced interest group opposition to healthcare reform and began to bend the cost curve downward, if slowly and over a multi-decade span. But the absence of
an employer mandate – a de facto tax on many employers, upon
which the Clinton administration had depended – meant that the
Obama scheme would have to rely far more than the Clinton
plan upon a set of tax increases to pay for both an expansion of
Medicaid and the subsidies necessary to make the state insurance
exchanges work, since large subsidies were now required for millions of middle-income families soon forced to either buy health
insurance or pay the penalizing mandate fee.

A few liberal fireworks should explode right here! The taxes
incorporated into the Obama ACA were highly progressive and

represented the most consequential redistribution of income, from the top to the bottom, that Americans had seen since the imposition of World War II-era hyper-taxes on the very rich. Unlike the regressive payroll taxes used to pay for Social Security and Medicare, Obamacare added a 3.8 percent additional tax on all incomes above US$250,0000 per family, not just on wages, but on investment income as well, including capital gains from stocks and real estate which have powered so many of the fortunes of the super-rich. In addition, Medicare payroll taxes were also increased .9 percent with no upper limit, thereby making the really wealthy pay an additional 4.7 percent tax to fund medical care for the poor and the lower middle class. Both of these taxes generated an additional US$230 billion to pay for the health reform, about a quarter of all new revenue over a ten-year span. The Congressional Budget Office estimated that another US$106 billion would come from employers who failed to offer adequate insurance for their own workers.[25] As the key Senate staffer and Edward Kennedy aide John McDonough put it in his 2013 account of how the ACA was muscled through Congress: "For progressives, this is an enormous and positive breakthrough in tax policy heretofore considered untouchable; to conservatives the policy is anathema." Theda Skocpol concurred: "Affordable Care's funding represents the most progressive tax reform in several generations."[26]

The new taxes, especially the uncapped levy on the investment and dividend income that generated so much wealth for the one percent, could never have been passed in a bipartisan fashion. The GOP boycott of the ACA negotiations in the fall and winter of 2009–2010 meant that the Democrats were negotiating with themselves, and therefore shifted tax policy leftward. Thus, when Republican-controlled Congresses in the years after 2011 repeatedly called for a repeal of Obamacare, most news reportage saw their ire directed at the sometimes-clunky state insurance exchanges and the individual mandate burdening some middle-class families. But those were fiscal sideshows when compared to the truly progressive, redistributive tax regime that paid for so much of the health reform.

The revenue raised by those taxes went straight from the top of the American income pyramid to the bottom – paying for a dramatic

expansion and improvement of Medicaid, a means-tested program
with a reputation that seemingly discredited any effort to directly
provide health provision for the poor and near poor. In 1965, when
the Johnson administration enacted Medicare, Medicaid seemed
almost an afterthought. It was conceived as an addition to state-run
welfare programs, and like other forms of "welfare" it was stigma-
tized, underfunded, and a political whipping boy. The federal government provided between 50 and 75 percent of its funding, with
the higher proportion going to the poorer states, but those administrative units set the criteria for eligibility and the kind of benefits
that might be awarded. Doctors and hospitals were reimbursed at
a lower rate than for Medicare's seniors, so many refused to take
Medicaid patients at all. Various scams and corruptions were rife
among those physicians and other medical personnel who saw these
neglected patients and then sent the bill to poorly regulated state
Medicaid administrators. Republicans, and not a few liberals, were
contemptuous of this quasi welfare program and the role it was des-
tined to play in the ACA. Republican Senator Richard Burr called
Medicaid "the most dysfunctional delivery system that exists in the
American health care system," while Texas Senator John Cornyn
called it a "health care 'gulag.'"[27]

But the ACA greatly transformed and improved Medicaid,
moving it a considerable distance from "welfare" and planting
it firmly within a national system of health provision. The first
thing that Obamacare did was to establish a set of national eligibility standards, which vastly improved access among the poor
and near poor in Southern and Plains states. No longer would
eligibility be limited to mothers with small children or the disabled. Instead, anyone with an income less than 138 percent of
the poverty line (in 2018, US$16,753 for an individual, not far
below many full-time Walmart clerks) could enroll. Second, payment schedules were improved for physicians and health services
expanded.[28] They did not reach Medicare standards, but there
was now much more money in the system because under the
ACA the federal government assured states that it would pay
for 100 percent of the additional cost of enrolling new recipients under the expanded Medicaid system during the years 2014
through 2016, and then progressively less each year until 2020

when fully 90 percent of expenses would be from the federal treasury.[29]

The expansion of Medicaid proved an outstanding success, with enrollments 50 percent greater than those projected by the Congressional Budget Office in 2010. By the end of 2015 Medicaid and the closely-linked Children's Health Insurance Plan enrolled almost 71 million people, a 14.1 million increase since the plan was expanded in 2013. In Arkansas, which accepted ACA funding and expanded eligibility standards, enrollment rose by 60 percent, in West Virginia by 61 percent, in Nevada by 83 percent, and in populous California by 54 percent.

Meanwhile, another 5 million people would almost certainly have been enrolled if the Supreme Court in 2012 had not allowed states to reject Medicaid money and the new eligibility standards under ACA. Thus, in Texas and Florida alone, where Republican governors and legislatures turned down ACA Medicaid expansion, more than two and a half million lower-income people have no access to the new program. In those states, enrollment rose by just 17 percent and 6 percent respectively. But when a Southern state did adopt the new program, the results were dramatic. In Kentucky, where a Democratic governor was an ACA partisan, Medicaid and CHIP enrollment leaped more than 101 percent in less than three years, with almost half a million new people covered in 2016. By way of contrast, Kentucky enrollment in the ACA health insurance marketplaces, where more than 75 percent of those purchasing private insurance policies were subsidized by the federal government, remained quite modest, with just over 100,000 signing up.[30] Indeed, marketplace enrollment has been a disappointment nationwide. Although the Congressional Budget Office once estimated that by 2016 21 million individuals would purchase health insurance through these regulated exchanges, the actual number was far lower, about 13 million, including 11 million with subsidized coverage and 2 million without.[31]

The Medicaid experience might well be something of a "natural experiment" in which a single-payer system has demonstrated its superiority over that of the hybrid public/private ACA insurance exchanges. Unlike the exchanges, one could enroll in Medicaid at any time during the year: there was no time-limited open enrollment period. Medicaid requires no deductibles and no co-pays. And while insurance companies were sometimes involved in administering state-level Medicaid programs, enrollees did not pay any premiums. This was the responsibility of the government, federal and local. Where state officials have championed the program, especially on the West Coast, in New England, and in poor states where liberals were in charge, Medicaid constitutes something close to "socialized" medicine for the bottom half of the American working class. In Kentucky almost a third of all residents are in the program, thus dropping the state's uninsured rate to 7.5 percent in 2016, from 20 percent in 2013. In some former mining counties 60 percent of all residents are covered by Medicaid.[32]

Why Obamacare remains divisive

Yet Obamacare remains utterly divisive, and not just in partisan Republican circles but among those who benefit most from its provisions. While Donald Trump's victory in Appalachia and the Rust Belt might seem to exemplify this phenomenon, it is even more clearly evident in the 2015 gubernatorial victory of Republican Matt Biven, who promised to dismantle Kentucky's insurance exchange and roll back much of the Medicaid expansion that had benefitted so many in his state. Indeed, Biven's success was most notable in the very Eastern Kentucky counties where Medicaid expansion held the most impact. In desperately poor Clay County, where 60 percent of the 21,000 residents are covered by Medicaid, Trump won 87 percent of the vote in 2016 while Biven took 70 percent the year before. By all accounts Medicaid was a popular program in Clay County, but it did not build a constituency that translated that sentiment into political support.[33]

The same proved true throughout the nation. Majorities did like key aspects of the health insurance plan, like guaranteed issue and the enrollment of children up to age twenty-six on their parent's health insurance policy, but during the Obama presidency the popularity of the law never rose much above the 45 percent approval it achieved when first introduced to the American public in 2009.[34] Bill Kristol was wrong in Clay County and similar localities and so too were his liberal opponents who thought that once Obamacare reached the grassroots, it would sink deep into the nation's political topsoil. So why were both liberals and conservatives wrong on this score? Why did Obamacare take so long to win a constituency commensurate with the transformation it made in American healthcare provision?

There were four reasons. First, Obamacare was thoroughly politicized by its opponents from day one. GOP leaders in Congress and conservative activists elsewhere were determined to make this expansion of the welfare state an utterly partisan phenomenon and demonize the law even before the Democrats framed the legislation and sent it on to the president for his signature. In a twenty-eight-page memo written by pollster Frank Luntz in the spring of 2009, Republicans were urged to use the phrase "government takeover" when referencing the Democratic healthcare bill.[35] Other GOP militants, including those funded by the Koch brothers, mobilized by the Tea Party, or lobbied by the Heritage Action (the Heritage Foundation's political arm) were determined to "lock in" conservative opposition to the law, which explains the seemingly endless series of votes, seventy by some counts, designed to put Republicans on the record in favor of "repeal." No reforms or modifications, even when helpful to employers or other elements of the Republican coalition, would be proffered because such adjustments merely served to legitimize the legislation and relieve the pressure for its complete abolition.[36]

Thus, in an era of intense polarization, such partisan demonization was enough to divorce the actual social and economic impact of the scheme from the political allegiances one might expect it to generate. "The campaign by the Affordable Care Act critics against it has been very effective in demonizing the phrase Obamacare and anything to do with the president," remarked the pro-ACA Kentucky Governor Steven Beshear who in 2014 was then in the process of expanding Medicaid coverage despite much legislative opposition. "So I think you find a reluctance on the part of people, even though the law is benefitting them, to publicly acknowledge it."[37]

Second, the corporatist deal-making which helped give birth to Obamacare continued to impact the program throughout its short history. Many identified the concessions made to Big Pharma, the insurance companies, and the rest of the health industrial complex with the extraordinarily unpopular bailouts of the big financial institutions that inaugurated the Obama presidency. Republican Senator John McCain called all this "unsavory deal-making," a charge later amplified at scores of Tea Party protests and citizen confrontations with Democratic legislators during home district meetings held during the 2009 congressional recess.[38] The insurance exchanges did work, but they were cumbersome to use and they represented a wager on the efficient functioning of the insurance marketplace, which in effect made a core welfare state function dependent upon an oligopolistic set of for-profit businesses whose financial health stood in a fundamental tension with the social purposes of the ACA.

Third, Obamacare, unlike that of its Clintonite predecessor, had been designed to have as little impact as possible on the workings of the employer-provided system whereby most Americans still found their health insurance. Some liberals had expected a steady migration of individuals from the world of employer-provided health insurance to the exchanges, but this did not happen, possibly because of the economic recovery that gained momentum after 2013. This meant that for good or ill, the ACA barely touched the lives of the vast majority of employed Americans or those on Medicare. The ACA was an abstraction, especially in the years before 2014, when Medicaid was expanded and the insurance exchanges finally came on line. That long delay gave conservatives an imaginative field when it came to the law's shortcomings. The opposition could say "This will kill jobs, pestilence will come, vermin will fall from the sky," remembered Kathleen Sebelius, the Obama administration's Health and Human Services Secretary at the time. Meanwhile, supporters of the law could only say, "Wait and see."[39] Indeed, even after the ACA had been in existence for many years, few ordinary Americans could explain how the insurance exchanges worked or what was involved in the extension of Medicaid to newly eligible individuals.

And finally, the very progressivity of the ACA worked against it. The people who were helped the most, those enrolled in Medicaid or those who received generous subsidies on the insurance exchanges, were the least vocal, the least engaged, and the least likely to vote, a disposition of which Republican governors and legislators were well aware. After visiting his home state, Kentucky, right after the Biven gubernatorial victory in 2015, *New York Times* reporter Alec MacGillis explained the dramatic conservative tilt of Eastern Kentucky and other impoverished counties this way, "the people who most rely on the safety net programs secured by Democrats are, by and large, not voting against their own interests by electing Republicans. Rather, they are not voting, period. They have, as voting data, surveys and my own reporting suggest, become profoundly disconnected from the political process."[40] Republican politicians understood this all too well. When a top advisor to Senator McConnell was asked if Republicans were afraid of the electoral consequences of depriving health insurance to four or five hundred thousand people newly covered by the Obamacare, he replied, "People on Medicaid don't vote."[41]

Meanwhile, those with the most difficult relationship to the new program – families earning above US$92,000 a year – paid unsubsidized insurance premiums that bought them policies that often included high deductibles and co-pays as well as seemingly unpredictable rate hikes. But these were precisely the strata of families and individuals who were the vocally engaged voters, certainly far more than those whose ACA benefits were more generous.

Saving the Affordable Care Act

All this would seem to have made Obamacare's demise a near certainty once the unexpected election of Donald Trump gave Republicans control of both Congress and the presidency after the 2016 elections. And, indeed, on his first full day in the White House Trump signed an executive order to "seek the prompt repeal" of the Affordable Care Act.[42] When it came to Social Security and Medicare, previous Republican administrations had promised to "save" these programs by raising the age of eligibility, reducing benefits, restricting coverage, or privatizing and contracting out key provisions, but Trump and the conservatives he now appointed to administer Obamacare repeatedly described the law as a "disaster," ready to "implode" and in a "death spiral." Repeal and replacement were the only solutions.

Although Trump himself might well have been somewhat less hostile to the welfare state than many GOP legislators, he also wanted a legislative "win," and so too did the Republicans who had defined their party over four election cycles as the steadfast advocate of Obamacare repeal. It was foundational, like the anti-Communism of the Cold War era. Any equivocation would in the words of Josh Holmes, a Republican strategist and former aid to the Senate Majority Leader, create a "catastrophic narrative" that would demoralize and fragment the Republican base. The cold reality, said Holmes in the spring of 2017, was that the phrase "President Trump's efforts to repeal Obamacare" still held the approval of more than 90 percent of core Republicans.[43]

But the Republicans, who were crafting repeal legislation in the spring of 2017, were not just driven by ideology. The Party sought a drastic tax reduction for the donor class, and tax reduction for the rich remained one of the few planks upon which party moderates and conservatives could unequivocally agree. Medicaid, both the expanded version legislated by the Affordable Care Act and traditional Medicaid that had existed for decades before the new law, is expensive and paid for by some of the most progressive taxes enacted since World War II. Thus, it was not surprising that every iteration of the GOP repeal bills put forward in 2017 took direct aim at Medicaid, slashing about US$750 billion out of its budget over a ten-year span. Add to this the US$425 billion that the GOP repeal bill sought to cut from the exchanges, mainly subsidies designed to make the individual market affordable for those families earning less than US$92,000 a year, and more than US$1.2 trillion was at stake over the next decade. All this would reduce the federal deficit by several hundred billion dollars, money that Republican leaders planned to "spend" when they got around to their big tax cut initiative once Obamacare repeal was out of the way.[44]

Another feature of GOP repeal legislation, the effort to end Obamacare's prohibition against denying insurance coverage to people with pre-existing medical conditions, was extraordinarily unpopular in early 2017 and in the run-up to the 2018 midterm elections. But from the Republican perspective, there was a certain demographic and political logic to this seemingly suicidal policy gambit. "Guaranteed issue," the legal and economic mandate that required insurance companies to sell a comprehensive policy to anyone regardless of pre-existing health conditions, had been one of the few parts of Obamacare that enjoyed near universal applause. And for good reason, because by some estimates 133 million Americans suffered from a chronic malady or injury. There was no obvious price tag attached to this mandate, nor any obvious class bias. Indeed, the proscription against denial of coverage on account of a pre-existing condition had a particularly beneficial impact on those middle-aged and more affluent Americans who before Obamacare had been shut out of the health insurance market, even when they could afford it. Under Obamacare, all exchange policies had to offer ten essential benefits to any policyholder. This increased the overall cost of the average insurance policy, but also made sure that those with pre-existing conditions could actually buy one.

It therefore seemed that conservatives were shooting themselves in the foot when they demanded, first in a House bill that passed in early May 2017, and then in legislation that came before the Senate in July of that same year, that the government no longer mandate that insurance companies cover such essential benefits or guarantee issue of an affordably priced policy for all. Most on the left thought of this GOP gambit as another example of free market ideology run amuck, which was not really at variance with the ultra-conservative House Freedom Caucus efforts to eviscerate any and all Obama-era regulations governing the sale and subsidy of private insurance. In the Senate, Texas Republican Ted Cruz put forth an amendment allowing insurers to once again sell whatever bare-bones coverage they desired, with just one ineffectual condition: that insurance companies would have to offer one plan that complied with Obamacare's existing comprehensive benefits standard.[45]

Most insurance companies, not to mention any and all defenders of Obamacare, denounced this plan, decrying the perversity and irresponsibility of such a dichotomous scheme, arguing that it would segregate the insurance market into one for the young and healthy, who are unlikely to need or want comprehensive coverage, and a smaller and much more expensive market for the old and sick, who will see their premiums, even with government subsidies, skyrocket. But from the GOP point of view there was much to gain from the Cruz/Freedom Caucus gambit. One of the real problems with the exchanges, especially for those not eligible for a government subsidy, has been the high premiums and even more burdensome deductibles. By allowing insurance companies to sell stripped-down policies to healthy young adults, the GOP right-wingers would demonstrate that for a considerable slice of the population, perhaps 30 or 40 million in all, a bare-bones plan would reduce unsubsidized insurance costs, even as a smaller and less healthy slice found themselves in what amounted to a high-risk pool inadequately funded by federal or state governments. GOP partisans thought they could head into the 2018 campaign season with legislation that might well appeal to tens of millions: elimination of the individual mandate, deregulation of the insurance market, and a reduction of premiums for many grateful – and healthy – constituents. And the Congressional Budget Office agreed, forecasting that within a few years insurance premiums would decline by 20 percent, albeit for policyholders with a bare-bones, high-deductible policy.[46]

The GOP effort to repeal Obamacare failed, not once but twice. The first failure achieved a Hollywood-like climax when John McCain, whose fatal brain cancer had become known just a week earlier, left an Arizona hospital and flew back to Washington in order to join GOP moderates Lisa Murkowski and Susan Collins in a July 28 early-morning vote against the most recent iteration of their own party's gut-Obamacare effort.[47] What seems remarkable is that only three Republican Senators voted no, given the extraordinary unpopularity of the GOP bill (it was supported by just 17 percent in contemporary polls) and by the opposition of every substantial stakeholder, including hospitals, insurance companies, Big Pharma, and virtually every association of medical professionals in the country. A decentralized but widespread set of citizen protests, largely uncoordinated by the Democrats or former Obama-era health experts, made life exceedingly uncomfortable for many Republican Congressmen and senators in their home districts. Add to that the well-advertised CBO estimate that defunding the ACA would throw upwards of 22 million off the insurance rolls, and it would have seemed that repeal of Obamacare was overdetermined. But in the end, it lacked just one Senate vote to pass.[48]

But that was not the end of the story and there would be a second GOP failure to repeal or cripple the law. The McCain vote assured that tax revenues would continue to sustain Obamacare, but administration of the law remained firmly in the hands of people like Secretary of Health and Human Services Tom Price, who as a Republican Congressman from Georgia had been a leader of the drive to repeal Obamacare, and Seema Verma, Administrator of the Centers for Medicare & Medicaid Services, who as a health administrator in Indiana had worked with then governor Mike Pence to implement the nation's most highly restrictive Medicaid expansion program, one which required premium payments and work obligations from the newly covered population. Along with President Trump and most other Republicans, who continued to claim that Obamacare was imploding, these administrators had a political and personal investment in making the ACA as dysfunctional as possible, so as to rob it of the public support the law had won during the repeal fight in the spring of 2017.

Thus the Trump administration slashed the Obamacare advertising and outreach budget by 90 percent in the weeks leading up to the health insurance enrollment period in the fall of 2017, a time window that itself had been cut in half by the new administration. The Trump administration also tossed aside an Obama-era effort to overturn a lower court ruling that eliminated ACA subsidies to insurers designed to aid low-income families. Meanwhile, Verma's Centers for Medicare & Medicaid Services encouraged conservatively led states to impose work requirements and premium fees for those individuals eligible for Medicaid. These "waivers" were designed to make signing up for Medicaid more onerous, as in the pioneering Indiana program, thereby reducing the size of the Medicaid population and eroding its character as a universal entitlement for those earning below the poverty threshold. For those with a higher income, the administration sought to create a set of more loosely regulated insurance plans that would appeal to the young and healthy. These would be cheap, but

257

because they promised to distort the market for those who still bought high-standard insurance on the Obamacare exchanges, the new plans threatened to increase premiums for everyone else, especially those with a pre-existing condition.[49] And, finally, the Republicans eliminated the individual mandate as part of their big tax reduction bill that Congress approved and President Trump signed in December 2017. Over the next decade, the Congressional Budget Office estimated that elimination of the mandate might well reduce insurance coverage by 13 million people and spike premiums for those remaining on Obamacare roles.[50]

The Democrats and other supporters of the ACA charged the Trump administration with attempting to "sabotage" the healthcare law. But despite those efforts, the essential structure of Obamacare remained largely intact. By the end of 2018 about 20 million people still held insurance directly subsidized through the ACA, of which three-fifths were covered via the expansion of Medicaid. And federal dollars continued to flow: nearly US$1.6 trillion forecast between 2019 and 2028. Insurance companies raised their rates in 2016 and 2017 and enrollment among unsubsidized customers in the individual market plummeted nearly 30 percent as premiums rose, but among the much larger group of subsidized exchange enrollees, participation actually rose by six percent between 2015 and 2017. Indeed, most exchange customers hardly noticed because of the large subsidies that were still funded and available through the federal government.[51]

Meanwhile, public support for Obamacare rose steadily in the months after Congressional Republicans failed to repeal the law in July 2017. By the time the 2018 midterm election season got fully underway, many GOP stalwarts no longer campaigned to repeal the ACA outright but instead promised to preserve key provisions, especially those mandating that insurance companies cover everyone with a pre-existing condition, a central pillar of the law and a provision that all GOP repeal efforts, both legislative and legal, would have either eliminated or greatly reduced. In an election which returned Democrats to the majority in the House of Representatives, more than 40 percent of all voters declared healthcare their most important issue, far above immigration or the economy. Thus, for the first time in nearly a decade, Democrats actually campaigned on a promise to secure and expand Obamacare, with many advocating "Medicare for All," a single-payer extension of the ACA. Although progressive Democrats in the South campaigned on platforms that put expansion of Medicaid at the top of their agenda, failure to win governorships in Georgia and Florida or more state legislative seats in key Southern states meant that the old Confederacy remained a bastion of resistance to an expansion of health provision. But in the rest of red-state America, the expansion of Medicaid had become a winning issue. Democrats pledged to Medicaid expansion won governorships in Kansas, Maine, and Wisconsin, while in conservative Utah, Idaho, and Nebraska voters overwhelmingly approved referendums mandating expansion of the program.[52] "Republicans Abandon the Fight to Repeal and Replace Obama's Health Care Law," ran a *Washington Post* headline the day after the 2018 elections. "Health care was on the ballot," rejoiced House Democratic leader Nancy Pelosi, "and health care won."[53]

Conclusions

Three conclusions arise from this brief Obamacare history. First, Bill Kristol was right. It took nearly a decade, but the Affordable Care Act finally achieved popular legitimacy, if only because its near-death experience at the hands of a Republican Congress seemed to concentrate the public mind. Democratic success in the 2018 midterm elections seemed to ratify Kristol's fears that near-universal health insurance would indeed "revive the reputation of the party that spends and regulates, the Democrats, as the generous protector of middle-class interests." Second, this achievement was a product not just of popular sentiment but also arose out of the deal-making corporatism that gave birth to Obamacare in the first place. Because the Obama-era architects of the ACA had carefully bought off all the key stakeholders within a sprawling healthcare industry, the law appeared unseemly, but it was also remarkably sturdy. Despite all their hyper-partisanship and their denunciation of the healthcare law as anti-capitalist, Republicans failed to detach any of the powerful players – the drug and insurance companies, hospitals, medical societies, and medical device makers – from support of the law. It might offend left-wing sensibilities, but all of these money-making enterprises had a large stake in the success of an entitlement that promised to send their profits skyward.

Finally, and perhaps ironically, the one significant failure of the law promised to ease the path toward an even more robust and universal welfare state. The insurance exchanges, especially those administered by the federal government, were relative failures. They enrolled but half the number initially forecast, they were dependent on the goodwill and profitability of a shifting series of private insurance companies, deductions were far too high, and government subsidies were too low – or nonexistent – to relieve the healthcare cost burden on families that were barely middle class. Meanwhile, the ACA's expanded and enhanced Medicaid program had proven an unexpected success. Although not all those enjoying its benefits credited Obamacare itself with their good fortune, the program worked, especially in those states that actually tried to make it work. Its single-payer simplicity contrasted starkly with the Rube Goldberg complexity of the insurance exchanges, which were also more easily distorted and subverted by GOP efforts to rewrite the rules and sabotage this public–private collaboration. All this has spurred on progressive efforts to let the exchangers fall by the wayside and transform Obamacare into a truly universal, single-payer program. And this renewed social democratic impulse may well be the most important legacy to emerge out of the travail endured by the social entitlement that bears the name of America's 44th president.

Notes

1. Stephanie Marken, "U.S. Uninsured Rate at 11.0%, Lowest in Eight-Year Trend," Gallup.com Health, April 7, 2016.
2. Among the key books on the Clinton Health Care Plan and its origins, see Marie Gottschalk, *The Shadow Welfare State: Labor, Business, and the Politics of Health Care in the United States* (Ithaca, NY: Cornell University Press, 2000); Jacob Hacker, *The Road to Nowhere: The Genesis of President Clinton's Plan for Health Security* (Princeton, NJ: Princeton University Press, 1997); Theda Skocpol, *Boomerang: Clinton's Health Security Effort and the Turn Against Government in U.S. Politics* (New York: W.W.Norton, 1996); Colin Gordon, *Dead*

on Arrival: The Politics of Health Care in Twentieth-Century America (Princeton, NJ: Princeton University Press, 2003); and Jill Quadagno, *One Nation Uninsured: Why the U.S. Has No National Health Insurance* (New York: Oxford University Press, 2005).

3. As quoted in Gordon, *Dead on Arrival*, 252. And see Nelson Lichtenstein, *The Retail Revolution: How Wal-Mart Created a Brave New World of Business* (New York: Picador, 2010), 286–295.

4. John Judis, "Abandoned Surgery: Business and the Failure of Health Reform," *American Prospect* online, spring 1995.

5. Skocpol, *Boomerang*, 136–137. At that time, the big five insurance companies were Prudential, Met Life, Aetna, CIGNA, and John Hancock, all of whom were involved with managed care reforms and willing to deal on government regulations.

6. Paul Starr, *Remedy and Reaction: The Peculiar American Struggle over Health Care Reform* (New Haven, CT: Yale University Press, 2013), 112–119.

7. William Kristol, "Defeating President Clinton's Health Care Proposal," Project for a Republican Future, December 2, 1993. Reprinted in *Talking Points Memo Online*, September 24, 2013.

8. Norman Ornstein, "The Real Story of Obamacare's Birth," *The Atlantic*, July 6, 2015.

9. See for example Andrea Louise Campbell, "Policy Makes Mass Politics," *Annual Review of Political Science*, 15, June 2012: 333–351.

10. Starr, *Remedy and Reaction*, 146–151.

11. For a good blow-by-blow account of passage of the ACA see Lawrence R. Jacobs and Theda Skocpol, *Health Care Reform and American Politics: What Everyone Needs to Know* (New York: Oxford University Press, 2016), 50–67; and Starr, *Remedy and Reaction*, 235–238.

12. Ezra Klein, "The Lessons of '94," *American Prospect* online, January 20, 2008.

13. Paul Starr makes the point that by the time he assumed office, President Obama had been convinced by Hillary Clinton, during the long 2008 Democratic primary, that her framework for health reform, including the necessity of an individual mandate, was the proper policy choice. Obama had been the most conservative of the three Democratic presidential candidates and had opposed the mandate idea during the primaries.

14. John McDonough, *Inside National Health Reform* (Berkeley: University of California Press, 2011), 81.

15. Starr, *Remedy and Reaction*, 228.

16. Jacobs and Skocpol, *Health Care Reform and American Politics*, 69.
17. Paul Starr, *Remedy and Reaction*, 218.
18. McDonough e-mail to author, November 17, 2016.
19. N. C. Alzenman, "Health-care Provision at Center of Supreme Court Debate was a Republican Idea," *The Washington Post*, March 26, 2012. However, the conservative columnist Ramesh Ponnuru argues that the individual mandate was hardly a universally supported idea on the right even in the early 1990s, "The History of the Individual Mandate," *National Review*, March 27, 2012.
20. Jacobs and Skocpol, *Health Care Reform and American Politics*, 73–74.
21. McDonough, *Inside National Health Reform*, 76; W. James Antle III, "The Irony of ObamaCare: How Liberals Came to Love Big Business," *The Week*, February 18, 2015.
22. McDonough, *Inside National Health Reform*, 164–166.
23. Starr, *Remedy and Reaction*, 220; and McDonough e-mail to author, November 17, 2016.
24. Not all retailers were on board. Although the National Retail Federation represented many high-benefit, unionized firms, it condemned Walmart's endorsement of the ACA as "quite possibly the most unwelcome development to date of the health care debate for us." The sense of betrayal carried over to the Chamber of Commerce, whose senior manager for healthcare policy denounced the Walmart initiative as "the worst incarnation" of the mandate idea, "the most dangerous policy." Pamela Lewis Dolan, "Wal-Mart Backs Employer Mandate for Health Coverage," *American Medical News*, July 27, 2009; Janet Adamy and Ann Zimmerman, "Wal-Mart Backs Drive to Make Companies Pay for Health Coverage," *The Wall Street Journal*, July 1, 2009.
25. Patrick O'Mahen, "Obamacare and Tax Reform: A Progressive Double Play," *The Makeshift Academic* online, October 22, 2013.
26. Jacobs and Skocpol, *Health Care Reform and American Politics*, 135.
27. McDonough, *Inside National Health Reform*, 140.
28. Ricardo Alonso-Saldivar, "As Medicaid Loses Stigma Election May Cloud its Future," *Associated Press* online, October 20, 2016.
29. Ezekiel Emanuel, *Reinventing American Health Care* (New York: Public Affairs, 2014), 206–209; McDonough, *Inside National Health Reform*, 142–144.
30. "Medicaid & CHIP (Childrens Health Insurance Program) in Kentucky," Medicaid.gov, accessed November 22, 2018; "5 Years Later: How the Affordable Care Act is Working for Kentucky," U.S.

Department of Health & Human Services, HHS.gov, February 23, 2016.

31. Kimberly Leonard, "Under Obamacare, Government Insurance Thrives More than Private Plans," *US News*, March 25, 2016; Timothy Jost, "CBO Lowers Marketplace Enrollment Projections, Increases Medicaid Growth Projections," Health Affairs Blog, January 26, 2016.

32. Phil Galewitz, "In Depressed Rural Kentucky, Worries Mount Over Medicaid Cutbacks," *Kaiser Health News* online, November 19, 2016.

33. Charles Pierce, "Saddened, Angry, Sickened, Defeated," *Esquire*, November 21, 2016. In the 2019 gubernatorial election, Republican Governor Matt Bevin was defeated by Democrat Andy Beshear, who ran on a platform pledged to protecting Medicaid expansion. But Clay County voted just as heavily for Bevin in 2019 as it had in 2015, not unlike most of the other impoverished, Medicaid dependent counties in Eastern Kentucky. Beshear's narrow victory was a product of a shift in the allegiance of more affluent voters in the suburbs. "Live: Kentucky Election Results," *The New York Times* online edition, November 6, 2019.

34. "Kaiser Health Tracking Poll: The Public's View of the ACA," *Kaiser Health News* online, October 2016.

35. Robert Draper, "The Obamacare Operation," *The New York Times Magazine*, February 19, 2017: 35.

36. Ibid.: 36. Although passed by Congress and signed by President Obama, a bill that in 2011 relieved small businesses of a burdensome reporting requirement – that employers submit 1099 tax forms for all transactions exceeding US$600 – was opposed by Heritage Action because it would "whittle off various constituencies that we want to keep as part of the full-repeal platform."

37. Abby Goodnough, "Where Health Law Helps Voters but Saps Votes," *The New York Times*, September 17, 2014: A1. Support for Medicaid expansion remained high in Kentucky, despite the electoral success of a governor determined to curb it. Abby Goodnough, "Poll Finds Support for Kentucky Medicaid Expansion," *The New York Times*, December 12, 2015: A14.

38. Jonathan Oberlander, "Long Time Coming: Why Health Reform Finally Passed," *Health Affairs*, 29, 6 (June 2010): 1112–1116.

39. Ibid.: 50.

40. Alac MacGillis, "Who Turned My Blue State Red?" *The New York Times*, November 22, 2015: SR 1.

41. Ibid. An Arkansas political observer more sympathetic to Medicaid expansion reached the same conclusion. Commenting on Governor Asa Hutchinson's interest in block granting the program and thereby "shrinking dramatically the number of poor people served with health coverage," Max Brantley wrote, "So what? They don't vote. Or at least not in great enough numbers to be a political concern." Max Brantley, "Governor to Release Budget. Suddenly, What About Obamacare?" Arkansas Blog, November 9, 2016.
42. Robert Draper, "The Obamacare Operation," *The New York Times Magazine*, February 19, 2017: 34.
43. Arron Blake, "Why Would the GOP Want to Pass a Hugely Unpopular Health-Care Bill? Let's Debate," *The Washington Post* online, July 16, 2017.
44. These tax savings were politically useful. In the Senate version of the Obamacare repeal bill, Majority Leader McConnell sought to restore about US$200 billion of the taxes over the next decade to pay off moderates like West Virginia Republican Shelly Capito, whose vow to "push for policies that result in affordable health care coverage for West Virginians, including those who are in the Medicaid population and those struggling with drug addiction" sounds very much like she is courting a legislative bribe. Thomas Kaplan, Robert Pear, and Reed Abelson, "Senate Health Care Decision: Pence Breaks Senate Tie," *The New York Times*, July 25, 2017: A1.
45. "Insurers Want Ted Cruz's Low-Cost Proposal Dropped from Republican Health Bill," *Reuters* online, July 15, 2017; Jon Greenberg, "Understanding Ted Cruz's Health Care Amendment and Pre-existing Conditions," *Politifact* online, July 17, 2017.
46. Haeyoun Park and Wilson Andrews, "The C.B.O. Did the Math: These Are the Key Takeaways from the Senate Health Care Bill," *The New York Times*, June 26, 2017.
47. Peter Jacobs, "John McCain: Here's Why I Voted No and Killed the 'Skinny Repeal,'" *Business Insider* online, July 28, 2017. The so-called "skinny repeal" was a hastily concocted GOP bill that would have retained many Obamacare provisions, including its progressive funding formula. But both opponents and supporters knew that once this version was debated in a House–Senate conference committee, the more draconian House version was almost certain to emerge largely intact as the Republican bill.
48. Andrew Sprung, "The Healthcare Miracle that this Election Could Ratify," in healthionsurance.org online, November 2, 2018.

49. Margaret Sanger-Katz, "Number of Uninsured Isn't Going Up, or Down," *The New York Times*, May 22, 2018: A16.
50. Sy Mukherjee, "The GOP Tax Bill Repeals Obamacare's Individual Mandate. Here's What That Means for You," *Fortune* online, December 20, 2017.
51. Paul Demko and Adam Cancryn, "Trump's Losing Fight Against Obamacare," *Politico* online, August 1, 2018.
52. "What Does the Outcome of the Midterm Elections Mean for Medicaid Expansion?" *The Henry J. Kaiser Foundation* online, November 7, 2018. Available at: https://www.kff.org/medicaid/fact-sheet/what-does-the-outcome-of-the-midterm-elections-mean-for-medicaid-expansion/ (accessed August 2019).
53. Sean Sullivan, "Republicans Abandon the Fight to Repeal and Replace Obama's Health Care Law," *The Washington Post*, November 7, 2018.

Part 3

MOVEMENT POLITICS

9

Criticize and thrive: The American left in the Obama years

Michael Kazin

A change is going to come

On election night in 2008, Bob Dylan happened to be giving a concert in Minneapolis, the same city where he began his career half a century earlier singing folk music at a scruffy coffeehouse. "I was born in 1941," he told the audience in a voice turned sandpapery with age. "That was the year they bombed Pearl Harbor. I've been living in darkness ever since. It looks like things are going to change now."[1]

The icon of 1960s rebellion rarely speaks with such passion, at least in public. But that night, most of his fellow Americans on the liberal and radical left could second his emotion. Nearly seventy million voters had just chosen an eloquent, hip, youngish black man with a background as an anti-apartheid activist, community organizer, and opponent of the Iraq War to govern the most powerful nation on earth. Not since Franklin D. Roosevelt's re-election in 1936 had nearly everyone who identified with the quarrelsome, perpetually embattled American left given more than grudging support to a victorious presidential nominee. In Chicago's Grant Park, where forty years earlier police had beaten up anti-war demonstrators come to protest the Democratic convention, an exuberant throng composed of all ages and races gathered to glory in what they believed would be a new dawn of progressive social change. "He stands on the shoulders of the crowds of four decades ago," commented Todd Gitlin, a professor of journalism who was

269

a leader of radical students in the 1960s, "His rebellion takes the form of practicality. He has the audacity of reason." The president-elect was, if anything, more popular overseas than at home. As the French philosopher Pascal Bruckner, normally a critic of the multi-cultural left, put it, "Barack Obama etait le candidat du monde."[2] A confirmation of sorts arrived less than a year after the election when Obama was awarded the Nobel Peace Prize.

But in the US, the celebration did not last that long. By the summer of 2009, many liberals were denouncing the new president's appointments of such Wall Street "insiders" as Lawrence Summers and Timothy Geithner and wondering why he had not broken up the banks and insurance companies they blamed for causing the Great Recession. That August, Katrina van den Heuvel, editor of *The Nation*, faulted Obama for not emulating FDR in using "this moment of crisis . . . to restructure – not simply resuscitate – the smug financial sector." For their part, most radicals had already written off Obama as what Tariq Ali, the veteran British Marxist, damned as a "messenger-servant of the country's corporations . . . ensuring that no obstacles are placed in their way."[3]

Such harsh judgments from the left remained the norm as the president stumbled through his first term, then won re-election but saw his party lose control of the House and the Senate, as well as a majority of governorships and state legislatures. The most salient criticisms – whether voiced in sorrow or anger or contempt – included: Obama's failure to fight for a public option in the Affordable Care Act, his reluctance to boldly protest an upsurge in racist talk and police killings of unarmed black men, his refusal to pull US forces out of Afghanistan and to abandon the surveillance regime accompanying the unending "war on terrorism," his lack of support for legislation that would have made it easier for unions to organize or to do anything else of significance to attack economic inequality, and his persistent attempts to compromise with the same Republicans in Congress who – backed by a large and well-funded network of right-wing groups like the Tea Party – sought to defeat him at every turn. In August 2014, Cornel West, perhaps Obama's most prominent black critic, summed up the radical indictment: "he posed as a progressive and turned out to be counterfeit. We ended up with a Wall Street presidency, a drone presidency, a national security presidency . . . he's just another neoliberal centrist with a smile and a nice rhetorical flair."[4]

Yet the disappointments and cynicism helped produce an ironic result. The left revived in numbers, spirit, and creativity during the Obama years – due, in no small part, to the gap between what most liberals and radicals had hoped for (and some expected) from his administration and what actually took place. With his bracingly progressive rhetoric and activist biography, the first African-American president had raised expectations among leftists of nearly every stripe. Their frustrations proved to be productive ones: they helped fuel an upsurge of protest and organizing that propelled issues like police killings of black men and economic inequality to the forefront of national politics. They also did much to make what became a heated, two-person battle within Obama's party to succeed him a contest to prove who could sound more progressive than the other.

Something like this had happened twice before in modern US political history. During the 1930s and 1960s, the left also mushroomed when avowedly liberal presidents were in office. There were, of course, significant differences between what occurred during Obama's presidency and those of Franklin D. Roosevelt, John F. Kennedy, and Lyndon B. Johnson. In the earlier periods, major social movements on the left enabled Democratic Congresses to pass and Democratic presidents to sign landmark pieces of legislation that became pillars of the liberal state. Not until late in the 1960s did conservatives gain the legitimacy and the resources to apply counter-pressure from the right. Still, in all three eras, the left responded to reformist chief executives in similar ways. Intellectuals and organizers found their voice on issues they could use to build their movements both in numbers and confidence. However, those previous lefts used a mix of hope and discontent to build institutions that sustained their activism and won signal victories that altered the politics and, to a degree, the culture of the nation. The left that began to thrive during the Obama presidency did not develop into such a mature, enduring force. It is still too early to know whether its spirited mobilization against the Trump administration and Republican party's dominance of the federal government will produce that result.

A half-correct critique

Before describing how the left grew, one first ought to evaluate its criticisms of Obama's presidency. Were the charges valid? The answer depends on what one thinks the President actually wanted to accomplish, how he went about it, and what, given the political context he inherited, Obama realistically could have done. Those who saw him as a stalwart progressive impatient to launch a New Deal or Great Society for the twenty-first century and to denounce and defy anyone who got in his way did not take an accurate measure of the man. As Gitlin suggested – and as historian James T. Kloppenberg argued in an intellectual biography written midway through Obama's first term – the President was an instinctive pragmatist who believed that only patient, empathetic deliberation could generate beneficent change. These qualities of mind had helped him become the first African-American president of the *Harvard Law Review* and then a skillful community organizer in Chicago where he learned, in Kloppenberg's words, "to coax from groups a sense of what they shared, an awareness that proved sturdy because it was their doing, not his." Then, in the 2004 keynote at the Democratic convention that vaulted Obama to national prominence, he famously declared while "there are those who are preparing to divide us, the spin masters and negative ad peddlers," the reality was "there's not a liberal America and a conservative America; there's the United States of America." Alas, when he got to the White House, this exponent of consensus-building took far too long to understand that neither he, nor any other president, could effectively govern that way. Driven by ideological conviction and electoral self-interest, his Republican opponents had no intention of making deals.[5]

Yet, Obama's left critics also ignored obstacles that would have confronted any serious reformer who moved into the White House near the beginning of an economic crisis severe enough to be compared to the Great Depression. When FDR took office in 1933, more than three years after the stock market crash, no one blamed him for the millions of unemployed or the thousands of banks that were in danger of going broke. But Obama had to weather the inevitable decline of the economy and so he reaped less credit from the slow recovery that followed. If Roosevelt had been elected in, say, 1930, he surely would have struggled mightily to enact the New Deal programs that became keystones of the modern liberal state.

Neither should one ignore, or quickly disparage, reforms that Obama and a Democratic Congress managed to enact during the first two years of his administration – reforms which the Trump administration has quickly sought to dismantle. The economic stimulus plan, the ACA, the Dodd-Frank regulation of high finance, and the beginning of a serious effort to stall or reverse global warming were serious attempts to solve some of the nation's and one of the world's most serious problems. And, on climate change, the executive orders Obama issued, the international pacts he spearheaded, and the Keystone and North Dakota pipeline projects he halted (if only temporarily) were enough to cheer even most radical environmentalists. If these were the acts of a corporate "messenger-servant," why did the pro-corporate Republicans who blasted Obama as a "socialist" not get the message?[6]

Most of the President's left critics also neglected the fact that he had to cope with much smaller majorities in Congress than FDR and LBJ enjoyed – and unbending opposition from nearly every GOP lawmaker in both houses. This was a stark contrast with the relative bipartisanship that prevailed during earlier liberal heydays. A sizeable minority of Republicans had voted for such signature programs of the New Deal as Social Security and the GI Bill as well as for such pillars of the Great Society as Medicare and the Civil Rights Act.[7]

Yet, Obama's left critics were certainly correct about one big thing: the president did not live up to the image of a bold movement leader that had done much to win him both his party's nomination and, perhaps, the general election. As the recession predictably worsened in 2009, he stuck to managing the crisis from the White House instead of traveling around the nation to empathize with Americans who had lost their homes, their jobs, and their life savings. As Theda Skocpol commented, in an otherwise positive evaluation of Obama's first two years in office, the President's "failure to engage more consistently in high-profile public leadership on the economy constitutes, in an important sense, democratic political

273

malpractice." Organizing for America, the group Democrats created just before the inauguration to harness the momentum of the Obama campaign to their legislative program, failed to keep the party's young, multicultural base mobilized against the Republican onslaught that followed.[8]

How Black Lives Mattered

Yet, soon, members of that base in communities around the nation began to mobilize themselves. The most impressive effort was made by young African Americans who had celebrated Obama's election but quickly realized the president would or, perhaps, could do little to dismantle racist practices in government and the economy. Criminal justice became their primary target. Activists rallied first in the summer of 2013 under the twitter hashtag #BlackLivesMatter after a jury in Florida acquitted George Zimmerman for the killing of Trayvon Martin. Over the next three years, the protests grew, in decentralized fashion, from smartphone to smartphone, and city to city, as the murders of individual black men were caught on amateur videos and then viewed everywhere.

In a trajectory familiar from the black freedom movement of the 1960s, activists moved swiftly from protesting specific outrages (lack of civil and voting rights then, police killings now) to a bold assault on the norms and structures of American society itself. The three young individuals who launched the original presence on social media proudly identified themselves as "queer Black women" and insisted the new freedom movement "affirm the lives" of African-Americans of all genders, sexualities, and national origins. Their language testified to the remarkable legitimacy and influence the cause of LGBT rights and identity had gained in the early years of this century. The trio roundly condemned both "hetero-patriarchal society" and a "narrow" black nationalism of the past that had taken those norms for granted.[9]

In the summer of 2016, some fifty black-led groups, assembled under the Movement for Black Lives (MBL), issued a platform of demands and policies on taxes, reparations, the military budget, education, incarceration, and, of course, police conduct that was

as sweepingly radical as any group on the left – aside from dog-
matic sects – had issued since the 1960s. Some of its planks were
borrowed from the think-tank Demos and other liberal organizations. Still, the platform writers made clear their distance from
Obama and his party. Their movement might be "focused on
domestic policies," but nothing short of an international uprising
would repair "the ravages of global capitalism and anti-Black racism, human-made climate change, war, and exploitation."[10]

To have an African American as president gave the new black
freedom movement both a sense of hope and a target on which to
train its frustrations with the slow pace of change. Many lashed
out at the President and other members of the black elite, in and
out of government, for preaching to young African Americans
in poor communities a gospel of "respectable" speech and dress
instead of enacting policies that would give them a good education and secure jobs at living wages.[11]

At the same time, the enthusiasm for Obama's presidency,
which never flagged among most non-activist African Americans,
did help gain the black left a nationwide audience for the first time
in decades. The organizers of mass protests could point to the gap
between Obama's rhetoric about racism and his lack of progress in
combatting the suffering it caused. A month after Trayvon Martin
was killed in Florida, the President declared, "If I had a son, he'd
look like Trayvon . . . When I think about this boy, I think about
my own kids." But Obama had also made clear that he could not
do more to address and remedy the problems of African Americans than he would for the concerns of other citizens. BlackLives-
Matter thus became the latest progressive movement to advance
when it could challenge a president who either did not, or could
not, fulfill his promises – instead of having to combat one who had
no sympathy at all with its cause.[12]

There was a critical difference, however, between this upsurge
and that of the large black reform and radical left whose actions
did much to shape the history of postwar America. No equivalent
of the NAACP, SCLC, CORE, or SNCC emerged to raise money
and plan strategy for BlackLivesMatter; no facsimile of Martin
Luther King, Jr., Malcolm X, Stokely Carmichael, Angela Davis,
or Fannie Lou Hamer thrilled mass rallies with his or her rhetoric

and became a familiar name in the mass media. The young activists who spearheaded the new movement did not attempt to build a durable local or national organization or choose leaders who could represent their cause to the country at large. They were sharply critical of the "old guard" of men like Jesse Jackson, Sr. and Al Sharpton who seldom showed up at street protests they did not initiate. The "new guard" also had little faith that their elders were sincerely committed to "intersectionality" – a determination to fight all forms of oppression which quickly became a cherished goal for young leftists of all races. As a group called Ferguson Action explained late in 2014, "We are decentralized, but coordinated . . . We do not cast any one of ours to the side in order to gain proximity to perceived power. Because this is the only way we will win." Such a "horizontalist" approach seemed only natural for a movement launched and diffused on social media.[13]

However, a movement that eschews durable organizations and depends on police murders to sustain itself may also speed its own decline. As the sociologist Jo Freeman warned decades ago during the upsurge of radical feminism, "The more unstructured a movement is, the less control it has over the directions in which it develops and the political actions in which it engages . . . diffusion of [its] ideas does not mean they are implemented; it only means they are talked about."[14] With Trump as president, it is quite unlikely that BlackLivesMatter, with its combination of local protests and a radical vision, will spur statutory change, much less anything as far-reaching as the Civil Rights and Voting Rights acts of the 1960s. But the brash, independent spirit of the new black movement certainly inspired a national debate about policing and incarceration, in which the 2016 presidential nominees of both major parties engaged. No meaningful change in politics occurs without a catalyst that, in most cases, does not endure.

The limits of Occupy

The Occupy uprising launched in September 2011 provided a similar jolt from the left without building a structure equipped to organize for systemic reform. Responding to the call of *ADBUSTERS*, a Canadian anti-corporate magazine, several dozen radicals began camping out in Zuccotti Park in Lower Manhattan. They declared themselves the tribunes of the 99 percent of the people against the 1 percent who ruled the global economy and whose reckless investment schemes had, they charged, brought on the Great Recession. Within days, the group in the renamed Liberty Park swelled into the thousands. Soon, protestors inspired by their example were occupying parks and other locations in dozens of other locales; suddenly, thanks to blanket media coverage, "economic inequality" had become as inescapable an issue as civil rights had been during the 1960s.[15]

However, unlike any anti-racist movement past or present, Occupy really did express the sentiments of most Americans, if not quite 99 percent of them. A poll that November reported that six-tenths of the public "supported government efforts to reduce disparities in wealth"; another survey taken that same month found that the same proportion of registered voters agreed it was necessary "to reduce the power of major banks and corporations" and give neither "financial aid to corporations" nor "provide tax breaks to the rich." For decades, labor union officials and left-wing journalists and academics had been demanding changes in a status quo that favored the wealthy. But it took an unplanned protest by a group composed mainly of young, middle-class whites without steady jobs to make a dent in what the historian Steve Fraser dubbed "the Age of Acquiescence."[16]

How Occupy activists viewed Barack Obama also tended to differ from how their counterparts in BlackLivesMatter regarded the president. Many of the African Americans who took to the streets of Ferguson, Baltimore and other cities complained that the first black chief executive was too much of a bystander to their cause. But they could not realistically accuse him of abetting the crimes they were protesting. In contrast, those who kept the Occupy encampments going – what Todd Gitlin called "the inner movement" – viewed Obama as yet another shill for the "neoliberal" order, decidedly part of the problem instead of the solution, to borrow a phrase favored by the New Left of the 1960s.[17]

Besides a loathing for finance capitalism and its political enablers, the Occupiers articulated no specific ideology. Yet some of the most vocal among them embraced an updated form of anarchism – one refashioned to embrace the strict environmentalism, multicultur-alism, and gender neutrality that nearly every young leftist now takes for granted. They were the cyber-clever progeny of Henry David Thoreau and Emma Goldman, streaming video and orga-nizing flash mobs instead of penning essays about the wilderness or traveling around the country touting feminism and free love. The horizontal nature of a movement brought to life and sustained by social media fit snugly inside the anarchist vision of a future in which autonomous, self-governing communities would link up with one another – voluntarily of course.[18]

But the quite un-anarchistic resident of the White House had helped set the stage for the radicals who condemned him. In the latter months of 2008, Obama had the ironic good fortune to be running in the midst of an economic debacle. In his acceptance speech in Denver, he set aside his bent for compromise to blame the "old, discredited Republican philosophy" of "trickle-down economics" for causing millions of Americans to lose their jobs, their homes, and enough money to pay credit card bills and col-lege tuition. The attack was reminiscent of that which Franklin D. Roosevelt, accepting the Democratic nomination, had hurled at the Hoover administration seventy-six years before.[19]

Yet, in both cases, presidential practice lagged behind campaign rhetoric. When they took office, neither FDR nor Obama had a strategy for winning higher wages, enhanced bargaining power, or job security for wage earners. Instead, both concentrated on restoring the health of a badly ailing macroeconomy. Roosevelt vowed to cut federal spending and expended most of his ener-gies on rescuing banks and manufacturing firms from the abyss. Although in 2008 Obama had the support of nearly every union in the country, he made no attempt to get Congress to enact the Employee Free Choice Act, labor's main legislative priority. Even when, in December 2011, the president devoted an entire speech to the issue of economic inequality – an implicit nod to Occupy – he addressed it to a politically safe demographic, "the middle class," and essentially repeated the critique of conservative economics he had made during his 2008 campaign.[20]

Midway through his own first term, Franklin Roosevelt had benefitted from, and began to appeal to, a larger and far better organized class-conscious left. From the mass strike wave of 1934 to the sit-down strikes of 1936–1937, working-class activists – some of whom belonged to one or another Marxist party – nurtured an environment in which the president and Democrats from industrial states could win more votes by supporting unions than they lost to Americans who feared social unrest. At the same time, non-left figures like Francis Townsend were gaining a mass following with the demand to create a federal pension for the elderly. Huey Long and Charles Coughlin rose to national prominence with calls to redistribute the wealth. The ability to channel this resistance into legislation and Democratic majorities in Congress and industrial states was a vital element in the construction of the New Deal order.[21]

In contrast, Occupy mainly generated a shift in political rhetoric. Many local unions did hail the encampments and supplied them with food and other resources. But labor was hardly the vigorous, growing force it had been from the 1930s through the 1950s. In the wake of Occupy, the Service Employees International Union (SEIU) – the largest private-sector union in America – organized one-day strikes among fast food workers for a wage of US$15 an hour. Soon, Bernie Sanders and other left Democrats took up the demand as well. But by the time Obama left office, it had not led to a rebirth of unions among the men and women who need them most.

How marriage equality won

The most successful movement on the broad left during Obama's presidency – that of LGBT activists – managed to appear less radical in its key demand and was far better equipped to win it. During his 2008 campaign, the Democratic nominee had affirmed the position on legal matrimony taken by nearly every politician from both major parties: "I believe marriage is between a man and a woman. I am not in favor of gay marriage." However, back in 1996, when he was running for a seat in the Illinois Senate, Obama had endorsed such unions and even told a gay magazine that he "would fight efforts to prohibit" them. Running for re-election in 2012, he changed his mind again or, more likely, decided to help increase the speed at which the winds of politics were already blowing. In June 2016, by a 5–4 decision, the Supreme Court, in *Obergefell* v. *Hodges*, agreed, and marriage equality became the law of the land.[22]

This remarkable victory was not merely the result of an increased tolerance of sexual diversity in American culture; it depended upon a shrewd strategy that LGBT activists carried out with persistence and an acute sense of how to shift public opinion their way. In the 1990s, gay rights attorneys filed suit in liberal states like Hawaii and Vermont where they could establish precedents. Then they challenged the Defense of Marriage Act, easily passed in 1995 by Congress and signed by President Bill Clinton, and were able to convince Obama's Justice Department not to defend the law in court. Accompanying these legal maneuvers was a change of message: instead of talking about marriage as a "right," the movement's literature stressed that same-sex couples wanted to get married for the same reasons that straight couples did: for "love and commitment." That helped break down the resistance of people who had bridled at the idea of overturning a legal norm as old as civilization itself.[23]

Although Barack Obama's gradual "evolution" toward backing same-sex marriage frustrated its supporters, his change of position accelerated the pace of their victory. The president's new stance immediately became that of his party. It helped win over black churchgoers as well as bind most young people of all races to the Democrats – when they bothered to vote. By 2015, it had become inconceivable to imagine that the administration would side with the four conservative justices who dissented from the landmark ruling. No major expansion of individual freedom in US history has occurred without a presidential blessing, however tardy it may be.

Why the anti-war movement disappeared

In sharp contrast, few leftists of any stripe devoted much effort to opposing Obama's continuation of military intervention or proposed alternatives of their own. During the 1960s, protest against the US war in Indochina had been a signature cause for radicals, and, eventually, for most liberals too. By 2014, opinion polls showed that most Americans opposed the ongoing US war against the Taliban in Afghanistan; support had been declining steadily since Obama took office.[24] But no protest was large or creative enough to gain the attention of anyone outside a small circle of activists. In the spring of 2015, on the twelfth anniversary of the invasion of Iraq, a nationally advertised Spring Rising Anti-War Intervention attracted only a few hundred demonstrators to Washington, DC and received no coverage at all in the mainstream media and barely any mention in left-wing outlets.

Perhaps the most obvious, and most significant, reason for the absence of a large and persistent anti-war movement is the nature of the enemies the United States has been fighting since the fall of 2001. There are, of course, many distinctions between al-Qaeda and the Taliban, Saddam Hussein's regime and ISIS. But nearly all Americans sensibly regard each of these groups (Hussein's, retrospectively) with loathing. So anti-war activists sensibly sought to focus on innocent victims: how US military actions kill and maim large numbers of civilians, particularly with drones often directed from buildings located in Northern Virginia.

But the flourishing of the peace movement during the 1960s did not depend solely on having an unpopular war to stop. Many of its most talented and committed activists came from other movements on the broad left – against poverty, for civil liberties, for nuclear disarmament, and especially for black liberation. They had learned to define their politics as a moral undertaking that could transform the world. Slogans like SNCC's "One Man, One Vote—Mississippi, Vietnam," and Muhammad Ali's statement, "I ain't got no quarrel with them Viet Cong. No Viet Cong ever called me nigger," when he applied (unsuccessfully) to be a conscientious objector, helped forge the link between black freedom and anti-war movements. For both groups, a passionate internationalism was taken for granted.

Contemporary foes of US action in the Muslim world did not have such an expansive, optimistic vision. Most feminist and LGBT activists objected to the size of the military budget, but few drew connections between the violence in the Middle East and the injustices they combat at home. After all, misogynistic groups like ISIS and the Taliban burn to reverse every achievement that activists for gender equality hold dear. Neither did any spokesperson for BlackLivesMatter or the movement to halt climate change link his or her cause to that of pulling all foreign troops out of Afghanistan. The one exception to this pattern is the BDS (Boycott, Divestment and Sanctions) movement campaign to punish Israel for its occupation of Palestinian lands – which became the left's anti-imperialist cause of choice. But no US soldiers are patrolling the West Bank.

Perhaps one reason few leftists spent their time agitating against US military intervention abroad is that issue was not the property of the left alone. Rand Paul and other libertarians on the right spoke out against "imperial overreach" and NSA surveillance as consistently as did anyone on the left. In his 2016 campaign, Donald Trump sometimes echoed their views and vowed to take care of America First. All opponents of intervention, whatever their ideology, agree that US military power does little or no good in the world; they do not agree about why. Meanwhile, President Obama often seemed apologetic about committing US forces. In foreign affairs, the president showed more enthusiasm for recognizing the Communist regime in Cuba – a step universally applauded on the left. With such ambiguous realities and contradictory motivations, any hope for mass anti-war protest fizzled. The result was that, by the end of Obama's term, left internationalism had become close to an oxymoron on any issue other than climate change. As Michael Walzer puts it, "the default position of the left is that the best foreign policy is a good domestic policy."[25]

The Bernie boom

The best evidence that a left focused on domestic concerns was thriving with Obama in the White House emerged during the final year of his presidency – in the extraordinary campaign for the Democratic nomination by an independent senator in his seventies who had criticized the president for not following through on his progressive promises. An avowed socialist, Bernie Sanders received 43 percent of the Democratic vote in his 2016 run and won an overwhelming majority of votes cast by people of all races under thirty years old. His popularity was a testament both to his principled "authenticity" and to the hunger for egalitarian change stoked by the left upsurge that began during the final years of George W. Bush's administration but accelerated greatly under Barack Obama – whom many conservatives accused of being a "socialist" too.

Ironically, Sanders might be the most unchangeable politician in America. By the time he announced for president, Sanders had spent over half a century advocating a reform agenda that would turn the US into a social-democratic nation – a Finland with a lot more people and much warmer summers. His rhetoric rarely altered from his tenure as mayor of the largest city in Vermont in the 1980s to his campaign for the White House more than thirty years later. Sanders bashed millionaires and billionaires for corrupting democracy and strongly supported labor unions and public health insurance; he paid less attention to racial inequality and the degradation of the environment. Like his hero, Eugene V. Debs, he viewed every political issue through the lens of class injustice. Unlike Obama, Sanders never abandoned the passionate leftism of his youth.[26]

Inevitably, this led him to disparage the president during his first term in office. "I think that there are millions of Americans who are deeply disappointed" in Obama, Sanders claimed in 2011, "who believe that with regard to Social Security and a number of other issues, he has said one thing as a candidate and is doing something very much else . . . [they] cannot believe how weak he has been . . . in negotiating with Republicans." Sanders even mused, at the time, about challenging the president in several primaries. In the summer of 2016, after losing to Hillary Clinton in the Democratic race, he refreshed his critique: "After Obama became president," Sanders told an interviewer, "he severed his ties with the grassroots that got him elected."[27] Despite losing the nomination, Sanders and his followers wielded a good deal of influence over a party the Senator had never actually joined. Hillary Clinton seconded his opposition to the Trans-Pacific Partnership bill backed by President Obama and embraced Sanders's call for a big boost in the minimum wage, debt-free tuition in public colleges, and a reversal of the Supreme Court ruling in the *Citizens United* case. As a result, the platform adopted by the Democratic Party in 2016 leaned farther leftward than any since the days when party leaders were proud to wear the liberal label.

Conclusion: what future for the left?

Where does the left go from here? In 2017, its resurgence during Obama's time in office helped prepare both Democrats shattered by Hillary Clinton's defeat and radicals who had grudgingly supported her, if at all, to organize a sizable movement of "resistance" to President Donald Trump and his policies. In the first year after the celebrity billionaire was inaugurated, they staged an impressive variety of protests – on the streets, in airports, and at congressional town halls – on a scale not seen on the broad left since the heyday of the anti-war movement at the end of the 1960s. Young "millennials" who voted for Sanders played a prominent role in the movement. They also challenged the Democratic leaders in Congress and officials at the Democratic National Committee to embrace a sweeping platform that would include single-payer health insurance, higher taxes on the rich, and other stands the Vermont Senator had taken during his 2016 campaign.

In the midterm elections of 2018, Democrats won back control of the House of Representatives they had lost two years into Obama's first term in office. Moderate candidates provided the party's margin of victory in close races. But early in 2019, it was a self-proclaimed democratic socialist – Alexandria Ocasio-Cortez, a charismatic thirty-year-old new Congresswoman from a safely Democratic district in New York City – and her young left-wing colleagues who captivated the mass media and drove debate within their party. Democratic Socialists of America, to which Ocasio-Cortez belongs, grew from 6,000 to some 60,000 members between 2015 and 2019. In the United States, no explicitly socialist organization has been so large since the 1930s. Several weeks after taking office, Ocasio-Cortez co-sponsored The Green New Deal, a tremendously ambitious plan to restructure the American economy in order to combat climate change. It quickly became both an urgent priority of the left as well as a weapon President Donald Trump wielded to brand the Democrats as dangerous radicals out to undermine the nation's prosperity.

Despite the upsurge of the left in the first two years of the Trump administration, it is not yet clear that contemporary leftists will be able to emulate the achievements of their predecessors in the 1930s and the 1960s. During those eras, the Democratic Party was a more truly national party than it is today when its strength lies in big cities, nearby suburbs, and the states of the Northeast and West Coast. And the "resistance" to President Trump and the GOP majority in Congress is not yet the equivalent of the industrial labor upsurge of the 1930s or the black freedom movement of the early to mid-1960s, each of which gave left activists a sense of common purpose and helped elect durable liberal Democratic majorities in Congress and many key states. But the American left needed Barack Obama's presidency to thrive again – even if most activists today regard the administration of the first black president as a profound disappointment.

As ever, a president is an ally of the left only when the left makes it difficult for him (or someday, she) not to be so. During the 2008 campaign, a black community organizer from New Orleans remarked that Obama "is a man who can be accommodated by America, he is not my hero, because a politician, by nature, has to surrender."[28] The question is which forces the president will bargain with, whose rhetoric and demands he will amplify, and which he will surrender to.

Notes

1. Andrea Swensson, "Bob Dylan: 'Things are going to change now'," *CITYPAGES* (Minneapolis): http://www.citypages.com/music/bob-dylan-things-are-going-to-change-now-6632216
2. John M. Broder and Monica Davey, "Celebration and Sense of History at Chicago Party," *The New York Times*, November 5, 2008: http://www.nytimes.com/2008/11/05/us/politics/05chicago.html?_r=0 (accessed August 2019); Eric Coller, "Un 11 septembre à l'envers," *Le Monde*, November 5, 2008: http://www.lemonde.fr/elections-americaines/article/2008/11/05/un-11-septembre-a-l-envers_1114930_829254.html (accessed August 2019).
3. Katrina Vanden Heuvel, "Let's Get Real About Obama," a column published August 13, 2009. Reprinted in Vanden Heuvel, *The Change I Believe In: Fighting for Progress in the Age of Obama* (New York: Nation Books, 2011), 17. Of course, the title of her book is a variation on Obama's 2008 campaign slogan, "Change

We Can Believe In"; Tariq Ali, *The Obama Syndrome: Surrender at Home, War Abroad* (London: Verso, 2010), 75.

4. West interview with Thomas Frank, http://www.salon.com/2014/08/24/cornel_west_he_posed_as_a_progressive_and_turned_out_to_be_counterfeit_we_ended_up_with_a_wall_street_presidency_a_drone_presidency/. By the summer of 2016, the tone of criticism from the far left had not changed. See the introduction by C. J. Polychroniou to his interview in *Truthout* with Noam Chomsky (June 2, 2016), in which he labels Obama's regime "a neoliberal regime in overdrive." Chomsky, himself, was a bit more ambivalent. Available at: http://www.truth-out.org/news/item/36260-a-mixed-story-ranging-from-criminal-to-moderate-improvement-noam-chomsky-on-obama-s-legacy (accessed August 2019).

5. Brad Berenson quoted in David Remnick, *The Bridge: The Life and Rise of Barack Obama* (New York: Knopf, 2010), 207; James T. Kloppenberg, *Reading Obama: Dreams, Hope, and the American Political Tradition* (Princeton, NJ: Princeton University Press, 2011), 28–29. For a splendid analysis of the institutional obstacles to a new New Deal, see Eric Alterman, *Kabuki Democracy: The System vs. Barack Obama* (New York: Nation Books, 2011).

6. In a 2015 interview, Klein acknowledged that Obama "sounds like a climate leader": http://www.democracynow.org/2015/11/30/video_naomi_klein_extended_interview_on (accessed August 2019).

7. Theda Skocpol, *Obama and America's Political Future* (Cambridge, MA: Harvard University Press, 2012), 8.

8. Ibid., 37–38. In part, the failure of OFA was due to the changing make-up of the ACA as its backers struggled to gain support for it in Congress. But Skocpol also makes the cogent point that "grassroots activism works better when it is relatively spontaneous and at most loosely linked to official institutions" (ibid., 32).

9. See http://blacklivesmatter.com/herstory/. The three women are Alicia Garza, Patrisse Cullors, and Opal Tometi.

10. See https://policy.m4bl.org/platform/. For a friendly analysis, see Vann R. Newkirk, II, "The Permanence of Black Lives Matter," *The Atlantic*, August 3, 2016: http://www.theatlantic.com/politics/archive/2016/08/movement-black-lives-platform/494309/ (accessed August 2019).

11. See Fredrick C. Harris, "The Rise of Respectability Politics," *Dissent*, winter 2014, 33–37.

12. For a left-wing critique of Obama's presidency which understands his enduring appeal, see Keeanga-Yamahtta Taylor, *From #Black-LivesMatter to Black Liberation* (Chicago: Haymarket Books, 2016), 135–152.
13. Quoted in ibid.
14. Jo Freeman, "The Tyranny of Structurelessness," originally published in1970: http://struggle.ws/pdfs/tyranny.pdf (accessed August 2019).
15. For a list of and documents from occupations in the US and abroad, see http://occupyarchive.org/items
16. Polls quoted in Todd Gitlin, *Occupy Nation: The Roots, the Spirit, and the Promise of Occupy Wall Street* (New York: It Books, 2012), 37. Steve Fraser, *The Age of Acquiescence* (New York: Little Brown, 2015).
17. Gitlin, *Occupy Nation*, 28.
18. This paragraph is adapted from a *New Republic* column I wrote in early November, 2011: https://newrepublic.com/article/97114/anarchy-occupy-wall-street-throwback (accessed August 2019).
19. See for instance: http://www.foxnews.com/politics/2012/09/06/transcript-obama-speech-at-dnc.html (accessed August 2019).
20. Transcript of Obama speech in Osawatomie, Kansas, December 6, 2011: http://articles.latimes.com/2011/dec/06/news/la-pn-text-obama-speech-kansas-20111206/2 (accessed August 2019).
21. Steve Fraser, *The Age of Acquiescence*, 410–411.
22. See http://www.politifact.com/truth-o-meter/statements/2012/may/11/barack-obama/president-barack-obamas-shift-gay-marriage/ (accessed August 2019).
23. Most of this paragraph is based on David Cole, *Engines of Liberty: The Power of Citizen Activists to Make Constitutional Law* (New York: Basic Books, 2016), 15–93.
24. See http://www.gallup.com/poll/116233/afghanistan.aspx (accessed August 2019).
25. Jon Lee Anderson, "The Cuba Play," *The New Yorker*, October 3, 2016, 53. The previous section on the absence of protest against US wars is adapted from my article, "Why Is There Not Antiwar Movement?" *Dissent* (summer 2015): https://www.dissentmagazine.org/article/michael-kazin-why-no-antiwar-movement-iraq (accessed August 2019). Michael Walzer, "A Foreign Policy for the Left," *Dissent*, spring 2014: https://www.dissentmagazine.org/article/a-foreign-policy-for-the-left (accessed August 2019).
26. See the rather critical narrative of Sanders's career during the 1970s and 1980s in Greg Guma, *The People's Republic: Vermont and*

the Sanders Revolution (Shelburne, VT: The New England Press, 1989). Sanders quoted in Eric Bates, "Bernie Looks Ahead," *The New Republic*, November 2016, 32.

27. Evan McMorris Santoro, "The Obama Campaign Remembers 2012 Very Differently Than Bernie Sanders," BuzzFeed News, November 8, 2015: https://www.buzzfeed.com/evanmcsan/the-obama-campaign-remembers-2012-very-differently-from-bern?utm_term=.wbreRG11q#.lhaM07yyZ (accessed August 2019); Eric Bates, "Bernie Looks Ahead," 31.

28. Quoted in my review essay, "Too Many Obamas?" *Raritan,* 30 (winter 2011), 93.

10

"Stop killing us": Mobilizing against structural racism in the United States from Black Lives Matter to the Movement for Black Lives

Audrey Célestine and Nicolas Martin-Breteau

For more than seven years, Black Lives Matter (BLM) has emerged as a broad social movement seeking to reveal and dismantle what its militants regard as the institutional violence directed at racial minorities in the United States. In July 2013, the controversial acquittal of the vigilante George Zimmerman in the death of seventeen-year-old African American Trayvon Martin was at the origin of the rallying cry #BlackLivesMatter, first disseminated on social networks. While not limited to the issue of police brutality, the movement has grown and structured itself alongside the outrage provoked by the public revelation of the deaths of hundreds[1] of unarmed African Americans at the hands of the police.

The BLM movement thus presents a historical paradox: how to understand that during the mandate of Barack Obama, the first black US president, the African-American community has risen in what turned out to be the largest social movement since the Civil Rights movement of the 1950s and 1960s.

Since its inception, the BLM movement has been designed and structured as a horizontal network of grassroots activist organizations working in communities of color. Although leaders have emerged within the movement, its decentralized structure has facilitated the proliferation of new and dissident voices and actions, notably through the use of social networks and collective mobilizations.

In 2016, more than fifty of these organizations formally gathered in a large coalition called the Movement for Black Lives (M4BL).

In its analyses and objectives as well as its structure and deployment, BLM and M4BL voluntarily organized in an intersectional movement.[2] This term must be understood in a twofold meaning. On the one hand, by combining analyses in terms of race, ethnicity, class, gender, sexuality, and nationality, BLM and M4BL seek to circumscribe a structure of domination characterized by the intersection of various forms of oppression that are mutually reinforcing. On the other hand, to combat this structure of domination, the movement tries to connect, without any kind of hierarchical order, multiple initiatives emerging from grassroots political mobilization.

Like any intersectional movement, BLM and M4BL are, in practice, confronted with key strategic issues regarding the struggles that must be waged first. The police and justice issues concerning primarily the figure of the young black male have constituted the core of the political demands formulated by the movement. Nevertheless, the leadership of other traditionally marginal or invisible groups (women, LGBTQ persons) reveals the heterogeneity of the actors of the movement as well as the age and class tensions that cleave it.

Based on a body of recent primary and secondary documents produced by the leaders and organizations of the movement, the US and international press, as well as academic works, this chapter proposes a synthesis intended to open avenues for future empirical and interdisciplinary studies of the BLM movement and M4BL. First, this chapter will analyze the many-faceted historical and sociological origins of the movement. Second, the examination of BLM then M4BL as an organization, a coalition, and a movement will highlight the plural mechanisms of their development. Finally, the study of the movement's declared objectives and solutions will reveal how the lines of division within the African-American community have redefined the traditional strategy of its established political organizations.

Black Lives Matter: the intersection of multiple causes

In the early 2010s, the emergence and structuring of the BLM movement and subsequently the M4BL have resulted from an intersection of multiple and age-old causes, which reinforced each other in their social, economic, and political consequences.[3] While the activists of the Occupy movement in the early 2010s had put economic inequality at the heart of their mobilization, BLM and M4BL militants have shed a broader light on the multifaceted situation that they believe has been characterizing American society.[4]

The emergence of Black Lives Matter is directly related to the repetition and media coverage of news revealing the extent of police brutality against men and women of color in the United States.[5] This phenomenon, however, is old: since the slavery era, the violence of white-dominated law enforcement agencies has constituted a structuring aspect of African-American history.[6] Since 2012, the phenomenon has nevertheless gained an unprecedented visibility in mainstream media due to the revelation of video recordings crudely displaying the killing of unarmed people. As a result, the main demand of the movement was summarized as "Stop killing us."[7]

Black Lives Matter began in July 2013 following the acquittal of George Zimmerman for the death of Trayvon Martin in Sanford, Florida on February 26, 2012.[8] The scandal caused by the verdict and posthumous insinuations blaming Martin for his own death were so intense that Barack Obama had to publicly address the nation, claiming that Martin could have been his son, or himself.[9] This indirect condemnation of the verdict did not appease those who considered that Martin had been "executed" because of the suspicion caused by the presence of his black body dressed with a hoodie in a gated community.[10]

Following the verdict, many civil rights organizations were created or mobilized to denounce the criminalization of young African-American males. The Dream Defenders in Florida, The Million Hoodies Movement in Washington, DC, The Black Youth Project (BYP100) in Chicago were some of these initiatives. As for the rallying cry "Black Lives Matter" it was launched on the internet by three activists, Alicia Garza, Patrisse Cullors, and Opal Tometi, claiming that "Our Lives Matter, Black Lives Matter."[11]

The movement grew following other deaths of African Americans caused by the police. In particular, the deaths of Michael Brown in Ferguson, Missouri (August 2014) and Freddie Gray in Baltimore

(April 2015) led to mass uprisings in both cities, the largest since the 1992 acquittal of the police officers involved in the videotaped beating of Rodney King, a black motorist in Los Angeles. The deaths of Eric Garner in New York, Laquan McDonald in Chicago, and Tamir Rice in Cleveland (2014), Eric Harris in Tulsa, Oklahoma, Sandra Bland in Prairie View, Texas, and Walter Scott in Charleston, South Carolina (2015), Philando Castile in Minneapolis-St. Paul, Alton B. Sterling in Baton Rouge, Louisiana, and Terence Crutcher in Tulsa, Oklahoma (2016), and hundreds of others killed during interactions with the police have been described as "extralegal killings" even "lynchings" seeking to terrorize whole neighborhoods to keep blacks "in their place."[12]

Therefore, the movement gained widespread public attention by revealing the extent of police violence against African Americans. The figures concerning the deaths caused by police forces being not precisely reported by the US government (the Bureau of Justice Statistics and the FBI in particular), private associations such as KilledByPolice.net, FatalEncounters.org, and MappingPoliceViolence.org, joined by national or foreign media outlets such as *The Washington Post* and *The Guardian*, launched such counting, primarily based on the (inaccurate and underestimated) collection of police shooting cases covered in the local press.[13] Figures may differ from one counting to the other. For example, in 2015, *The Washington Post* recorded 259 African Americans killed by the police, while *The Guardian* recorded 300, and Mapping Police Violence recorded 336. But these databases agree on one fact: between 2013 and 2017, about 25 percent of all persons killed by the police were African Americans, twice their share in the total US population. According to the 2017 report of Mapping Police Violence, "Black people were more likely to be killed by police, more likely to be unarmed and less likely to be threatening someone when killed."[14]

The movement has also highlighted the relative impunity of police officers for these deaths. The American jurisprudence tolerates a large freedom of appreciation in the necessity of the use of physical and lethal force by police officers in case of danger.[15] Despite their recent increase due to media coverage, the indictments and even more so the convictions of a police

officer involved in the death of an individual remain extremely
rare.[16] In addition, police departments and city halls regularly
pay enormous financial compensation to the victims' families
to settle the case. Between 2004 and 2015, the City of Chicago
spent more than half a billion dollars in financial compensation to victims and their families in order to avoid lawsuits, in
particular for acts of torture.[17] One of the tactics of BLM and
M4BL militants seeks to have prosecutors reluctant to sue police
officers dismissed, an endeavor which turned out to be successful in Chicago and Cleveland in 2016.[18] As a result, in 2018 a
jury convicted Chicago police officer Jason Van Dyke for the
murder of seventeen-year-old Laquan McDonald in 2014.

In recent years, this quasi absence of judicial sanctions has
legitimized the rapid militarization of US police forces, favoring
tactics and equipment (massive deployment, special forces, snip-
ers, armored vehicles, assault rifles, combat uniforms, and so on)
used in the wars of Iraq and Afghanistan. Applied to contain uprisings in poor black neighborhoods since the 1960s, these measures
have transformed the police into an "occupation army" whose
objective is to "hold" enemy territory.[19] This situation explains
why many black police officers can themselves participate in the
violence denounced by the BLM and M4BL militants.

For these activists, such a repressive policy is responsible for the
dramatic growth of the US penal state, a situation which has been
denounced under the concept of "mass incarceration."[20] Since the
1970s, stimulated by the "war on drugs" launched by Richard
Nixon and further pursued by Ronald Reagan, George H. Bush,
and Bill Clinton, this policy has resulted in an unprecedented
increase in arrests, convictions, and length of prison sentencing.[21]
In thirty years, the US prison population has increased more than
fourfold (500,000 inmates in 1980; 2.2 million in 2012) – a situation which disproportionately affects African Americans who
account for nearly 33 percent of the incarcerated population in
the country. Today, while the racial gap has decreased, the impris-
onment rate for black people is nearly six times the imprison-
ment rate for whites.[22] At the beginning of the 2000s, one in three
black men was expected to be put in prison during his lifetime[23] –
a statistic that has not been updated since then. Conversely, the

financial benefits generated by for-profit private actors in the "prison-industrial complex" (jobs and wages, investments and dividends) are analyzed as a central aspect of the neoliberal state in the post-industrial era.[24]

Due to felon disfranchisement laws, about six million Americans including more than two million African Americans lost some of their civil rights – such as their right to vote, and their ability to apply for jobs and housing – after a prison sentence.[25] Amid unfavorable demographic trends for the rapidly shrinking white majority, felon disfranchisement laws exclude more people from the vote than voter ID laws and other schemes aimed at restricting minority voting rights.[26] The massive scope of incarceration of the American population is therefore seen as a cause and a consequence of the political and economic dispossession of many among disadvantaged Americans. After having been firmly supported by politicians, the media, and public opinion for more than half a century, this aggressive criminal policy is now condemned by a few on the right and most on the left, like *The New York Times*, which deemed it a "disaster" in 2014.[27]

These phenomena allow BLM and M4BL to point out the increase of wealth inequality in the United States. According to the Bureau of Labor Statistics, from 1972 until 2017 the unemployment rate of African Americans was consistently twice as high as that of whites (in 2017 it was 7.5 percent for African Americans and 3.8 for whites). Similarly, the economic crisis that began in the late 2000s hit racial minorities hard, as revealed in their unemployment and eviction rates which fueled their revolt in return.[28] The continuing social deprivation which has been affecting most black American families since the end of slavery (the almost impossible access to land ownership and to credit for example) has prevented intergenerational accumulation of wealth, notably real estate. As a result, despite undeniable progress over the last half-century, particularly in terms of income, the black median family owns only 8 percent of the wealth of the white median family (US$11,000 versus US$140,000). Likewise, about 25 percent of the African-American population lives below the poverty line, which affects nearly 40 percent of African-American children, that is, 4 million people.[29]

Finally, these phenomena are accentuated by a process of intense spatial segregation. Since the Civil Rights movement, racial segregation of places of residence has never decreased, remaining very high especially in urban areas, North and South.[30] While public schools have experienced a period of racial desegregation following the *Brown* v. *Board of Education* decision in 1954, they have been undergoing a dramatic process of "resegregation" since the late 1980s, generating disproportionate drop-out rates among disadvantaged black youth who are funneled to prison as a seemingly logical outcome of their "failure" at school – a process commonly referred to as the "school-to-prison pipeline."[31] One of the major consequences of racial segregation is the relatively rare interactions across racial and class lines, which leads to mutual fear and distrust between many white police officers and minority city dwellers among whom they work.

Together, these patterns are mutually intersecting and reinforcing. BLM and M4BL militants aimed at demonstrating that young African Americans were the victims rather than the cause of the brutal state repression in the US. The death of young black men and women at the hands of the police triggered a revolt against a century-old and deep-seated institutional oppression affecting the poorest among the African-American community. In that regard, this situation does not reveal a "crisis" – that is, a critical but transient period of maladjustment – but the structural culmination of age-old trends. In response, BLM and M4BL activists have sought to bring together a broad coalition of organizations to address the various aspects of this situation.

Black Lives Matter: a diverse political coalition

It is not easy to characterize the nature of Black Lives Matter. Launched as a slogan in 2013, Black Lives Matter at first referred to a network of more than twenty branches throughout the United States, now called the Black Lives Matter Network.[32] Second, it was initially an informal coalition of local organizations, some of which existed before the mobilization while others have been created since, and which gathered into the Movement for Black Lives in 2016.[33] Finally, Black Lives Matter can be seen as a social movement welcoming anyone who believes that the value of black lives should be defended by means of political action.[34]

The question of participation in the movement is therefore a key dimension in the understanding of Black Lives Matter's boundaries. Apart from the Black Lives Matter branches themselves, the movement is made up of a coalition of old and new progressive organizations working locally on issues of social justice. These organizations are spread across a broad political spectrum, work on national and international issues, and resort to different modes of action.

On this last point, we find supporters of community control working toward a subversion of power relations at the local level in favor of the oppressed through radical political slogans such as the Malcolm X Grassroots Movement or the Dream Defenders.[35] Other organizations, such as the Organization for Black Struggle or BYP100, are doing more traditional community organizing in a tradition of radical grassroots democracy that sees social change as the result of the counter-power exercised by ordinary people against the political establishment.[36] Beyond their differences, each of these approaches is characterized by empowerment, that is, the acquisition by everyone of the means to reinforce one's capacity for action.[37]

Moreover, in a traditional way, the militant roles within the various organizations of BLM and M4BL seem to be clearly defined: individuals from the community organize themselves following a collective grievance; the most active members become the leaders; a coordinator of the group, sometimes from outside the community, assumes the role of organizer.[38] This is the pattern that was put in place in Ferguson. For example, Brittany Packnett, director of Teach for America in St. Louis and an active member of Black Lives Matter, is an organizer for Teach for Ferguson, an organization created in the aftermath of the 2014 uprisings.[39] Whether in their fight against mass incarceration, for education in poor neighborhoods, for migration policy reform, or for the end of US military intervention in the Middle East, this militant model tends to position BLM and M4BL in the long tradition of social conflicts in the United States.

In the wake of pan-African decolonization movements and more recently the Arab Spring movement, the Black Lives Matter project is not limited to the United States alone. Its activists denounce in particular the structural relationship between police violence related to the "war on drugs" in the United States and military violence related to the "war on terror" abroad. According to them, this situation of permanent war commands the inflation of state violence at the local and global levels. Stimulated by the Black Lives Matter movement, several historians reinterpret these inner and outer racial wars as the twin aspects of a unique "long war" characterizing the US imperial, racial, and capitalistic republic.[40] Also, in seeking to address the social and political problems faced by people of color around the world, Black Lives Matter focuses on a still emerging international political coalition.[41]

With community organizing as a model of local organization and structural change as a horizon for national and international action, BLM and M4BL are a political catalyst for their participants. By building on a coalition of local grassroots organizations, the movement benefits from solid militant support and practices, and a broad media presence. At the same time, by presenting BLM and M4BL as a political, social, and cultural movement, its leaders offer a multitude of local actions a visibility, a slogan, and a global political direction. Thus, among the movement's grassroots activists, many are already involved in progressive militant movements and networks.[42]

These militant trajectories in favor of marginalized populations (migrants, prisoners, LGBTQ people, and so on) can be found in the main figures of the movement. This is the case of the three founders of the Black Lives Matter movement: Opal Tometi, Alicia Garza and Patrisse Cullors. Tometi is the director of the Black Alliance for Just Immigration organization. Originally from Nigeria, she grew up in Arizona where she completed a Bachelor's degree in History and a Master's degree in Communication. At the time of Black Lives Matter's inception, she had extensive professional experience in community organizing as an employee of an association working in the area of domestic violence and then as director of communication for the organization she heads today. Presenting herself as a feminist with a transnational commitment, she participated in campaigns against the withdrawal of citizenship of Dominican citizens of Haitian origin in the Dominican Republic. Alicia Garza was also an organizer in the field of domestic workers' rights in California before founding Black Lives Matter. She is now director of the National Domestic Workers Alliance. As such, she has received several professional awards in the field of organizing and community work. Identifying as queer, she has long been engaged in the fight against violence against LGBTQ people. In the aftermath of the 2016 presidential election, she launched the Black Futures Lab, a project dedicated to the building of "independent political power for Black communities."[43] Patrisse Cullors is an artist also based in California, where she studied at UCLA. A former Fulbright scholar, she also has a history of organizing in the defense of the rights of people in prison. She is now director of the Coalition to End Sheriff Violence in LA Jails. Like Garza, she identifies as queer.[44]

As shown by the emergence of leaders from traditionally marginalized population groups (women, LGBTQ people), BLM and M4BL favors a highly inclusive coalition whose slogan is sometimes summed up as "All Black Lives Matter." While the construction of collective identities in social movements traditionally tends to circumscribe the population concerned by the mobilization for purposes of strategic cohesion, the intersectional character of BLM and M4BL makes this movement original.[45]

On the one hand, the movement offers a very broad definition of "black lives" as people of color, associating African Americans and non-European immigrants from Africa, the Caribbean, Latin America, the Middle East, and South and Southeast Asia. In fact, the population identified as black in the United States has changed significantly since the end of the twentieth century with the arrival of migrants from sub-Saharan Africa or the Caribbean (particularly Nigeria, Jamaica, Haiti, and Ethiopia). Caribbean immigrants today account for almost 10 percent of the black population.[46]

On the other hand, the emphasis on women, homosexual, transsexual, and queer populations accentuates this inclusive dimension in a new way when it comes to the tradition of African-American political struggles. Announced in February 2016, the candidacy for Baltimore Mayor of a central figure of the movement, DeRay Mckesson, was seen as a way to help establish the possibility for a young black gay to be recognized as a legitimate representative of the movement on the institutional political scene.[47] The absence of a restrictive collective identity imposed on sympathisers makes Black Lives Matter an original case study of the articulation between the internal cohesion and external representation of a social movement.

In this perspective, the interracial mobilization of the academic world in the Black Lives Matter movement is interesting. The year 2015 was marked by a series of racist incidents leading to black and white student mobilization, first at the University of Missouri before the movement spread from Princeton to Claremont McKenna, Georgetown, Yale, or Stanford. These mobilizations, which are part of a renewal of student activism since the Occupy movements, have been galvanized by Black Lives Matter, bringing students from dozens of universities to claim a greater diversity of the student body and faculty, to call for a renaming of campus buildings bearing the names of notorious slavers, or to advocate greater support from university governance toward more satisfactory living and working environments for minority students.[48] In 2017 and 2018, in a political climate marked by the public resurgence of the US far right, Black Lives Matter activists tried to prevent or disrupted several talks and events organized by white supremacists – for instance neo-Nazi Richard Spencer – on various US campuses.[49] Academics have also been involved in teaching the historical and sociological issues of the movement through the #FergusonSyllabus initiative, which brings together scientific references that can be used to understand and analyze racial violence in the United States. The articulation between campuses and the movement is also reflected in the leadership's reflexive and pedagogical efforts at fully establishing the historical and sociological sense of BLM and M4BL.[50]

Speeches and the positions of movement leaders purportedly use academic categories. They mention notions such as intersectionality, systemic racism, and so on, initially forged at the margins of academia, such as Black Studies, Race Studies, Gender Studies, LGBTQ Studies, and so on. Such a framing undoubtedly matched the resumes of the leaders of the movement, representatives of an elite familiar of critical theory programs. It also corresponds, as we shall see, to the abandonment of a religious framework traditionally imposed through the preeminence of churches in African-American mobilizations.

The scope of the coalition and the absence of a restrictive definition of identity do not, however, prevent leaders of BLM and M4BL from prioritizing their claims by formulating specific objectives.

Black Lives Matter: a structural political project

The coalition behind the Black Lives Matter movement is rooted in an understanding of racial injustice as a long-term structural phenomenon. In that regard, the movement rejects the dominant psychological paradigm in the political, media, and scientific fields considering racism as the consequence of individual will.[51] For sure, the expression "Black Lives Matter" is both a cry of indignation and mobilization seeking to assert and impose the value of black lives in the public space by appealing to the moral conscience of the individual.[52] However, the movement seeks above all to defend a materialist political program in the fight against racial inequalities. Expressions such as "The New Jim Crow" and "From the auction block to the cell block"[53] show such attention to the concrete mechanisms of transformation and preservation of racial oppression over generations.

By understanding racism as a structural or institutional phenomenon – that is to say, a phenomenon which reproduces within social systems (the school system, the justice system, the political system, the economic system, the healthcare system, and so on) – the movement aims at changing the power structures in society, even provoking a revolution. Alongside classic concepts such as "institutional racism" and "white supremacy," the movement uses newer concepts such as "state-sponsored racism" and "state-sanctioned violence" that specifically emphasize the direct and indirect role of the state in the perpetuation of racial violence against communities of color.[54] From this point of view, the deaths caused by the police are not analyzed in terms of individual mistakes but as the results of a concerted public policy. Besides, the elaboration of the concept of "state violence" to explain the perpetuation of structural poverty, including among Latino and white working-class people, has made it possible to

300

identify common political interests between Black Lives Matter and the American labor movement.[55]

In 2015, Darsheel Kaur of the Ohio Student Association, and Alicia Garza, said in these terms:

> DK: It's more than just police brutality. It's about systems in place that continue to devalue the lives of black and brown people in different aspects including the prison industrial complex, economic and food systems, the housing market, voting rights. The energy that came together as this movement is a collective energy that has been building up through frustration about these many issues. It all comes down to the value of human life and what we're willing to put on the line to fight for it.
>
> AG: I agree. State violence is much bigger than police violence, though police enforce the needs of the state.[56]

In that regard, BLM and M4BL enrich the intellectual and political framework of the Black Power movement of the 1960s and 1970s. Unlike the Civil Rights movement of the 1950s and 1960s, which considered the federal government as the best remedy against racist oppression, the Black Power movement sought to attack the "institutional racism" lodged in the core of American state structures. Through multiple local mobilizations, the Civil Rights movement aimed above all to overturn the Jim Crow laws in services, whether public (schools, transportation, libraries, parks, and so on) or private (restaurants, hotels, cinemas, churches, and so on). In this sense, the passing of the Civil Rights Act in 1964 declaring racial discrimination and segregation to be illegal was the apogee of the movement. In the mid-1960s, persistent poverty and large-scale uprisings in black ghettos forced civil rights activists like Martin Luther King, Jr. to direct their action against the mutually reinforcing social structures of capitalism and racism.[57]

By targeting the structures of the US social system, the actions undertaken by BLM and M4BL militants are both symbolic and practical. On the one hand, the movement seeks to disrupt the daily functioning of society to revolutionize the status quo ante. Like television in the 1950s and 1960s, the use of social networks allows for the effective mobilization of activists and a massive diffusion of their message, sometimes with lurid videos embedded. Disruption as a means of direct action inherited from the LGBTQ and Occupy movements is another remarkable feature of BLM's militant repertoire. Voluntarily provocative, thousands of collective mourning gatherings, die-ins, and Freedom Rides have, since 2014, sought to subvert the usual functioning of the public space by blocking traffic on roads, railways, bridges, and tunnels, interrupting political speeches, occupying shopping centers, encircling city halls and police stations, delaying sports events, or kneeling during the national anthem, as did Colin Kaepernick and many other professional football players and athletes. These actions responded to the slogan "Shut It Down!"[58]

On the other hand, the movement advances practical proposals, particularly on police issues. Following Michael Brown's killing in August 2014, the Ferguson Action coalition released a list of specific requests for the St. Louis metropolitan area, soon to be followed by each major city and campus throughout the country.[59] Ferguson Action also established national demands in its "Our Vision for a New America" program, directly inspired – and repeating sometimes verbatim – the program of the Black Panther Party for Self-Defense published in 1966, in a similar context made of police violence and urban uprisings.[60] The collective We The Protesters, led by DeRay Mckesson, Samuel Sinyangwe, and Brittany Packnett, also published national demands while launching MappingPoliceViolence.org and CampaignZero. CampaignZero was inaugurated in August 2015 as a platform providing both precise and ambitious solutions to "law and order" issues in disadvantaged African-American neighborhoods. Likewise, in 2016, the M4BL established a similar platform in favor of political, economic, and social justice, including highly contentious demands such as reparations for past racial injustices and the condemnation of the Israeli colonization of Palestinian territories.

Obama's actions to reform criminal justice were limited as they mainly applied to federal prosecutions and inmates, which represent only a small fraction of cases nationwide. Also, his 2015 task force in twenty-first-century policing mainly presented recommendations and non-binding suggestions. While these were indeed limited steps to reform US law enforcement agencies, some of the measures outlined by CampaignZero and the M4BL (the abandonment of "broken glass" policies, citizen representation in the local justice system, the demilitarization of police forces, the establishment of independent investigations on police violence, and so on) were incorporated into the Democratic program for the 2016 presidential election.[61] After the resounding election of Republican candidate Donald Trump in November 2016, the deadly use of force against minorities of color had largely vanished from public debates, so it seemed. The popular and mediatic tsunami following the killing of George Floyd by a White police officer in May 2020 proved, if need be, that the simmering racial scars had not closed. Further, Trump's highly controversial and continually commented on policies and statements, notably on racial and immigration issues, during his presidency led many commentators to wonder whether BLM and M4BL can win or even be heard in the "Trump Age."[62]

The actions and demands promoted by BLM and M4BL highlight the deep division along class and age lines that fracture the African-American community.[63] The social polarization of this community divides its political interests between, on the one hand, integrated elites holding political power and economic resources since the 1960s and 1970s (President of the United States, elected members in the US Congress and state assemblies, mayors, judges, businessmen, professionals, and so on) and, on the other hand, poor people relegated to the margins of the American capitalist democracy.[64] In March 2015 Baltimore black mayor, Stephanie Rawlings-Blake, scolded the poorest segments of the African-American community in her city for being "complacent" toward "black-on-black crime" – what many considered an unbearable declaration inspired by white conservative rhetoric after the death of Freddie Gray a month later, in April 2015.[65]

In particular, this tension is reflected in the refusal of young BLM and M4BL activists to adopt the codes of "respectability politics."[66] Linked to the "racial uplift" strategy designed by the African-American upper classes at the end of the eighteenth century, the public display of black respectability sought to reform the supposed immorality of the black working classes in order to prove the dignity of the whole community and thus obtain equal civil rights and social integration. By privileging "passing" and assimilation to put an end to racial injustice, this strategy of emancipation neglected the transformation of social structures at the origin of the reproduction of racial injustice. Today this political program is still a pivot of African-American political culture, particularly through its churches, but, promoted by African Americans now in a position of power, it seems all the more scandalous for many BLM and M4BL activists.[67]

Barack Obama himself has spoken out for racial respectability as a legitimate political tactic. In his most famous speech, "A More Perfect Union," Democratic presidential candidate Barack Obama certainly pointed to the structural persistence of racial inequality: "But we do need to remind ourselves that so many of the disparities that exist in the African American community today can be directly traced to inequalities passed on from an earlier generation that suffered under the brutal legacy of slavery and Jim Crow."[68] Yet, once elected, Obama defended a moralizing and conservative vision in which black social oppression was often explained by black deviant culture and lack of personal responsibility.[69] Obama's analytical ambivalence has been coupled with a political reluctance to implement programs specifically targeted for the African-American community – such as affirmative action programs – in order to favor color-blind initiatives, like the reform of the healthcare system designed to reunify the country around "common" values and ideals. In *The Audacity of Hope*, published ahead of his first presidential campaign, Obama sought to overcome the entrenched political and racial divisions in the United States by making extensive use of the adjective common (common values, common sense, common good, common ground, common hopes, and so on), a trope which tends to downplay social conflicts and depoliticize public action.[70] This tactic, however, did not disarm accusations of anti-white racism coming from his right, and racial treason coming from his left.[71]

Resulting from the criticism aimed at the politics of respectability, the diminished political role of churches in BLM and M4BL is arguably the most notable historical difference with the Civil Rights movement. Traditionally, mass political mobilizations in the African-American community have been organized with the help of the different black protestant denomination. The presence of women and queer people in positions of responsibility within the movement, the suspicion toward the moral conservatism of certain religious leaders, the mobilization of younger and less religious generations, as well as the use of both profane and radical concepts like intersectionality and systemic racism show the relative marginalization of the black church in the current mobilization.[72] From this perspective, BLM and M4BL appear as the first African-American political movement since the Black Panther Party that is not explicitly supported by the message and the network of black churches. In its demands and modes of action, BLM and M4BL part ways with the traditional political strategy based on the networks of hundreds of religious organizations, hierarchically directed, led by a charismatic leader, and playing by the rules of democratic respectability, such as the Rainbow PUSH Coalition and the National Action Network of pastors Jesse Jackson and Al Sharpton.[73]

As racial issues are ultimately unable to unify the whole African-American community around common political objectives, many activists in the movement favor the intersectional paradigm instead. However, like any movement fueled by an intersectional ambition, BLM and M4BL face the dilemma of how to decide over their political priorities. The demarginalizing exhortation of 1970s–1980s black feminists, i.e. placing women and LGBTQ people at the heart of the protest, remains a challenge, given the powerful issues of race, class, and age which are still polarizing the movement.

Conclusion

Fifty years after the Civil Rights movement, the rise of BLM and M4BL highlights the persistence of racial inequality in the United States. The 2008 and 2012 elections of Barack Obama did not signal the "end of black politics," as *The New York Times* announced in 2008.[75] On the contrary, the recent emergence of large-scale political mobilizations marked a revival of African-American struggles over race issues.[76]

During his two terms in office, in the context of a major economic crisis that severely affected communities of color in the United States, Barack Obama attempted to tackle the issue of racial inequality through racially neutral policies such as the reform of the healthcare system, the revaluation of overtime pay, the debate on minimum wage, and justice system reform. More than his centrist prudence and conservative rhetoric, Obama's relative failure to reform American society has primarily been the result of the racial resentment triggered by his election in large sections of the white electorate.[77] Like all racial gains since the Civil War, Obama's two terms as President of the United States have stimulated reactionary racial trends that fueled, among other things, the rise of the Tea Party movement, the systematic obstructionism of Republicans in Congress, and the 2016 election of Donald Trump. In that regard, BLM and M4BL are the consequences of the increased polarization of the American public arena since the early 2000s, and a powerful refutation of the consensus narrative on the success of US civil rights history. Finally, BLM and M4BL appeared not in spite of, but because of, the presence of an African-American president in the White House.

In this context, BLM and M4BL emerged as a movement driven by a global "strategic project" seeking to address the intersection of the multiple causes that explain the persistence of racial inequality in American society.[78] BLM and M4BL have been conceived of as the political formulation of a multi-sided and century-old social problem. By positing a lucid narrative based on undeniable empirical facts, in particular about police brutality and mass incarceration, the movement articulates renewed analyses of the structure of racial inequality and advanced practical solutions for the reform of state institutions by providing more power to local communities. This sort of structural analysis, relatively marginal in the United States, has been gradually gaining favor among Democratic sympathizers and Americans under thirty years of age.[79]

To achieve its political objectives, the BLM and M4BL coalition have attempted to redefine the nature of collective minority struggles. On the one hand, the movement relies on mobilization strategies outside established institutional channels, which have been experienced by major American social movements for more than half a century, such as the Civil Rights movement, the Black Power Movement, the feminist movement, the gay and lesbian movement, Occupy Wall Street, and so on. Above all, BLM and M4BL seek to fuse diverse identities and particular interests within a plural and collective movement. The visibility of many women and LGBTQ people in leadership positions within the movement demonstrates how new forms of activism are taking shape that are independent from traditional African-American mobilizations.

The plurality of political projects in the movement raises the question of its cohesion and its representation over the long term, a problem that is inherent to any movement self-defined as intersectional. The challenge for BLM and M4BL is therefore to build among its activists and supporters a "collective subject of representation" able to discern its own interests in a multiplicity of circumscribed and sometimes contradictory but interconnected struggles.[80] In this respect, the historically problematic alliance between the black and white working classes whether in trade unions or political mobilization is not the least of the challenges encountered by BLM and M4BL.

The slogans "All Lives Matter" and "Blue Lives Matter" promoted by opponents of the movement seek precisely to stiffen racial tensions by refuting the specificity and centrality of black oppression. Yet, given the current social context in the United States today, all lives (including white lives) will really matter only if black lives are valued. In the same vein, by focusing on the fight against the violence of the justice system against racial minorities – of which black men are known to be the main victims – BLM and M4BL favor a struggle that is both specific and central to advance them all, and achieve its main goal: to redefine the contours of American and international democracy.

Notes

1. Given the lack of reliable data on police killings, several newspapers including *The Washington Post* and *The Guardian* have set up websites to count the number of people killed by police and other law enforcement agencies in the US. The Counted, a project launched by *The Guardian*, is considered to be one of the most reliable. For 2015, it counted seventy-nine unarmed black persons killed by the police. For 2016, it counted forty-two unarmed black persons killed by the police. See https://www

.theguardian.com/us-news/ng-interactive/2015/jun/01/about-the-counted (last accessed November 17, 2019).

2. Crenshaw, "Mapping the Margins," 1991, and "Demarginalizing the Intersection," 1989.
3. De Jong, *Invisible Enemy*, 2010; Taylor, *From #BlackLivesMatter to Black Liberation*, 2016.
4. Calhoun, "Occupy Wall Street," 2013; Gitlin, "Occupy's Predicament: The Moment," 2013, and *Occupy Nation*, 2012; Taylor, *From #BlackLivesMatter to Black Liberation*, 2016.
5. Chatelain and Asoka, "Women and Black Lives Matter," 2015.
6. Hadden, *Slave Patrols*, 2001; Alexander, *The New Jim Crow*, 2010; Muhammad, *The Condemnation of Blackness*, 2010; Gray et al., *Killing Trayvons*, 2014.
7. Elzie, "'Our Demand Is Simple: Stop Killing Us,'" 2015.
8. Smith, "How Trayvon Martin's Death Launched a New Generation of Black Activism," 2014.
9. Obama, "Remarks by the President on Trayvon Martin," 2013b.
10. Harris-Perry, "Trayvon Martin: What It's Like to Be a Problem," 2012.
11. Garza, "A Herstory of the #BlackLivesMatter Movement," 2014; Ruffin, "Black Lives Matter: The Growth of a New Social Justice Movement," 2015; Cullors, "#BlackLivesMatter Will Continue to Disrupt the Political Process," 2015; De La Cruz, "#BlackLivesMatter Co-Founders Say Their Org is 'A Love Note to Black People,'" 2015.
12. Kelley, "Why We Won"t Wait: Resisting the War Against the Black and Brown Underclass," 2014; Wilkerson, "Mike Brown's Shooting and Jim Crow Lynchings Have too Much in Common," 2014; Hill, "Are Police Shootings Really Like Lynchings?" 2016.
13. Malcolm X Grassroots Movement, "Operation Ghetto Storm," 2013; *The Washington Post*, "Police Shootings," 2015; *The Guardian*, "The Counted: People Killed by Police in the US," 2018; McCarthy, "US Government Database Hopes to Tell 'Whole Story,'" 2015.
14. Mapping Police Violence, "2017 Police Violence Report," 2017.
15. *Tennessee v. Garner* (1985) and *Graham v. Connor* (1989) are the two Supreme Court decisions which set up a framework for determining when deadly force by police officers is reasonable. The two cases have to do with the legitimacy of police officers shooting when defending their life or the lives of others and when a violent felon is fleeing. What matters is not that there is an actual threat but that the officer has an "objectively reasonable" belief that there is a threat.
16. Kindy and Kimbriell, "Thousands Dead, Few Prosecuted, 2015.

17. Davey and Eihorn, "Settlement for Torture of 4 Men by Police," 2007; Davey and Williams, "Chicago Pays Millions but Punishes Few in Killings by Police," 2015; Spielman "Chicago Pays $5.5M in Reparations to 57 Burge Torture Victims," 2016.
18. *The New York Times Editorial Board*, "Voters Tell Prosecutors, Black Lives Matter," 2016.
19. Balko, *Rise of the Warrior Cop*, 2013; Keller and Simon, "David Simon on Baltimore's Anguish," 2015; Police Accountability Task Force, "Recommendations for Reform," 2016.
20. Alexander, *The New Jim Crow*, 2010; Thompson, "Why Mass Incarceration Matters," 2010; National Research Council, "The Growth of Incarceration in the United States," 2014; Gottschalk, *Caught: The Prison State and the Lockdown of American Politics*, 2015; Hernandez et al., "Historians and the Carceral State," 2015; Muller, "Northward Migration," 2012; Quigley, "40 Reasons Why Our Jails are full of Black and Poor People," 2015; Hinton, *From the War on Poverty to the War on Crime*, 2016.
21. Cullors, "#BlackLivesMatter Will Continue to Disrupt the Political Process," 2015.
22. Calhoun, "Occupy Wall Street," 2013; Gitlin, "Occupy's Predicament: The Moment," 2013 and *Occupy Nation*, 2012; Taylor, *From #BlackLivesMatter to Black Liberation*, 2016.
23. Sentencing Project, *Report of the Sentencing Project to the United Nations*, 2013.
24. Gilmore, *Golden Gulag*, 2007; Wacquant, *Les prisons de la misère*, 2011.
25. Pager, *Marked*, 2007; Manza and Uggen, *Locked out*, 2008; Wood and Bloom, "De Facto Disenfranchisement," 2008; Wood, "Restoring the Right to Vote," 2009.
26. Anderson, *One Person, No Vote*, 2018.
27. *The New York Times Editorial Board*, "End Mass Incarceration Now," 2014.
28. Desmond, *Evicted*, 2016.
29. Pinkney, *The Myth of Black Progress*, 1984; Wacquant, *Parias urbains*, 2006; King and Smith, *Still a House Divided*, 2011; Wilson, *When Work Disappears*, 2012; Sugrue, A House Divided," 2013; Shapiro et al., "The Roots of the Widening Racial Wealth Gap," 2013; Coates, "The Case for Reparations," 2014; Pew Research Center, "On Views of Race and Inequality," 2016.
30. Massey and Denton, *American Apartheid*, 1992.

31. Clotfelter, *After Brown*, 2004; Logan et al., "The Geography of Inequality," 2012; Fiel, "Decomposing School Resegregation," 2013; Hannah-Jones, "Segregation Now," 2014.
32. The full list of BLM chapters is available at blacklivesmatter.com/take-action/find-a-chapter/
33. Movement for Black Lives, "About Us," 2017.
34. Fletcher, "From Hashtag to Strategy," 2015.
35. Talpin, *Community Organizing*, 2016a.
36. Ransby, "Black Lives Matter is Democracy in Action," 2017.
37. Bacqué, "Association 'communautaires' et gestion de la pauvreté," 2005.
38. Talpin, *Community Organizing*, 2016a.
39. King, "A Conversation with Brittany Packnett of Teach for America St. Louis," 2015; Reilly, "Meet the Teach for America Official Charged with Bringing Change to Ferguson and Beyond," 2014.
40. Singh, *Race and America's Long War*, 2017.
41. Ruffin, "Black Lives Matter: The Growth of a New Social Justice Movement," 2015; Beydoun and Ocen, "Baltimore and the Emergence of a Black Spring," 2015; Khan, "Black Lives Matter Has Become a Global Movement," 2015; Chitnis, "Meet the Indian Women Trying to Take Down 'Caste Apartheid,'" 2015; Zappi, "Une Marche de la dignité à Paris contre les violences policières," 2015; Taylor, From #BlackLivesMatter to Black Liberation, 2016; Davis, *Freedom Is a Constant Struggle*, 2016.
42. Greene, "The Southern Strategy," 2015.
43. See blackfutureslab.org/
44. Armstrong, "The New Civil Rights Leaders," 2014.
45. On political representation as a performative process, see Bourdieu, "La délégation et le fétichisme politique," 1984.
46. Anderson, "A Rising Share of the US Black Population is Foreign Born," 2015.
47. On political representation as an interactional process, see Dutoya and Hayat, "Prétendre représenter: la représentation politique comme revendication," 2016; Talpin, "La représentation comme performance," 2016b. Mckesson eventually finished sixth in the Democratic primary for Baltimore mayor.
48. Wilder, *Ebony and Ivy*, 2013.
49. Burch, "Colleges Brace for Tumult in 2018 as White Supremacists Demand a Stage," 2018.

50. See for instance, sociologistsforjustice.org/ferguson-syllabus/ and college.georgetown.edu/collegenews/the-ferguson-syllabus.html (last accessed 12 August 2018).
51. Bonilla-Silva, "More than Prejudice," 2015.
52. Fletcher, "From Hashtag to Strategy," 2015; Harris, *The Price of the Ticket*, 2012; Fassin, "Economie morale de la protestation," 2015a.
53. Alexander, *The New Jim Crow*, 2010.
54. Tometi, "Staying Focused in the Movement for Racial Justice," 2014.
55. On the necessary and yet difficult dimension of interracial political coalitions for African Americans, see Wilson, *The Bridge Over the Racial Divide*, 1999; Sugrue, *Not Even Past*, 2010; King and Smith, *Still a House Divided*, 2011; Coates, "The Enduring Solidarity of Whiteness," 2016.
56. Chatelain, "#BlackLivesMatter: An Online Roundtable with Alicia Garza, Dante Barry, and Darsheel Kaur," 2015; Tometi and Lenoir, "Black Lives Matter Is Not a Civil Rights Movement," 2015.
57. Ture and Hamilton, *Black Power*, 1967; Jackson, *From Civil Rights to Human Rights*, 2007; Joseph, *Neighborhood Rebels*, 2010.
58. Petersen-Smith, "Black Lives Matter: A New Movement Takes Shape," 2015; Oluo, "Bernie Sanders, Black Lives Matter and the Racial Divide in Seattle," 2015; Cullors, "#BlackLivesMatter Will Continue to Disrupt the Political Process," 2015.
59. WeTheProtesters, "The Demands," 2014.
60. Ferguson Action, "Our Vision for a New America," 2014.
61. CampaignZero, "Solutions," 2015.
62. McClain, "Can Black Lives Matter Win in the Age of Trump?" 2017.
63. Wilson, *The Declining Significance of Race*, 1980, and *When Work Disappears*, 2012.
64. Taylor, "In Baltimore and Across the Country," 2015, and From #BlackLivesMatter to Black Liberation, 2016.
65. Wenger and Broadwater, "Mayor Calls on Black Men to Do More to Stop Violence," 2015; Carmon, "Under Fire, Baltimore Mayor Stephanie Rawlings-Blake Stays 'No Drama,'" 2015.
66. Gaines, *Uplifting the Race*, 1996; Harris, *The Price of the Ticket*, 2012, and "The Rise of Respectability Politics," 2014; Squire, "The End of Respectability Politics," 2015.
67. Taylor, "What Divides Black America," 2014, and *From #BlackLivesMatter to Black Liberation*, 2016.

68. Obama, "Remarks by the President on Trayvon Martin," 2013b; Obama, "Candidate Barack Obama Remarks in Selma," 2007; Obama, "Obama's Father's Day Remarks," 2008a; Obama, "Remarks by the President at the 'Let Freedom Ring' Ceremony Commemorating the 50th Anniversary of the March on Washington," 2013a; Obama, "Remarks By The President On Strengthening The Economy For The Middle Class," 2013c; Obama, "Remarks by the President at Morehouse College Commencement Ceremony," 2013d.
69. Obama, "Candidate Barack Obama Remarks in Selma," 2007; Obama, "Obama's Father's Day Remarks," 2008a; Obama, "Remarks by the President at the 'Let Freedom Ring' Ceremony Commemorating the 50th Anniversary of the March on Washington," 2013a; Obama, "Remarks By The President On Strengthening The Economy For The Middle Class," 2013c; Obama, "Remarks by the President at Morehouse College Commencement Ceremony," 2013d. For sociological analysis combining structural and cultural explanations, see the work of Wilson, *More than Just Race*, 2009, who deeply influenced Obama.
70. Obama, *The Audacity of Hope*, 2006.
71. Sugrue, *Not Even Past*, 2010; Diamond, "Color Blindness and Racial Politics in the Era of Obama," 2010; Coates, "On the Death of Dreams," 2013; Taylor, *From #BlackLivesMatter to Black Liberation*, 2016.
72. On the relative declining influence in the early twenty-first century of traditional political elites who came from the Civil Rights Movement, see Cobb, *The Substance of Hope*, 2010. See also Green, "Black Activism, Unchurched," 2016.
73. Paybarah, "Amid Tensions, Sharpton Lashes Out at Younger Activists," 2015; Petersen-Smith, "Black Lives Matter: A New Movement Takes Shape," 2015; Thrasher, "'We're winning': Jesse Jackson on Martin Luther King, Obama and #blacklivesmatter," 2015; Reynolds, "I Was a Civil Rights Activist in the 1960s," 2015. On the important role of churches in the building of the civil rights movement, see Morris, *The Origins of the Civil Rights Movement*, 1984.
74. Crenshaw, "Mapping the Margins," 1991.
75. Bai, "Is Obama the End of Black Politics?" 2008.
76. Coates, *Between the World and Me*, 2015; West and Yancy, "Cornel West: The Fire of a New Generation," 2015; Kazin, "Introducing Our Summer Issue: American Movements," 2015.
77. Willer et al., "Threats to Racial Status Promote Tea Party Support Among White Americans," 2016.

78. Chauvin and Jaunait, "L'intersectionnalité contre l'intersection," 2015.
79. On the mixed vision of Black Lives Matter – and racial issues in general – in public opinion in the US, see Pew Research Center, "On Views of Race and Inequality," 2016.
80. Chauvin and Jaunait, "L'intersectionnalité contre l'intersection," 2015.

11

The Obama administration's labor and employment legacy

David Bensman[†] and Donna Kesselman

Barack Obama's ascendency to the presidency gave rise to aspirations for a higher ground through racial tolerance and social justice. He was the new-age statesman who would deliver the economy from quagmire and once more place institutions of government in the service of the people and provide American workers with decent jobs. The American labor movement felt it could rightfully claim its due, having once again, as in every election for generations, contributed massive campaign contributions and countless hours of volunteer footwork to ensure the victory of Democratic Party candidates. Wasn't it, after all, Nevada's unions that brought about the surprise jump-start to the Obama campaign in the second primary contest of 2008?

Although President Obama won as a progressive, he pursued neoliberal policies throughout most of his presidency. He disappointed labor allies by not going to bat for longed-for legislation that would have facilitated union organizing. Nor did he adopt a public sector-based model for landmark healthcare reform. Other neoliberal-era policies included free trade agreements, refusing to punish the perpetrators of financial fraud, and supporting corporate educational "reform" which attacked public education.

The subprime mortgage crisis triggered the Greater Recession and led to high levels of unemployment and underemployment, and to the withdrawal of masses from the labor market. Millions of Americans lost their homes in bankruptcy and millions of formerly middle-class families were plunged into poverty; the ripple effect ravaged industrial communities into fiscal default, causing them to neglect essential infrastructure. The slow "jobless" recovery was blamed squarely on the Obama administration. Its monetary rather than Keynesian fiscal policy, and notably the underfunded Recovery Act (aka "the stimulus plan"), were sharply criticized by prominent neo-Keynesians.[1] The setbacks absorbed by the Obama presidency in its early years, and the Republican victory in the 2010 midterms, placed unprecedented strains on the historical Labor–Liberal alliance[2] and paved the way toward Right-To-Work laws passed by Republican governors in highly unionized Midwest states.

It is in this context of impasse at the federal level and disappointments and attacks on both political and labor strongholds that counter-movements broke out, initiated by rank-and-file unionists and non-union workers at state and local levels, just as from the shop floor. Protests against Right-To-Work in Wisconsin, against mass unemployment, wage stagnation, housing foreclosures, mass incarceration, and a corporate trade agenda, highlighted by the Occupy movement, were followed by progressive denunciations of worsening economic inequality, and by the mobilization of workers in the fast food, home-care and domestic work industries. Successful campaigns for the US$15 minimum wage and paid sick leave, and innovative local legislation such as "fair workweek" took place within urban areas where strong progressive coalitions were emerging. In response, the second term Obama administration began adopting programs aimed at strengthening labor regulations and protecting workers. In particular, the Labor Department began developing new strategies for enforcing the labor laws and regulations after decades of neglect. Development of these strategies amounted to some of the most pro-labor measures since the New Deal.

The dominant narrative for Obama's inability to fulfill progressive ambitions, even during the heyday of the Democratic Party majority in Congress, lays the blame upon systematic obstructionism engaged in by congressional Republicans.[3] It is nevertheless worth noting that Barack Obama had deliberately refused to be the candidate of minorities and that he was not the flag-bearer of the Democratic Party leadership that had endorsed Hillary Clinton in the primaries, a group that included the leadership of the AFL-CIO and most of its national affiliates. In addition,

Obama did not subsequently attempt to mobilize these constituencies in support of presidential initiatives. Research has begun to emphasize other explanations, especially that of the influence of business interests, and more specifically from the financial sector, upon the Obama administration and its policy agenda.[4] This hypothesis is in line with the historical context of the crisis that took place in the dominant financial sector. It is also in line with the fact that, due to financialization, the balance of social forces was quite contrary to that which had given birth to social redistribution through twentieth-century welfare states in response to massive working-class mobilizations.

Our approach takes a deep look at the consequences of finance influence upon labor issues, as well as on Obama's own neoliberalism to explain his administration's policies and thereby to help explain the gap that existed between the aspirations aroused by the inspiring leader and the policies carried out. It delves into what we believe to be a decisive episode whose significance tends to be underplayed in the overall picture of the Obama legacy toward labor, one that brings to light the intimate relationship between this presidency and the world of finance to promote financial rationale in collective bargaining during the 2009 automobile industry bailout. We also place this presidential agenda in historical context. Ever since the Carter administration, in the late 1970s, and going through the Clinton administration, the Democratic Party had been a party of neoliberalism.

The first part of this chapter deals with how Democratic presidencies faced the agony of what Fraser and Gerstle dubbed the New Deal Order.[5] This helps specify the policy precedents to the actions taken by Obama in his first term. The second part deals with the president's first term landmark legislation that would distance the presidency from labor's agenda. Particular focus is placed upon the administration's handling of the automobile industry bailout, which constituted unprecedented government intervention into industrial relations. Focus will then be placed upon the social movements which emerged during the Obama years, and on how they influenced the administration's about-face to devote executive power to strengthen workplace regulations and protect workers. At best it might be said that Obama had no clear agenda for labor at the outset, a glaring example of what had early on been deemed as "presidential ambiguity."[6] Whatever the administration's intentions, its neoliberalism would strain the historical progressive alliance to an unprecedented degree and was a factor in US labor's turn toward new strategies and alliances.

The Democratic Party as a party of neoliberalism

The Democratic Party's embrace of neoliberalism went back to the Carter administration and its strategic choice in the face of stagflation – the simultaneous existence of mass unemployment and rapid inflation. Labor liberals organized to turn the economic policy-making of the administration to the fight against the mass unemployment that followed the Arab oil embargo. Two leading labor liberals in Congress, Senator Humphrey and Congressman Hawkins, wrote legislation to make full employment the nation's policy priority. They met resistance even within the Democratic Party, however. Full employment, which had been a goal of progressives since the Great Depression, now faced competing priorities from Democrats not tightly tied to the labor movement, a group that was soon to solidify as the New Democrats. A series of compromises was negotiated in Congress to produce not the original bill of Labor Liberal champions, but an act that had four potentially competing priorities: full employment, price stability, balance of trade, and budget deficit reduction. The legislation did set requirements for government policy, but never gained the influence that Labor Liberals had hoped for.[7] Looking back, the 1978 Full Employment and Balanced Growth Act was the last stand for a policy which had been the political trademark of Labor Liberalism. Subsequently, the Carter administration chose to fight inflation rather than unemployment. By adopting a monetary policy which kept interest rates high, Federal Reserve Board Chairman Paul Volcker precipitated the collapse of thousands of industrial enterprises, with massive unemployment being the inevitable fallout.[8] The predictable result was the undermining of labor bastions in traditional industries and so of union membership and clout.

During the Carter administration, the Democrats' shifting stance on regulation further signaled that the Democrat's liberal ideology was in flux. During the New Deal Order, regulation of markets was a priority, necessary to eliminate "destructive competition" and to ensure orderly markets. But in 1980, Senator Ted Kennedy (D-MA), though a leader of Democratic liberalism, sponsored a bill to deregulate the trucking industry, arguing that the Interstate Commerce Commission's setting of freight rates and oversight of freight routes created an inefficient market that stifled competition. Ralph Nader, the champion of America's consumers after successful battles with the automobile industry over the issue of car safety, joined with Kennedy. This was a momentous turn from the days when consumer advocates had sided with labor to regulate markets by creating institutions like the Interstate Commerce Commission, which set freight rates and approved freight routes. By 1980, it had become an article of faith among consumer advocates that regulation created market distortions, raising prices and impeding growth. The business lobby, which had long advocated for freeing the trucking market in order to reduce the burden of high transport prices on commerce, was a bastion of the deregulatory movement. The voices of black truck drivers, who complained about being excluded from the industry's workforce, added strength to the call for deregulation. The International Brotherhood of Teamsters' defense of the regulatory framework and the orderly markets it maintained in operation for more than thirty years was drowned out, harmed by the Brotherhood's reputation of being Mafia dominated.[9] Deregulation of airlines and telecommunications followed during the Reagan presidency, and Wall Street escaped regulation by the end of the Clinton administration.

After President Carter's 1980 re-election bid was defeated, Democrats went into opposition. While the Party was out of power, a new caucus was formally organized under the name of New Democrats in 1985. It responded to the Reagan campaign's success in winning substantial white working-class support by calling for the Party to move away from the New Deal politics espoused by Walter Mondale in his unsuccessful run for the presidency in 1984. In 1990, Governor William Clinton of Arkansas became the head of the Democratic Leadership Council, as the group called itself. The DLC urged the Democratic Party to adopt free trade, market deregulation, and pro-growth policies. During the Clinton administration, it played a role in the battle to ratify NAFTA and in support of reform of the welfare and criminal justice systems.[10]

When Clinton was elected president in 1992, his administration neoliberal's cast was apparent. Although the economy was in recession when he took office, Clinton refrained from stimulating the economy via fiscal policy. Instead, he relied on Wall Street financier Robert Rubin's advice to opt for monetary policy. Clinton signed the New American Free Trade Agreement, which had been negotiated during the Bush administration, in 1992, after adding "side agreements" on the environment and labor rights meant to appease liberals. To get NAFTA approved by Congress, Clinton, in an unprecedented political turn, relied on Republican votes, since labor organized massive opposition to the treaty, and a sizeable majority of Democrats outside the DLC orbit opposed ratification.[11] NAFTA was just the beginning of the Clinton administration's embrace of neoliberalism. It adopted education policies that all but abandoned apprenticeship and technical education in favor of "higher education" as the solution to unemployment and the sole path to individual advancement. It deregulated agriculture, "reformed" welfare in favor of workfare, and revised the criminal justice system in a manner that sharply increased incarceration. These policies threw millions of American industrial workers out of work, tolerated mass unemployment, and weakened federal regulation.

By the time Obama ascended to the presidency in 2009, the world of work and employment had become a "grey zone"[12] where workers' rights were either ambiguous or nonexistent, unions in the private sector were nearly defenseless, and precarious work seemed to be becoming the norm. Transformations toward financial capitalism undermined the economy's industrial base and the labor leadership's alliance with an ever-less liberal Democratic Party. The working class was left behind, caught in a representation gap.

The neoliberalism of the Obama presidency

Though President Obama won as a progressive opposing Hillary Clinton's centrist stance, he embraced neoliberal policies throughout most of his presidency. He demonstrated his commitment to neoliberalism by telling a meeting of DLC members in 2009 that he was a New Democrat.[13] He repeatedly disappointed labor allies by proposing pro-corporate trade agreements, by continuing to rely on monetary policy rather than Keynesian fiscal policy, by accepting high levels of unemployment (the rate of unemployment rose from 9.3 in 2009 to 9.6 in 2010), underemployment, and massive defections from the labor market as the new normal (the labor force participation rate dropped from 65.7 percent at the beginning of the Obama administration to 62.7 percent in 2016), and by supporting corporate educational "reform" which attacked public education.[14] As he, among other liberal allies, had warned at the passage of the 2009 Reinvestment Act (ARRA), while the stimulus package did ameliorate the effects of the Great Recession, Paul Krugman later wrote, with hindsight: it was "too small and too short-lived" to overcome the "dire legacy of the giant housing bubble."[15] Finally, the Obama administration failed to address the moral issues raised by the financial crisis. "Assuming office in the midst of the financial crisis, he appointed economic advisers who had promoted financial deregulation during the Clinton years. With their encouragement, he bailed out the banks on terms that did not hold them to account for the behavior that led to the crisis and offered little help for ordinary citizens who had lost their homes," comments Michael J. Sandel.[16] Robert Kuttner, who had expected "a transformative progressive president," later argued toward the end of the first term that Obama's presidency was "shaping up as one of American history's epic missed moments."[17]

Especially disturbing to the labor movement was the Obama administration's refusal to go to bat for labor's key agenda items. The first was EFCA, the Employee Free Choice Act, which the labor movement deemed essential for the success of its organizing campaigns. Over the decades, labor leaders believed, the Taft-Hartley Act's institution of Right-To-Work, court interpretations, and National Labor Relations Board (NLRB) rulings had created an uneven playing field. EFCA was proposed to even that playing field by allowing for card check as an alternative to NLRB elections, by speeding up those elections, by allowing unions to enter binding arbitration to produce a collective agreement if a bargaining agreement was not reached, by raising penalties for employers who committed unfair labor practices, and so on. President Obama ignored EFCA entirely; he presented virtually no support for EFCA during the first two years of his presidency, and he failed to use his political influence to move the bill through a Congress where Democrats were the majority.[18]

The second labor priority was universal healthcare. The passage of Obamacare will certainly follow its founder throughout history. It should be noted, however, the extent to which this dire flaw in the US social state was foremost on the country's historical agenda. The 2008 election witnessed the unprecedented fact that all candidates running, whatever their party, placed a national healthcare plan on their platform. The model that would ultimately be passed was similar to the market-based healthcare system Republican Mitt Romney put in place as Governor of Massachusetts.[19]

The Affordable Care Act was momentous, extending insurance coverage to over thirty million people and providing hundreds of billions of dollars of subsidies to low- and middle-income families. However, despite some new restrictions, private insurers retained – to the chagrin of labor and liberals – their primary role. These medical providers and manufacturers (including the big pharmaceutical firms) agreed to certain concessions but received in return millions of new patients and substantial new sources of revenue and profits, exerting increasingly powerful influence on lawmakers to achieve these ends. And many of the feared perverse effects of the market-based system quickly became apparent: beneficiary out-of-pocket cost increases, reports of the decreasing quality of health plans, and involuntary part-time employment imposed immediately after the laws passed to exclude access for many workers.[20] From the outset, the Act showed no regard for the progressive agenda single-payer healthcare system, universal healthcare financed by taxes that cover essential costs for all residents, through a single public system (hence 'single-payer'), called for in a unanimous September 2009 AFL-CIO Convention motion. Such a plan would be nothing more than an extension of Medicare.[21] A *New York Times*/CBS poll at the time showed wide support for this: "Americans overwhelmingly support substantial changes to the health care system and are strongly behind one of the most contentious proposals Congress is considering, a government-run insurance plan to compete with private insurers."[22] Except for this bill (H.R.676, sponsored by Rep. John Conyers, Jr., Michigan), proposals for either a single-payer plan or a government-run insurance option "were discarded before serious formulation began."[23] And to the dismay of unionists, Obamacare ended up including the dreaded "Cadillac tax" on contractually negotiated healthcare. This provision was named by advocates to give the impression that employer-sponsored health benefits reflected the status and greed of organized workers. According to the Tax Policy Center of the Brookings Institution, comprehensive coverage of employer-sponsored health benefits will be subject to a 40 percent excise tax starting in 2022. The ". . . so-called Cadillac tax will be levied on insurance companies, but the burden will likely fall on workers. The tax will effectively limit the tax preference for employer-sponsored health insurance."[24] Among the main union slogans in 2008 to vote for Barak Obama had been denouncing John McCain who would "Bring In the Cadillac Tax."

Newly elected President Obama made good on promises to appoint progressive figures to key positions to defend worker rights. California Representative Hilda Solis as Secretary of Labor and former Department of Labor (DOL) policy advisor Seth Harris as Deputy Secretary were popular with labor. Pro-labor appointments were made to the NLRB, the Occupational Health and Safety Administration (OSHA) and the Mine Safety and Health Administration (MSHA).

To name a few pro-labor actions accomplished, the NLRB adopted a rule in 2011 that recognized micro-units in companies and allowed the members of micro-units to vote on union representation even though the main body of the workplace remained non-union. This rule had been sought by labor and overturned the Board's previous preference for "wall-to-wall" elections. OSHA hired additional inspectors, increased penalties for violations, and instituted more rigorous enforcement of safety violations in the mining industry.[25]

At least as prominently, the first Obama administration policy was also host to bank-friendly advisors who framed federal financial policy. They included Timothy Geithner, New York Federal Reserve president, as Treasury Secretary; Lawrence Summers, managing director of a hedge fund, who critics contend supported positions that helped foster the financial crisis, as Chief Economic Advisor; Diana Farrell, financial analyst at Goldman Sachs, and as Assistant on Economic Policy, Rahm Emanuel, former investment banker, as White House chief of staff.[26]

The auto industry bailout serves as a telling example. This singular episode of the Obama legacy toward labor is a prime instance of business, notably finance, influence upon administration policy. The in-depth study presented here illustrates how government intervention served as the vehicle for promoting financial rationale in industrial relations and subsequently impacting the very nature of automobile trade unionism.

The government enters the "collective bargaining business"[27]

Tripartite negotiations took place in Washington in 2009 to bail out an industry facing a cyclical downturn of sales combined with a credit crisis that resulted in the sharpest decline in production and sales since World War II, down over one-third in just two years. Things were particularly bad for the Detroit 3, whose market share slid from 50 percent to 44 percent in the same period.[28] This public intervention, an exceptional circumstance in the United States, can be likened to those that took place throughout Western countries to ward off financial collapse.[29] This context helps explain the concessions the auto workers union made in the name of saving jobs while they were under state injunction. While much reference has been made, when commenting on the bailout, of the "US government going into the automobile business," less attention is paid to its going into the "collective bargaining business." And the administration's strategy was anything but neutral: its policies were directly targeted to introduce financial rationale. Its main vehicle was the VEBA, the Voluntary Employee Benefit Association. The question explored here is how Democratic government policy ultimately affected trade unionism in the automobile industry as it confronted the challenges of the twenty-first-century global marketplace.

This exceptional public intervention occurred at a critical juncture between the automobile collective bargaining negotiations in 2004 and 2007 which introduced employment norm transformations and the new socio-political consensus reached in 2015 Detroit 3 contracts. Since the government's first Chrysler bailout in 1979, the UAW (United Auto Workers) – the previous trendsetter for workers' gains – attempted to limit its losses through "concession bargaining."[30] Two major concessions made in 2007 Detroit 3 contracts led to what has been called a historical turn.[31] The introduction of the two-tier career scale, which consisted of a lower-wage scale, and lesser benefits and career paths for entry-level workers, fractured the single employment norm that had traditionally applied to all auto workers. Second, the national UAW accepted to take over the management of the VEBA healthcare trust for retirees: for the first time, employers were relieved of the responsibility for providing a vital social gain. As it concerned only one category of beneficiaries, it undermined the single employment norm as well.

First introduced in 2004 when it was managed by the companies, the Voluntary Employee Beneficiary Association (VEBA) set up a distinct healthcare regime for retirees in lieu of the more generous active employees plan they had enjoyed. Contract terms in 2007 allowed companies to pay off the sums corresponding to their liabilities for retiree healthcare to the VEBA as a means of eradicating this debt from their accounting and relinquishing their role as provider. While independent according to tax law, with five out of eleven governing trustees coming from the union, including its main officers, and the others named by the courts, it is the UAW that actually assumed the management of the fund and so the attribution of this social benefit.[32] The tax-exempt, non-profit, stock market-based trust for providing employee benefits has been promoted as a new solution for social insurance, one that is de-linked from employers and that promises greater assurances of continuity in benefits. One specialist called the VEBA the "New Treaty of Detroit," referring to the 1950 UAW-GM accord, symbol of the US contract model. This potential ". . . employee benefit of the future [would] help unions attract workers and employers."[33]

The 2008 stock market crash placed bailing out the auto industry on top of the crisis management agenda. An ad hoc task force appointed by the president negotiated in the name of the Obama administration with GM and Chrysler, Ford deciding to go it alone. The resumes of its members reflected the administration's negotiating strategy. Comprised mostly of Wall Street and private equity firm executives and lawyers with experience in restructuring troubled companies, it was headed by Steven Rattner, a prominent investment banker, whose nomination was contested by Michigan elected officials and trade unionists.[34]

This task force rejected the firms' initial restructuring plans. As a condition for receiving public loans, it demanded tougher conditions so the companies would "become financially viable."[35] The Obama administration and Congress demanded that the bailout cut indebtedness by two-thirds: reduce production costs to those comparable to foreign automaker transplants, and finance the VEBA not from company cash payments but through stock equity ownership in New GM and New Chrysler after restructuring.[36] The extent of concessions demanded by the task force met staunch opposition from financial fund creditors, resulting in bankruptcy.[37] According to *The New York Times*, "By pushing the matter into bankruptcy court, the [Obama] administration is assuming that the judge will also reject the holdouts' demands." Chapter 11 of the US Bankruptcy Code allows company protection from creditors while restructuring, including the possibility to reject or modify collective bargaining agreements, under control of the judge. In this case, the latter replaced the federal government by requiring the same conditions.[38]

The two "new" firms, restructured in less than two months, pocketed US$85 billion in public loans. The new automobile labor contracts were crafted to reduce labor costs: pay freeze for workers, elimination of contractual overtime pay and bonuses, suspension of cost of living adjustments and Job Bank remuneration, and six-year contracts with a no-strike pledge. Thousands of layoffs and factory closures were planned. Despite Ford's not entering bankruptcy, it received the same concessions.[39]

The two firms were partially nationalized: the US government became 60.8 percent owner of General Motors, and Canada

10 percent. As for Chrysler, the two governments became part-owners, but also imposed a partnership with Italian automaker Fiat.[40] The most innovative – and controversial – feature was the role of the VEBA: the fund became 17.5 percent owner of General Motors and 67.7 percent owner of Chrysler. According to government prescribed terms, the cash liabilities promised in 2007 to finance the VEBA were reduced and payment would be made in the form of shares in the new firms.[41]

Thus, the automobile workers union, through its management of the retiree health insurance trust fund, now financed by automobile company stock, became de facto owner – majority owner in the case of Chrysler – of the two companies. As the UAW president stated at the time, if Chrysler went bankrupt – a possible, if not probable, scenario – that would be 67 percent of "0." A VEBA trustee entered the board of directors of each firm.[42]

In January 2010 the independent UAW-VEBA was launched. By the end of 2014, Fiat had bought out the government's stake and the UAW-VEBA shares to become the new, fully independent firm Fiat Chrysler Automobiles (FCA), and the US government sold its remaining shares of General Motors on the market. The UAW-VEBA continued to own 8.85 percent of GM stock.

Contracts bargained in 2015, the first negotiation after the bailout, restored social compromise in the automobile industry, a situation that both depends on and reinforces social peace.[43] However, it did not come without a fight. On October 1, 2015, for the first time in a generation, autoworkers voted down a UAW-negotiated national contract at FCA, by an almost two to one margin (65 percent), despite the fact that it contained substantial pay rises, for it perpetuated two-tier wages and proposed a new healthcare plan for active workers.[44] Deep-going rank-and-file opposition to concessions – lost wages, the two-tier system, and the VEBA – had grown and crystalized in the spectacular campaign of an opposition candidate for union president against the UAW leadership caucus at the 2010 convention.[45]

The final Detroit 3, 2015 contracts reversed the trend of previous concessions. Entry-level workers would reach top wage scales after eight years; the two-tier system, if not totally eliminated, commented Kristen Dziczek, Director of the Center for Automotive

Research, started to be "phased out."[46] Moreover, a UAW-proposed Healthcare Cooperative for active employees, presented as modeled after the VEBA, was rejected outright by the membership, and withdrawn. While contracts are complex constructions, these were major concessions that the companies had to make, inasmuch as two-tier wages and the UAW takeover of the VEBA for retirees had been the two main sources of cost cutbacks.[47]

What are the implications for the union of years of vested interest, if not de facto ownership, of two Detroit 3 firms through the VEBA? The UAW president explained the membership's rejection of the proposed healthcare cooperative as a "communication problem." Some observers took the analysis further. For Gary Chaison, professor of Industrial Relations at Clark University: "The UAW is now more involved in administering employee and retiree benefits than in bargaining for substantial economic gains . . . It presents something of a conflict of interest."[48] The *Detroit Free Press* wrote: "UAW President Dennis Williams made it a priority to help the Detroit Three automakers control or reduce healthcare costs," thereby expressing the union leader's concern for company interests.[49]

By making the UAW-VEBA a shareholder in General Motors and Chrysler, the 2009 automobile bailout created a precedent for auto union relations with companies. The autoworkers union had taken on the role of social benefits provider when accepting to manage the VEBA trust in 2007; it henceforth became a stakeholder in company profits. One expert observer, Teresa Ghilarducci, saw the VEBA as a vehicle for the UAW to reposition itself as a player in the emerging market landscape. It had become ". . . a tool in its own strategy to establish labor standards in the industry."[50] After a rocky start, the UAW-VEBA cut drug costs, added preventive care and partially restored dental and vision benefits while also increasing assets. At another level, it has become an influential shareholder on corporate governance issues, pressuring major firms – McDonald's, Walgreens – toward greater transparency in political donations, joint lobbying for lower drug and medical treatment prices, and so on. It has become an actor in a growing debate over the progressive role unions can play, through pension and healthcare funds, as stock market activists.[51]

Whatever one's view of the UAW-VEBA, its internal contradictions remain. The trust is market based and so bears investment risks. It redistributes resources available: benefits are extended or reduced according to stock and bond market values (section 3.5 of trust agreement) and in the case of collapse, no one is responsible for providing healthcare to UAW retirees (section 6.5). During 2015 contract negotiations, the announcement that the UAW-VEBA's estimated worth had dropped by almost half by May 2009 before rebounding was exploited by opponents of the new healthcare scheme.[52]

What is the significance for the Obama administration's legacy with labor of its direct intervention into the sphere of automobile labor relations through policies based on financial rationale? Freeman points to a systemic difference between industrial relations systems in Europe and the United States: "The EU model uses social dialogue institutions to help determine economic outcomes, particularly in the labor market, whereas the US relies more on market forces."[53] The US government intervention in the 2009 automobile industry bailout through ad hoc tripartism, however, did aim to determine economic outcomes. Government strategy explicitly aimed to impact employment norms and also promote the competitive automobile market positioning of favored national sons. To do so, the government became a direct player in industrial relations to the point of dictating contract clauses.

To influence automobile market standards of competition, the government-managed bailout introduced new, post-Fordist norms regarding corporate revenue redistribution. Labor costs – wages and benefits – would no longer be based upon workers' productivity or, even less so, on workers' buying power as consumers, through the traditional auto reference to cost-of-living increases, as was the case for the Fordist standard employment relationship.[54] They would be determined through the market-based notion of aligning labor costs to the level of foreign car manufacturer competitors producing in the United States. The discriminating feature of these Asian and European firms is that they are mostly located in Southern Right-To-Work states, do not use union labor or bargain collectively, and therefore provide significantly lower benefits.[55]

In addition to this attempt to impact industrial market standards, state action also promoted financial rationale within industrial relations. The Obama administration placed the UAW-VEBA at the heart of the auto industry bailout strategy and thus of the financial logic that impelled the state to engage in the extreme form of interventionism, that of nationalization. It should be noted that the bailout strategy was endorsed and implemented by all three branches of government – there was continuity between outgoing and incoming presidents, and from all branches of the government. The result was to undermine historical gains and, most significantly, the single employment norm that granted equal benefits to all autoworkers, including retirees. Via the VEBA, the bipartisan automobile bailout compelled the recodification of automobile employment relations toward associating workers' gains with corporate share results.

This financial logic was in line with the 1974 ERISA law on pension funds and the 1993 law on VEBAs, framed to incite the development of trusts as a harbor for workers' savings and more risk-taking investments by trust managers. For S. Montagne this "pre-eminence of finance over other institutional forms contributes to the development of a new, 'financialized', wage-labor nexus (*relation salariale*) as opposed to that existing during Fordism."[56] The UAW-VEBA embodies this logic and coincides with the union's attempt to play a role in employment norm transformations in globalization.

What is comparable among state interventions in Western countries in 2007–2008 is not just their form, state-mandated trilateralism, but their substance. In the United States as elsewhere, rather than upholding demands framed around workers' interests, as was previously customary in most European countries, public measures were "focused on competitive conditions for businesses, traded off for job maintenance: wage moderation, flexibilized labor markets, and changed pension and healthcare rules," meaning neoliberal standards.[57] The trend reflects the growing influence of the financial elite upon government policy, notably during the global financial crisis.[58]

In the specific case of the Obama administration, the automobile industry bailout is a key juncture in its legacy. It illustrates, just as in the course taken by Obamacare discussed above, the extent of influence of business interests upon the Obama administration and its policy, especially from financial spheres.[59] This singular episode, where government intervened as a direct stakeholder in industrial relations would alter the nature of trade unionism in the automobile industry.

The fact remains that the extraordinary tripartite moment in 2009 would end up counterpoising top-down political injunctions with rank-and-file resistance in the auto industry. This discontent, along with disappointments with Obama administration labor and employment policy and political gridlock at the federal level, coincides with the grassroots upsurge that would place social movements on the offense. The national AFL-CIO would find itself at a crossroads.

US labor and new social movements during the Obama years

The faded hopes that organized labor had placed in the Obama administration, and Republican victory in the House of Representatives in the 2010 midterms – one of the worst Democratic losses in seventy years – led to political impasse at the federal level. The stakes for workers and labor then played out on local grounds, in the states, cities, shop floors and, in a milestone development, among low-paid service sector workers. Consensus at these scales spanned from conservative backlash to progressive legislation and emerging social movements that culminated in a strategic turn taken by the national AFL-CIO.[60]

In 2011, Republican governors in the Midwest launched a coordinated campaign to limit or eliminate the right to collective bargaining for public workers by extending Right-To-Work, previously the hallmark of the union desert South, to labor bastion states. From 2011 to 2012, public worker union rates in Wisconsin and Indiana dropped from 50.3 to 37.4 percent and from 28.3 to 22.8 percent respectively.[61] Its adoption in Wisconsin, where labor rights for public workers had pioneered the Kennedy administration executive order authorizing collective bargaining in this sector nationally, was a severe setback and a symbolic blow. Despite the massive occupation of protesters at the state capitol building in Madison for three weeks and the call for a general strike launched by local unions, the national AFL-CIO and teachers' union's choice to shift the fightback to electoral grounds ended in failure with the aborted special recall election to oust Governor Walker.[62] Even the automobile union state of Michigan passed Right-To-Work laws for private and public sector employment in 2012.

Despite the difficulties and historically low union density – 6.6 percent of the private sector in 2012 – organized labor pursued its mission of defending and organizing workers, even scoring victories. The signature industrial action during the Obama years was the 2012 Chicago teachers' strike. Thousands of unionized teachers walked picket lines in front of 600 schools for seven exhilarating days to fend off the neoliberal austerity school reform – drastic cutbacks in wages and benefits and privatization – promoted by Democratic mayor and former Obama aide Raul Emmanuel. The Chicago Teachers Union became the new model of social movement unionism. Grassroots leaders worked with parents and community activists who shared a stake in protecting public education.[63] These strategies of "organizing," rank-and-file activism, and community outreach to mobilize public support have energized labor struggles since the epic Justice for Janitors unionization campaign conducted by the SEIU (Service Employees International Union) in the early 1990s, and portrayed by Ken Loach in the film *Bread and Roses*.

The Obama years witnessed the emergence of social forces which adopted innovative approaches to protest and which began to converge: Fight For $15 fast food and Our Walmart retail workers. In the wake of Occupy Wall Street, new social movement organizations also came increasingly to the social forefront. They all represented challenges for US labor.

After mutual skepticism, notably on the part of the national AFL-CIO, the federation developed open alliances with civil society associations such as "Worker Centers," or new social movement organizations that organize workers who do not fall under the juridical category of "employees," i.e. that can legally be unionized according to US labor law.[64] These growing categories of workers, like the misclassified independent contractors getting work from digital platforms, which are labor market transformations in the new economy, tend to undermine social rights. In response to these challenges, the 2013 AFL-CIO national convention engaged a strategic turn to formally embrace non-traditional labor groups and progressive community alliances.[65]

Worker Centers welcome precarious workers, what some have called today's main alternative form of organization to labor unions for the "new precariat."[66] Worker Centers address the needs of low-wage workers, mostly immigrants, often undocumented. They do not engage in workplace organizing but provide a wide range of services including legal aid (payment of wage theft, immigration procedures) and other types of services, such as English lessons, writing resumes, and so on.[67] They seek social justice through city, county, and state legislation.

Unions backed the National Domestic Workers Alliance, a Worker Center whose Domestic Workers Bill of Rights became a New York state law in 2010. It grants new rights for nannies, housekeepers, and home healthcare workers, who are excluded from basic labor protections: it mandates overtime pay, a minimum one day off per week, three paid vacation days per year after a year in a workplace, protection under state human rights laws, and so on. Similar laws followed suit in California and Hawaii. The Alliance was instrumental in the passage of ILO Convention No. 189: "Decent Work for Domestic Workers," in 2011.[68]

The New York Taxi Workers Alliance, founded in 1998 in collaboration with the New York City AFL-CIO Central Labor Council, was granted a union charter in 2011, and at the 2013 convention its chairwomen joined the National Labor Federation's Executive Committee. While taxi drivers are independent contractors, and not employees, the NYTWA defends their demands and fights for collective bargaining rights. It does so as well for Uber and Lyft drivers who make up one-third of the membership, and demand that they should be reclassified as employees. A campaign launched in 2015 against Uber, supported by a large progressive coalition, resulted in a landmark city legislative measure in 2018 establishing the country's first cap on ride-sharing vehicles which essentially requires companies to pay their drivers a minimum wage.

Unions are active stakeholders in campaigns for living wage ordinances and for paid family and sick leave laws. New York City is the vanguard "Fortress City," where a strong union presence helps to promote progressive policies.[69] The city and the state enjoy the highest levels of union density in the country, one-fourth of the workforce in 2013, and the greatest presence of new social movement organizations.[70] New York City workers earned US$15 minimum wage by 2018 and, due to state legislation, surrounding counties will progressively follow suit by 2021. In 2017, progressive Mayor Bill de Blasio, elected in 2013, stewarded the city's Fair Workweek law, the fifth US city to do so, improving working conditions for fast food and retail workers. Employers must give workers good faith estimates of when and how much they will work, predictable work schedules, and the opportunity to work newly available shifts before hiring new workers. In 2016, New York state passed the most generous law in the country for paid family leave. For the first time in a generation the state is directly intervening to regulate shop floor working conditions and for the first time in the country's history, it – alongside a few other vanguard states[71] – is obliging employers to grant paid gains to workers.

Grassroots social movements as drivers of legacy

In September 2011, Occupy Wall Street held rallies throughout Manhattan's financial district to decry the inequalities due to financial capitalism that preclude the possibility of genuine democracy. Claiming to represent the 99 percent of the population excluded from financial wealth, Occupy protests broke out in over 600 communities in the United States and in over 951 cities across 82 countries in a month's time. Occupy took inspiration from the Arab Spring, the 2009 Iranian Green Movement, the Spanish Indignados Movement and other anti-austerity protests of 2010. The role of labor was uneven. Many labor activists took part, and while most official unions held back, the spirit of revolt was contagious.

Widespread and unpredictable rolling strikes in the fast food and retail industries nationwide grew with each passing year until the end of the Obama administration, and captured the public imagination. They were triggered by 200 fast food restaurant workers who, in the wake of Occupy Wall Street, went on a one-day strike in November 2012 with demands for a US$15 an hour federal minimum wage, more than twice the current U$7.25 an hour that had not been raised since 2009, and the right to unionize. The demand was coined from the MIT Living Wage Calculator estimation that the living wage in New York county at the time was US$15.50 dollars an hour for an adult working full time and US$29.61 for an adult with a dependent child. In 2014, 42 percent of workers earned less than US$15 an hour, including 48 percent of women, 36 percent of whites, 54 percent of African Americans, and 59 percent of Hispanics. Among them, at least half were thirty-five years old or older.[72] A grassroots campaign was meticulously planned and financed by SEIU leadership in early 2011. It deployed 1,500 organizers in seventeen cities around the country: fights broader than individual shop floors would be necessary to take on corporations and organize workers on a mass scale.[73]

A year later tens of thousands of low-wage workers took to the streets, and protested outside banks and inside shareholders meetings in hundreds of cities.[74] Low-wage workers from other sectors joined the movement, including healthcare workers, childcare workers, gas station attendants, and small business employees, often on specially targeted dates. Airport workers joined the strikes, during Thanksgiving weekend for example. The OUR Walmart movement was launched and financed by the United Food and Commercial Workers International Union in 2012; it mounted coordinated strikes in major cities and targeted Black Friday, the most profitable day for retail, to strike. Community allies mobilized public support through rallies in support of strikers in cities large and small, from North to South.[75] The protests bore fruit. In four years, almost twenty-two million wage earners, mostly African American and Hispanic, received wage increases through contracts or laws. It was undoubtedly the campaign which improved conditions for the widest range of working people in fifty years in the United States and can be directly traced back to Fight for $15.[76]

The strikes were part of a larger, incipient movement that included acts of civil disobedience, such as occupations, that resulted in hundreds of arrests and gave birth to coalitions in civil society.[77] In 2014, Fight for $15 joined Black Lives Matter in protests in Ferguson Missouri, after Michael Brown was fatally shot by local police. Other innovative forms of protest emerged, such as Moral Mondays. Launched in 2013 by religious progressives in North Carolina with claims of unfair treatment and discrimination by state government legislation, the grassroots social justice movement, featuring marches and acts of civil disobedience, spread the next year to other Southern states like Georgia and South Carolina, and then more broadly to Illinois, New Mexico, and elsewhere.

In response, retail titans like Walmart, Target, and Gap granted across-the-board wage and benefit hikes. Unparalleled, such conspicuous concessions cannot be ascribed to financial loss, which was minimal, nor to the number of strikers, which was proportionally insignificant.[78] The first motivation for these ultra-conservative employers, renowned for their hostility to organized labor and their ability to defeat unionization attempts, was to prevent unionization. This attests to the deeply engrained creed of corporate US anti-unionism as well as to the persistence of labor organization despite the obstacles that alone can explain the sustained prosperity of the multi-billion dollar union-busting industry in the United States. Over three-quarters of employers hire consultants when confronted by organizing campaigns, and large union avoidance firms are increasingly seeking export markets for their "expertise."[79] This credo has extended to the tech world culture. Robert Noyce, cofounder of Intel, famously stated, "remaining non-union is essential for survival for most of our companies."[80]

The sector-wide social movement in fast food and retail, so rare in the United States, directly confronted the multinational firms with demands, rather than immediate employers. By doing so it undermined the business model of franchising and subcontracting that corporations depend on in the service industries to avoid acknowledging their obligations as employers, allowing them to capitalize on a low-wage and precarious workforce.[81] The second Obama administration would draw upon this dimension of the social movement underway to advance one of its most progressive measures that workers would seize upon to take McDonald's to court in 2015 as a joint employer, together with its franchisees.

Along the same lines, while Occupy Wall Street shifted the terms of the national debate toward economic inequalities due to corporate greed, Fight for $15 directly framed it in class terms through the need to fight for better working conditions. Striking low-wage workers sparked the sympathy of public opinion and brought people into the streets on their behalf. The media portrayed workers walking out of fast food restaurants and neighborhood stores or engaging in civil disobedience at corporate shareholder meetings as the heroism of ordinary workers whose plight was working multiple jobs and struggling to support their families.[82] Worker confidence and consciousness escalated through internet-based communication such as video conference calls, chat groups, voting apps to take collective decisions, and videos of charismatic leaders and totemic actions.[83]

The fervor of corporate reaction to this mobilization attests to the significance of its impact. The Seattle Chamber of Commerce and the International Franchise Association (IFA), the largest trade association of its kind in the country, brought a lawsuit against an ordinance that would increase the minimum wage in the city to US$15 by 2017. Outbursts from business and conservatives followed minimum wage increases in Chicago, San Francisco, and San Diego, and even in red states like Alaska and Arkansas, where minimum wage increases were passed by popular referendum during the 2014 midterm elections.[84] Conservative countermovements to progressive gains included state legislatures voting "preemption" laws that prevent local governments from raising the minimum wage or passing paid leave and rent control laws, and so on. Forty-four states have passed preemption laws that target worker rights. New York state prevents the nation's biggest city from raising its own minimum wage without approval from the state government. This preemption movement goes back two decades but has picked up significantly since 2013.[85]

Progressives energized the Democratic Party, which campaigned for these ballot issues and legislative gains at local levels. In characteristically impassioned rhetoric, President Obama took the forefront in condemning inequalities as the major flaw in American democracy. The urgency of resolving them marked the Democratic Party's electoral platform in 2016. Militant unionists had succeeded in mobilizing grassroots hostility to globalization's rush-to-the bottom within a worldwide context of social and political upsurge. The subsequent polarization of social forces has been increasingly institutionalized through legislation.

The Obama administration takes a progressive turn toward the labor agenda

The Obama administration reacted to this social movement mobilization by taking a progressive turn in its second term, adopting measures aimed at strengthening labor regulations and protecting workers. President Obama signaled the turn in policy by nominating Thomas Perez to be Secretary of Labor in April, 2013. Perez had been Assistant Attorney General during the first Obama administration, during which time he compiled a record that provoked Republican opposition. Republican members of the Senate, backed by the business community, mounted a campaign opposing Perez's nomination, delaying the vote on his confirmation until July. After the majority Democrats in the Senate passed a cloture resolution, Perez's nomination was confirmed by a partisan vote of 54–46. It was the first time that a Cabinet member's confirmation received a party-line vote.[86]

As Secretary of Labor, Perez pushed for policies to protect the nation's workers, often in the face of intense opposition. For example, from the start of his tenure he championed the fiduciary rule, which forbade retirement advisers from receiving any commissions that created a conflict of interest. Perez's push for the fiduciary rule was fiercely opposed by the financial services community, and it only became law three years later, on June 9, 2016.[87] During Perez's term in office he also issued the Home Care Final Rule, which required that home care workers for people with disabilities or for the elderly receive the minimum wage and compensation for overtime.[88]

Two key appointments enabled the Labor Department to carry out an agenda strengthening the Department's reform of labor law and regulation. David Weil, a professor at Boston University, became the Administrator of the Wage and Hour Division, a position that had remained vacant for ten years. The vacancy symbolized how the Division had become ineffective in recent years, with its budget remaining flat while the number of employers grew, and its enforcement staff reduced to the point that employers faced a "trivial" likelihood that they would be investigated in a given year.[89] Before his appointment to the post, Weil was the principal investigator on a report for the DOL, recommending that the Wage and Hour Division focus its enforcement energies on industries in which companies had been outsourcing employment by subcontracting, franchising, or setting up supply chains, a practice Weil termed "fissuring." Weil's report had put him in the cross-hairs of business concern about the direction of the Labor Department, and his nomination spurred a furious lobbying campaign to defeat his confirmation. While Professor Weil was nominated in September, 2013, the Senate didn't allow a vote on his confirmation until May, 2014.[90] Before he assumed his post, Weil published an immediately influential book entitled *The Fissured Workplace: Why Work Became So Bad For So Many and What Can Be Done About It* that virtually set out his program.[91]

Under Weil's leadership, the Wage and Hour Division expanded its inspection staff and undertook market research to determine in which industries companies had carried out fissuring most extensively and were therefore most likely to have committed violations of the law and regulations, including notably misclassifying employees as independent contractors to avoid paying benefits, or bringing in temporary staffing agencies that could be replaced as soon as they get too expensive. The Division issued new guidelines making it clearer whether workers were or were not independent contractors in July, 2015, and initiated a joint agency task force to crack down on tax avoidance that was often the result of misclassification.[92]

Richard Griffin was the second appointee who helped chart a reform agenda during Obama's second term. Griffin had been General Counsel to the International Union of Operating Engineers until he was confirmed as General Counsel to the National Labor Relations Board on November 4, 2013.[93] As General Counsel, Griffin took two actions that challenged the way companies' franchise arrangements allowed franchisors to avoid legal liability for the misdeeds of their franchisees. In *Browning-Ferris*, the

Board ruled that a company and the temporary staffing agency that recruited and managed its workers were joint employers; as a result, the company could be held responsible for violations of legal workplace standards. This reintroduces the missing link in the franchising chain of externalization. In the *McDonald's* case, the Board argued that the company was a joint employer with its franchisees when it attempted to block union organizing efforts. These cases stirred up furious opposition from franchising industries.[94] The rulings shed light on the dark side of franchising and represented, on a more modest scale, the first time since the Civil Rights Act in 1964, and the New Deal before it, that social movement and federal regulation coalesced toward constraining employer prerogatives and advancing social justice in the workplace.

In addition to these initiatives, the Department of Labor began capitalizing on local activism and legislative initiatives by advocating for new labor standards for paid sick leave and paid family leave. It began embracing technical education through partnerships with community colleges and it even called for free tuition for students at those colleges.[95] In the face of fierce opposition, it updated the rule exempting white-collar workers from overtime by raising the threshold for the exemption by more than double.[96]

The National Labor Relations Board adopted new regulations to provide for timely representation elections and began taking to court employers who disregarded workers' right to organize and bargain collectively. And on May 31, 2016, the Board ruled that an employer illegally hired replacement workers during a strike to punish the union and its striking members. The importance of this ruling needs to be understood in historical perspective: the balance of social forces had not allowed employers to take advantage of the 1938 Supreme Court decision allowing employers to hire replacement workers during a strike until the 1990s, during the massive onslaught against collective bargaining agreements; replacement workers have been widely used since then. The 2016 Board ruling was a big step away from the status quo. In addition to these NLRB actions, the president issued executive orders to extend labor rights and protections to LGBT employees of federal contractors.[97] He issued an executive order setting a minimum wage of US$10.10 for jobs on federal contracts, and an executive order barring companies with significant, repeated, and unremedied violations of labor and employment laws from receiving federal contracts.[98]

Taken together, the Obama labor agencies reinvigorated the government's role in regulating labor markets. This record incorporated actions taken to help labor unions directly, by reducing obstacles to union organizing, for example. The record also aimed to provide labor rights to unorganized workers who were not protected by labor regulations. The order protecting LGBT workers on federal contracts might serve as an example of this type of action. The Obama labor agencies thus took a stance which mirrored that of organized labor, which gave more attention to the needs and rights of unorganized workers during this period than at any time since the Great Depression. This harmony of the two institutions' approach to labor rights and regulations brought organized labor closer to the Obama administration than it had been to any Democratic administration since the Democratic Party took its turn toward neoliberalism in the late 1980s and reinvigorated labor support for party candidates in the 2016 election. Thus, a 2016 article in the *Washington Examiner* wrote that "President Obama has been arguably the most pro-labor chief executive since Harry Truman. He has appointed staunch labor allies to the federal agencies that watch unions, and he has tilted the regulatory field in organized labor's favor through reinterpreting old rules and implementing new ones." "'President Obama has been a good president for working people,' AFL-CIO President Richard Trumka said at a Sept. 1 Christian Science Monitor breakfast," in 2016.[99]

Conclusion

The "polarization of our politics"[100] is one legacy left by the 44th President of the United States who in many ways was a largely divisive figure himself too, albeit unwittingly. This was due to the divisive primary when he took on the party establishment candidate. It was also due to Republican obstructionism that heightened with the Tea Party insurgency during the 2010 midterms, to the nation's cleavage around race, to the tough policy choices required to manage a systemic crisis, and to political gridlock for issues of concern to working people and their families that fueled the eruption of grassroots social movements. In this context, the two Obama administrations adopted radically different policy approaches.

The landmark policies implemented during the 2008–2009 recession were neoliberal by design; they made a clear break with the liberal agenda that had founded the Party's erstwhile alliance with US labor and its allies. This was true of the Recovery Act, healthcare reform, financial sector reform or, as we highlight here, the automobile industry bailout. Though he enjoyed a Democratic majority in both Houses of Congress, the newly elected president passed up the opportunity to go to bat for the Employee Free Choice Act, which would have given unions the opportunity to run organizing campaigns on a more even playing field.

Through its management of the VEBA, the United Automobile Workers Union became a provider of market-based social benefits. As a government-imposed condition for bailing out the automobile industry, the union-run healthcare fund became part owner of Chrysler for four years. It continues to be part owner of General Motors. And it had union leaders on both companies' boards. After the UAW-VEBA sold company shares in 2018, the *Detroit News* noted that it is "still likely GM's largest stakeholder ... The 2009 agreement says the UAW trust must own at least 50 percent of the shares it initially acquired following the automaker's federally-induced bankruptcy."[101] What will be the long-term consequences of introducing financial rationale into the very nature of automobile unionism by linking social benefits for automobile retirees to corporate stock market results? The Obama administration introduced financial logic into the very nature of automobile unionism and did this by becoming a direct stakeholder in industrial relations. As for the course taken with Obamacare, these instances highlight the influence of business interests, notably from financial spheres, upon the Obama presidency policies, and legacy, toward employment and labor issues.

The setbacks absorbed by the Obama presidency in its early years placed unprecedented strains on the historical Labor–Liberal alliance and paved the way toward Right-To-Work laws passed by Republican governors in highly unionized Midwestern states. Republicans gained control of Congress in the 2010 midterms. It is in this context of impasse at the federal level and attacks on both political and labor strongholds that counter-movements broke out, initiated by rank-and-file unionists and non-union workers. Placed at a crossroads, the AFL-CIO would embrace these new social movements and allies.

In response to these movements, Obama's second term administration delivered ground-breaking labor law enforcement strategies and executive orders that improved government effectiveness in implementing workplace regulations and helped to advance many progressive social rights campaigns engaged at local levels. While some of these advances have since been reversed, the 45th President of the United States has not been able to stop their momentum. The Trump-appointed NLRB, for instance, has not yet been able to reverse the Obama-era *Browning-Ferris* standard. Rather, it was reinforced in December 2018 when the US Court of Appeals for the D.C. Circuit determined that a business could be considered a "so-called joint-employer" if it exercised a certain level of "indirect control" over employees' working conditions. A few months previously, an administrative law judge rejected a settlement negotiated between the NLRB and McDonald's: the corporation agreed to make payments to individual workers who were fired for Fight for $15 protests, although it did not agree to being designated as a joint employer. Whatever their outcomes, these rulings shed light on the dark side of franchising in the public eye. And while modest in comparison, they mark the first time since the Civil Rights Act in 1964, and the New Deal before it, that social movement and federal regulation have coalesced toward constraining employer prerogatives and advancing social justice in the workplace. This is historical legacy in the making. On an opposite note, the new social movement upsurge during the Obama years was a lever for polarizing politics around issues related to the role of government in the redistribution of wealth, such as state-mandated paid vacation time, workers' pay, working conditions, and union rights. The result, however, has been to intensify the institutionalization of increasingly contrasting rights through rapidly proliferating legislation at various local levels that results in further deepening the fragmentation of the US social state.

The reorientation of the Obama administration brought the Democratic Party closer to labor than it had been at any time since the Party began adopting neoliberalism with the advent of globalization. This did not mean that the Labor–Liberal alliance was reborn. The polarizing years of Obama's America had their expression within the party whose inner tensions as to how to face the challenges of neoliberalism crystallized during the 2016 primaries when the presidential party found itself deeply divided. The 37 percent of union members who voted for the next Republican president – 52 percent of households including a white unionized worker, with higher proportions in Midwest deindustrializing states, unprecedented since Ronald Reagan's election – placed the AFL-CIO in a political quandary. It would turn toward new strategies and alliances and enter the 2016 elections with deeply splintered ranks.

The Obama legacy toward workers and labor presents a mixed balance sheet. On the one hand, missed opportunities. Union density in the two terms of the Obama presidency declined from 12.4 percent in 2009 to 10.8 percent in 2017.[102] On the other hand, the second term saw the production of a strategy for labor law enforcement that can be the program of future, pro-labor Democratic administrations.

Notes

1. "Stiglitz Says Government Misses Mark on Economy," *All Things Considered*, January 15, 2010. Paul Krugman, "The Stimulus Tragedy," *The New York Times*, February 20, 2014.
2. Kevin Boyle (ed.), *Organized Labor and American Politics: The Labor-Liberal Alliance* (Albany, State University of New York Press, 1998).
3. Theda Skocpol and Lawrence Jacobs (eds.), *Reaching for a New Deal* (New York: Russell Sage Foundation, 2011).
4. Banerjee Tarun et al., "Capital Strikes as a Corporate Political Strategy: The Structural Power of Business in the Obama Era," *Politics & Society*, 46(1), 2018, pp. 3–28.
5. Steven Fraser and Gary Gerstle (eds.), *The Rise and Fall of the New Deal Order* (Princeton, NJ: Princeton University Press, 1989).

6. Michael Foley, "Barack Obama and the Calculus of Presidential Ambiguity," *Political Studies Review*, 11, 2013, pp. 345–357.
7. Thomas Edsall, *The New Politics of Inequality* (New York: Norton, 1985).
8. William Greider, *The Secrets of the Temple* (New York: Simon Schuster, 1987).
9. Shane Hamilton, *Trucking Country* (Princeton, NJ: Princeton University Press, 2008); Dorothy Robyn, *Breaking the Special Interests* (Chicago: University of Chicago Press, 1987); David Bensman, "Port Trucking as a Test Case of Precarious Work in the Grey Zone of Work and Employment," *Revue Interventions Economiques/ Papers in Political Economy*, 58, 2017.
10. Jon F. Hale, "The Making of the New Democrats," *Political Science Quarterly*, 110(2), summer 1995, pp. 207–232; DLC, "The New American Choice Resolutions" (New York: Democratic Leadership Council, 1995).
11. John R. MacArthur, *The Selling of Free Trade* (Berkeley: University of California Press, 2000).
12. Jean-Yves Boulin and Donna Kesselman, "Work and Employment Grey Zones: New Ways to Apprehend Emerging Labour Market Norms," *Transfer*, 24(3), August 2018.
13. Carol E. Lee and Jonathan Martin, "Obama: I am a New Democrat," *Politico*, March 3, 2009. Available at: https://www.politico.com/story/2009/03/obama-i-am-a-new-democrat-019862 (accessed August 2019).
14. Sandel, Michael J. "Populism, Liberalism, and Democracy," *Philosophy and Social Criticism*, 44(4), 2018; Hershman, Brett, "A Look at the Unemployment Rate Since Obama Took Office," *Benziga*, November 4, 2016. Available at:https://www.benziga.com/news/16/11/8653903/a-look-at-the-unemployment-rate-since-obama-took-office
15. Krugman, *art. cit.*
16. Sandel, *art. cit.*, p. 355.
17. Robert Kuttner, "Unequal to the Moment," *American Prospect*, February 2011. Available at: https://prospect.org/culture/unequal-moment/ (last accessed December 2019).
18. Anne-Marie Lofaso, "Promises, Promises, Assessing the Obama Administration's Record on Labor Reform," *New Labor Forum*, 20(2), spring 2011, pp. 65–72; Stanley Aronowitz, *The Death and Life of American Labor: Toward a New Worker's Movement* (New York: Verso, 2015).

19. Available at: https://www.motherjones.com/politics/2015/10/mitt-romney-obamacare-romneycare/ (last accessed March 3, 2018).
20. Malini Cadambi Daniel and Erica Rafford, "Noyes Obamacare and Collective Bargaining: The Massachusetts Experience," *New Labor Forum*, 22(1), winter 2013, pp. 37–43. William E. Even and David A. Macpherson, "The Affordable Care Act and the Growth of Involuntary Part-Time Employment," *ILR Review*, 72(4), 2018, pp. 955–980.
21. Renamed "Medicare for All," the proposal became controversial during the Democratic presidential primaries in 2019–2020.
22. Available at: https://www.nytimes.com/2009/06/21/health/policy/21poll.html
23. Tarun et al., pp. 3–28.
24. Available at: https://www.taxpolicycenter.org/briefing-book/what-cadillac-tax (last accessed June 10, 2018).
25. Available at: https://www.lhsfna.org/index.cfm/lifelines/october-2012/what-has-the-obama-administration-done-on-occupational-safety-and-health/ (last accessed March 22, 2019).
26. Jonathan Alter, *The Promise: President Obama, Year One* (New York: Simon & Schuster, 2010), p. 52.
27. This section borrows from Donna Kesselman, "The Great Recession and New U.S. Automobile Employment Norms: Financial Rationale in the Work and Employment Grey Zone," *Interventions Economiques/Papers in Political Economy*, 58/2017. See https://interventionseconomiques.revues.org/3204, in the special issue on "The Grey Zones of Work," edited by Corinne Siino and Sid Soussi.
28. The term "Detroit 3," referring to General Motors, Ford, and FCA (Fiat Chrysler Automobiles) replaced the previous term "The Big Three" (automobile manufacturers) when Toyota became the market leader in 2008. For figures, see Thomas H. Klier et al., "Restructuring of the U.S. Auto Industry in the 2008–2009 Recession," *Economic Development Quarterly*, 27(2), 2013, pp. 144–159.
29. IRES, "La démocratie sociale à l'épreuve de la crise. Un essai de comparaison internationale," *Ires*, Report no. 04.2013 (translation), Frédéric Lerais et al., www.ires-fr.org/images/files/Rapports/CONFERENCE INTER ANGLAIS.pdf
30. Nelson Lichtenstein, *Walter Reuther: The Most Dangerous Man in Detroit* (Urbana-Champaign: University of Illinois Press, 1995); Harry Katz et al., "Crisis and Recovery in the U.S. Auto Industry: Tumultuous Times for a Collective Bargaining Pacesetter," in Howard R Stanger et al. (eds.), *Collective Bargaining Under Duress: Case*

Studies of Major North American Industries (Ithaca, NY: Cornell University Press, 2013).

31. Catherine Sauviat, "Restructurations et négociations collectives chez les trois grands de l'automobile américaine: un véritable tournant," *Chronique internationale de l'IRES*, 110, January 2008, pp. 17–32.

32. Thomas H. Klier and Jonathan M. Rubinstein, "Detroit Back from the Brink? Auto Industry Crisis and Restructuring, 2008–2011," *Economic Perspectives*, Federal Reserve Bank of Chicago, 2012, pp. 35–54.

33. Teresa Ghirladucci, "The New Treaty of Detroit: Are VEBA's Labor's Way Forward?" in Claire Brown et al. (eds.), *Labor in the Era of Globalization* (New York: Cambridge University Press, 2010), pp. 241–263; Aaron Bernstein, "Can VEBAs Alleviate Retiree Healthcare Problems? *Pensions and Capital Stewardship Project*," April, Cambridge, Harvard Law School. Available at: http://www.law.harvard.edu/programs/lwp/pensions/publications/occpapers/occasionalpapers_Ap9_fin2.pdf (last accessed August 2019).

34. Paul Ingrassia, *Crash Course: The American Automobile Industry's Road to Bankruptcy and Bailout – and Beyond* (New York: Random House, 2011); Bill Vlasic, *Once Upon a Car: The Fall and Resurrection of America's Big Three Automakers – GM, Ford, and Chrysler* (New York: HarperCollins Publishers, 2011); Klier and Rubenstein, 2012.

35. Klier and Rubinstein, 2012.

36. Vlasic, 2011; Ingrassia, 2011; White House, "Fact Sheet on Obama Administration Auto Restructuring Initiative for General Motors," 2009, www.whitehouse.gov/the-press-office/fact-sheet-obama-administration-auto-restructuring-initiative-general-motors (last accessed August 2018).

37. Klier and Rubinstein, 2012.

38. *The New York Times*, 1 May 2009.

39. Katz et al., 2013.

40. Steven Rattner, *Overhaul: An Insider's Account of the Obama Administration's Emergency Rescue of the Auto Industry* (New York: Houghton Mifflin Books, 2010).

41. White House, 2009; Vlasic, 2011.

42. Rattner, 2010; Austan Goolsbee and Alan B. Krueger, "A Retrospective Look at Rescuing and Restructuring General Motors and

Chrysler," *The Journal of Economic Perspectives*, 29(2), spring 2015, pp. 3–23.

43. Stewart, P., "Forward," in Jean-Pierre Durand and Nicolas Hatzfeld (eds.), *Living Labor. Life on the Line at Peugeot-France* (New York: Palgrave Macmillan, 2003).

44. For an in-depth account of shop floor tensions between full-benefit and newly hired two-tiered workers during the divisive 2009–2015 period, and other consequences of the bailout contracts, the VEBA, etc., on autoworker families, see Kesselman, 2015.

45. Gary Walkowitz, a Ford local bargaining committeeman, ran for UAW president on a dissident slate opposing two-tier contacts and the VEBA.

46. Kristin Dziczek, "Process & Outcomes of 2015 Auto Negotiations," *Center for Automotive Research*, January 14, 2016. The 2015 contract introduced an eight-year "grow-in" provision for two-tier workers to reach tier-one wages. One gain from the six-week 2019 General Motors strike was a reduction of that period to four years for currently employed workers. Future hires, however, will take eight full years to achieve this wage scale. So the two-tier status remains, but with the perspective of "grow-in" over time.

47. Joel Cutcher-Gerschenfeld et al., "The Decline and Resurgence of the U.S. Auto Industry," *EPI Briefing Paper*, no. 399, May 6, 2015.

48. *Detroit Free Press*, September 16, 2015.

49. *Detroit Free Press*, October 8, 2015.

50. Ghilarducci, 2010, p. 258.

51. *Bloomberg Businessweek*, December 27, 2015; Michael A. McCarthy, "Turning Labor into Capital: Pension Funds and the Corporate Control of Finance," *Politics & Society*, 42(4), 2014, pp. 455–487; John Adler and Jay Youngdahl, "The Odd Couple: Wall Street, Union Benefits Funds, and the Looting of the American Worker," *New Labor Forum*, 19(1), winter 2010, pp. 81–89.

52. *Automotive News*, October 13, 2015.

53. Richard B. Freeman, "Searching for the EU Social Dialogue Model," *National Bureau of Economic Review*, Working Paper no. 12306, June 2006.

54. Frank Levy and Peter Temin, "Institutions and Wages in Post-World War II America," in Claire Brown et al. (eds.), *Labor in the Era of Globalization* (New York: Cambridge University Press, 2010), pp. 15–50; Harry C. Katz, *Shifting Gears: Changing Labor Relations in the U.S. Automobile Industry* (Cambridge, MA: The MIT Press, 1987).

55. Cutcher-Gerschenfeld et al., 2015.
56. Sabine Montagne, "Le Trust, fondement juridique du capitalisme patrimonial," in Frédéric Lordon (ed.), *Conflits et pouvoirs dans les institutions du capitalisme* (Paris: Les Presses de Sciences Po, 2008), pp. 221–250, our translation.
57. IRES, *op. cit.*, pp. 9–10; Anne Dufresne and Jean-Marie Pernot, "Les syndicats européens à l'épreuve de la nouvelle gouvernance économique," in Anne Dufresne and Jean-Marie Pernot (eds.), special issue *Chronique internationale de l'IRES*, no. 143–144, November, pp. 3–29, www.ires-fr.org/images/files/Chronique/C143-144/c143-144-1.pdf
58. Bob Jessop, *The State: Past, Present, Future* (Cambridge, UK: Polity Press, 2016).
59. Tarun et al., 2018.
60. This section borrows from Donna Kesselman and Catherine Sauviat, "Les enjeux de la revitalisation syndicale face aux transformations de l'emploi et aux nouveaux mouvements sociaux," *Chronique internationale de l'IRES*, 160, December 2017, pp.78–96.
61. Barry T. Hirsch and David Macpherson, "Union Membership and Coverage Database from the CPS." Available at: http://unionstats.gsu.edu/UnionStats.pdf
62. Thomas Geoghegan, *Only One Thing Can Save Us: Why America Needs a New Kind of Labor Movement* (New York: The New Press, 2014); Steve Early, *Save Our Unions: Dispatches from a Movement in Distress* (Chicago: Haymarket Books, 2013).
63. Jonathan Rosenblum, "Labor Needs a Bold Vision to Inspire Workers in the New Economy," *New Labor Forum*, 25(3), 2016, pp. 82–84; Micah Uetricht, *Strike for America! Chicago Teachers Against Austerity* (New York: Verso Books, 2014); Steve Early, 2013.
64. Jean-Christian Vinel, *The Employee: A Political History* (Philadelphia: University of Pennsylvania Press, 2013).
65. Convention Resolution, Sunday September 8, 2013. Available at: https://aflcio.org/resolutions/sunday-sept-8-2013 (last accessed March 3, 2018).
66. Ruth Milkman and Ed Ott (eds.), *New Labor in New York: Precarious Workers and the Future of the Labor Movement* (Ithaca, NY: Cornell University Press, 2014); Guy Standing, *The Precariat: The New Dangerous Class* (London: Bloomsbury, 2011).
67. Janice Fine, *Worker Centers: Organizing Communities at the Edge of the Dream* (Ithaca, NY: ILR Press/Cornell University Press, 2006);

Steve Jenkins, "Organizing, Advocacy, and Member Power: A Critical Reflection," *WorkingUSA*, 6(2), 2002, pp. 56–89, https://doi.org/10.1111/j.1743-4580.2002.00003.x-i1

68. Eileen Boris et al., *Women's ILO: Transnational Networks, Global Labour Standards and Gender Equity, 1919 to Present* (Leiden, Netherlands: Brill Publishing, 2018).

69. Rich Yeselson, "Fortress Unionism," *Democracy Journal*, 29, summer 2013.

70. Milkman and Ott, 2014.

71. Ten states, plus Washington, DC require paid sick leave for employees, following the lead of Connecticut in 2011: Arizona, California, Connecticut, Maryland, Massachusetts, New Jersey, Oregon, Rhode Island, Vermont, Washington, Washington, DC. Six states require paid family leave: California, Washington, DC, Massachusetts, New Jersey, New York, Oregon, Rhode Island.

72. Mitchell Hirsch, "Fight for $15 Movement Grows with Largest Low-Wage Worker Protests in US History," *National Employment Law Project* (NELP), April 20, 2015. Available at: https://goo.gl/5UdR6p

73. Ibid.

74. Ibid.

75. Various press. Interviews with Donna Dewitt, then President of South Carolina AFL-CIO, August 2015.

76. Kate Andrias, "The New Labor Law," *The Yale Law Journal*, 126(1), October 2016. Available at: www.yalelawjournal.org/article/the-new-labor-law>

77. Various press.

78. Ben Becker, "Under the Radar," *New Labor Forum*, 22(1), 2013, pp. 7–9.

79. John Logan, "The Union Avoidance Industry in the United States," *British Journal of Industrial Relations*, 44(4), December 2006, pp. 651–675.

80. Julianne Tveten, "Silicon Valley's Techno-Capitalists Have a Low-Wage Worker Revolt on Their Hands," *In These Times*, August 15, 2017.

81. Max Fraser, "Franchise Fratricide and the Fight for $15," *New Labor Forum*, 24(3), 2015, pp. 95–98.

82. Jonathan Rosenblum, "Labor Needs a Bold Vision to Inspire Workers in the New Economy," *New Labor Forum*, 25(3), 2016, pp. 82–84.

83. Becker, 2013.

84. Fraser, 2015.
85. Available at: https://www.epi.org/preemption-map/ (last accessed March 21, 2019).
86. Available at: http://www.msnbc.com/rachel-maddow-show/the-historical-oddity-thomas-perezs, MSNBC, July 18, 2013 (last accessed December 28, 2018).
87. Available at: https://obamawhitehouse.archives.gov/the-press-office/2016/04/06/fact-sheet-middle-class-economics-strengthening-retirement-security (last accessed December 28, 2018).
88. Available at: https://www.nytimes.com/2013/09/18/business/us-to-include-home-care-workers-in-wage-and-overtime-law.html (last accessed March 20, 2019).
89. David Weil, *The Fissured Workplace: Why Work Became So Bad for So Many and What Can Be Done About It* (Cambridge, MA: Harvard University Press, 2014).
90. Available at: https://www.littler.com/publication-press/publication/david-weil-nominated-head-dol%E2%80%99s-wage-and-hour-division (last accessed March 20, 2019).
91. David Weil, 2014.
92. Lydia DePillis, "Meet the Government Guys Standing up for Franchise Workers and Contractors," *The Washington Post*, March 9, 2016. Available at: https://www.washingtonpost.com/gdpr-consent/?destination=%2fnews%2fwonk%2fwp%2f2016%2f03%2f09%2fmeet-the-government-guys-standing-up-for-franchise-workers-and-contractors%2f%3f (last accessed August 2019).
93. Available at: https://www.nlrb.gov/news-outreach/news-story/richard-f-griffin-jr-sworn-nlrb-general-counsel (last accessed March 20, 2019).
94. DePillis, L., "Department of Labor Sends Warning Shot to Clients of Temp Staffing Agencies," *The Washington Post*, January 20, 2016. Available at: https://www.washingtonpost.com/gdpr-consent/?destination=%2fnews%2fwonk%2fwp%2f2016%2f01%2f20%2fdepartment-of-labor-sends-warning-shot-to-clients-of-temp-staffing-agencies%2f%3f (last accessed August 2019).
95. Available at: https://www.dol.gov/newsroom/releases/eta/eta20161117 (last accessed March 20, 2019).
96. Available at: https://www.dol.gov/whd/overtime/final2016/faq.htm (last accessed December 28, 2018).
97. Available at: https://www.govexec.com/contracting/2014/07/obama-signs-executive-orders-protecting-lgbt-feds-and-contractors/89183/ (last accessed March 20, 2019).

98. "Testimony of Christine L. Owens, Hearing Before the United States Congress Workforce Protection Subcommittee, House of Representatives Education and Workforce Committee," December 9, 2016. Available at: https%3A%2F%2Fedworkforce.house. gov%2Fuploadedfiles%2Ftestimony_owens.pdf&usg=AOvVaw2 cwZF4SV3kUnsTO5KILj0u

99. Sean Higgins, "How Obama has Tilted the Workplace for Unions," *Washington Examiner*, September 12, 2016.

100. Todd Makse and Anand Sokhey, "Revisiting the Divisive Primary Hypothesis: 2008 and the Clinton–Obama Nomination Battle," *American Politics Research*, 38(2), 2010, pp. 233–265; Robert C. Smith and Richard A. Seltzer, *Polarization and the Presidency: From FDR to Barack Obama* (Boulder, CO: Lynne Rienner Publishers, 2015).

101. *Detroit News*, March 5, 2018.

102. Barry T. Hirsch, David A. MacPherson, and Wayne G. Vroman, "Estimates of Union Density by State, 1964–2018, Unionstats. gsu.edu/monthlylaborreviewarticle.htm (last accessed December 2019).

12

Why wasn't there a twenty-first-century "new" New Deal? Historical perspectives for the hope for and reality of Obama's presidency

Elizabeth T. Shermer

"Suddenly, everything old is New Deal again." Economist and *New York Times* editorialist Paul Krugman made that observation less than a week after Barack Obama's 2008 presidential win. That liberal commentator was not the only one wondering if the Illinois Senator would become "Franklin Delano Obama."[1] In the last months of Obama's campaign, in the wait for his swearing in, and throughout the first months of his presidency, there were constant references to the Great Depression, the New Deal, and FDR. Left-wing commentators wanted Obama to ambitiously experiment in his first hundred days.[2] Liberal pundits expected a president capable of updating liberalism for the twenty-first century as Roosevelt had remade it for the twentieth,[3] whereas mainstream journalists generally emphasized similarities in style.[4] Those hopes and predictions terrified many conservatives who saw another ambitious liberal president coming into office with, at least on paper, a Democratic supermajority. Weeks before the election, *Wall Street Journal* editors warned that "Liberals would dominate the entire government in a way they haven't since 1965, or 1933 . . . mark[ing] the restoration of the activist government that fell out of public favor in the 1970s."[5]

Those assumptions seemed foolish eight years later when populist, right-wing firebrand Donald Trump won districts that Obama had carried and Republicans maintained their narrow hold over

Congress.[6] But liberal, progressive, and left-wing hopes for a second New Deal had started to vanish early in Obama's first term during the protracted battle to pass the Affordable Care Act, colloquially known as Obamacare. Favorable comparisons between FDR and Obama all but disappeared after the first midterm election when Democratic Congressional losses were catastrophic. That defeat almost surpassed the seats Democrats lost in the now infamous 1938 midterms during Roosevelt's second term.[7]

The parallels between the 1938 and 2010 results should not have ended the comparisons between the Roosevelt and Obama administrations. Scholars and journalists should have continued to notice the parallels between them and the other liberal Democrat, Lyndon Baines Johnson, who briefly presided with and then lost the liberal majorities in Congress necessary to enact sweeping legislative reforms. The dreams, fears, and comparisons made between Roosevelt and Obama rested on persistent myths that still surround FDR, his first 100 days, and the entire New Deal as well as the lore surrounding the failures of the Johnson White House. Journalists and even academics, who should know better, still reflexively describe Roosevelt as a universally liked, crusading liberal who single-handedly upended American politics and governance. Political scientists even considered him to be responsible for a new chapter in the history of the American presidency when the public increasingly expected the president to be highly visible, central to setting the nation's agenda, and capable of single-handedly making policy.[8]

Decades of historical research has undermined the nevertheless persistent mythos surrounding Roosevelt and the realities of the modern presidency. Chief executives have struggled to manage the executive branch, contend with federalism, work with a fractious divided Congress, deal with the press, win over the citizenry, and prevent the judiciary from threatening their signature achievements. Comparing the constraints on the Roosevelt, Johnson, and Obama administrations' domestic agendas highlights how American mores and the Constitution's checks and balances have continued to determine chief executives' ability to preside, which has been at odds with how the press, academy, and public have described presidential power for decades.

The various social and legal limits on the executive branch have also increasingly paralyzed American governance over the course of what was predicted to be the American Century. All three of these Democratic presidents struggled to pursue their domestic agendas even though their party held a supermajority in Congress for at least a part of their respective administrations. Despite FDR's fabled first 100 days, journalists, everyday citizens, leading business executives, and career politicians undermined reforms throughout his administration. Their efforts left the New Dealers' domestic agenda circumscribed, incomplete, and embattled, much to the frustration of later liberal presidents with ambitious agendas, like Johnson, who had plans to complete the New Deal, and Obama, who many expected to herald its return. Obama instead had to govern a former superpower whose rising mortality rate,[9] decaying infrastructure,[10] and widening inequality[11] made Trump's 2016 promise, to "Make America Great Again," alluring to many voters.[12]

The real Roosevelt

The academy was just as complicit as the press in feeding expectations that Obama would be able to create and personally oversee a second New Deal. Scholars have been remiss in describing the authority modern presidents have had, including FDR.[13] That carelessness has fed a public expectation that the media and the academy often perpetuates.[14] Celebratory accounts of and popular references to FDR's first 100 days correctly recognize that the president certainly signed a dizzying number of executive orders in that short period. He, in fact, retains the record for the most issued, although chief executives have increasingly used them since the Civil War. FDR also spent his early months in office simply signing laws that Congress had quickly passed.[15]

Yet many of his administration's long-standing achievements, such as the 1935 Social Security Act and 1938 Fair Labor Standards Act, actually came after the 1934 midterm and 1936 presidential elections. Those victories strengthened congressional support for his administration's agenda. Popular lore still holds that citizens and journalists celebrated reforms, new social welfare programs,

354

and even the men and women, but particularly the president, trying to first give them a New Deal and then turn the country into
an Arsenal of Democracy that would sit atop of a new world order
during what, Henry Luce predicted in 1941, would be the American
Century.[16]

Scholars have shown that neither the press nor the public universally loved Roosevelt, which frustrated his ability to preside.
Despite contemporary knee-jerk assumptions and right-wing news
organizations' claims, journalists have never been liberal stalwarts.[17] Researchers have uncovered that 65 percent of American
newspapers opposed Roosevelt's administration. That number
reflected widespread unease and opposition to 1930s experiments
as well as Depression-era changes to the industry. Dailies across
the country folded during the 1930s, when powerful publishers,
such as Roy Howard and William Randolph Hearst, bought failing
outfits and built veritable media empires that dictated the tenor,
tone, and politics of papers across the country. Both Howard and
Hearst grew increasingly hostile to the Roosevelt administration,
which very much shaped their many publications' coverage of the
president. Hearst, for example, demanded reporters uses phrases
such as "soak the successful" or "Raw Deal" to build opposition
to the president.[18]

Those indictments limited the Roosevelt administration's
power. Roy Howard, for example, eagerly published investigations into malfeasance within the labor movement, whose
power had grown exponentially after Roosevelt signed the
1935 Wagner Act. Pulitzer prize-winning reporter Westbrook
Pegler's devastating exposés into the building trade and theat-
rical unions in 1939 and 1940 not only challenged the legitimacy of those protections but called all New Deal programs
into question. Many Americans still considered him a hero:
Time reported that he had garnered the third highest number of
votes for the annual "Man of the Year" contest. Although Roosevelt won, the president would increasingly distance himself
from the New Deal. For example, he proclaimed that Dr. New
Deal had retired to make room for Dr. Win the War. Scholars
have contended that his proclamation did not reflect how FDR
would preside during World War II but instead symbolized how

much the broad initiative had always been but was increasingly attacked in the late 1930s.[19]

That political turmoil reflected widespread discomfort, distrust, and even opposition to FDR. He had high approval ratings throughout his years in office and is still remembered as one of the country's most popular presidents.[20] However, those ratings and the mythology surrounding FDR masked twelve years of ongoing, building opposition. For example, Louisiana's Huey Long's popularity seemed a real threat to FDR's ability to win the 1936 primary and general elections. The Kingfish ran the state like a dictator as governor and then from afar as a US Senator. His populist promise to "Share the Wealth" with every white American endeared him to millions across the country who started and joined Share the Wealth clubs before his 1935 assassination. Long partly built that following on attacking the wealthy who detested him as much as Roosevelt. Executives, most notably the DuPont brothers, considered Roosevelt a traitor to his class. Their political organization, the American Liberty League, funded Republican political challengers and lawsuits against the laws that Congress passed and FDR signed.[21]

The Roosevelt administration struggled to transcend the business-funded, journalist-stoked divides that commentators today might label "tribalism."[22] Historians have long called the 1920s tribal and shown how those divisions limited FDR's ability to preside over a vast, disparate, and desperate land filled with many remote towns as well as isolated immigrant neighborhoods within major cities, like New York, Chicago, and Los Angeles.[23] When journalist Lorena Hickok traveled the country to observe the devastation for Roosevelt-insider Henry Hopkins, her many letters indicated that America was, at best, one-third a nation, which needed reconstruction (not just relief).[24]

The Roosevelt administration certainly started such an ambitious overhaul. Historians have noted, for example, that new federally guaranteed labor rights, social welfare supports, and work opportunities gave residents an unprecedented sense of citizenship and belonging. FDR certainly helped. He delivered his famous fireside chats over the radio, which helped him reach more Americans than previous presidents had. FDR also forsook his blue-stocking accent to outline new policies in a clear, accessible manner for the American people whom New Dealers needed to make these programs work.[25]

Many citizens enthusiastically participated in making their own New Deals. For example, young people traveled the country to study through the National Youth Administration's work-study program, to improve the nation's basic infrastructure through the Civilian Conservation Corps, or to defend democracy during World War II, an effort that the government continually emphasized was All-American. Total mobilization did bring Americans from all over the country together in far-flung colleges, military bases, and war-production factories. The War Department also created programs to assuage the shock of meeting fellow citizens from different parts of the country who were nothing like them. Policy-makers also used those educational initiatives to provide basic civic lessons to the many Americans whose schooling had never given them such basic knowledge.[26]

Even though those programs reflected the Roosevelt administration's overarching effort to empower the citizenry in the name of democracy, FDR's critics still attacked him as a would-be dictator. Researchers have noted how much the New Deal expanded the executive branch's power.[27] Yet experts and journalists have overstated how much he personally oversaw policy. FDR did not have much day-to-day oversight over the popular programs that those laws created. Throughout his administration, he gave his aides the ability to experiment. FDR also insisted on significant input and oversight from local, state, and national advisory boards, which highlighted the president's preference for respecting the balance of powers between local, state, and federal governments as well as institutions, such as schools, churches, and unions. He even included that deference in programs that he created through executive orders, such as the National Youth Administration. FDR publicly insisted that the head of this agency had carte blanche to start initiatives designed to offer relief to 16-to-25-year-olds but also mandated that the director coordinate with local groups and answer to a National Advisory Committee that included representatives from the government, business, and labor.[28]

The Roosevelt administration also devolved power over initiatives in an effort to empower the many Americans who had been relatively powerless against the country's largely white, Anglo-Saxon, Protestant, moneyed elite. Catholic, Jewish, African-American, and immigrant industrial workers, for example, eventually sat confidently across the bargaining table from their managers because of a new federal guaranteed right to organize a union of their choosing. Other Americans flocked to Washington in order to serve in New Deal agencies. These young men and women had been left out of the halls of power, despite their education and hard work in their communities. Religion, ethnicity, and poverty had often kept them from full participation in public life. In the 1930s and 1940s, these young reformers found new positions of power in local branches of federal agencies and in Washington. Lyndon Baines Johnson, for example, had earned a degree from a small teacher's college, the only local option for this impoverished Texan. That experience helped him run NYA's Texas office, an important moment in the future president's thirty-year political career.[29]

The Roosevelt administration also deferred to locals like Johnson because the Supreme Court, Congress, the Democratic Party, and the country were more divided than most Americans realize. Both the Constitution and political tradition gave judges significant power over the president's agenda, which they used to strike down many laws quickly passed during FDR's storied first 100 days. Five–four majorities decided most of those cases, which highlighted how divided the judiciary was, even before what came to be known as "FDR's court-packing plan." FDR publicly endorsed the infamous, unpopular 1937 congressional bill that would have enabled him to appoint additional justices, but it never left the Senate Judiciary Committee. Historians still debate why Owen Johnson surprisingly voted to uphold a minimum wage law in *West Coast Hotel Co. v. Parrish* (1937), a case popularly remembered as "the switch in time to save nine." That ruling also inaugurated a new era in jurisprudence that enabled the Roosevelt administration to experiment, build a social welfare state, and create a new liberal political order for a century that seemed, at the time, predestined to be America's.[30]

That case did nothing to end Congress's ability to check the president's power, particularly the Southern and Western delegates who had what scholars consider a veto over New Deal legislation. Even when liberal Democrats' power peaked between the 1934 and 1938 midterms, they still had to compromise with many of the Southern and Western Democrats who insisted that far-reaching landmark legislation, like the 1935 Wagner and Social Security Acts, not cover agricultural, domestic, or government workers. Those caveats effectively left women and minorities without a New Deal. Those retrograde representatives could insist on such exclusions because no one would have been helped if they had voted "no" with the many conservative Republicans from across the country who disdained liberals in both parties.[31]

The Constitution's fixed election schedule also bedeviled the Roosevelt administration. Liberals won important seats in 1934 and 1936 but lost many votes in the 1938 midterms. Those losses created the opportunity for what scholars have deemed a "conservative coalition," which frustrated the Roosevelt administration throughout his third and fourth terms. Recalcitrant Representatives and Senators launched investigations into well-known policies, New Dealers, and bureaucracies, like the National Youth Administration, its director, and its popular work-study initiate. Southern Democrats tarred and feathered left-wing Alabaman Aubrey Williams before Congress and in the press before tense 1942 budget negotiations dramatically cut the funding for the NYA as well as many other New Deal bureaucracies that had continued to pursue reform as a part of the war effort.[32]

Roosevelt appointees had struggled to roll out programs at the local level long before Congress exercised its budgetary power in 1942. For example, Tennessee Valley Authority director David Lilienthal promised that the water project would put democracy "on the march." He envisioned the 1933 legislation enabling the creation of community land-use associations that would determine equitable renting agreements for government property, helping experts advise small farmers who would have access to federally funded fertilizers, and ensuring local cooperatives would manage the profits from the federal hydroelectric infrastructure.

Those dams and power states would offer well-paying jobs to poor white and black Southerners who would finally have both electrical and electoral power. But the grassroots never oversaw TVA. Management was instead undemocratically ceded to the "grass tops," sociologist Philip Selznick's moniker for this local elite. The NAACP accordingly damned TVA as "Lily-white Reconstruction" because community representatives provided service to white communities first and most African-American TVA employees worked in low-paid, unskilled positions.[33]

Minorities likewise found themselves spottily protected after Roosevelt's sweeping Executive Order 8802, which created the Federal Employment Practices Commission to bar racial and religious discrimination in defense industries. Many Americans filed claims in the name of guaranteeing what many hoped would be a "Double V" over fascism abroad and racism at home. Historians have noted that enforcement proved difficult across the country, not just the South. Many at the time knew how much the Roosevelt administration struggled to implement policies. For example, Chester Himes's famous 1945 novel about the violent Los Angeles shipyards, *If He Hollers Let Him Go*, emphasized that union organizers, federal officials, defense contractors, and war production workers never took this storied decree seriously.[34]

The White House's last New Dealer

Few Americans, journalists, and scholars remember the criticisms of, opposition to, and limits of the New Deal, the war effort, or FDR. That mythology has paradoxically left successive presidents unable to live up to his larger-than-life reputation of presiding over the supposed start of the American Century. But citizens, academics, and journalists also reflexively describe modern chief executives as directly overseeing far more than they wanted to or could do as the size, reach, and power of the federal government grew.

That contradiction has hidden how the system of checks and balances as well as political fights continued to stop sweeping federal reforms. For example, scholars once deemed the 1940s and 1950s as a relatively dull period in domestic policy-making since Congress did not pass major legislation pertaining to civil rights, women's equality, healthcare, education, or any of the other issues animating postwar social movements. More recent scholarly assessments have highlighted how those issues actually roiled American politics and society in those decades, when there were still dramatic fights over labor rights and citizenship guarantees supposedly secured during the Roosevelt administration.[35]

Disagreements among politicians, journalists, and voters checked the power of even the twentieth and twenty-first century's few genuinely popular presidents, like LBJ and Obama, from achieving what many predicted they could do when their parties had overwhelming control of Congress. For example, Johnson had a well-deserved reputation of strong-arming politicians in order to get his way through the infamous "Johnson treatment." Yet LBJ, like FDR, also struggled to manage the executive branch, work with a fractious Congress, and win over the press to fulfill his ambitious promise to complete the New Deal through a War on Poverty that would help build a Great Society for all Americans.[36]

That pledge highlighted how much the New Dealers had not been able to do but what seemed possible for this superpower in the 1960s. Many historians now consider that decade to mark the American Century's apogee and the beginning of the superpower's decline.[37] Those arguments in some ways capture the public, the media, and the academy's sense that the Texan's controversial administration ushered in a rightward shift in American politics.[38]

A different ending seemed likely when Johnson inherited the office in 1963 and enjoyed a landslide victory a year later. He presided during what many scholars now consider the "Rights-Conscious Sixties," the high-watermark of everyday Americans' participation in civic and political life.[39] Public demand for individual rights and opportunity befit a moment when Johnson signed into law still-popular programs, like Head Start, as well as additions to New Deal programs, such as Medicare and Medicaid. The latter eventually became political third rails that rival the public pensions in the 1935 Social Security Act that Congress amended in the mid-1960s in order to include healthcare for the poor and elderly.[40]

The Johnson White House and the Democratic Party started to unravel long before those programs became sacred cows. Even though Democrats retained their control of Congress in 1966, the party still lost forty-seven seats in the House and three in the Senate. Two years later, Johnson declined to seek re-election. Public anger over and media coverage of the Vietnam conflict, War on Poverty, and Great Society tore apart the Democratic Party and made another electoral victory doubtful.[41]

That ending obscures that Johnson, like FDR, faced the monumental task of presiding over a disparate, desperate, and divided country. Although Americans usually consider the 1960s an affluent era, politicians, journalists, and citizens at the time openly discussed inequality's persistence.[42] For example, journalist Edward R. Murrow's 1960 *Harvest of Shame* shocked viewers with the story of the impoverished, East Coast, African-American farm workers who had likely picked the crops cooked for the Thanksgiving feasts devoured the night before CBS aired this documentary. Pickers' struggles for subsistence highlighted how many Americans, particularly in the rural South, had not received the New Deal necessary for prosperity.[43]

Hardship also persisted among those who the 1930s legislation had directly helped. John F. Kennedy's well-publicized meeting with West Virginia coal miners on the 1960 campaign trail provided a stark reminder of Southern poverty's persistence. Union members seemed to live in another time and country but their struggles exemplified how politicians, the courts, and business interests had already begun to incrementally disassemble the New Deal, particularly the labor rights that had done so much to enable blue-collar workers to have white-collar living standards.[44]

Those concerted efforts to undermine union guarantees highlighted that, despite the persistent mythology surrounding Roosevelt and the New Deal order, the country remained politically divided over what remained of his administration's policies and programs. Liberalism's critics had continued their assaults after World War II but did not really begin to fashion a concerted movement until the mid-1950s. As in the 1930s, journalists, executives, and politicians played an outsized role in stopping and rolling back liberal legislation. Right-wing CEOs, like GE's Lemuel Boulware, funded conservative journalists, most notably William Buckley, and their publications, including *National Review*, which profiled firebrands, such as Arizona Republican Barry Goldwater. The retailer had first been elected to Congress by attacking FDR and his successor, Harry Truman. But the Senator made a name for himself nationally in the 1950s by attacking moderate Republicans, like President Dwight Eisenhower, and top trade unionists, like United Auto Workers president Walter Reuther. By the 1960s, Goldwater served as the standard bearer for a growing conservative movement within the Republican Party, which had already frustrated liberal Democrats and Republicans' agendas at local, state, and federal levels, stymied congressional efforts to expand on New Deal promises for economic security, and made political inroads in Southern, Western, and Steel Belt suburbs.[45]

This gradual party realignment frustrated LBJ long before his famous prediction that the 1964 Civil Rights Act would "deliver the South to the Republican Party for a long time to come."[46] The Texan had cut his political teeth during the New Deal and had fought to defend Williams and the National Youth Administration from both Southern Democrats and right-wing Republicans.[47] Less than twenty years later, he faced a formidable conservative Republican opponent for his Senate seat in 1960. Former Southern Democrat John Tower lost that race but handily won the 1961 special election to replace LBJ after he assumed the vice-presidency. The foreign policy hawk occupied that seat for almost twenty-five years, when the GOP slowly won over Southern Democrats, white suburbanites across the country, and a growing, but still small, number of minorities.[48]

The Republican Party's new base was evident during the 1964 primary and general elections, which highlighted how stark political divisions had persisted, deepened, and shifted. Right-wing activists, most notoriously Phyllis Schlafly, damned GOP kingmakers who ignored the many Republicans disdainful of Northeastern and Midwestern Republicans' moderation or even liberalism. Frustrated conservatives eagerly traded earmarked copies of her self-published 1964 tract. *A Choice, Not an Echo* spoke to many white homeowners, including Californians, who shocked the nation when they overwhelmingly chose Goldwater over liberal establishment Republican Nelson Rockefeller in the primary. But the raucous San Francisco Republican National Convention perplexed top journalists who struggled to capture an event that historians later labeled the "Woodstock for Conservatives." So-called "Goldwater Girls" dressed as cowgirls and the Senator's delegates (predominately white men over fifty) drank carbonated Gold Water, wore clear plastic water-drop-shaped jewelry with gold flakes inside, plastered their cars with AuH20 bumper stickers, and enthusiastically roared when he declared in his acceptance speech, "Extremism in the defense of liberty is no vice" and "Moderation in pursuit of justice is no virtue!" That spectacle fueled concerns that far-right organizations, like the stridently anti-communist John Birch Society, drove the Senator's campaign. He refused to rebuke these supporters even though leading conservatives, most notably William Buckley, attacked them as extremists, not conservatives.[49]

Tribal-like social divisions became even more apparent during the general election. Johnson forced Goldwater to stray from his tried-and-true denunciations of liberal economic policy. The president solicited corporate support and coffers through summits, pledges to make specific cuts in the federal budget, and assurances of his support for Kennedy's tax cuts for businesses. CEOs, for their part, backed and funded LBJ because many, who may have agreed with Goldwater politically, feared wasting their vote on the obvious loser and thus sacrificing their influence.[50]

Losing this constituency pushed the Arizonan's handlers to abandon the battle over economic policy in favor of a war over culture. Staffer Clifton White called it "the moral crisis" when he privately urged Goldwater to approve the documentary *Choice*. Historians eventually deemed that film the opening salvo in what pundits would later christen the Culture Wars. Over shots of a topless dancer, gyrating teenagers, arrested black protestors, the narrator announced, "There are two Americas." Citizens for Goldwater groups received the film, but NBC refused to air the graphic production. Goldwater vetoed any mass showings. "I'm not going to be made out to be a racist," he declared after a viewing. But even though he bristled at comparisons to those he considered backwards segregationists, he nonetheless issued statements that fell in line with their politics and demands. He decried drug abuse and urban violence and called busing an infringement on individual liberty and local control.[51]

Goldwater's sputtering campaign ended in a dramatic defeat. He only carried Arizona, Alabama, Louisiana, Georgia, Mississippi, and South Carolina. The returns certainly looked grim for Republicans: LBJ had won more than 60 percent of the popular vote and Democrats had secured sixty-eight-seat and 295-seat majorities in the Senate and the House, respectively. But historians later recognized that Goldwater had solidified a new Republican base that would be steadily expanded so that, sixteen years later, Goldwater protégé Ronald Reagan easily triumphed in the 1980 presidential election.[52]

Scholars have also noted that Johnson presided knowing that both the Constitution and partisanship limited his time to pursue an agenda arguably as ambitious as the New Deal. The Texan already used national grief over his slain predecessor to proclaim a popular mandate for pursuing a War on Poverty and building a Great Society. Both initiatives hinged, like New Deal experiments, on Democratic supermajorities in Congress in order to overwhelm the conservative Republican and Southern Democratic opposition that had frustrated liberals in both parties since the 1930s. The Texan pressed both staffers and party stalwarts to pass a lot before the upcoming 1966 midterms. That legislation included historic federal guarantees for voting, immigration, education, healthcare, and other issues that the New Dealers had pursued, Johnson proudly signed into law, and liberals on the Supreme Court largely upheld.[53]

Johnson-era programs survived such scrutiny because they, like many 1930s and 1940s initiatives, preserved the general balance of power between all levels and branches of government. Even laws which journalists and scholars celebrated for extending the federal government's reach and attributed to Johnson's political prowess retained long-standing deference to American federalism. For example, historians still celebrate the 1965 Higher Education Act as a historic national guarantee for broad federal funding for higher education. Yet states and schools had a lot of say on how that money was spent. University financial aid officers decided which students received the new federal loans, grants, and work-study opportunities. Johnson never mandated that rule nor those programs but instead left his staff to negotiate with congressional representatives fighting out the details. Like a lot of Great Society legislation, the president ended up signing a bill that he did not entirely like despite his reputation of being the "Master of the Senate."[54]

That nickname belied White House efforts to empower ordinary Americans to participate in implementing change as liberals had done during the New Deal. Enabling poor white and black Southerners to control dams, farms, and power grids through the TVA proved as difficult as waging the War on Poverty thirty years later. Journalist Jonathan Rowe, for example, credited Volunteers in Service to America (VISTA) with making him a "Spear carrier for the War on Poverty." Though he gained notoriety as a left-wing activist, he had been raised in a Republican household that abhorred Roosevelt but cherished voluntarism and civic engagement. VISTA embodied both American traditions and, as Rowe admitted, helped him avoid going to Vietnam in the 1960s. He instead spent a bitterly cold New York winter organizing poor African-American renters to finally force a recalcitrant landlord to fix the heat in their Harlem apartment building. Twenty years later the journalist credited that experience with ending his naivety about political change. "The revolution is exhilarating," he opined, "Running the state afterwards is something else."[55]

Journalists and scholars have spent decades criticizing how the Johnson administration ran the government and looked to everyday citizens to fight the War on Poverty. For example, celebrated writer Tom Wolfe's infamous 1970 essay, "Mau-Mauing the Flak Catchers," gave the public a word that is still used to lampoon the Johnson administration in particular and liberal policy-making in general. Even though the public still celebrates Wolfe's New Journalism, his avant-garde style masked starkly racist portrayals of civil rights activists intimidating well-meaning white bureaucrats, like Rowe, into providing a handout, not a hand up.[56]

Such indictments have shaped popular memory and scholarly understanding of the Johnson administration far more than critical coverage of the New Deal's efforts to empower unionists and Southerners. Journalists, regardless of where they fell on the political spectrum, considered more to have gone wrong than right when they covered that initiative's fiftieth anniversary and noted poverty has persisted despite far more government spending.[57] Some historians have also described the entire War on Poverty as a disorganized farce; Allen Matusow even considered it a part of the *Unraveling of America*.[58] Although there have been more measured assessments of the Johnson administration since Matusow's 1984 book,[59] the recent work on the history of conservatism has often fallen back on these presumptions about the Johnson White House's record in order to explain the country's supposed political drift to the right after 1968.[60]

Franklin Delano Obama or Barack Hussein Johnson?

Fifty years later, that shift looked more like a constitutionally enforced tribal stalemate, which had helped turn the country into a former superpower. Scholars and journalists once conflated the 1970s with political scandals and voter apathy, which the so-called Reagan Revolution replaced with sunny reassurances of "Morning Again in America."[61] Peace, international hegemony, and economic prosperity seemed to define the 1990s, when the Soviet Union collapsed and the US economy boomed.[62]

Scholars now consider that decade to have been "A Fabulous Failure," which obscured a sustained crisis in American democracy.[63] Americans' trust in government, interest in voting, and participation in civic life had started to decline before Watergate but really fell after that scandal.[64] Voters have also steadily lost the ability to be civically and politically engaged. Americans increasingly worked longer hours but without a real increase in their wages.[65] Inequality has instead soared at the same time that courts, local governments, and state legislatures have dismantled the protections in the historic 1965 Voting Rights Act.[66] That disassembly exemplified the overall trend toward the courts and government bureaucracies governing more than elected leaders, who have been bogged down in partisan fights.[67] Political antagonism and power struggles in Washington have created a reliance on presidential executive orders and congressional budget reconciliation negotiations to pass legislation, which has not stopped costly, increasingly common government shutdowns.[68]

That political quagmire fueled wars between and within the two parties, which have alienated voters and instigated third-party challenges for decades. The 1968 election provided a hint of that new status quo. Most Americans and journalists remember that Richard Nixon prevailed over a fractured Democratic Party but rarely mention Alabama Governor George Wallace's stunning independent run. His populist denunciations of both major parties and promises to restore law and order won over voters across the country and helped him carry five Southern states. That showing provoked the last serious effort to rid the country of the Electoral College but did little to stop the acrimony building within and toward the Democratic and Republican Parties. Voter antipathy continued and helped Ross Perot win almost 20 percent of the popular vote in the 1992 presidential election. That result helped Bill Clinton win that race but also inspired Donald Trump to first run for the Reform Party's 2000 presidential candidacy before he fought for the 2016 GOP nomination.[69]

The 2008 primaries and general elections were also contentious. Obama promised both hope and change, the kind of impossible-to-fulfill vow that voters expect from modern presidents.[70] That message energized the electorate even though the race indicated that he would hardly have an easy time changing the status quo. He struggled to win the Democratic Party's nomination. He faced a crowded field of candidates and an extended primary battle with Hillary Clinton who made veiled attacks on his youth, inexperience, and race.[71] Republicans also viciously assailed Obama in ways that echoed the historic divisions between Americans that pundits had started to label cultural after the 1964 election and described as tribal after the 2016 race. Sarah Palin, the 2008 vice-presidential nominee, for example, presented herself as a folksy hockey mom who mocked Obama's work as a Chicago community organizer in a manner that evoked Wolfe's condemnations of the War on Poverty. Other Republicans insisted that Obama was a socialist or communist, not a liberal or a centrist. Only at the end of the campaign did his Republican opponent, Arizona Senator John McCain, publicly correct a supporter who insisted that Obama was a foreign-born Muslim unfit for the presidency.[72]

Election returns seemed to bode well for predictions that Obama had a Great Recession mandate on par with FDR's mythic Depression-era popularity. The Chicago transplant won almost 53 percent of the vote and twenty-eight states. Democrats also increased their hold on the House and Senate since the previous midterms, a rare feat since the Roosevelt era. The party's fifty-seven and 257 respective seats in the Senate and House made it seem possible that Obama might actually deliver on the change he had promised on the campaign trail.[73]

The incumbent's coat-tails were too short for him to have a first 100 days as dizzying as FDR's or first two years as productive as LBJ's. The political divisions and constitutional constraints that had hamstrung Roosevelt and Johnson had only continued to paralyze the government, divide the citizenry, and make presiding even more difficult. By 2008, many political experts still focused on a new president's first months in office but also recognized what LBJ had learned decades before in the Senate: presidents have little time to pursue an agenda before the midterm elections.[74] Johnson had faced that reality by entrusting his aides to fight for numerous bills to complete the Roosevelt administration's many experiments to reconstruct the nation. Obama concentrated on a few reforms in the midst of the Great Recession and received criticism for prioritizing healthcare. Many also did not like his reliance on staff to work with Senators and Representatives, who did much of the work drafting bills that they would send to Obama to sign.[75]

Such rebukes reflected misguided expectations for presidents. Commanders in chief have been presumed to be far more involved in crafting policy than modern presidents (including FDR and LBJ) have been as well as an unwillingness to consider how much Obama's power rested on a deeply divided Congress. His administration needed two independent Senators, Vermont's left-wing Bernie Sanders and Connecticut's right-leaning Joe Lieberman, to vote with Democrats in order to secure the Patient Protection and Affordable Care Act's (ACA) 2010 passage. The former vice-presidential candidate infuriated leading Democrats, who damned him for holding the bill hostage over the so-called public option, a scrapped federal insurance program that, like the TVA for the electricity market, would have acted like a public competitor for the private health insurance market.[76]

Southern and Western representatives also retained a kind of veto over such liberal legislation. In the new millennium, these recalcitrant representatives were largely in the GOP, whose hold over these states had only increased since Democrat-turned-Republican Tower had won Johnson's Senate seat in 1961. But a Democrat, Nebraska Senator Bill Nelson, threatened to sink the final omnibus bill until he decided not to run for re-election. He used his power to ensure that the legislation included more Medicaid money for his state. Pundits quickly labeled that provision the "Cornhusker Kickback," a nickname symbolic of the political machinations contributing to a long-standing legislative logjam.[77]

A special election highlighted this long-standing political quagmire even more. Republicans almost aborted the ACA after liberal lion Ted Kennedy succumbed to brain cancer in August 2009. Democrats assumed that they would easily prevail in the special election to fill his Senate Seat. Massachusetts Republican Scott Brown instead won that unexpectedly close special election.[78] His victory gave Republicans the forty-one votes needed to defeat the ACA in the Senate. As a result, despite months of wrangling and compromises within the party that controlled Congress, Obama and the Democrats only passed healthcare reform through budget reconciliation, a once obscure, filibuster-proof process that Democrats and Republicans have increasingly used to enact legislative change since the Johnson administration.[79]

The press, as under FDR and Johnson, also did a lot to frustrate the Obama White House's domestic agenda. Scholars have shown that the right-wing media grew dramatically after Johnson prevailed over Goldwater in 1964. By the 2000s, political scientists boldly proclaimed, "what America has right now is a thousand-pound-gorilla media juggernaut on the right . . . coexisting with other news outlets trying to keep up while making fitful efforts, twentieth-century style, to check facts and cover 'both sides of the story.'" The largest, most-watched, and wealthiest right-wing source was Fox News, whose reach far surpassed *National Review* in the mid-1960s and the Hearst empire in the 1930s. Fox had the money to conduct the polls that financially struggling so-called mainstream competitors (like CNN) had to use. Fox's enormous viewership also helped the network set the terms of debate over incendiary issues and promote the right's preferred news stories, candidates, and opinions in other conservative, moderate, and liberal, and left-wing media outlets.[80]

Fox News's power made words a powerful weapon against healthcare reform. For example, the earliest usage of the term "Obamacare" appeared in February 2007, when a self-described "contrarian" blogger used it in a post about Democratic candidates' campaign promises. Left, right, and center journalists steadily adopted the space-saving shorthand in their news stories, but Republicans started using it to openly disparage the Senator's proposals by September. Fox News helped the GOP keep the word an epithet during the congressional fights over the ACA, when some leading news outlets, including NPR, refused to use a term that captured Republicans' hostility to the bill and the president. That phrase epitomized citizens' presumptions and fears of the seemingly all-powerful modern president, who the courts, Congress, and lower levels of governance could not constrain.[81]

Obama subsequently struggled to prove his dedication to federalism and individual choice. Congress proposed and the Chicagoan endorsed state exchanges that allowed Americans to shop for insurance. The president also constantly promised that "if you like your doctor, you can keep your doctor." Yet journalism, historical memory, and academic scholarship had cemented the image of modern presidents as emperors, even though archetypes like FDR and LBJ hardly presided in such a manner. The word, "Obamacare," hardly contradicted those presumptions. As such, right-wing fearmongering about government death panels, tax increases, small-business layoffs, and clauses that would enable Obama to create a private army terrified many Americans.[82]

Fox and other right-wing reporters also intensified partisan divides by proclaiming the president's sharpest and loudest critics to be the country's true patriots. For example, Fox's excessive coverage of the supposedly grassroots Taxed Enough Already parties made this movement seem far larger than it actually was. These protests sprang up after a CNBC reporter's fabled February 2009 rant against the Obama administration's plans to save the imploding mortgage industry. He had demanded a "Chicago Tea Party" of capitalists but conservative radio shock jocks and bloggers used the clip and social media to urge ordinary Americans to come together in order to protest the just-elected president's policies. Small crowds gathered in a handful of cities on February 27, 2009 to protest a range of issues; six weeks later, hundreds of thousands rallied on April 15 when tax returns were due. Tea Partiers seemed as raucous as the delegates to the 1964 GOP convention, which some of these generally older, white Americans remembered as spurring their interest in politics. Almost fifty years later, insurgents fastened unused tea bags to their clothes (sometimes Revolutionary costumes), brandished dog-eared copies of the Constitution, and perplexingly demanded the government stop interfering with Medicare, the national health insurance scheme for the elderly that LBJ had signed into law. The right-wing media lauded them as the conservative movement's shock troops, the ordinary Americans taking a stand against the un-American forces of spending, taxation, and big government. The mainstream, liberal, and left-wing press (as during the 1964 election) dismissed protestors as retrograde, racist, morons, who may have been able to quote the Founders but had not grasped the very basic facts of history or current events.[83]

Researchers later uncovered that all of this coverage made the Tea Party look far larger and more boisterous than it actually was. Those who shouted the loudest made headlines, but they were a cantankerous minority who often attended televised rallies but not local meetings. Only a fifth of voting-age Americans strongly agreed with Tea Partiers' principles. Roughly 1,000 local Tea Parties existed and 800 remained active in summer 2011. Most local groups were quite small with only a few dozen attendees; those with larger rosters usually had just a handful of true activists. Women led the overwhelmingly older, white, male membership, who may have been comfortable but painfully aware of their middle-class existence's precariousness. Their insistent cry of "I want My Country Back" bespoke an outrage that New Deal and Great Society old-age provisions that they had paid into over their lifetimes would disappear before they could retire. Tea Partiers feared that Democrats wanted to extend benefits to immigrants, minorities, and young people, who had not spent years being taxed for entitlements that seemed increasingly unable to guarantee the kind of New Deal or Great Society that FDR and LBJ had promised decades before. Fox News and other news outlets also ignored the fact that Tea Partiers often also wanted the GOP back. Patriots, even those registered as Republicans, generally considered themselves to the right of Republicans in office. Tea Partiers even saw themselves as "watch dogs," who would force party allegiance to the Tea Party's brand of American conservatism.[84]

That agenda created tension on the right. Republican politicians feared Tea Party primary challenges but wealth billionaires, DC-based lobby organizations (such as Freedom Works), and GOP-affiliated Political Action Committees (most notably the Tea Party Express) spent millions supporting Republican candidates in the movement's name. Some Patriots welcome the attention and support. Many more bristled at the policy proposals being made in their name and the manufactured rallies, which stole attention from the local meetings and grassroots initiatives.[85]

That turmoil did not prevent Republicans from triumphing in the 2010 midterms, when the comparisons between FDR and Obama wrongly ceased. Scholars still cannot agree on how to interpret these results because presidents' parties have been expected to lose seats in the midterm elections. That trend, in fact, made the 1934 midterms historic. Yet the 2010 losses were dramatic. Some considered it a referendum on Obamacare, whereas others have credited Republican strategists for turning out their supporters. At the end of his administration, Obama actually blamed himself for not doing more to use his influence and popularity to build up support for and nurture talent within the Democratic Party. The party could do little to help him govern after Republicans retook Congress and made themselves into "the party of no." The proudly obstinate GOP even managed to deny Obama his right to appoint a Supreme Court justice after Anton Scalia's sudden 2016 death.[86]

That denial had real consequences and meaning for Americans hoping for a "new" New Deal. The courts, as during Roosevelt's and subsequent administrations, had the power to determine the fate of legislation that bore Obama's signature. The ACA, for example, faced numerous legal challenges immediately after its passage. The first before the Supreme Court challenged the individual mandate that required Americans to buy insurance from state exchanges. Journalists called the ruling a "Victory for Obama," a headline that captured the general sense that modern presidents have become all-powerful but obscured the 5–4 decision's details. Chief Justice John Robert's vote upholding the law shocked many commentators. Yet even though his majority opinion upheld the law's constitutionality under Congress's ability to tax, he (like the dissenting jurists) did not think that Congress's authority over interstate commerce gave it that authority. Three judges, including the supposedly moderate Anthony Kennedy, wrote a dissent contending that the entire law should have been struck down. Seven justices also rejected the ACA's broad expansion of Medicaid. States were allowed to opt out. Mostly Southern and Western states did, which left many Americans struggling to afford health insurance.[87]

However, many Democrats proclaimed Obamacare to have been "signed, sealed, and delivered" during his 2012 election bid.[88] Yet the program's successes, like New Deal and Great Society breakthroughs, came from the hard work of civil servants and ordinary Americans. Federal and state officials initially struggled to set up the websites for Americans to buy their health insurance, but they did impressive work recruiting young web-savvy professionals to fix the glitches.[89] Volunteer groups across America helped citizens enroll. Their ranks included college students eager to help deliver change, like Rowe had been when he joined VISTA and LBJ had been when he ran NYA's Texas branch. In the 2010s, millennials helped the uninsured defy yearly enrollment expectations. Many newly covered Americans found themselves receiving the medical treatments and services that they had long needed but were never able to afford because they did not have insurance.[90]

But federalism and partisanship forced Obama, like FDR and his successors, to reluctantly rely on executive orders and his bureaucratic appointees to govern. He used both, for example, to police the student loan industry, which his administration had first gone after through the budget reconciliation process that secured the ACA's passage. Democrats had been able to include a provision ending the original Johnson-ra federal loan program, which, unlike the New Deal's work-study program, had created a sizeable, profitable, and pernicious financial sector. Legislative reform was unlikely after the midterms, so the president and Education Department staffers continued to push for smaller reforms. For example, a 2014 executive order eased requirements for a loan forgiveness program, whereas Education Department staff used their authority to simplify enrollment in favorable repayment plans, draft rights for borrowers, and centralize how loans were serviced in order to save indebted Americans both time and money. Federal officials also went after the difficult-to-police for-profit colleges and student-aid lenders, who often colluded to offer private loans for shady institutions peddling worthless degrees. Under Obama, Department of Education staff also sued other large for-profits, including the sizeable Corinthian College. The predatory school ended up dissolving as part of the settlement with federal officials, who had evidence of substantial abuses that saddled alumni with useless but expensive degrees. Those seemingly small changes mattered a lot to the forty-four million Americans still trying to pay back more than US$1.5 trillion, but they hardly represented the kind of sweeping overhaul that Obama had promised in his 2008 run.[91]

But voters, journalists, and academics should not have expected a revolution or even a second New Deal after Obama's win. All modern presidents have faced constitutional and practical limits on their power, including those like FDR, LBJ, and Obama who had sizeable Democratic majorities in Congress. The public nevertheless had and still has unrealistic expectations for modern presidents, which journalists have perpetuated and scholars have rarely publicly corrected.

Decades of unrealistic hopes, unfulfilled promises, powerful courts, fractured parties, partisan divides, irresponsible reporters, and frustrated citizens helped pave the way for the third-party challengers who inspired Trump. The Queens native personified the danger of widespread misconceptions of the New Deal and presidential power. The realtor, after all, guaranteed a lot during Day 1 of his administration, the kind of increasingly common presidential campaign promises that no chief executive can actually deliver.

Journalists even started to worry during the primaries that the Republican candidate did not actually know what presidents could actually do.[92]

Those fears seemed warranted after Trump took office. He issued executive orders intended to ban Muslims, pressed for the ACA's repeal, and claimed, "In two years, we have accomplished more than almost any administration in the history of our country." That remark provoked laughter among United Nations General Assembly members, whose giggles made clear that the American Century had undeniably ended.[93] The world, after all, had been watching as thousands of Americans flooded airports to protest the Muslim bans, the courts fought the travel restrictions that the Supreme Court narrowly upheld, the Republican-controlled Congress could not agree on legislation to destroy Obamacare, and the media doggedly covered, despite threats from the White House, Trump's propensity to lie, exaggerate, and fulfill his over-the-top promises. Yet Republicans still managed to increase their seats in the Senate during the 2018 midterms, when Democrats took back control of the House. Even though that outcome increased lawmakers' ability to check the executive branch's power, many noted that a divided Congress likely guaranteed more political gridlock, which has and will continue to prevent Americans from getting the kind of deal that would make the country great for everyone.[94]

Notes

1. Paul Krugman, "Franklin Delano Obama?" *The New York Times*, November 10, 2008, https://www.nytimes.com/2008/11/10/opinion/10krugman.html (accessed August 2019).
2. Tony Badger, "FDR: A Model for Obama?" *The Nation*, January 26, 2009, https://www.thenation.com/article/fdr-model-obama/ (accessed August 2019).
3. George Packer, "The New Liberalism," *The New Yorker*, November 17, 2008, https://www.newyorker.com/magazine/2008/11/17/the-new-liberalism (accessed August 2019).
4. Kate Zernike, "The Charisma Mandate," *The New York Times*, February 17, 2008, https://www.nytimes.com/2008/02/17/weekinreview/17zernike.html (accessed August 2019).

5. "A Liberal Supermajority," *The Wall Street Journal*, October 17, 2008, https://www.wsj.com/articles/SB122420205889842989https://www.wsj.com/articles/SB122420205889842989 (accessed August 2019).
6. Mark Fahey and Nicholas Wells, "The Places that Flipped and Gave the Country to Trump," CNBC, undated, https://www.cnbc.com/heres-a-map-of-the-us-counties-that-flipped-to-trump-from-democrats/ (accessed August 2019).
7. Chris Cillizza, "Election 2010: Republicans Net 60 House Seats, 6 Senate Seats and 7 Governorships," *The Washington Post*, November 3, 2010, http://voices.washingtonpost.com/thefix/morning-fix/2010-election-republican-score.html (accessed August 2019).
8. Sidney Milkis, "The Presidency, Democratic Reform, and Constitutional Change," *PS* 20:3 (summer 1987), 628–636.
9. Olga Khazan, "A Shocking Decline in American Life Expectancy," *The Atlantic*, December 21, 2017, https://www.theatlantic.com/health/archive/2017/12/life-expectancy/548981/ (accessed August 2019).
10. James Surowiecki, "System Overload," *The New Yorker*, April 18, 2016, https://www.newyorker.com/magazine/2016/04/18/inside-americas-infrastructure-problem (accessed August 2019).
11. Robert Reich, "Political Roots of Widening Inequality," *American Prospect*, April 28, 2015, http://prospect.org/article/political-roots-widening-inequality (accessed August 2019).
12. George Packer, "Head of the Class," *The New Yorker*, May 16, 2016, https://www.newyorker.com/magazine/2016/05/16/how-donald-trump-appeals-to-the-white-working-class (accessed August 2019).
13. Fred Greenstein (ed.), *Leadership in the Modern Presidency* (Cambridge, MA: Harvard University Press, 1995), 296–352 (but all chapters in this book illustrate the authority that presidents have been increasingly presumed to have).
14. There are few examples of trying to correct this record in the press see: Tamara Keith, "The First 100 Days: A Standard that Not Even Roosevelt Achieved," NPR, April 29, 2017, https://www.npr.org/2017/04/29/525810758/the-first-100-days-a-standard-that-not-even-roosevelt-achieved (accessed August 2019).
15. Jonathan Alter, *The Defining Moment: FDR's First 100 Days and the Triumph of Hope* (New York: Simon & Schuster, 2007); Anthony Badger, *FDR: The First Hundred Days* (New York: Hill and Wang, 2009); Adam Cohen, "The First 100 Days," *Time*, June 24, 2009, http://content.time.com/time/specials/packages/

article/0,28804,1906802_1906838_1906979,00.html (accessed August 2019); Zach Carter, "After 84 Years, FDR's First Hundred Days Remain a Benchmark," *The Huffington Post*, April 28, 2017, https://www.huffingtonpost.com/entry/fdr-100-days_us_58ff825ce4b0c46f0782b0c4 (accessed August 2019); Dhrumil Mehta, "Every President's Executive Actions in One Chart," *FiveThirtyEight*, November 20, 2014, https://fivethirtyeight.com/features/every-presidents-executive-actions-in-one-chart/ (accessed August 2019).

16. Jason Scott Smith, *A Concise History of the New Deal* (Cambridge: Cambridge University Press, 2014), 62–98, 149–182.

17. Theda Skocpol and Vanessa Williamson, *The Tea Party and the Remaking of Republican Conservatism* (Oxford: Oxford University Press, 2012), 121–154; Nicole Hemmer, *Messengers of the Right: Conservative Media and the Transformation of American Politics* (Philadelphia: University of Pennsylvania Press, 2016).

18. David Witwer, *Shadow of the Racketeer: Scandal in Organized Labor* (Urbana-Champaign: University of Illinois Press, 2009), 147–174.

19. David Witwer, "Westbrook Pegler and the Anti-Union Movement," *Journal of American History* 92: 2 (2005), 527–552; Elizabeth Tandy Shermer, *Sunbelt Capitalism: Phoenix and the Transformation of American Politics* (Philadelphia: University of Pennsylvania Press, 2013), 71–73; John Jeffries, "The 'New' New Deal: FDR and American Liberalism, 1937–1945," *Political Science Quarterly* 105:3 (Autumn 1990), 397–418; Smith, *A Concise History of the New Deal*, 124–148.

20. Brandon Rottinghaus and Justin Vaughn, "New Ranking of U.S. Presidents puts Lincoln at No. 1, Obama at 18; Kennedy Judged Most Overrated," *The Washington Post*, February 16, 2015, https://www.washingtonpost.com/news/monkey-cage/wp/2015/02/16/new-ranking-of-u-s-presidents-puts-lincoln-1-obama-18-kennedy-judged-most-over-rated/?utm_term=.49ec30b3acc5 (accessed August 2019); Ashley Alman, "Only Two Presidents In Recent History Have Gained Approval During Their Time in Office," *The Huffington Post*, December 10, 2014, https://www.huffingtonpost.com/2014/12/10/president-approval-ratings_n_6303960.html (accessed August 2019).

21. Shermer, *Sunbelt Capitalism*, 39–92; Alan Brinkley, "Huey Long, the Share Our Wealth Movement, and the Limits of Depression Dissidence," *Louisiana History: The Journal of the Louisiana Historical Association* 22:2 (spring 1981), 117–134; Kim Phillips-Fein,

Invisible Hands: The Businessmen's Crusade Against the New Deal (New York: W. W. Norton & Co., 2010), 3–25.

22. Amy Chua, "Destructive Dynamics of Political Tribalism," *New York Times*, February 20, 2018, https://www.nytimes.com/2018/02/20/opinion/destructive-political-tribalism.html (accessed August 2019).

23. Leo Ribuffo, *The Old Christian Right: The Protestant Far Right from the Great Depression to the Cold War* (Philadelphia, PA: Temple University Press, 1983), xi–24.

24. Shermer, *Sunbelt Capitalism*, 39–40.

25. Margaret O'Mara, *Pivotal Tuesdays: Four Elections That Shaped the Twentieth Century* (Philadelphia: University of Pennsylvania Press, 2015), 59–83; Nelson Lichtenstein, *State of the Union: A Century of American Labor* (Princeton, NJ: Princeton University Press, 2013), 54–97.

26. Lizabeth Cohen, *Making a New Deal: Industrial Workers in Chicago, 1919–1939* (New York: Cambridge University Press, 2008); Robert Fleegler, "'Forget All Differences until the Forces of Freedom Are Triumphant': The World War II-Era Quest for Ethnic and Religious Tolerance," *Journal of American Ethnic History* 27:2 (winter 2008), 59–84; Elizabeth Tandy Shermer, "From Educator- to Creditor-In-Chief: The American Presidency, Higher Education, and the Student Loan Industry," in Mark Rose and Roger Biles (eds.), *The President and American Capitalism* (University of Florida Press, 2018), 123–147; Christopher Loss, *Between Citizens and the State: The Politics of American Higher Education in the 20th Century* (Princeton, NJ: Princeton University Press, 2012), 91–120.

27. For an overview of that growth as well as scholarly assessments of the executive branch's growth under Roosevelt, see Joanna Grisinger, *The Unwieldly American State: Administrative Politics since the New Deal* (Cambridge: Cambridge University Press, 2012), 1–13.

28. Shermer, "From Educator- to Creditor-In-Chief," 126–130.

29. Lichtenstein, *State of the Union*, 20–53; John Salmond, *Southern Rebel: The Life and Times of Aubrey Willis Williams, 1890–1965* (Chapel Hill: University of North Carolina Press, 1983), 43–56; Loss, *Between Citizens and the State*, 53–90.

30. AHR Forum, "The Debate over the Constitutional Revolution of 1937," *American Historical Review* 110:4 (October 2005), 1046–1115.

31. Ira Katznelson and Kim Geiger, "Limiting Liberalism: The Southern Veto in Congress, 1933–1950," *Political Science Quarterly* 109:2 (summer 1993), 283–306; Shermer, *Sunbelt Capitalism*, 39–70.

32. Smith, *Concise History of the New Deal*, 124–148; Shermer, *Sunbelt Capitalism*, 39–70; Salmond, *Southern Rebel*, 141–161.
33. Shermer, *Sunbelt Capitalism*, 41–48, quoted 42 and 47.
34. Lichtenstein, *State of the Union*, 54–97; Chester Himes, *If He Hollers Let Him Go* (New York: De Capo Press, 2002 reprint).
35. Julian Zelizer, *The Fierce Urgency of Now: Lyndon Johnson, Congress, and the Battle for the Great Society* (New York: Penguin Books, 2015), 11–61.
36. Ibid.; Tom Wicker, "Remembering the Johnson Treatment," *The New York Times*, May 9, 2002, https://www.nytimes.com/2002/05/09/opinion/remembering-the-johnson-treatment.html (accessed August 2019).
37. Donald White, «Mapping Decline: The History of American Power,» *Harvard International Review* 27:3 (2005), 60–65; Allen J. Matusow, *The Unraveling of America: A History of Liberalism in the 1960s* (Athens: University of Georgia Press, 2009), ix–xviii.
38. Zelizer, *Fierce Urgency of Now*, 1–10, 303–324; Vaughn Bornet, "Reappraising the Presidency of Lyndon B. Johnson," *Presidential Studies Quarterly* 20:3 (1990), 591–602.
39. Nelson Lichtenstein, *State of the Union*, 178–211; Matusow, *Unraveling of America*, 376–440.
40. Zelizer, *Fierce Urgency of Now*, 163–224.
41. Ibid., 225–302.
42. Daniel Horowitz, *Anxieties of Affluence: Critiques of American Consumer Culture* (Amherst: University of Massachusetts Press, 2005), 101–161.
43. Elizabeth Blair, "In Confronting Poverty, 'Harvest of Shame' Reaped Praise and Criticism," NPR, May 31, 2014, https://www.npr.org/2014/05/31/317364146/in-confronting-poverty-harvest-of-shame-reaped-praise-and-criticism (accessed August 2019).
44. Robin Muncy, "Coal-Fired Reforms: Social Citizenship, Dissident Miners, and the Great Society," *Journal of American History* 96:1 (June 2009), 72–98; A. H. Raskin, "A Depressed Area Looks to Kennedy," *The New York Times*, September 29, 1960, 25; Richard Johnson, "Kennedy Hailed in Mining Region," *The New York Times*, April 27, 1960, 26.
45. Phillips-Fein, *Invisible Hands*, 68–149; Elizabeth Tandy Shermer, "Sunbelt Patriarchs: Lyndon B. Johnson, Barry Goldwater, and the New Deal Dissensus," in Robert Mason and Iwan Morgan (eds.), *The Liberal Consensus Reconsidered: American Politics and Society*

in the Postwar Era (Gainesville: University of Florida Press, 2017), 167–186.

46. Wicker, "Remembering the Johnson Treatment."
47. Salmond, *Southern Rebel*, 141–161.
48. Shermer, "Sunbelt Patriarchs."
49. Shermer, *Sunbelt Capitalism*, 289–292, quoted 290.
50. Ibid., 289–292.
51. Ibid., 289–292, quoted 291.
52. Ibid., 289–292.
53. Zelizer, *Fierce Urgency of Now*, 61–84, 163–224.
54. Shermer, "From Educator- to Creditor-In-Chief"; Hugh Davis Graham, *Uncertain Triumph: Federal Education Policy in the Kennedy and Johnson Years* (Chapel Hill: University of North Carolina Press, 1984), 53–83.
55. Paul Glastris, "Remembering Jonathan Rowe," *Washington Monthly*, May/June 2011, https://washingtonmonthly.com/magazine/mayjune-2011/remembering-jonathan-rowe/ (accessed August 2019); Jonathan Rowe, "I was a Spear Carrier in the War on Poverty," *The Washington Monthly* 16:10, 1984, 38–47, quoted 46.
56. Tom Wolfe, *Radical Chic & Mau-Mauing the Flak Catchers* (New York: Farrar, Straus & Giroux, 1970); Deirdre Carmody and William Grimes, "Tom Wolfe, 88, 'New Journalist' With Electric Style and Acid Pen, Dies," *The New York Times*, May 15, 2018, https://www.nytimes.com/2018/05/15/obituaries/tom-wolfe-pyrotechnic-nonfiction-writer-and-novelist-dies-at-88.html (accessed August 2019).
57. "War on Poverty Still Worth Fighting?" *Tell Me More*, NPR, September 19, 2013, https://www.npr.org/templates/story/story.php?storyId=224084191 (accessed August 2019); NR Symposium, "The War on Poverty at 50," *National Review*, January 8, 2014, https://www.nationalreview.com/2014/01/war-poverty-50-nro-symposium/ (accessed August 2019); Here & Now, "'War on Poverty' Remains Controversial," NPR, January 8, 2014, http://www.wbur.org/hereandnow/2014/01/08/war-on-poverty (accessed August 2019); Albert Hunt, "Remembering L.B.J. for More Than Vietnam," *The New York Times*, April 13, 2014, https://www.nytimes.com/2014/04/14/us/politics/remembering-lbj-for-more-than-vietnam.html (accessed August 2019).
58. Matusow, *Unraveling of America*, ix–xviii, 217–243.
59. Zelizer, *Fierce Urgency of Now*, 303–324; Bornet, "Reappraising the Presidency of Lyndon B. Johnson."

60. Kim Phillips-Fein, "1973 to the Present," in Eric Foner and Lisa McGirr (eds.), *American History Now* (Philadelphia, PA: Temple University Press, 2011), 175–200.
61. Ibid.
62. Timothy Canova, "Legacy of the Clinton Bubble," *Dissent* (summer 2008), https://www.dissentmagazine.org/article/the-legacy-of-the-clinton-bubble (accessed August 2019); Nelson Lichtenstein, "Fabulous Failure: Clinton's 1990s and the Origins of Our Times," *American Prospect*, January 29, 2018, http://prospect.org/article/fabulous-failure-clinton%E2%80%99s-1990s-and-origins-our-times (accessed August 2019).
63. Canova, "Legacy of the Clinton Bubble"; Lichtenstein, "Fabulous Failure."
64. Cooper, Mary H. "Low Voter Turnout," *CQ Researcher* 10:36 (October 20, 2000), 833–856.
65. Lichtenstein, *State of the Union*, 212–245.
66. Jim Rutenberg, "A Dream Undone," *The New York Times*, July 29, 2015, https://www.nytimes.com/2015/07/29/magazine/voting-rights-act-dream-undone.html (accessed August 2019).
67. Jonathan Turley, "Rise of the Fourth Branch of Government," *The Washington Post*, May 24, 2013, https://www.washingtonpost.com/opinions/the-rise-of-the-fourth-branch-of-government/2013/05/24/c7faaad0-c2ed-11e2-9fe2-6ee52d0eb7c1_story.html?utm_term=.94d1aa6fb798 (accessed August 2019); Greg Weiner, "Power of the Courts is Messing Up Politics," *The New York Times*, November 11, 2017, https://www.nytimes.com/2017/11/11/opinion/sunday/the-power-of-the-courts-is-messing-up-politics.html (accessed August 2019); Christopher Ingraham, "Congressional Gridlock Has Doubled since the 1950s," *The Washington Post*, May 28, 2014, https://www.washingtonpost.com/news/wonk/wp/2014/05/28/congressional-gridlock-has-doubled-since-the-1950s/?utm_term=.02247bb36f2c (accessed August 2019).
68. Amber Phillips, "Budget Rule You've Never Heard of that Ties Republicans' Hands on Obamacare," *The Washington Post*, March 9, 2017, https://www.washingtonpost.com/news/the-fix/wp/2017/03/09/the-budget-rule-youve-never-heard-of-that-ties-republicans-hands-on-obamacare/?utm_term=.a46940d28baf (accessed August 2019); Ryan Struyk and Joyce Tseng, "The History of US Government Shutdowns in 1 Chart," CNN, January 13, 2018, https://www.cnn.com/2018/01/13/politics/us-government-shutdowns-budget-chart/index.html (accessed August 2019); Kenneth Mayer and Kevin Price,

"Unilateral Presidential Powers: Significant Executive Orders, 1949–99," *Presidential Studies Quarterly* 32:2 (June 2002), 367–386.

69. Elizabeth Tandy Shermer, "Party Crashers: How Far-Right Demagogues Took Over the GOP," *Dissent*, spring 2017, 144–148; Tom Squitieri, "A Look Back at Trump's First Run," *The Hill*, October 7, 2015, https://thehill.com/blogs/pundits-blog/presidential-campaign/256159-a-look-back-at-trumps-first-run (accessed August 2019).

70. Conor Friedersdorf, "The Decline and Fall of Hope and Change," *The Atlantic*, January 30, 2014, https://www.theatlantic.com/politics/archive/2014/01/the-decline-and-fall-of-hope-and-change/283454/ (accessed August 2019); Rick Hampson, "When it Comes to Campaign Promises, Presidents Usually Try, Often Fail," *USA Today*, July 6, 2016, https://www.usatoday.com/story/news/politics/elections/2016/07/06/campaign-promises-trump-clinton/86134898/ (accessed August 2019).

71. Patrick Healy and Julie Bosman, "Clinton Campaign Starts 5-Point Attack on Obama," *The New York Times*, February 26, 2008, https://www.nytimes.com/2008/02/26/us/politics/26clinton.html (accessed August 2019); Joan Walsh, "2008 Democratic Primary Was Far Nastier than 2016's," *Nation*, April 11, 2016, https://www.thenation.com/article/the-2008-democratic-primary-was-far-nastier-than-2016s/ (accessed August 2019).

72. Tom Curry, "'Community Organizer' Becomes a Punch Line," NBC-NEWS, September 4, 2008, http://www.nbcnews.com/id/26547877/ns/politics-decision_08/t/community-organizer-becomes-punch-line/#.W7_FOfF95E4 (accessed August 2019); Adam Serwer, "What Right Wingers Mean When They Call Obama a 'Socialist,'" *American Prospect*, October 13, 2008, http://prospect.org/article/what-right-wingers-mean-when-they-call-obama-socialist (accessed August 2019); Jonathan Martin and Amie Parnes, "McCain: Obama not an Arab, Crowd Boos," *Politico*, October 10, 2008, https://www.politico.com/story/2008/10/mccain-obama-not-an-arab-crowd-boos-014479 (accessed August 2019).

73. Nathan Gonzales and Stuart Rothenberg, "From Coast to Coast, Democrats Rule the Day," CNN, November 7, 2008, http://www.cnn.com/2008/POLITICS/11/07/rothenberg.elections/ (accessed August 2019).

74. David Greenberg, "The Folly of the 'Hundred Days,'" *The Wall Street Journal*, March 21, 2009, https://www.wsj.com/articles/SB123759302359600669 (accessed August 2019); John Steele

Gordon, "A Short History of Midterm Elections," *The Wall Street Journal*, November 6, 2010, A13.

75. Norm Ornstein, "The Real Story of Obamacare's Birth," *The Atlantic*, July 6, 2015, https://www.theatlantic.com/politics/archive/2015/07/the-real-story-of-obamacares-birth/397742/ (accessed August 2019); William Galston, "President Barack Obama's First Two Years: Policy Accomplishments, Political Difficulties," *Governance Studies at Brookings*, November 4, 2010, https://www.brookings.edu/wp-content/uploads/2016/06/1104_obama_galston.pdf (accessed August 2019).

76. Chris McGreal, "Why Joe Lieberman is Holding Barack Obama to Ransom over Healthcare," *The Guardian*, December 16, 2009, https://www.theguardian.com/world/2009/dec/16/joe-lieberman-barack-obama-us-healthcare (accessed August 2019).

77. Jason Millman, "Ben Nelson to Work on Obamacare," *Politico*, January 23, 2013, https://www.politico.com/story/2013/01/nelson-from-60th-vote-to-acas-implementation-086646 (accessed August 2019).

78. Michael Cooper, "G.O.P. Senate Victory Stuns Democrats," *The New York Times*, January 19, 2010, https://www.nytimes.com/2010/01/20/us/politics/20election.html (accessed August 2019).

79. Lawrence Jacobs and Theda Skocpol, *Health Care Reform and American Politics: What Everyone Needs to Know* (New York: Oxford University Press, 2012), 101–120; David Reich and Richard Kogan, *Introduction to Budget 'Reconciliation* (New York: Center on Budget and Policy Priorities, 2016), https://www.cbpp.org/sites/default/files/atoms/files/1-22-15bud.pdf (accessed August 2019).

80. Theda Skocpol and Vanessa Williamson, *The Tea Party and the Remaking of Republican Conservatism* (New York: Oxford University Press, 2013), 121–154, quoted 126.

81. Edward Schumacher-Matos, "What We Hear When NPR Refers to 'Obamacare,'" NPR, September 6, 2013, https://www.npr.org/sections/ombudsman/2013/09/06/219765368/what-we-hear-when-npr-refers-to-obamacare (accessed August 2019); Elspeth Reeve, "Who Coined 'Obamacare'?" *The Atlantic*, October 26, 2011, https://www.theatlantic.com/politics/archive/2011/10/who-coined-obamacare/335745/ (accessed August 2019).

82. Jamelle Bouie, "Obamacare Fear-Mongering Hall of Fame: Death Panels and More," *The Daily Beast*, September 30, 2013, https://www.thedailybeast.com/obamacare-fear-mongering-hall-of-fame-death-panels-and-more (accessed August 2019); Jason Millman,

"This is Obama's Explanation for Why You Might Not Get to Keep Your Doctor," *The Washington Post*, March 14, 2014, https://www.washingtonpost.com/news/wonk/wp/2014/03/14/this-is-obamas-explanation-for-why-you-might-not-get-to-keep-your-doctor/?utm_term=.dcb47e8be9a5 (accessed August 2019).

83. Skocpol and Williamson, *The Tea Party and the Remaking of Republican Conservatism*, 3–44.

84. Skocpol and Williamson, *The Tea Party and the Remaking of Republican Conservatism*, 45–82.

85. Skocpol and Williamson, *The Tea Party and the Remaking of Republican Conservatism*, 121–188.

86. Chris Cillizza, "What Effect Did Health-care Reform Have on Election?" *The Washington Post*, November 7, 2010, http://www.washingtonpost.com/wp-dyn/content/article/2010/11/07/AR2010110705311.html (accessed August 2019); Jennifer Rubin, "Did Obama Make It All About Him?" *Chicago Tribune*, December 27, 2016, https://www.chicagotribune.com/news/opinion/commentary/ct-obama-democrats-future-20161227-story.html (accessed August 2019); Michael Grunwald, "The Party of No: New Details on the GOP Plot to Obstruct Obama," *Time*, August 23, 2012, http://swampland.time.com/2012/08/23/the-party-of-no-new-details-on-the-gop-plot-to-obstruct-obama/ (accessed August 2019); Adam Liptak, "Study Calls Snub of Obama's Supreme Court Pick Unprecedented," *The New York Times*, June 13, 2016, https://www.nytimes.com/2016/06/14/us/politics/obama-supreme-court-merrick-garland.html (accessed August 2019).

87. Adam Liptak, "Supreme Court Upholds Health Care Law, 5–4, in Victory for Obama," *The New York Times*, June 28, 2012, https://www.nytimes.com/2012/06/29/us/supreme-court-lets-health-law-largely-stand.html (accessed August 2019); Scott Lemieux, "How the Supreme Court Screwed Obamacare," *New Republic*, June 26, 2017, https://newrepublic.com/article/143524/supreme-court-screwed-obamacare (accessed August 2019).

88. Mike Green, "The Obama Legacy: Signed, Sealed . . . Delivered," *The Huffington Post*, December 3, 2012, https://www.huffingtonpost.com/mike-green/the-obama-legacy_b_2209919.html (accessed August 2019).

89. Robinson Meyer, "The Secret Startup That Saved the Worst Website in America," *The Atlantic*, July 9, 2015, https://www.theatlantic.com/technology/archive/2015/07/the-secret-startup-

saved-healthcare-gov-the-worst-website-in-america/397784/ (accessed August 2019).

90. Ian Reifowitz, "Helping People Enroll in Obamacare is a Way to Volunteer," *The Huffington Post*, December 6, 2017, https://www.huffingtonpost.com/ian-reifowitz/helping-people-enroll-in-obamacare_b_4975875.html (accessed August 2019); Claire Bolderson, "Obamacare in Kentucky: The Luxury of Seeing a Doctor," *BBC Magazine*, July 21, 2014, https://www.bbc.com/news/magazine-28337867 (accessed August 2019).

91. Binyamin Appelbaum and Michael Shear, "Once Skeptical of Executive Power, Obama Has Come to Embrace It," *The New York Times*, August 13, 2016, https://www.nytimes.com/2016/08/14/us/politics/obama-era-legacy-regulation.html (accessed August 2019); Shermer, "From Educator- to Creditor-In-Chief"; Office of the Vice-President, "Factsheet: Making Student Loans More Affordable," June 9, 2014, https://obamawhitehouse.archives.gov/the-press-office/2014/06/09/factsheet-making-student-loans-more-affordable (accessed August 2019); Kevin Carey, "Programs That Are Predatory: It's Not Just at For-Profit Colleges," *The New York Times*, January 13, 2017, https://www.nytimes.com/2017/01/13/upshot/harvard-too-obamas-final-push-to-catch-predatory-colleges-is-revealing.html?smid=nytcore-ipad-share&smprod=nytcore-ipad (accessed August 2019); Kaitlin Mulhere, "Here's What Obama's New Student Loan Moves Could Mean for You," *Time*, April 28, 2016, http://time.com/money/4310765/student-loans-new-consumer-protections/ (accessed August 2019).

92. David Graham, "How Many of His 'Day One' Promises Did Trump Fulfill," *The Atlantic*, January 24, 2017, https://www.theatlantic.com/politics/archive/2017/01/trump-day-one-promises/514184/ (accessed August 2019); Libby Nelson, "Donald Trump Seems to be Stunningly Ignorant about what a President Actually Does," *Vox*, November 14, 2016, https://www.vox.com/policy-and-politics/2016/11/14/13624858/donald-trump-transition-presidency (accessed August 2019).

93. Quoted Zack Beauchamp, "UN Audience Literally Bursts Out Laughing at Trump's Speech," *Vox*, September 25, 2018, https://www.vox.com/policy-and-politics/2018/9/25/17900980/un-trump-laughed-at (accessed August 2019).

94. Richard Wolf, "Travel Ban Timeline," *USA Today*, April 25, 2018, https://www.usatoday.com/story/news/politics/2018/04/25/

trump-travel-ban-timeline-supreme-court/547530002/ (accessed August 2019); Leigh Ann Caldwell, "Obamacare Repeal Fails," NBC News, July 28, 2017, https://www.nbcnews.com/politics/congress/senate-gop-effort-repeal-obamacare-fails-n787311 (accessed August 2019); Glenn Kessler, Salvador Rizzo, and Meg Kelly, "President Trump has Made More Than 5,000 False or Misleading Claims," *The Washington Post*, September 13, 2018, https://www.washingtonpost.com/politics/2018/09/13/president-trump-has-made-more-than-false-or-misleading-claims/?utm_term=.c5913680bbe7 (accessed August 2019); Avery Anapol, "Trump Ramps Up Attacks on Journalists," *The Hill*, August 5, 2018, https://thehill.com/homenews/administration/400433-trump-attacks-reporters-as-enemy-of-the-people-says-they-cause-wars (accessed August 2019); John Bennett and D. A. Banks, "With the Midterms Over, Get Ready for Investigation Nation and Congressional Gridlock," *Roll Call*, November 8, 2018, http://www.rollcall.com/video/with_the_midterms_over_get_ready_for_investigation_nation_and_congressional_gridlock (accessed August 2019).

13

Coda – Obama's fractured legacy

Sidney M. Milkis

This volume began as an international conference of scholars of American politics who gathered in Paris in December 2016 to consider Barack Obama's legacy. When first invited, most of us, expecting Hillary Clinton, whom the president anointed as his heir apparent, to be elected, looked forward to a stimulating but serene conversation about the first African-American president's important but fragile record of accomplishment. As the final essays reveal, most of those who tackled the assignment viewed Obama as a victim of harsh partisan polarization, but someone whose progressive vision was proscribed by a willingness to temporize – to compromise with an administrative state denigrated by "neoliberal forces" that weakened public accountability and fomented appalling economic inequality. This verdict, as Nelson Lichtenstein's chapter argues, is best framed by the promise and limitations of Obama's signature policy achievement: the Affordable Care Act (ACA). Highlighting especially its progressive tax structure and the expansion of Medicaid, he acknowledges the ACA marked an "expansion of the U.S. welfare state unmatched since the Great Society" (see p. 236). At the same time, Lichtenstein laments Obamacare's limited redistributive potential. Truth be told, its most formative feature, the expansion of Medicaid, was dramatically circumscribed by the Supreme Court, which gave states the right to choose whether to accept expanded coverage that would cover the working poor. But the bill that Obama signed, with "corporate deals" that empowered predatory private insurance companies and lacked a "public option," he claims, was "structured in a radically discordant fashion" (p. 236).

Once we convened in Paris, however, the remarkable and unsettling results of the 2016 election overawed our attempt to calmly reflect on the accomplishments and disappointments of Obama's two terms. Had Secretary of State Hillary Clinton been elected, the conference participants and their essays might have debated whether Obama's failure to live up to his transformative promise was due to personal leadership failings or the nettlesome political context he faced. Placing Obama's presidency in "political time," Steven Skowronek's analysis suggests that the first African-American president entered office after George W. Bush's two terms exposed a vulnerable conservative political order, but not one on the brink of disaster. Or we might have reflected, reverently and critically, on the venerable strains of the "Madisonian System," reprised by Elizabeth Shermer, which has limited all transformative presidents and has remained strong in the face of an emerging modern executive.

But the election and re-election of the first African-American president ensured that race also would have loomed large in our discussions. In fact, Audrey Célestine and Nicolas Martin-Breteau, in their chapter for this volume on the Black Lives Matter movement, argue that Obama's "relative failure to reform American society has primarily been the result of racial resentment" (see p. 306). The results of the 2016 elections brought this issue to the forefront of the conference – and this volume. Like all racial gains since the Civil War, Célestine and Martin-Breteau aver, "Obama's two mandates as president of the United States have stimulated reactionary racial trends that fueled, among other things, the rise of the Tea Party, the systematic obstruction of Republicans in Congress, and the election of Donald Trump" (p. 306).

The election of a bombastic, iconoclastic real estate mogul and reality television star, spewing a message of fear, aroused a sense of urgency that, as disappointing as it might have seemed to many of the volume's authors, would not have followed from the election of a pragmatic problem solver like Hillary Clinton. Trump's America First slogan aroused deep concern that a clever demagogue had moved a right-wing authoritarian strain, once considered marginal in a "liberal" nation, to the mainstream of politics in the United States. His promise, sounding more like a threat, to Make America Great Again cast a fearful pale over conference deliberations and this volume's essays. Did, we fretted, the complacency and recalcitrance of "neoliberalism" bring into question the norms and institutions of a constitutional republic? Was the pragmatic progressive tradition of Roosevelt, Johnson, and Obama strong enough to hold right-wing populism at bay? Could the Madisonian System – metaphorically characterized as "guard rails," which Shermer views as so intractable – save America from the excesses of the right, just as it has circumscribed left-wing reform since the 1930s? These questions have intruded on our attempt to understand Obama's legacy – and they force us to contemplate developments that have fractured the country and weakened the national resolve.

In seeking to shed light on the momentous developments that roiled Obama's two terms and abetted the rise of Trump, this concluding chapter stresses how – to use Skowronek's framework – *secular* time has overtaken *political* time. Although the enduring constitutional features stressed by Shermer and the political cycles emphasized by Skowronek are still significant, I think the causes of our present discontents are best understood as the consequence of critical changes over the course of the past five decades that have transformed the United States – once praised or criticized for its centrist politics and pragmatism – into a deeply divided country rattled by widespread dissatisfaction with government, strong and intensifying polarization, and high-stakes battles over the basic direction of domestic and foreign policy. More concretely, Obama's legacy – and the threat the 2016 election and Trump's presidency poses to it – should be viewed as a new and highly disturbing episode in an ongoing contest between liberalism and conservatism – one that can be traced back to the 1960s, but took more definite shape during the George W. Bush and Obama presidencies. During these administrations, long simmering conflicts were further aroused in the wake of September 11 and the Great Recession, thus setting the stage for the remarkable and unsettling events of the past four years.

From this perspective, this coda makes three points about where we are in the stream of American political development. First, I think that for all the craziness and bellicosity of the 2016 election, the final results did not look very different from 2012; or, for that matter, from every presidential election since 2000. Recent presidential elections have occurred amid the demise of the Democratic New Deal consensus and the failure of either party to build an enduring basis of national support. Second, these elections and political conflicts have been joined to a transformation of partisanship, from the localized and patronage-based politics of the late nineteenth and early twentieth centuries to the executive-centered battles that began to take shape during the New Deal but have come into full realization during the Obama and Trump presidencies. Third, the 2016 election and its aftermath have confirmed that the New Deal conflict between the advocates and enemies of a strong national state, which dominated the New Deal political order, has been displaced by a battle for the services of the administrative state forged during Franklin Roosevelt's protracted presidency and elaborated during the pursuit of a Great Society during the 1960s. Since Richard Nixon, Republicans have been dedicated to the proposition that the modern presidency can be, ideologically, a two-edged sword that can serve conservative causes. Aroused by issues such as trade, undocumented immigration, and law and order, Trump and his loyal supporters have practiced a harsh partisanship that has engaged the country in an all-consuming struggle for the power to shape the national identity.

The fracturing of the New Deal political order and the rise of a red and blue nation

Shermer rightfully reminds us that Franklin Roosevelt's protracted presidency was constrained by constitutional forms and a conservative coalition of Southern Democrats and Republicans. But there is no gainsaying that Roosevelt was a "reconstructive" president, one of the country's transformative leaders, who Skowronek credits with forging a new governing coalition, formulating a new governing philosophy, reordering political institutions, and adopting new policies. Most important, the New Deal political order consolidated developments that began during the end of the nineteenth century and that gave rise to an executive-centered administrative

SIDNEY M. MILKIS

state, a structural change that brought into view the "contretemps of political and secular time" that frames Skowronek's analysis of contemporary developments in American politics. Even as the New Deal marked a momentous development in political time, it significantly advanced secular forces that appear to have dimmed "the prospects for any abrupt repudiation or wholesale transformation of the terms and conditions of legitimate national government" (see p. 34). Indeed, the rise of the New Deal state seemed to subordinate the conflicts of partisan strife that mark political time to administration – as Skowronek puts it, to a "political universe of presidential action that has grown progressively more inclusive in its interests and purview, more interdependent in its operations, thicker in its institutional environment, and more reliant on central management" (p. 34).

The resilience of the New Deal state – and the diminishment of political time – followed in no small measure from the way the Roosevelt Reconstruction redefined the terms of the social contract. The development of the modern American State during the Great Depression and World War II involved not just the creation of new programs and administrative agencies but a new public philosophy. In his iconic 1941 State of the Union Address, FDR argued that America's traditional freedoms such as speech and religion needed to be supplemented by two new "essential human freedoms": "freedom from want" and "freedom from fear." This was not mere rhetoric. "Freedom from fear" was embodied by the national security state in the fight against global communism, while "freedom for want" took institutional form in domestic programs like Social Security, the cornerstone of the welfare state. These commitments, the charter of the modern American State, Roosevelt argued during the 1932 campaign, should not be subject to partisanship, but to "enlightened administration" – to the creation of an administrative state, anchored by a "modern" executive, that would supplant limited constitutional government and the decentralized party politics that accommodated it. Tempered by economic crisis and total war, American politics was endued with pragmatic policy-making.[1] The enactment of the 1939 Executive Reorganization Act, which created the White House Office (the West Wing) and strengthened the president's control over the

392

expanding administrative core, is the organic statute of the New Deal political order.

The consolidation of executive power under Franklin Roosevelt was hotly contested and far from complete; nonetheless, the rise of an executive-centered administrative state reflected a fragile consensus that for a time obscured partisan conflict over national administrative power. Beginning in the progressive era, reformers collectively scorned the political practices and institutions built during the nineteenth century, which were dominated by local issues and a spoils system that supported a highly-decentralized "state of courts and parties" as Skowronek terms it.[2] Following World War II, many conservatives and liberals alike celebrated Roosevelt's vision of a new American State. Partisan politics reached a low ebb as citizens held high trust in government and majorities of both parties largely agreed about the direction of domestic and foreign policy, so long as national programs did not disturb a racialized political order with major civil rights reforms.

Dwight Eisenhower, the first Republican president – the first "opposition leader" – elected during the New Deal regime, for a time epitomized the bipartisan legitimacy that underpinned the liberal political order. Two years after his 1952 campaign victory he worked with the Congress to pass an expansion of Social Security, thereby rendering America's nascent welfare state more inclusive.[3] More telling of a bipartisan commitment to the fledgling national state was the creation of a national highway system, first proposed in 1944, which Eisenhower celebrated as "the biggest peacetime construction project ever undertaken by the United States or any other country."[4] Against the powerful strain of isolationism in the Republican Party, Eisenhower also retained Roosevelt and Truman's commitment to liberal internationalist institutions like NATO, the United Nations, and global financial institutions.

Although Eisenhower's two terms in office bestowed a measure of bipartisan legitimacy on the liberal state, many GOP loyalists and Democratic conservatives detested his "modern Republicanism." Old guard stalwarts such as "Mr. Republican," Robert A. Taft, as Melvyn Leffler has observed, "seemed little concerned with conditions abroad; their intent was to crush communism at home, besmear the New Deal, and thwart the activist state."[5] Western conservatives, fueled by the population boom in the Sunbelt states, rallied around a libertarian creed that denounced federal intervention in land management, business regulation, and civil rights enforcement. Southern Democrats feared that Roosevelt's 1941 order to prohibit racial segregation in war industries was the opening wedge of an assault on Jim Crow, a fear confirmed by Harry Truman's decision to integrate the armed services and issue an *amicus curia* in support of the NAACP's suit against forced segregation in education. Republicans made deep inroads into the South throughout the 1950s, challenging the dominance of one-party rule and enhancing the prospects of a vote-rich, multi-region party.

Nevertheless, the New Deal administrative state seemed to have rendered less meaningful the categories of political time. The election of John F. Kennedy in 1960 and his pursuit of a New Frontier appeared to sanctify the pragmatic administration governing the welfare and national security states. Addressing a White House Conference on National Economic Issues in May 1962, Kennedy declared:

> Most of us are conditioned for many years to have a political viewpoint – Republican or Democratic – liberal, conservative, moderate. [But] most of the problems or at least many of them that we now face are *administrative problems*. They are very sophisticated judgments which do not lend themselves to the great sort of "passionate movements" which have stirred the country so often in the past.[6]

Reifying these developments, the Harvard sociologist Daniel Bell ideologically heralded the "end of ideology."[7] But civil rights leaders, anti-war protesters, and a woman's liberation movement rejected the working arrangements of the New Deal state for its egregious accommodation of racism, sexism, corporate greed, and the imperialism it pursued under the banner of protecting global freedom. Inured to America's simmering racial divisions and inequalities, neither Kennedy nor Bell foresaw the powerful social movements that would soon pressure the presidency to abandon incremental reform and throw American politics "off center."[8]

"Sixties Civics" – combining distrust of the government and a passion to expand its responsibilities – envisaged the American State in a multicultural society whose government would actively protect the rights of women, immigrants, and African Americans, and promote free society abroad through free-trade, diplomacy, and a commitment to human rights, not imperialism.[9] This ideal manifested itself most fully in the social causes championed by Lyndon Johnson's Great Society. The attempt to realize the Great Society exposed the liberal state's central fault lines, and with violent upheaval in Vietnam and in the nation's urban core, the pragmatic center that buttressed the New Deal disintegrated. The 1960s left many social and anti-war activists feeling alienated from the "establishment"; but they remained active in government during the 1970s through "public interest" groups, dedicated to remaking, rather than dismantling, administrative politics. Celebrating "participatory democracy," these public lobbyists gained access to the regulatory process, opened up the courts to further litigation, and democratized congressional procedures, with the consequence that programmatic liberalism was extended to affirmative action, environmental and consumer protection, and education.[10] As Paul Pierson argues, these policies gave rise to an activist and polarized state centered on "a range of profoundly contentious issues . . . The character of these issues made compromise difficult, and created incentives for polarizing forms of mobilization."[11]

In Skowronek's framework, Ronald Reagan resembled a reconstructive leader who repudiated the Liberal political order. Combining a celebration of the market and states' rights with a commitment to restore "traditional" values in foreign and domestic affairs, Reagan won landslide victories in 1980 and 1984 that many scholars and pundits viewed as the mainsprings of a new conservative political order. But unlike the New Deal and earlier party eras, voters reacted with ambivalence to the new Republican regime. With the exception of the Senate from 1981 to 1987, Congress stayed under Democratic control throughout the 1970s and 1980s. When Republicans finally did capture both chambers of Congress in 1994, Democrat Bill Clinton was in the White House, and his re-election two years later was widely interpreted as a reaction to Speaker of the House Newt Gingrich's attempt to bring the Reagan "Revolution" to fruition. Indeed, since Reagan's 1984 re-election, presidential contests have been highly competitive and the survivors of these bitter contests have had to manage, during at least part of their tenure, with a Congress controlled by the opposition party.[12]

The regular existence of divided government is due in large measure to the political landscape of post-New Deal politics – to the way that Republicans and Democrats have represented different regions of the country. The geographic division in party strength first became apparent to the media in the 2000 election, when it was labeled "the red state/blue state divide." What Donald Trump and Hillary Clinton proved in the rancorous 2016 campaign is that the regional party system that we thought defined red and blue America – with Republicans in the Southern, border, and mountain states, especially in small towns and exurban enclaves; and the Democrats along the East and West Coasts, especially in the major metropolitan areas – has been altered, with serious consequences for American democracy. With Hillary Clinton winning states like Nevada, Colorado, and Virginia (and coming very close in North Carolina, and even being competitive in Texas); and with Donald Trump winning states like Ohio, Pennsylvania, Wisconsin, and Michigan (the "Blue Wall"), the cultural divide in America has become more national and plebiscitary.

The combat between what the journalist Ronald Brownstein has called the coalition of ascension – young people, minorities, and educated whites, especially women, who embrace the massive demographic and social changes of the past five decades – and the coalition of restoration – blue-collar, religiously devout, and non-urban whites who are exceedingly anxious about losing their country – has now eroded regional enclaves and further weakened the rearguard of the New Deal political order.[13] It is telling that nearly one-third (206) of the more than 650 counties that voted for Obama both in 2008 and 2012 flipped to Trump in 2016; most of these counties are predominantly white, and outside of major metropolitan areas. These areas were critical not just to the cracking of the blue wall but also to Trump's victory in the key swing state of Florida.[14]

The emergence of the partisan divide between cosmopolitan and small town/rural America has made more likely not just divided government but also a discrepancy between the electoral college and popular vote. As in 2000, the Democrats won the popular vote in 2016 (this time by nearly three million votes), but lost the electoral college. Just as the Republicans won the popular vote in five of six presidential elections between 1968 and 1972, so Democrats have won the popular vote in six of the last seven presidential elections, which has never happened in history. Therefore, contrary to all the chatter on Fox News and other conservative media outlets after the 2016 election, there was no mandate – a mischievous, politically constructed concept that never has had clear meaning in American presidential politics. Indeed, Skowronek suggests that this unprecedented turn in American electoral politics might presage the emergence of a new progressive wave, and that Trump might be viewed as the rearguard of the conservative political order that the Reagan Revolution spawned. As Julia Azari and Scott Lemieux suggest, however, the polarizing cultural struggle in the country, rooted in red and blue communities, might not portend a "disjunctive" presidency, with Trump presiding over the implosion of the Republican conservatism:

> While it is true that Republicans have lost the popular vote in 6 of the last 7 presidential elections, they have also been the dominant congressional party since 1994, and the fact that the House, Senate and therefore the Electoral College all overrepresent predominantly white rural areas gives the Republican Party as currently constituted a very high electoral floor that will make its consignment to the political wilderness unlikely.[15]

Rather than a preface to a transformation of American politics, the 2016 campaign instead may very well have marked a culmination of sorts in the erosion of what Arthur Schlesinger, Jr. once called the "vital center" of American politics[16] – a breaking apart that has its origins in the cosmic crack-up of the 1960s, when the civil rights revolution, immigration reform, and recriminations over the Vietnam War launched a struggle not only over material things, but also over the very question of what it means to be an American: who are "We, the People"?

397

The transformation of partisanship

The struggle for the soul of American democracy, fought on the landscape of a sprawling administrative state, has sometimes resembled the trench warfare of World War I. Indeed, at first glance, Trump's first two years as president revealed the resilience of Obama's legacy. Against the claim of his highly experienced opponent, Secretary Hillary Clinton, that he was unqualified by temperament and background to occupy the White House, Trump retorted in his acceptance of the Republican nomination in Cleveland that only an outsider who had long jousted with the "establishment" could truly reform a "rigged system." "Nobody knows the system better than me," Trump claimed, "which is why I alone can fix it."[17] But for all his braggadocio during the 2016 campaign, Trump thus far has failed to translate most of his promises into legislation: Obamacare is still the law of the land; there is no "big, beautiful" wall on the border with Mexico; save for a massive tax bill, which threatens to ooze rather than drain the "swamp," the Republican Congress that prevailed during the first two years of the Trump presidency failed to enact any major program central to the White House's America First agenda; and Trump had the dubious honor of recording the lowest public approval ratings for a president's first two years in modern history.

Never, it seems, has there been such dramatic validation of Theodore Lowi's refrain that the modern presidency is trapped in an intractable dynamic of "Power Invested" and "Promise Unfulfilled."[18] Skowronek might attribute this disappointment to the thickening of institutions, just as Shermer could point to the gravitational pull of American constitutional government. The Democrats takeover of the House in 2018, moreover, makes clear that for all the talk of possible rapprochement on issues such as criminal justice and infrastructure, partisan gridlock will mark the rest of Trump's first term. Yet often overlooked among the disappointments and recriminations of Trump's frenzied first term is his administration's aggressive and deliberate assault on the liberal state. Since day one, Trump has forcefully – and sometimes successfully – taken aim at the programmatic achievements of his predecessor. In an effort, as one of Trump's supporters put it, to "erase Obama's legacy," the President has issued a blizzard of executive initiatives that have refashioned or seriously disrupted government commitments in critical policy arenas such as immigration, climate change, foreign trade, national security, criminal justice, civil rights, and healthcare policy. Moreover, Trump has appointed two Supreme Court justices – Neil Gorsuch and Brett Kavanaugh – who will likely shift the balance on the court toward greater acceptance of public action that advances conservative policies in national security, protection of the homeland, policing, and civil rights.

There are many features of Trump's shocking rise to the White House and his tumultuous presidency that represent novel features of American politics. However, the administrative aggrandizement that so far has dominated his time in office marks the continuation of a far-reaching development in American politics: the rise of an executive-centered partisanship.[19] Beyond the expansion of liberalism to social issues, the breaking apart of American democracy during the late 1960s and 1970s abetted the long-standing attack on regular party organizations. Change in campaign finance and the creation of a presidential primary system brought to a culmination the assault on the institutions and party leaders – or brokers – who acted as a buffer against unfiltered partisan combat. By the time Reagan, who was widely considered too extreme to be elected president, ascended to the White House, the decentralized, patronage-based party system – anchored by the quadrennial national party convention – had been replaced with a presidency-centered partisanship, with parties dependent on presidents and presidential candidates to raise funds, mobilize base supporters, convey a message, and advance party programs. We can trace the development of a presidency-centered partisanship back to Franklin Roosevelt – and the institutionalization of the modern executive office – but it was significantly advanced by the media-driven, plebiscitary politics loosed by Sixties Civics, and has taken more definite form due to the partisan politics of Reagan (the first Republican president to pose fundamental challenges to liberalism), George W. Bush (who, unlike his father, styled himself as an heir apparent of the Reagan "Revolution"), and Barack Obama (who bestowed bipartisan legitimacy on this executive-centered partisanship).

In fact, although he threw himself into the partisan fray somewhat reluctantly, Obama's creation of a presidential grassroots organization marked a new stage in the development of presidential partisanship. This fascinating experiment in top-down, bottom-up mobilization went through three phases over the course of Obama's two terms. It started with Obama and his allies building a digital-age grassroots organization that proved central to the success of his two presidential campaigns. Born during the 2008 campaign as Obama for America (OFA), this mass mobilization effort, unlike other presidential campaign organizations, was not dismantled once the 2008 campaign ended. Envisioning a post-election role for OFA, the president-elect, newly appointed chair of the Democratic National Committee (DNC) Tim Kaine, staffers, and volunteers engaged in extensive discussions, finally resolving that OFA should be inserted into the DNC as Organizing for America during the president's first term, where it was tasked with mustering support for the Patient Protection and Affordable Care Act, the president's signature program; working for Democratic candidates in the 2010 off-year election; and developing a ground game for Obama's re-election campaign. Due to its effectiveness in performing these tasks, OFA was rechristened Organizing for Action and spun off as a 501(c)(4) social welfare group dedicated to advocating for Obama's second term objectives: immigration reform, efforts to fight climate change, gun safety legislation, LGBTQ rights, and the implementation of healthcare reform. Removing his organization from the DNC, President Obama promised his followers, would further strengthen its potential as a grassroots advocacy group – one that would tie him directly to a widely scattered but potentially formidable coalition – the Coalition of the Ascendant that represents the maturing of the Great Society.[20]

Most of OFA's significance has been attributed to the sophisticated digital platform that Obama and his close political allies forged to mobilize support for the 2008 and 2012 campaigns. As important as the fascinating combination of internet-based targeting and old-fashioned canvasing was to Obama's election to two terms, the most innovative feature of OFA is how it was kept intact after both elections *and* redeployed as a deeply loyal and digitally savvy volunteer base to support the White House's programmatic ambitions. Candidate-centered campaigns had been a staple of presidential politics since John Kennedy utilized the "Irish Mafia" in the 1960 election; but Obama's organization was distinctive both in its capacity to mobilize supporters at the grassroots level and its adaption to policy advocacy during his presidency.

Taking account of the important role Republican presidents, especially Ronald Reagan, have played in forging a conservative coalition, scholars such as Daniel Galvin and Katherine Krimmel have viewed the White House Office, especially the Office of Public Liaison (OPL) – a White House institution developed by Gerald Ford and Jimmy Carter to provide outreach to a wide and bipartisan network of groups – as pivotal in the transition from "less structured, 'pluralist' party-group relations to more institutionalized, long-term linkages that hold together modern party networks."[21] Most significant, Reagan's partisanship enlisted Christian Right groups into the Republican Party – the key development in his forging of a decidedly right-of-center GOP, imbued with social and cultural commitments that played so large in the 2016 election. Like Reagan, the Obama administration used the White House Office to build connections with partisan groups. In fact, Obama renamed the OPL the Office of Public Engagement to signify its role in forming ties with Democratic advocacy groups like MoveOn.org, the National Women's Political Caucus, the Service Employees International Union, the National Council of La Raza, and the Human Rights Campaign. But OFA – a multi-issue group, with its state-of-the-art digital platform, thirty million e-mail addresses, three million donors and two million active volunteers – was an especially critical ally – virtually a surrogate party machine – in Obama's efforts to cultivate a formative relationship between the White House, progressive groups, and a new progressive coalition.

OFA enabled Obama to make innovative uses of the rhetorical and administrative powers of the modern executive; however, Michael Kazin argues that Obama did not "live up to the image of a bold movement leader" (see p. 273). Nor was he able to change the essential structural reality that grassroots activism is more likely to thrive when it emerges spontaneously to challenge, rather than collaborate with, the White House. But Reagan's relationship with the Christian Right revealed new possibilities for top-down, bottom up forms of mobilization; and Obama, who deeply valued his experiences as a community organizer, viewed OFA as a way to join more effectively executive prerogative and grassroots mobilization. In a toxic political environment, where he was attacked from the left and the right, OFA gave Obama a credible and far-flung voice within the progressive wing of the party that countered some of the right's rhetorical thunder and strengthened the White House's relationship with his base constituencies – especially on issues like healthcare, climate change, immigration policy, and LGBTQ rights: sometimes by nudging the White House toward more progressive positions.

Just as important, in the face of partisan gridlock that Obama faced in the aftermath of the "shellacking" the Republicans administered to his party in the 2010 midterms, which saw the Democrats lose sixty-two seats in the House and six seats in the Senate, OFA helped to promote Obama's "We Can't Wait Campaign," his commitment to promote progressive causes with unilateral executive action.[22] As Andrew Rudalevige's chapter details, during the final year of his first term, Obama took measures authorizing the Environmental Protection Agency (EPA) to implement greenhouse gas regulations that were stalled in the Senate; issued waivers releasing states from many of the requirements of No Child Left Behind, enacted during the George W. Bush administration, which Congress had failed to reauthorize, and without legal authorization, formed a grant program – Race to the Top – that pressured states to embrace new Common Core standards that his administration deemed more progressive than those of his Republican predecessor; and bypassed the usual confirmation process by granting recess appointments to four nominees whom Senate Republicans were filibustering. Finally, in June 2012 Obama announced an initiative – Deferred Action for Childhood Arrivals (DACA) – which granted legal status and work permits to an entire category of young undocumented immigrants, as many as 1.4 million people, who otherwise would have been subject to deportation. Obama thus elided Republican opposition to the DREAM Act, the administration's bill to provide a conditional pathway to citizenship for immigrants who were brought to America illegally as children.

Obama's adroit administrative maneuver contributed to his successful re-election campaign. Prior to DACA, Hispanic activists were ambivalent about the Obama administration, which had pursued so vigorous a deportation policy that they dubbed him "deporter-in-chief." A survey of Latinos following the DACA announcement revealed a significant turning of the tide: 58 percent of respondents indicated that DACA had made them "more enthusiastic" about Obama. Only 6 percent indicated it had made them less enthusiastic.[23] Obama went on to win about 70 percent of the Latino vote in 2012.

The 2010 elections, which gave Republicans control of the House, encouraged Obama and his grassroots political machine to pursue progressive causes unilaterally; so the 2014 midterms, which saw the Republicans take command of the Senate, further incited the president and OFA to exploit the powers of partisan administration. Most controversially, soon after the election, Obama announced an expansion of deportation relief to parents of permanent residents and citizens – composing an additional 4.3 million unauthorized immigrants. Concurrently, OFA roused its members to support the White House initiative and, more generally, to shift their focus almost exclusively to administrative politics. As OFA's executive director, Sara El-Amine wrote in an e-mail of December 12, 2014,

> The last month has been a [big deal] for those of us who want to see meaningful action to fix our broken immigration system. But it came towards the end of a frustrating year. House leaders had more than 500 days to hold one simple vote on bipartisan, comprehensive reform, and they failed to act, making it clear that they were just running out the clock on this Congress. That's why President Obama refused to wait any longer.[24]

The frustration Obama and OFA experienced owed in large measure to the fiercely divided polity that confronted them. But their response to this bitter factionalism – the celebration of partisan presidential action – was, as Rudalevige concludes, "inherently fragile." Executive actions can "be reversed simply by future Chief Executives, and President Trump was eager to do just that" (see p. 83). Isabelle Vagnoux, whose chapter traces the wayward path of comprehensive immigration reform, laments that Obama's immigration initiatives, which were advanced through memoranda promulgated by the Department of Homeland Security rather than the regulatory rule-making process, were especially vulnerable. Beyond the ease of reversing policies implemented by memoranda, these exercises of partisan administration poured salt in the wounds that had afflicted the country for much of the past two decades. The "deep anger" DACA and, especially DAPA, triggered in the country "were predictably [among] the first to be [rescinded] by President Trump" (see p. 171).

Beyond the fragility of policies carried out unilaterally lies a more fundamental hazard of partisan administration. As Kazin's chapter on social activism suggests, Obama's partisanship raised the fundamental question of whether the executive of a vast administrative state, even with the support of an information-age grass-roots organization and the tools of social media, can truly function as a democratic institution with meaningful links to the public. Obama's "family," as OFA staffers and volunteers referred to themselves, was a pioneering organization that beheld the possibility of a new form of executive-centered partisanship, one that joins executive prerogative, street-level politics, and collective responsibility. At the same time, OFA marked a new stage in a century-long development that has seen presidents subordinate collective party responsibility to their own policy and programmatic ambitions.

Tellingly, even as Obama won two presidential campaigns – and gained very impressive approval ratings by the end of his presidency – he saw his party lose more support "down ballot" in Congress and the states than any president since Dwight Eisenhower in the 1950s. Furthermore, although many people who were instrumental in building Obama's pioneering information age grassroots organization – Organizing for Action – worked for the Hillary "machine," and even though Obama campaigned more vigorously than any previous president for an heir apparent, he was unable to anoint a successor. Even Michelle Obama, the most impressive Clinton surrogate, could not persuade two key constituencies of the Obama coalition – millennials and African Americans – to turn out in numbers that would close the enthusiasm gap between Trump and Clinton supporters. Obama bequeathed the institutional apparatus of his information-age grassroots organization to the Clinton campaign; however, there was a serious decline in the activist volunteers who were central in making Obama's pioneering brand of top-down, bottom up mobilization so effective.

The anxiety which loomed over the conference's deliberations – and which is interwoven in many of this volume's chapters – testifies to the fear that Obama failed to achieve political and programmatic successes that would endure beyond his two terms in office. Indeed, the way Trump summoned his supporters, not by grassroots organizing, but by "populist," plebiscitary appeals through cable television, mass rallies, and social media – a mobilizing strategy that continued into Trump's presidency – raised the specter that Obama's executive-centered partisanship and pioneering presidential organization might have prepared the ground for a more dangerous, narcissistic cult of personality to emerge.

Trump and the conservative state

Unilateral presidential action became an indispensable feature of executive-centered partisanship during the George W. Bush and Obama years, fueled in no small part by their having to face a Congress when at least one of its chambers was controlled by the other party over substantial periods of their presidencies. So far, in fact, did Obama push the administrative envelope that after Republicans assumed command of the House in the 2010 elections, GOP strategists eagerly anticipated that the next president their party elected would seize the "loaded administrative weapon" Obama had left in the Oval Office.[25] One might think an aggressive administrative strategy would not have been so pivotal after the GOP won control of the Senate in 2014 and began this current Republican administration under unified government in 2017. Nevertheless, Trump resorted to administrative aggrandizement right from the start, often in the service of highly controversial measures that strained his relations with congressional Republicans who remained split in the areas of free trade and immigration.

Trump, therefore, continued – indeed radicalized – a tradition of conservatism that does not want to roll back the national state forged on the New Deal and Great Society, but instead wants to deploy national administrative power in the service of conservative objectives. During its first two years in office, the Trump administration eagerly wielded the power of the American State – to secure his pledge to "Make America Great Again." In Homeland Security, where action against undocumented immigrants has been systematically ratcheted up across the government; in trade – where Trump has eschewed free markets for tariffs; in healthcare, where the administration encouraged work requirements for Medicaid recipients; and in criminal justice, where bipartisan efforts to reform the carceral state have been compromised by a series of actions that mark a recrudescence of "law and order."

Most scholars and pundits – especially "Never Trump" Republicans – place Trump outside the tradition of American conservative thought; and many regard him as a disruptive force who is indifferent, if not avowedly hostile, to his party. In contrast, the association of conservative Republicanism and retrenchment fails to recognize the critical change in the relationship between party politics and executive power that has occurred since the Reagan era – a joining of mobilization and executive prerogative – such that partisanship in the United States is no longer a struggle over the size of the state. It has become a battle for the services of national administrative power.[26] Despite rhetorical appeals to "limited government," since the late 1960s conservatives have sought national administrative power just as ardently as liberals: liberals seek to build administrative capacity to design and implement social welfare policies; conservatives have sought to redeploy and extend that power in service of their own partisan objectives, most notably in the areas of criminal justice and national and homeland security.

As liberalism expanded to more polarizing causes like racial justice and anti-imperialism, conservative Democrats and Republicans, who prior to the late 1960s viewed the executive-centered administrative state as an existential threat to constitutional government, gradually came to embrace administrative power. This began with a roar in the wilderness: Senator Barry Goldwater's 1964 campaign. It summoned an aggressive, messianic version of conservatism, notably in the all-encompassing struggle against communism: "I would remind you that extremism in the defense of liberty is no vice," he told the GOP convention in 1964. "And let me remind you also," Goldwater continued, "that moderation in the pursuit of justice is no virtue."[27] Goldwater's crusade, which ended in a historic defeat to Lyndon Johnson, marked an important precursor to Richard Nixon's presidency, representing the first advance of an alternative form of administrative power. Since Nixon, self-styled conservative administrations have sought to demonstrate that modern executive prerogative is a double-edged sword, which can cut in a conservative as well as a liberal direction. Put most simply, liberals dedicated themselves to the Freedom from Want, while conservatives embraced the Freedom from Fear. The state persists because conservatives no less than liberals covet its power.

That ideology is central to understanding the contemporary dynamics of state development suggests that the idea of a "State" cuts more deeply than suggested by Max Weber's classic definition of "a human community that (successfully) claims the monopoly of the legitimate use of physical force within a given territory."[28] Beyond the powers of government, the state represents a centralizing ambition to cultivate, or impose, a vision of citizenship. In Randolph Bourne's words, the state is a "concept of power" that comes alive in defense of, or in conflict with, an ideal of how such foundational values of Americanism as "free and enlightened" are to be interpreted and enforced. It is symbolized not by the Declaration and the Constitution but rather in rallying emblems such as the flag and Uncle Sam. A key mobilizing force is patriotism, a concept at once centralizing and conflictual.[29]

Contests over American identity have historical roots but, with the cosmic crack-up of the 1960s, they have become a more routine part of politics in the United States. These culture wars gave rise to two competing visions of the national state, which animate the rancorous struggle between conservatism and liberalism and fueled Donald Trump's remarkable ascent to the White House. In large measure this struggle can be expressed as a battle for the soul of the New Deal state, with liberals embracing Freedom from Want and conservatives championing Freedom from Fear. However, the meanings of Freedom from Fear and Freedom from Want were significantly transformed by an existential struggle over American identity.

Just as post-New Deal liberalism followed from the fraught but effective alliance, described by Kazin, that formed between Lyndon Johnson and civil rights activists, so Goldwater's call for a more unyielding struggle against communism summoned grassroots activists who advanced the contemporary conservative movement's rightward shift.[30] Fellow crusaders rejected the liberal state as an insidious form of despotism that would destroy "rugged individualism" at home and America's "exceptional" global place. Along with communism, a principal demon of conservatives' apocalyptic vision was urban unrest and rioting during the "long hot summers" of the late 1960s. Goldwater, therefore, preached the gospel of law and order that would become a rallying cry for conservatives' redeployment of state power at home.

Although Goldwater was the prophet of conservative statist ambition, it was Nixon who welded the promise of American exceptionalism and law and order to state power. Goldwater was the rearguard of anti-statism: he viewed the twin diseases of communism abroad and domestic unrest at home as symptoms of an executive-centered administrative state that had to be fervently resisted. But the traditional faith in limited constitutional government had faded considerably by the time Nixon took office. Now the modern presidency was inextricably linked with the quagmire in Vietnam and three summers of rioting in Northern cities, which severely tested the nation's resolve. Nixon coupled conservative insurgency to the promise of presidential power – an institution originally designed to protect and extend the vision of a programmatic, liberal state. "The days of a passive presidency belong to a simpler past," he foretold during the 1968 campaign. "Let me be very clear about this: the next president must take an activist view of his office. He must articulate the nation's values, define its goals and marshal its will. Under a Nixon administration, the presidency

408

will be deeply involved in the entire sweep of America's public concerns."[31]

Nixon acted on these words. On entering office, he reorganized rather than curtailed the executive aggrandizement of the Johnson years. Goldwater and Nixon laid the groundwork for a conservative state; Ronald Reagan and his self-styled heir apparent, George W. Bush, further advanced policies that would remedy the New Deal state's failure to uphold private property, protect "family" values, and effectively fight foreign enemies of the American way of life. Johnson enlisted civil rights social movement organizations as the foot soldiers of a new liberalism; Reagan forged an alliance with the Christian Right, which became the core constituency of the push for conservative nationalism.

Each party now laid claim to a particular aspect of the New Deal state: conservatives embraced the mantra of fear and the national security state; liberals celebrated the promise of freedom from want and the welfare state. But the terrorist attacks of September 11, 2001 and the subsequent "war on terrorism" brought the foreign and domestic executive closer than they had ever been before, blurring though not eliminating the distinction. Democrats neither ignore public anxieties nor are Republicans indifferent to the individual's insecurities. The terrorist attacks fostered a permanent condition of crisis that posed novel threats to civil liberties and the rule of law.[32] Hitherto a marginal term, "homeland security," became ubiquitous. As a result, Republicans have accepted this state of perpetual war. George W. Bush exploited his party's ideology and organization to extend the conservative administrative state into a preventative war against terrorist states, or the "axis of evil." As Rudalevige points out, Obama's exercise of unilateral power in foreign affairs further attenuated constitutional and legal constraints on executive aggrandizement. His adoption of a "surge" strategy in Afghanistan in 2009 and use of covert drone strikes reveals resemblance rather than contrast with his predecessor. Yet the partisan rancor over Obama's refusal to define his objectives as a War on Terror and the enemy as "radical Islamic terrorism" indicates that the Democrats took a different approach and strategy to national and homeland security – multilateralism and diplomacy over brinkmanship (as best demonstrated in the Iranian nuclear deal), and surgical strikes rather than massive troop deployments (the strategy that informed the struggle with ISIS). Liberals and conservatives, therefore, bitterly contest how to protect "homeland security" from Middle East terrorists, and, increasingly, undocumented immigrants. The partisan conflict over homeland security that reached a fevered pitch in the 2016 election shows that the wounds festering since the 1960s have become all-encompassing, which populist "outsiders" can all too easily exploit.

Although Trump's conservative nationalism has historical roots, his "Make America Great Again" campaign represented the unprecedented influence of a populist right-wing strain in American politics. Previous embodiments of this strain – Huey Long in the 1930s, Charles Lindberg (the hero of the original America First movement) of the 1940s, Joseph McCarthy of the 1950s, and George Wallace of the 1960s – were disruptive figures. But none succeeded in capturing the presidential nomination of a major political party. Such right-wing populism has a long tradition in Europe; for example, there are strong parallels between Trump's ascendency and the Brexit movement in the United Kingdom. But it was startling to see this authoritarian tradition, with connection to an emergent white nationalist movement, move from the margins of what was once thought to be a moderate constitutional republic to the mainstream of American politics. Trump's appointment of Steven Bannon, a leading figure in the so-called alt-right movement in American politics, as his Senior White House Counselor only intensified fears that the conservative movement had been hijacked by a scheming demagogue who appealed to Republican supporters' worst instincts and prejudices. Trump fired Bannon in August 2017, amid fallout from the president's controversial response to a deadly white nationalist rally in Charlottesville, Virginia. But he has retained, indeed strengthened, America First proponents like Stephen Miller, a militant proponent of restrictive immigration policy, and Peter Navarro, a staunch defender of protectionism.

Never-Trump conservatives have lamented that Trump's war cry that America was no longer a great nation, but the stooge of our international trading partners and the victim of predatory immigrants, abandoned the more uplifting conservatism that Ronald Reagan expressed – a conservatism that insisted, in opposition to the post-1960s liberals' anti-imperialism, that America still was a "city on a hill." This message of resilience and religious tolerance inspired the position that Reagan heir-apparent George W. Bush projected in the wake of the attacks of September 11, 2001. The first sentence of the 2016 Republican platform read: "We believe in American exceptionalism," an uplifting sentiment that Trump virtually ignored during the long and bitter 2016 contest. But this nostalgia for the Reagan "Revolution" has overlooked how, under these kinder and gentler partisans, the Republican Party had built a conservative base whose foot soldiers, most notably the Christian Right (that Reagan enlisted in his administration's conservative crusade) and the Obama-era Tea Party, that Republican presidential candidates had been courting since its inception, rallied around the belief that liberalism had so corrupted the country that the national government had the responsibility to support "family values" (a view that permeates proposals to restrict abortion and same-sex marriage; to require work for welfare; and to impose standards on secondary and elementary schools).

Significantly, Trump, a thrice married and one-time New York liberal, received strong support not only from Tea Party activists but also from conservative evangelical leaders. One of his strongest champions was Ralph Reed, now Chairman of the Faith and Reform Coalition, who, recounting the Christian Right's long march toward a leading place in the conservative coalition, appreciated Trump's strong pledge to make appointments to the administration and the Supreme Court who would oppose abortion, stand up to for the traditional family, and protect Christian schools from the Department of Education.[33] Other crucial defenders included Liberty University President Jerry Falwell, Jr., Focus on the Family's James Dobson, and Family Research Council's Tony Perkins. "We're not electing a pastor-in-chief," Falwell, echoing the pragmatism his father expressed in championing the candidacy of Ronald Reagan, explained to Fox News during the campaign. "Sometimes you have to be pragmatic. You have to choose the one with the best chance of winning and who is closest to your views."[34]

In the wake of the September 11 attacks and the Great Recession of late 2007 to 2009, it is not surprising that the most pressing targets of conservative activists in the 2016 campaign became "radical Islamic terrorism" and unauthorized immigration. Appealing to a restive Republican base agitated by movement conservatives, the 2012 Republican candidate Mitt Romney embraced a punitive immigration policy – endorsing Arizona's ultimately unconstitutional "show-me-your-papers" law and calling on undocumented immigrants to "self-deport" by denying them public benefits and fostering a subclass status that would drive most to leave. In subsequent years, GOP state officials and congressional members embraced harsh crackdowns on unauthorized immigration and demonized undocumented immigrants. Against this backdrop, Trump's ascendance was more than a cult of personality or the discovery of anti-immigrant appeals. His political success must also be attributable to his giving unfiltered expression to the marriage of Republican presidents and right-wing social movements that was more than four decades in the making.

Despite their relative inexperience, Trump and his strategists recognize the importance and relish the exercise of partisan administration. Trump's commitment to "erase Obama's legacy" is not merely personal recrimination; his presidency builds on the sustained reliance of Reagan, Bush 43, and Obama on executive-centered partisanship. As a candidate, Trump denounced the Obama administration's "major power grabs of authority." But as president, he has not only rescinded Obama-era actions, he also has redeployed administrative power to serve conservative objectives. This strategy has primarily entailed pushing policies that uphold Freedom from Fear; but the Trump administration has also sought to recast those programs dedicated to Freedom from Want. Restricting restroom accessibility for transgender students; changing Title IX guidance for colleges and universities, which reduce legal protections for sexual assault "survivors"; and removing LGBTQ protections with which government contractors had to comply does not remove or reduce the state's presence. By the stroke of the presidential pen, some groups lost while others gained.

Trump has also acted in the states, most of which are controlled by Republicans, to redeploy resources for conservative objectives.

Thad Kousser's chapter on federalism argues that Obama's effort to enhance national power over healthcare, education, and environmental policy met fierce resistance. The mobilization of this discontent in the 2010 and 2014 midterm campaigns gave Republicans control of the Congress and most state governments, thus "setting in place conditions for the states to move in divergent directions if they were freed to do so" (see p. 120). Trump's reversal of Obama's programs and his significant influence on the courts, Kousser concludes, has resulted in an "accidental devolution revolution."

Yet Trump's states' rights rhetoric has proven to be just as, if not more, hollow than that of Ronald Reagan and George W. Bush. As Kousser acknowledges, Trump's pursuit of his signature issue of immigration has involved efforts to impose national conservative policy on the states, most notably in his executive order to cut off federal funding to sanctuary cities – an attempt to compel states like California to cooperate fully with federal immigration agents. In addition to redeploying national state power to serve conservative causes in homeland security, the Trump administration has sought to recast social welfare policies to serve national conservative objectives. For example, Trump's Department of Education (DOEd) Secretary Betsy DeVos has long championed local control of public schools, but once in power she did not hesitate to take administrative measures that encouraged market-driven education reforms such as charter schools and vouchers.[35] She thus weakened the authority of some department divisions, while retooling and empowering others. Not surprisingly, DOEd's Office of Civil Rights has lost much of the independent regulatory authority it built for itself over the last decade. Trump issued an executive order in April 2017 that called for a review of the department's regulations and guidance documents;[36] four months later, DeVos rescinded the Obama-era "Dear colleague letter" that universities and colleges used to adjudicate Title IX complaints.[37] While DeVos has curbed the Office of Civil Rights' authority, she has creatively used the department's student loan division to support for-profit colleges and universities, and to protect student loan providers. By rewriting the gainful employment regulations and contracting with private collection agencies to more aggressively recoup student loan debt, the Department has not been weakened; rather, it has been retooled to provide state support for market-driven education providers.[38]

Another noteworthy example to enlist the states in national policy, discussed in Nelson Lichtenstein's chapter, is the Trump administration's repurposing of the Affordable Care Act. After the Republican Congress failed to repeal and replace Obamacare, Trump resorted to an administrative approach to recast a centerpiece of the Affordable Care Act: the extension of Medicaid benefits to those with annual incomes below 138 percent of the federal poverty level. Almost one year after taking office, the Trump administration informed each state's Medicaid office of a new demonstration project, encouraged by Republican governors' demands. With the permission of the Centers for Medicare and Medicaid (CMS), states may rescind the Medicaid benefits of able-bodied adults if they are not seeking work or demonstrating active "community engagement." To this point, amid legal battles which have set aside work requirements in three states, six states have received approval and eight more states have waiver applications pending. These administrative changes to the Affordable Care Act have encouraged Republicans in the seventeen states that had previously opposed Medicaid expansion, including Virginia, to do so.

The press and pundits viewed the Republicans' inability to repeal Obamacare as a great failure. But with a waiver from CMS, state officials now have the opportunity to remake healthcare for the poor into a more conservative program – to redeploy the most redistributive features of "Obamacare" through administrative fiat. In fact, because of the incentives these waivers provide for red states, Medicaid is projected to expand as a result of this policy – but only for "the deserving poor."[39]

The resort to remaking Obamacare through unilateral action follows from practical necessity and the institutionalization of partisan administration. As Lichtenstein notes, Republicans faced powerful headwinds in their effort to repeal the Affordable Care Act. More broadly, however, Trump's eager deployment of executive power also reflects a strategy to obviate divisions within his party over America First conservatism. Indeed, Trump's estrangement from the GOP establishment over the tenets and policies of conservative nationalism has resulted in some striking evidence of how presidents now dominate their party's "brand" – how they can denigrate parties as collective organizations. Although Trump's harsh positions on immigration, trade, and national security might not have won over Washington, he has forged strong ties with the GOP's base through tweets, mass rallies, and administrative action – dramatically transforming GOP loyalists views on issues such as the "wall" and tariffs.[40]

Given the fractious state of American politics, and the vast network of progressive social movements and advocacy groups that had formed during the Obama presidency, Trump's executive actions in the service of conservative causes aroused a ferocious opposition from the Democratic Party's base. As Kazin notes, progressive activists who gained traction during the Obama administration employed grassroots protest, social media, and legal action to protect the hard-won programmatic achievements of the past eight years. From the first day of his presidency, therefore, the Trump presidency found itself governing in a political war zone, which grew all the more combative after Democrats took control of the House in the 2018 elections. Given the president's truculent temperament, it is hardly surprising that he responded in kind, using twitter and mass rallies in small towns and rural areas to attack, indeed declare illegitimate, the insurgent opposition to his program.

Although the relationship between presidents and social movement organizations had become commonplace since the 1960s, Trump appeared to become especially dependent on disruptive activists. As the president's poll numbers dropped to historically low levels during the first year of his presidency, and the administration became embroiled in a scandal that risked exposing collusion between his campaign and the Russian government and obstructive tactics to hinder the Special Prosecutor Robert Mueller's investigation of potential high crimes and misdemeanors, Trump sought to strengthen the relationship he had forged with the leaders of the conservative movement during the 2016 election. The Mueller Report was not sufficiently condemnatory to incite an impeachment inquiry. But revelations in the fall of

2019 concerning the president's attempts to pressure Ukraine to investigate the "corruption" of then leading Democratic candidate for the 2020 Democratic nomination, former vice-president Joe Biden, and his son Hunter, led to the eruption of a full-blown impeachment inquiry. Facing the prospect of becoming only the third president to be impeached by the House, the president found refuge among his political base. Despite his weak public support after three years in office, the president's approval rating among conservative Republicans, according to a Gallup poll, was 90 percent – almost exactly what it was on inauguration day.[41]

Indeed, during his first three years in office, Trump's efforts to take credit for a robust economy were overshadowed by his championing of the issues that had become the template of movement conservatives over the past four decades: "traditional" family values, law and order, enhanced border security, opposition to affirmative civil rights policy, and the war against "radical Islamic terrorism." Relentlessly emphasizing these issues in the 2018 elections and the run-up to his 2020 re-election effort, Trump has doubled down on the politics of fear – conservative statism – thus deflecting attention from an historically robust economy.[42]

Whither the American republic?

Given the high stakes in the current battles between progressives and conservatives, with the country engaged in what might be termed a cold civil war over the very meaning of what it means to be an American, the public – whether liberals, conservatives, or independents – ought to demand that the field of partisan battle be waged, at least somewhat, on competing principles rather than personal acrimony: the 2016 contest pitted "Crooked Hillary" vs. Donald the "Deplorable"; in the aftermath of the 2018 elections institutional combat has been framed as a contest between "Crazy Nancy" (the president's moniker for Nancy Pelosi, the Speaker of the House) and a president whose opponents denigrate as "deranged." Since the 1960s, however, with the advent of a culture war, a churning combative 24/7 media, and prolonged and bitter primaries, partisanship has been joined to a politics of recrimination, where candidates not only differ on principles and policies, but also challenge the character and motives of their opponent. In truth, Donald Trump's unsettling roar that the 2018 elections were "fraudulent" and his bitter denunciation of the investigations of the Special Prosecutor and Congress's impeachment inquiry as "witch hunts" are only the most dramatic expression of the people's deep distrust in their leaders and political institutions that has emerged from the falling apart of America's vital center. The view that the system is rigged is more pronounced among Republicans than Democrats; but as the surprising Bernie Sanders democratic socialist insurgency in the 2016 primaries made clear, this message resonates on the left as well, especially among young people. That the Democrats won the popular vote and witnessed the devastating intervention of the FBI – and maybe the Russians – in the campaign only fanned the flames of their discontent with America's governing institutions.

The politics of personal destruction might be understood as the collision that Skowronek describes between secular and political time. As his mentor Lowi foretold, the rise of an administrative state privileges interest groups who are indifferent, if not avowedly hostile, to any sense of a public interest. Many scholars, including several authors in this volume, have attributed the astounding and troubling rise of Trumpism to the mischievous effect of "neoliberalism" on political and social justice. Although surely not reinventing the wheel, these scholars might benefit enormously by revisiting (or discovering) Lowi's account of liberalism's "end." For all of the enormous differences between the supporters of Donald Trump and Bernie Sanders, they are united in the view that contemporary American politics alienates everyone except those organized interests that bore within the administrate state (popularly denounced as the "establishment"). These self-styled democratic socialists and authoritarian nationalists seem to intuit, if not fully grasp, Lowi's admonition that "the most accurate characterization [of the modern administrative state]" is not neoliberalism or neo-conservatism but, rather, a government-sponsored elitism that provides "socialism for the organized and capitalism for the unorganized."[43]

417

Perhaps Lowi – whose views were always brilliantly contrarian – might view the culmination of a rancorous contest between left and right as a positive development – a departure from the rank apathy ("the nightmare of administrative boredom") – that afflicts "interest group liberalism."[44] Lichtenstein and Kazin make the somewhat ironic observation that the inherent limits of Obama's pragmatism and "corporatist deal-making" have strengthened the progressive wing of the Democratic Party. As Kazin writes, the unfulfilled promise of Obama's presidency "helped fuel an upsurge of protest and organizing that propelled issues like police killing of black men" (see p. 271), the principal animating factor in the rise of the Black Lives Matter movement, and "economic inequality," trumpeted by the Occupy Wall Street uprising, "to the forefront of national politics." This grassroots activism did much to make the "heated, two-person battle" between Clinton and Sanders "a contest to prove who could sound more progressive than the other." Former vice-president Joe Biden, calling for a "return to normalcy," managed to rally moderate Democrats behind him in vanquishing the sprawling field of over twenty candidates in the 2020 primary contests, including the heroes of the progressive wing of the party – Sanders and Massachusetts Senator Elizabeth Warren. Nevertheless, seeking to mollify progressive Democrats and unify the party for the general election, Biden quickly moved to the left. Soon after becoming the presumptive Democratic presidential nominee, he announced proposals to expand access to healthcare and higher education, reform bankruptcy laws, and curtail student loan debt. Moreover, the Movement for Black Lives, a coalition of the disparate groups that gave birth to the Black Lives Matter movement, imbued progressive concerns about economic inequality with a commitment to address the structural infirmities that sustain discrimination against African Americans, Latinos, the LGBTQ community, and women. The challenge for progressive activists and the Democratic candidates who sought to make their causes consequential, as Célestine and Martin-Breteau conclude, is to build a "collective subject of representation" (see p. 307). This will be no easy task, but the endeavor suggests a realization of the new progressive program and coalition that Obama's candidacy and presidency appeared to promise.

The 2020 election, then, might bring the revitalization of "political time," as rendered by Skowronek – a full-scale struggle for the soul of American democracy that promises a possible escape from the bureaucratic indifference of the administrative state. Yet as Lowi's *The Personal President* presciently recognized, our partisan battles – dominated by ad hominem assaults, not only on the programs of the opposition's leader, but also on his or her character – have become too presidency-centered. The Republicans mobilized opposition to Obama by attacking him personally – most notoriously in the Donald Trump-led "birther movement." Similarly – and more reasonably – Democrats have mobilized support against Trump, not so much by revitalizing progressive principles (as intriguing as the Medicare for All and Green New Deal are) as by attacking the president's competence and moral character. After gaining control of the House in the 2018 elections, the Democrats brought two articles of impeachment against Trump that indicted him for withholding needed military assistance to Ukraine, and they made its release contingent upon a politically motivated investigation that would target his potential Democratic Party opponent in 2020, Joe Biden. This episode followed a predictable course when Trump was "acquitted" by the Republican-controlled Senate. At the same time, it gave further credence to the Democrats' charge that Trump was not fit for office – that he represented, as Biden put it, an "existential threat to America." Trump's presidency thus appears to mark a reckoning for the personalization of the presidency – a startling testimony to Lowi's warning that the greatest threat to modern liberalism (to its fragmented and insular character) is a symbolic, plebiscitary politics, which exposes the American people to leaders who scorn the institutional restraints that are a vital ingredient of constitutional government as well as the collaboration that is the *sine qua non* of organized party politics.[45] In coming to terms with Obama's fractured legacy, the great task is to ponder how we can restore the liberal consensus. Or perhaps in the spirit of the condemnation of neoliberalism or the administrative state that reverberates through this volume

419

we should be more brazen – and dare to ponder whether liberalism is really worth restoring.

Notes

1. Franklin Roosevelt, "Campaign Address on Progressive Government, Commonwealth Club, San Francisco, California, September 23, 1932," (http://www.presidency.ucsb.edu/ws/?pid=88391); "State of the Union Message, January 6, 1941." Retrieved January 3, 2018 (http://www.presidency.ucsb.edu/ws/?pid=16092).
2. Stephen Skowronek, *Building A New American State: The Expansion of National Administrative Capacities, 1870–1920* (New York: Cambridge University Press, 1982).
3. Wilbur J. Cohen, Robert M. Ball, and Robert J. Myers, "Social Security Act Amendments of 1954: A Summary and Legislative History," September, 1954. *Bulletin.*
4. This was no idle boast. Daniel Patrick Moynihan denominated the national highway program as "The largest public works program in history." David Mayhew, "Long 1950s as a Policy Era," in Jeffery A. Jenkins and Sidney M. Milkis (eds.), *The Politics of Major Policy Reform in Postwar America* (Cambridge, UK: Cambridge University Press, 2014), 35: 27–47.
5. Melvyn Leffler, "Crossroads of Liberal Internationalism: Harry Truman and the 1946 Election." Presented at the Miller Center, University of Virginia, April 10, 2018.
6. John F. Kennedy, "Remarks to Members of the White House Conference on National Economic Issues," May 21, 1962 (http://www.presidency.ucsb.edu/ws/?pid=8670), emphasis added.
7. Daniel Bell, *The End of Ideology* (Cambridge, MA: Harvard University Press, 1962).
8. With this point, I take issue with Jacob Hacker and Paul Pierson, who view the Republican Party that emerged from the Reagan "Revolution" as the fomenter of partisan polarization. See *Off Center: The Republican Revolution and the Erosion of American Democracy* (New Haven, CT: Yale University Press, 2005).
9. Hugh Heclo, "Sixties Civics," in Sidney M. Milkis and Jerome Mileur (eds.), *The Great Society and the High Tide of Liberalism* (Amherst, MA: University of Massachusetts Press, 2005).
10. Richard Harris and Sidney M. Milkis, *The Politics of Regulatory Change: A Tale of Two Agencies* (New York: Oxford University Press, 2nd edition 1996).

11. Paul Pierson, "The Rise of Activist Government," in Paul Pierson and Theda Skocpol (eds.), *The Transformation of American Politics: Activist Government and the Rise of Conservatism* (Princeton, NJ: Princeton University Press, 2007), 35.
12. Nicole Mellow, "Voting Behavior: Continuity and Confusion in the Electorate," in Michael Nelson (ed.), *The Elections of 2016* (Washington, DC: CQ Press, 2017).
13. Ronald Brownstein, "The Clinton Conundrum," *The Atlantic*, April 17, 2015. Last accessed January 3, 2018 (https://www.theatlantic.com/politics/archive/2015/04/the-clinton-conundrum/431949/).
14. Sabrina Tavernise and Robert Gabeloff, "They Voted for Obama, then voted for Trump. Can Democrats Win Them Back," *The New York Times*, May 4, 2018. Last accessed August 2019 (https://www.nytimes.com/2018/05/04/us/obama-trump-swing-voters.html).
15. Unpublished paper, cited in Thomas Edsall, "The Fight Over How Trump Fits in with the Other 44 Presidents," *The New York Times*, May 15, 2019. Last accessed August 2019 (https://www.nytimes.com/2019/05/15/opinion/trump-history-presidents.html).
16. Arthur Schlesinger, Jr., *The Vital Center: The Politics of Freedom* (New York: Routledge, 2017, first published in 1948).
17. Donald Trump, "Acceptance Speech at the Republican National Convention, July 22, 2016, Cleveland, Ohio." Last accessed August 2019. (http://edition.cnn.com/2016/07/22/politics/donald-trump-rnc-speech-text/index.html).
18. Theodore Lowi, *The Personal President: Power Invested, Promise Unfulfilled* (Ithaca, NY: Cornell University Press, 1986).
19. For a more complete discussion of presidential partisanship, see Sidney M. Milkis, Jesse H. Rhodes, and Emily J. Charnock, "What Happened to Post-Partisanship: Barack Obama and the New American Party System." *Perspectives on Politics* 10(1): 57–76 (2012).
20. Sidney M. Milkis and John W. York. "Barack Obama, Organizing for America, and Executive-Centered Partisanship." *Studies in American Political Development* 31(1): 1–23 (2017).
21. Daniel Galvin, "Presidents as Agents of Change." *Presidential Studies Quarterly* 44(1): 95–119, 112–116 (March 2014); Krimmel, Katherine, *Special Interest Partisanship: The Transformation of American Political Parties* (unpublished PhD dissertation, Columbia University, Department of Political Science).
22. Kenneth Lowande and Sidney M. Milkis, "We Can't Wait: Barack Obama, Partisan Polarization, and the Administrative Presidency." *The Forum* 12(1): 3–27 (2014).

23. "New Report: 2012 Elections Offer Takeaways for 2013 Immigration Debate," America's Voice, January 3, 2013. Last accessed August 2019 (http://americasvoice.org/research/new-report-2012-elections-offer-takeaways-for-2013-immigration-debate-2/).

24. Sara El-Amine, e-mail to OFA members and supporters, December 12, 2014.

25. David Klaidman and Andrew Romano, "President Obama's Executive Power Grab," *The Daily Beast*, October 22, 2012. Last accessed August 2019 (.www.thedailybeast.com/newsweek/2012/10/21/president-obama-s-executive-power-grab.html).

26. Much of this section is drawn from Nicholas F. Jacobs, Desmond King, and Sidney M. Milkis, "Building a Conservative State: Partisan Polarization and the Redeployment of Administrative Power." *Perspectives on Politics* 17(2): 453–469 (June 2019).

27. Barry Goldwater, "Speech Accepting the Republican Nomination, July 16, 1964, San Francisco, California." Last accessed August 2019. (http://www.washingtonpost.com/wp-srv/politics/daily/may98/goldwaterspeech.htm).

28. Max Weber, "Politics as Vocation," in H. H. Gerth and C. Wright Mills (ed. and trans.), *From Max Weber: Essays in Sociology* (New York: Oxford University Press, 1946, originally published in 1918).

29. Randolph Bourne, "The State," 2018. Last accessed August 2019 . (http://fair-use.org/randolph-bourne/the-state/).

30. For a more fully developed discussion of presidents and social movements, see Sidney M. Milkis and Daniel J. Tichenor, *Rivalry and Reform: Presidents, Social Movements, and the Transformation of American Politics* (Chicago: University of Chicago Press, 2019).

31. Richard M. Nixon, "Remarks on the NBC and CBS Radio Networks: 'The Nature of the Presidency,'" September 19, 1968. Online by Gerhard Peters and John T. Woolley, The American Presidency Project. Last accessed August 2019 (.http://www.presidency.ucsb.edu/ws/?pid=123874).

32. Mary Dudziak, *War Time: An Idea, its History, its Consequences* (Oxford, UK: Oxford University Press, 2012).

33. Katie Glueck, "Christian Leaders See Influence Growing on Trump," *Politico*, November 25, 2016. Last accessed August 2019 (https://www.politico.com/story/2016/11/christian-evangelicals-donald-trump-influence-231810).

34. Jerry Falwell, Jr., interview on Fox Business News, September 27, 2016. Last accessed August 2019 (https://video.foxbusiness.com/v/5143151433001/#sp=show-clips).

35. Erica L. Green, "DeVos's Hard Line on Education Law Surprises States," *The New York Times*, July 7, 2017. Last accessed August 2019. (https://www.nytimes.com/2017/07/07/us/politics/devos-federal-education-law-states.html?mcubz=0).

36. "Enforcing Statutory Prohibitions on Federal Control of Education," Executive Order 13791. April 26, 2017. *Federal Registrar*, vol. 82, no. 82, 20427–20428.

37. US Department of Education, "Department of Education Issues New Interim Guidance on Campus Sexual Misconduct," September 22, 2017. Last accessed August 2019. (https://www.ed.gov/news/press-releases/department-education-issues-new-interim-guidance-campus-sexual-misconduct).

38. Michael Stratford, "Education Department Forges Ahead with Loan Servicing Overhaul," *Politico*, May 9, 2017 (https://www.politico.com/tipsheets/morning-education/2017/05/education-department-forges-ahead-with-loan-servicing-overhaul-220209); Danielle Douglas-Gabriel, "Trump Administration Welcomes Back Student Debt Collectors Fired by Obama," *The Washington Post*, May 3, 2017 (https://wwwwashingtonpost.com/news/grade-point/wp/2017/05/03/trump-administration-welcomes-back-student-debt-collectors-fired-by-obama/?utm_term=.7bc1472cd35d). Last accessed August 2019.

39. Nicholas F Jacobs and Connor M. Ewing, "The Promises and Pathologies of Presidential Federalism." *Presidential Studies Quarterly* 48(3), 201, 2018: 552–569.

40. For example, during the 2016 presidential campaign, Pew tracked a massive drop in the share of Republicans and Republican-leaning independents claiming that free trade agreements had been a "good thing" for the United States, from 56 percent in early 2015 to 29 percent in October 2016; see Ashley Parker, "A Sturdy Plank in the GOP Platform: Trumpism," *The Washington Post*, March 25, 2018, A1, A21. During his first two years in office Trump also managed to make "the Wall" the core of Republican immigration policy, a partisan symbol of their support for border security. Colby Itkowitz, "Republicans Spent Two Years Resisting Trump's Border Wall. What Happened?" *The Washington Post*, January 15, 2019. Last accessed August 2019 (https://www.washingtonpost.com/politics/2019/01/15/republicans-spent-two-years-resisting-trumps-border-wall-what-changed/?utm_term=.2a2eed8bcf78).

41. Gallup, *Presidential Job Approval Center* (2019). Last accessed August 2019 (https://news.gallup.com/interactives/185273/r.aspx).

42. Jonathan Martin and Alexander Burns, "Abortion Fight or Strong Economy: Cultural Issues Undercut 2020 Message," November 14, 2019 (https://news.gallup.com/poll/203198/presidential-approval-ratings-donald-trump.aspx).

43. Theodore Lowi, *The End of Liberalism: The Second Republic of the United States* (New York: Norton, 2nd edition 1979), 278–279.

44. Ibid., 313.

45. Lowi, *The Personal President*, chapter 5.

Bibliography

Abramowitz, Alan I. (2010), *The Disappearing Center: Engaged Citizens, Polarization, and American Democracy* (New Haven, CT: Yale University Press).

Abramson R. Paul et al. (2012), *Change and Continuity in the 2008 and 2010 Elections* (Washington, DC: Sage/CQ Press).

Abramson, R. Paul et al. (2015), *Change and Continuity in the 2012 and 2014 Elections* (Washington, DC: Sage/CQ Press).

Ackerman, Bruce (2010), *The Decline and Fall of the American Republic* (Cambridge, MA: Harvard University Press).

Alexander, Michelle (2010), *The New Jim Crow Mass Incarceration in the Age of Colorblindness* (New York: The Free Press).

Alexander, Michelle (2012), *The New Jim Crow: Mass Incarceration in the Age of Colorblindness*, 2nd rev. ed. (New York: Free Press).

Alinski, Saul David (1989), *Rules for Radicals: A Practical Primer for Realistic Radicals*, 2nd rev. ed. (New York: Vintage Books).

Anderson, Carol (2018), *One Person, No Vote: How Voter Suppression Is Destroying Our Democracy* (New York: Bloomsbury).

Anderson, Monica (2015), "A Rising Share of the US Black Population is Foreign Born," *Pew Research Center*, April 9, http://www.pewsocialtrends.org/2015/04/09/a-rising-share-of-the-u-s-black-population-is-foreign-born/ (last accessed September 1, 2018).

Armstrong, Lisa (2014), "The New Civil Rights Leaders," *Essence*, October 31, http://www.essence.com/2014/11/03/new-civil-rights-leaders (last accessed September 1, 2018).

Ashbee, Edward and John Dumbrell (2017), *The Obama Presidency and the Politics of Change* (New York: Palgrave Macmillan).

Bacqué, Marie-Hélène (2005), "Association 'communautaires' et gestion de la pauvreté," *Actes de la Recherche en Sciences Sociales*, vol. 160, no. 5, pp. 46–65.

Bai, Matt (2008), "Is Obama the End of Black Politics?" *The New York Times*, August 6, http://www.nytimes.com/2008/08/10/magazine/10 politics-t.html> (last accessed September 1, 2018).

Balko, Radley (2013), *Rise of the Warrior Cop: The Militarization of America's Police Forces* (New York: Public Affairs).

Béland, Daniel, Philip Rocco, and Alex Waddan (2016), *Obamacare Wars: Federalism, State Politics, and the Affordable Care Act* (Lawrence: University Press of Kansas).

Bereni, Laure, Sebastien Chauvin, Alexandre Jaunait, and Anne Revillard (2012), *Introduction aux études sur le genre*, 2nd ed. (Bruxelles: De Boeck).

Beydoun, Khaled A. and Ocen Priscilla (2015), "Baltimore and the emergence of a Black Spring," *Al-Jazeera*, May 5, http://www.aljazeera .com/indepth/opinion/2015/05/baltimore-emergence-black-spring-150504123031263.html (last accessed September 1, 2018).

Bonilla-Silva, Eduardo (2009), *Racism Without Racists: Color-Blind Racism and the Persistence of Racial Inequality in America* (Lanham, MD: Rowman & Littlefield Publishers).

Bonilla-Silva, Eduardo (2015), "More than Prejudice: Restatement, Reflections, and New Directions in Critical Race Theory," *Sociology of Race and Ethnicity*, vol. 1, no. 1, pp. 75–89.

Bourdieu, Pierre (1984), "La délégation et le fétichisme politique," *Actes de la recherche en sciences sociales*, vol. 52, no. 1, pp. 49–55.

Bruff, Harold H. (2015), *Untrodden Ground: How Presidents Interpret the Constitution* (Chicago: University of Chicago Press).

Burch, Audra D. S. (2018), "Colleges Brace for Tumult in 2018 as White Supremacists Demand a Stage," *The New York Times*, January 17, https://www.nytimes.com/2018/01/17/us/from-charlottesville-to-gainesville-how-colleges-manage-speakers-like-richard-spencer.html (last accessed September 1, 2018).

Calhoun, Craig (2013), "Occupy Wall Street in Perspective," *British Journal of Sociology*, vol. 64, no. 1, pp. 26–38.

CampaignZero (2015), "Solutions," http://www.joincampaignzero.org/ solutions/#solutionsoverview (last accessed July 17, 2018).

Carmon, Irin (2015), "Under Fire, Baltimore Mayor Stephanie Rawlings-Blake Stays 'No Drama,'" *MSNBC*, April 29, http://www.msnbc.com/ msnbc/under-fire-baltimore-mayor-stephanie-rawlings-blake-stays-no-drama (last accessed July 17, 2018).

Chatelain, Marcia (2015), "#BlackLivesMatter: An Online Roundtable with Alicia Garza, Dante Barry, and Darsheel Kaur," *Dissent*, January 19, https://www.dissentmagazine.org/blog/blacklivesmatter-an-online-roundtable-with-alicia-garza-dante-barry-and-darsheel-kaur (last accessed July 17, 2018).

Chatelain, Marcia and Asoka Kaavya (2015), "Women and Black Lives Matter," *Dissent*, vol. 63, no. 3, pp. 54–61.

Chauvin, Sébastien and Alexandre Jaunait (2012a), "Intersectionnalité," in C. Achin and L. Bereni (eds.), *Dictionnaire genre & science politique* (Paris: Presses de Sciences Po), pp. 286–297.

Chauvin, Sébastien and Alexandre Jaunait (2012b), "Représenter l'intersection. Les théories de l'intersectionnalité à l"épreuve des sciences sociales," *Revue française de science politique*, vol. 62, no. 1, pp. 5–20.

Chauvin, Sébastien and Alexandre Jaunait (2015), "L'intersectionnalité contre l'intersection," *Raisons Politiques*, vol. 58, pp. 55–74.

Chishti, Muzaffar, Sarah Pierce, and Jessica Bolter (2017), "The Obama Record on Deportations: Deporter in Chief or Not?" *Migration Policy Institute*, January 26, https://www.migrationpolicy.org/article/obama-record-deportations-deporter-chief-or-not (last accessed August 10, 2018).

Chitnis, Rucha (2015), "Meet the Indian Women Trying to Take Down 'Caste Apartheid,'" *Yes Magazine!*, October 23, http://www.yesmagazine.org/peace-justice/meet-the-women-trying-to-take-down-indias-caste-apartheid-and-finding-hope-in-black-lives-matter-20151023 (last accessed July 17, 2018).

Clotfelter, Charles T. (2004), *After Brown: The Rise and Retreat of School Desegregation* (Princeton, NJ: Princeton University Press).

Coates, Ta-Nehisi (2013), "On the Death of Dreams," *The Atlantic*, August 29, http://www.theatlantic.com/national/archive/2013/08/on-the-death-of-dreams/279157/ (last accessed July 17, 2018).

Coates, Ta-Nehisi (2014), "The Case for Reparations," *The Atlantic*, June, http://www.theatlantic.com/magazine/archive/2014/06/the-case-for-reparations/361631/ (last accessed July 12, 2016).

Coates, Ta-Nehisi (2015), *Between the World and Me* (New York: Spiegel & Grau).

Coates, Ta-Nehisi (2016), "The Enduring Solidarity of Whiteness," *The Atlantic*, February 8, http://www.theatlantic.com/politics/archive/2016/02/why-we-write/459909/ (last accessed July 17, 2018).

Cobb, William J. (2010), *The Substance of Hope: Barack Obama and the Paradox of Progress* (New York: Walker & Company).

Crenshaw, Kimberle W. (1989), "Demarginalizing the Intersection of Race and Sex: A Black Feminist Critique of Antidiscrimination Doctrine, Feminist Theory and Antiracist Politics," *University of Chicago Legal Forum*, 1989, 1, pp. 139–167.

Crenshaw, Kimberle W. (1991), "Mapping the Margins: Intersectionality, Identity Politics, and Violence against Women of Color," *Stanford Law Review*, vol. 43, no. 6, pp. 1241–1299.

Crotty William (ed.) (2012), *The Obama Presidency: Promise and Performance* (Lanham, MD: Lexington Books).

Cullors, Patrisse (2015), "#BlackLivesMatter Will Continue to Disrupt the Political Process," *The Washington Post*, August 18, https://www.washingtonpost.com/news/powerpost/wp/2015/08/18/opinion-blacklivesmatter-will-continue-to-disrupt-the-political-process/ (last accessed July 18, 2018).

Davey, Monica and Catrin Eihorn (2007), "Settlement for Torture of 4 Men by Police," *The New York Times*, December 8, http://www.nytimes.com/2007/12/08/us/08chicago.html (last accessed July 19, 2018).

Davey, Monica and Timothy Williams (2015), "Chicago Pays Millions but Punishes Few in Killings by Police," *The New York Times*, December 17, http://www.nytimes.com/2015/12/18/us/chicago-pays-millions-but-punishes-few-in-police-killings.html (last accessed July 19, 2018).

Davis, Angela Y. (2016), *Freedom Is a Constant Struggle: Ferguson, Palestine, and the Foundations of a Movement* (Chicago: Haymarket).

De Jong, Greta (2010), *Invisible Enemy: The African American Freedom Struggle after 1965* (Chichester, UK and Malden, MA: Wiley-Blackwell).

De La Cruz, Emmelie (2015), "#BlackLivesMatter Co-Founders Say Their Org is 'A Love Note to Black People,'" HerAgenda.com, May 22, http://heragenda.com/blacklivesmatter-co-founders-say-their-org-is-a-love-note-to-black-people/ (last accessed September 2, 2018).

Derthick, Martha (2011), *Up in Smoke*, 3rd rev. ed. (Washington, DC: CQ Press).

Desmond, Matthew (2016), *Evicted: Poverty and Profit in the American City* (New York: Crown).

Diamond, Andrew J. (2010), "Color Blindness and Racial Politics in the Era of Obama," *Books & Ideas*, December 8, http://www.booksandideas.net/Color-Blindness-and-Racial.html (last accessed July 19, 2018).

Dodds, Graham G. (2013), *Take Up Your Pen: Unilateral Presidential Directives in American Politics* (Philadelphia: University of Pennsylvania Press).

Dorrien, Gary (2012), *The Obama Question: A Progressive Perspective* (Lanham, MD: Rowman & Littlefield).

Dutoya, Virginie and Samuel Hayat (2016), "Prétendre représenter: la représentation politique comme revendication," *Revue Française de Science Politique*, vol. 66, no. 1: 7–26.

Dyson, Michael E. (2016), *The Black Presidency: Barack Obama and the Politics of Race in America* (New York: Houghton Mifflin Harcourt).

Edelson, Chris (2013), *Emergency Presidential Power* (Madison: University of Wisconsin Press).

Edelson, Chris (2013), "In Service to Power: Legal Scholars as Executive Branch Lawyers in the Obama Administration," *Presidential Studies Quarterly*, vol. 43, September, pp. 618–640.

Edwards, George C. (2009), *The Strategic President: Persuasion in Presidential Leadership* (Princeton, NJ: Princeton University Press).

Edwards, George C. (2012), *Overreach. Leadership in the Obama Presidency* (Princeton, NJ: Princeton University Press).

Elzie, Johnetta (2015), "Our Demand Is Simple: Stop Killing Us," *The New York Times*, May 4, http://www.nytimes.com/2015/05/10/magazine/our-demand-is-simple-stop-killing-us.html?_r=0 (last accessed September 3, 2018).

Ezekiel, Emanuel (2014), *Reinventing American Health Care* (New York: Public Affairs).

Fassin, Didier (2015a), "Économie morale de la protestation. De Ferguson à Clichy-sous-Bois, repenser les émeutes," *Mouvements*, vol. 83, no. 3, pp. 122–129.

Fassin, Eric (2015b), "Les langages de l'intersectionalité," *Raisons politiques*, vol. 58, no. 2, pp. 5–7.

Ferguson Action (2014), "Our Vision for a New America," http://fergusonaction.com/demands/ (last accessed July 18, 2018).

Fiel, Jeremy E. (2013), "Decomposing School Resegregation: Social Closure, Racial Imbalance, and Racial Isolation," *American Sociological Review*, vol. 78, no. 5, pp. 828–848.

Finnemore, Martha and Duncan D. Hollis (2016), "Constructing Norms for Global Cybersecurity," *American Journal of International Law*, vol. 110, no. 3, pp. 425–479.

Fisher, Louis (2007), "Presidential Inherent Power: The 'Sole Organ' Doctrine," *Presidential Studies Quarterly*, vol. 37, March, pp. 139–152.

Fisher, Louis (2012), "Military Operations in Libya: No War? No Hostilities?" *Presidential Studies Quarterly*, vol. 42, March, pp. 176–189.

Fisher, Louis (2018), *President Obama Constitutional Aspirations and Executive Actions* (Lawrence: University Press of Kansas).

Fletcher, Bill (2015), "From Hashtag to Strategy: The Growing Pains of Black Lives Matter. Movement Activists Discuss Strategy and Sactics in #BlackLivesMatter," *In These Times*, September 23, http://inthesetimes.com/article/18394/from-hashtag-to-strategy-the-growing-pains-of-black-lives-matter (last accessed September 3, 2016).

Gaines, Kevin K. (1996), *Uplifting the Race: Black Leadership, Politics, and Culture in the Twentieth Century* (Chapel Hill: The University of North Carolina Press).

Garrow, David J. (2017), *Rising Star: The Making of Barack Obama* (New York: William Morrow).

Garza, Alicia (2014), "A Herstory of the #BlackLivesMatter Movement," *The Feminist Wire,* October 7, http://www.thefeministwire.com/2014/10/blacklivesmatter-2/ (last accessed June 1, 2018).

Gilmore, Ruth W. (2007), *Golden Gulag: Prisons, Surplus, Crisis, and Opposition in Globalizing California* (Berkeley: University of California Press).

Gitlin, T. (2012), *Occupy Nation: The Roots, the Spirit, and the Promise of Occupy Wall Street* (New York: HarperCollins).

Gitlin, T. (2013), "Occupy's Predicament: The Moment and the Prospect for the Movement," *British Journal of Sociology*, vol. 64, no. 1, pp. 3–25.

Gitterman, Daniel P. (2017), *Calling the Shots: The President, Executive Orders, and Public Policy* (Washington, DC: Brookings Institution Press).

Godet, Aurélie (2012), *Le Tea Party. Portrait d'une Amérique désorientée*, (Paris: Vendémiaire).

Gottschalk, Marie (2015), *Caught: The Prison State and the Lockdown of American Politics* (Princeton, NJ: Princeton University Press).

Graham, John David (2016), *Obama on the Home Front. Domestic Policy Triumphs and Setbacks* (Bloomington: Indiana University Press).

Gramlich, John (2019), "The Gap Between the Number of Blacks and Whites in Prison is Shrinking," *Pew Research Center,* April 30, https://www.pewresearch.org/fact-tank/2019/04/30/shrinking-gap-between-number-of-blacks-and-whites-in-prison/ (last accessed November 17, 2019)

Gray, Kevin A. *et al.* (2014), *Killing Trayvons: An Anthology of American Violence* (Petrolia, CA: CounterPunch).

Green, Emma (2016), "Black Activism, Unchurched," *The Atlantic,* March 22, http://www.theatlantic.com/politics/archive/2016/03/black-activism-baltimore-black-church/474822/ (last accessed September 2, 2018).

Greene, Robert (2015), "The Southern Strategy," *Dissent*, vol. 63, no. 3, pp. 67–71.

Greenstein, Fred I. (2011), "Barack Obama: The Man and his Presidency at the Midterm," *PS: Political Science and Politics*, vol. 44, no. 1, pp. 7–11.

Grover, William F. and Joseph G. Peschek (2014), *The Unsustainable Presidency: Clinton, Bush, Obama, and Beyond* (New York: Palgrave Macmillan).

Grunwald, Michael (2012), *The New New Deal: The Hidden Story of Change in the Obama Era* (New York: Simon and Schuster).

Hadden, Sally E. (2001), *Slave Patrols: Law and Violence in Virginia and the Carolinas* (Cambridge, MA: Harvard University Press).

Hannah-Jones, Nikole (2014), "Segregation Now: The Resegregation of America's Schools," *ProPublica*, April 16, https://www.propublica.org/article/segregation-now-the-resegregation-of-americas-schools#intro (last accessed September 3, 2018).

Harris, Fredrick C. (2012), *The Price of the Ticket: Barack Obama and the Rise and Decline of Black Politics* (New York: Oxford University Press).

Harris, Fredrick C. (2014), "The Rise of Respectability Politics," *Dissent*, vol. 61, no. 1, pp. 33–37.

Harris, Fredrick C. (2015), "The Next Civil Rights Movement?" *Dissent*, vol. 63, no. 3, pp. 34–40.

Harris, Fredrick C. and Robert Lieberman (2013), *Beyond Discrimination: Racial Inequality in a Post-Racist Era* (New York: Russel Sage Foundation Press).

Harris-Perry, Melissa (2012), "Trayvon Martin: What It's Like to Be a Problem," *The Nation*, March 28, http://www.thenation.com/article/trayvon-martin-what-its-be-problem/ (last accessed July 12, 2016).

Hernandez, Kelly L., Heather Ann Thompson, and Khalil G. Muhammad (eds.) (2015), "Special Issue: Historians and the Carceral State," *The Journal of American History*, vol. 2, no. 1.

Hill, Karlos K. (2016), "Are Police Shootings Really Like Lynchings?" *History News Network*, March 2, http://historynewsnetwork.org/article/162172 (last accessed September 4, 2018).

Hinton, Elizabeth (2016), *From the War on Poverty to the War on Crime: The Making of Mass Incarceration in America* (Cambridge, MA: Harvard University Press).

Hopkins, Daniel J. and John Sides (eds.) (2015), *Political Polarization in American Politics* (New York: Bloomsbury).

Jackson, Thomas F. (2007), *From Civil Rights to Human Rights: Martin Luther King, Jr., and the Struggle for Economic Justice* (Philadelphia: University of Pennsylvania Press).

Jacobs, Lawrence R. and Desmond S. King (2010), "Varieties of Obamaism: Structure, Agency, and the Obama Presidency," *Perspectives on Politics*, vol. 8, no. 3, pp. 793–802.

Jacobs, Lawrence R. and Theda Skocpol (2016), *Health Care Reform and American Politics: What Everyone Needs to Know* (New York: Oxford University Press).

Jacobson, Gary C. (2015), "Obama and Nationalized Electoral Politics in the 2014 Mid-Term," *Political Science Quarterly*, vol. 130, no. 1, pp. 1–25.

Jacobson, Gary C. (2016), "The Obama Legacy and the Future of Partisan Conflict: Demographic Change and Generational Imprinting," *The Annals of the American Academy of Political and Social Sciences*, no. 667, September, pp. 72–91.

Joseph, Peniel E. (2010), *Neighborhood Rebels: Black Power at the Local Level* (New York: Palgrave Macmillan).

Kantor Paul (2013), "The Two Faces of American Urban Policy," *Urban Affairs Review*, vol. 49, no. 6, pp. 821–850.

Kazin, Michael (2015), "Introducing Our Summer Issue: American Movements," *Dissent,* vol. 63, no. 3, pp. 23–25.

Keller, Bill and David Simon (2015), "David Simon on Baltimore's Anguish," *The Marshall Project*, April 29, https://www.themarshallproject.org/2015/04/29/david-simon-on-baltimore-s-anguish (last accessed September 4, 2018).

Kelley, Robin D. G. (2014), "Why We Won't Wait: Resisting the War Against the Black and Brown Underclass," CounterPunch, November 25, http://www.counterpunch.org/2014/11/25/why-we-wont-wait/ (last accessed September 4, 2018).

Kenski, Kate, Bruce W. Hardy, and Kathleen H. Jamieson (2010), *The Obama Victory: How Media, Money, and Message Shaped the 2008 Election* (New York: Oxford University Press).

Khan, Janaya (2015), "Black Lives Matter Has Become a Global Movement," *The Root*, August 7, http://www.commondreams.org/views/2015/08/09/black-lives-matter-has-become-global-movement (last accessed September 4, 2018).

Kinder, Donald R. and Allison Dale-Riddle (2012), *The End of Race? Obama, 2008, and Racial Politics in America* (New Haven, CT: Yale University Press).

Kindy, Kimberly and Kelly Kimbriell (2015), "Thousands Dead, Few Prosecuted," *The Washington Post*, April 11, http://www.washington-post.com/sf/investigative/2015/04/11/thousands-dead-few-prosecuted/ (last accessed July 12, 2016).

King, Chris (2015), "A conversation with Brittany Packnett of Teach for America St. Louis," *The Saint Louis American*, December 22, http://www.stlamerican.com/news/local_news/article_48c9b488-a8bc-11e5-ae4a-a3b141046be5.html (last accessed September 4, 2018).

King, Desmond S. and Rogers M. Smith (2011), *Still a House Divided: Race and Politics in Obama's America* (Princeton, NJ: Princeton University Press).

Kloppenberg, James T. (2012), *Reading Obama: Dreams, Hope, and the American Political Tradition* (Princeton, NJ: Princeton University Press).

Logan, John R. et al. (2012), "The Geography of Inequality: Why Separate Means Unequal in American Public Schools," *Sociology of Education*, vol. 85, no. 3, pp. 287–301.

Lowande, Kenneth and Sidney M. Milkis (2014), "We Can't Wait: Barack Obama, Partisan Polarization, and the Administrative Presidency," *The Forum*, vol. 12, no. 1, pp. 3–27.

McCarthy, Tom (2015), "US Government Database Hopes to Tell 'Whole Story' of Police Killings after Year of *Guardian* Count," *The Guardian*, December 13, http://www.theguardian.com/us-news/2015/dec/13/justice-department-database-police-killings-counted-statistics?CMP=share_btn_tw (last accessed September 4, 2018).

McClain, Dani (2017), "Can Black Lives Matter Win in the Age of Trump?" *The Nation*, September 19, https://www.thenation.com/article/can-black-lives-matter-win-in-the-age-of-trump/ (last accessed September 4, 2018).

McCoy, Austin (2015), "Black Lives Matter to Labor," *CounterPunch*, September 7, http://www.counterpunch.org/2015/09/07/black-lives-matter-to-labor/ (last accessed September 4, 2018).

McDonough, John (2011), *Inside National Health Reform* (Berkeley: University of California Press).

McNamara, Carol and Melanie M. Marlowe (eds.) (2011), *The Obama Presidency in the Constitutional Order: A First Look* (Lanham, MD: Rowman & Littlefield Publishers).

Malcolm X Grassroots Movement (2013), "Operation Ghetto Storm: 2012 Annual Report on the Extrajudicial Killing of 313 Black People," April 7, https://mxgm.org/operation-ghetto-storm-2012-annual-report-on-the-extrajudicial-killing-of-313-black-people/ (last accessed September 4, 2018).

Manza, Jeff and Christopher Uggen (2008), *Locked Out: Felon Disenfranchisement and American Democracy* (New York: Oxford University Press).

Mapping Police Violence (2015), "Police Violence Reports," "Police Violence Map," http://mappingpoliceviolence.org/ (last accessed February 15, 2016).

Mapping Police Violence (2017), "2017 Police Violence Report," https://policeviolencereport.org/ (last accessed September 4, 2018).

Massey, Douglas S. and Nancy A. Denton (1992), *American Apartheid: Segregation and the Making of the Underclass* (Cambridge, MA: Harvard University Press).

Maurer, Tim (2018), *Cyber Mercenaries, The States, Hackers and Power* (Cambridge, MA: Cambridge University Press).

Mettler Suzanne (2010), "Reconstituting the Submerged State: The Challenges of Social Policy Reform in the Obama Era," *Perspectives on Politics*, vol. 8, no. 3, pp. 803–824.

Mettler Suzanne (2011), *The Submerged State. How Invisible Government Policies Undermine American Democracy* (Chicago: University of Chicago Press).

Meyer, Alix (2015), "The Office Holder: John Boehner as Speaker of the US House of Representatives," in Agnès Alexandre-Collier and François Vergniolle de Chantal (eds.), *Leadership and Uncertainty Management in Politics. Leaders, Followers and Constraints in Western Democracies* (Basingstoke: Palgrave Macmillan), pp. 32–50.

Meyer, Alix (2019), *The Obama Presidency (2009–2017)* (Paris: Belin & CNED).

Milkis, Sidney M. (1993), *The President and the Parties. The Transformation of the American Party System since the New Deal* (New York, Oxford University Press).

Milkis, Sidney M. and Daniel J. Tichenor (2019), *Rivalry and Reform: Presidents, Social Movements, and the Transformation of American Politics* (Chicago: University of Chicago Press).

Milkis, Sidney M. and John Warren York (2017), "Barack Obama, Organizing for Action, and Executive-Centered Partisanship," *Studies in American Political Development*, vol. 31, no. 1, pp. 1–23.

Milkis, Sidney M., Jesse H. Rhodes, and Emily J. Charnock (2012), "What Happened to Post-Partisanship: Barack Obama and the New American Party System," *Perspectives on Politics*, vol. 10, no. 1, pp. 57–76.

Morris, Aldon D. (1984), *The Origins of the Civil Rights Movement: Black Communities Organizing for Change* (New York: Free Press).

Movement for Black Lives (2017), "About Us," https://policy.m4bl.org/about/ (last accessed September 4, 2018).

Muhammad, Khalil G. (2010), *The Condemnation of Blackness: Race, Crime, and the Making of Modern Urban America* (Cambridge, MA: Harvard University Press).

Muller, Christopher (2012), "Northward Migration and the Rise of Racial Disparity in American Incarceration, 1880–1950," *American Journal of Sociology*, vol. 118, no. 2, pp. 281–326.

National Research Council (2014), "The Growth of Incarceration in the United States: Exploring Causes and Consequences," Washington, DC, The National Academies Press, http://www.nap.edu/catalog/18613/the-growth-of-incarceration-in-the-united-states-exploring-causes (last accessed July 12, 2016).

Nelson, Michael (ed.) (2010), *The Elections of 2008* (Washington, DC: Sage/CQ Press).

Obama, Barack (2006), *The Audacity of Hope: Thoughts on Reclaiming the American Dream* (New York: Crown Publishers).

Obama, Barack (2007), "Candidate Barack Obama Remarks in Selma," March 7, http://edition.cnn.com/TRANSCRIPTS/0703/04/le.02.html (last accessed July 12, 2016).

Obama, Barack (2008a), "Obama's Father's Day Remarks," *The New York Times*, June 15, http://www.nytimes.com/2008/06/15/us/politics/15text-obama.html?_r=0 (last accessed September 4, 2018).

Obama, Barack (2008b), "Remarks of Senator Barack Obama: 'A More Perfect Union,'" March 18, https://my.barackobama.com/page/content/hisownwords/ (last accessed September 4, 2018).

Obama, Barack (2013a), "Remarks by the President at the 'Let Freedom Ring' Ceremony Commemorating the 50th Anniversary of the March on Washington," August 28, http://www.whitehouse.gov/the-press-office/2013/08/28/remarks-president-let-freedom-ring-ceremony-commemorating-50th-anniversa (last accessed September 4, 2018).

Obama, Barack (2013b), "Remarks by the President on Trayvon Martin," July 19, https://www.whitehouse.gov/the-press-office/2013/07/19/remarks-president-trayvon-martin (last accessed September 4, 2018).

Obama, Barack (2013c), "Remarks By The President On Strengthening The Economy For The Middle Class," February15, https://www.whitehouse.gov/the-press-office/2013/02/15/remarks-president-strengthening-economy-middle-class (last accessed September 4, 2018).

Obama, Barack (2013d), "Remarks by the President at Morehouse College Commencement Ceremony," May 19, http://www.whitehouse.gov/the-press-office/2013/05/19/remarks-president-morehouse-college-commencement-ceremony (last accessed September 4, 2018).

Oberlander, Jonathan (2010), "Long Time Coming: Why Health Reform Finally Passed," *Health Affairs*, vol. 29, no. 6, pp. 1112–1116.

Oluo, Ijeoma (2015), "Bernie Sanders, Black Lives Matter and the Racial Divide in Seattle," *Seattle Globalist*, August 9, http://www.seattleglobalist.com/2015/08/09/bernie-sanders-black-lives-matter-race-divide-in-seattle/40394 (last accessed July 12, 2016).

Pager, Devah (2007), *Marked: Race, Crime, and Finding Work in an Era of Mass Incarceration* (Chicago: The University of Chicago Press).

Parker, Christopher S. (2016), "Race and Politics in the Age of Obama," *The Annual Review of Sociology*, vol. 42, July, pp. 217–230.

Parker, Christopher S. and Matt A. Barreto (2013), *Change They Can't Believe In: The Tea Party and Reactionary Politics in America* (Princeton, NJ: Princeton University Press).

Paybarah, Azi (2015), "Amid Tensions, Sharpton Lashes out at Younger Activists," *Politico*, January 31, http://www.capitalnewyork.com/article/city-hall/2015/01/8561365/amid-tensions-sharpton-lashes-out-younger-activists (last accessed September 5, 2018).

Petersen-Smith, Khury (2015), "Black Lives Matter: A New Movement Takes Shape," *International Socialist Review*, vol. 95, http://isreview.org/issue/96/black-lives-mattery (last accessed September 5, 2018).

Pew Research Center (2016), "On Views of Race and Inequality, Blacks and Whites Are Worlds Apart," June 27, http://www.pewsocialtrends.org/2016/06/27/on-views-of-race-and-inequality-blacks-and-whites-are-worlds-apart (last accessed September 4, 2018).

Pinkney, Alphonso (1984), *The Myth of Black Progress* (New York: Cambridge University Press).

Police Accountability Task Force (2016), "Recommendations for Reform: Restoring Trust between the Chicago Police and the Communities they Serve," April, https://chicagotonight.wttw.com/sites/default/files/article/

file-attachments/PATF_Final_Report_4_13_16.pdf (last accessed September 5, 2018).

Quigley, Bill (2015), "40 Reasons Why Our Jails Are Full of Black and Poor People," *The Huffington Post*, June 8, http://www.huffington-post.com/bill-quigley/40-reasons-why-our-jails-are-full-of-black-and-poor-people_b_7492902.html (last accessed September 5, 2018).

Raghavan, Gautam (ed.) (2018), *West Wingers: Stories from the Dream Chasers, Change Makers, and Hope Creators Inside the Obama White House* (New York: Penguin Books).

Ransby, Barbara (2017), "Black Lives Matter Is Democracy in Action," *The New York Times*, October 21, https://www.nytimes.com/2017/10/21/opinion/sunday/black-lives-matter-leadership.html (last accessed September 5, 2018).

Reilly, Ryan J. (2014), "Meet the Teach for America Official Charged with Bringing Change to Ferguson and Beyond," *The Huffington Post,* November 9, http://www.huffingtonpost.com/2014/11/19/ferguson-commission-teach-for-america_n_6183138.html (last accessed September 5, 2018).

Reynolds, Barbara (2015), "I Was a Civil Rights Activist in the 1960s. But it's Hard for Me to Get Behind Black Lives Matter," *The Washington Post*, August 24, https://www.washingtonpost.com/posteverything/wp/2015/08/24/i-was-a-civil-rights-activist-in-the-1960s-but-its-hard-for-me-to-get-behind-black-lives-matter/ (last accessed September 5, 2018).

Richomme, Olivier and Michelot, Vincent (eds.) (2012), *Le bilan d'Obama* (Paris: Presses de Sciences-Po).

Rid, Thomas and Ben Buchanan (2015), "Attributing Cyber Attacks," *Journal of Strategic Studies*, vol. 38, nos. 1–2, pp. 4–37.

Rockman, Bert A. and Rudalevige, Andrew (eds.) (2019), *The Obama Legacy* (Lawrence: Kansas University Press).

Rockman, Bert A., Andrew Rudalevidge, and Colin Campbell (eds.) (2012), *The Obama Presidency: Appraisals and Prospects* (Washington, DC: Sage/CQ Press).

Rudalevige, Andrew (2005), *The New Imperial Presidency* (Ann Arbor: University of Michigan Press).

Rudalevige, Andrew (2012), "'A Majority is the Best Repartee': Barack Obama and Congress, 2009–12," *Social Science Quarterly*, vol. 93, December, pp. 1272–1294.

Rudalevige, Andrew (2016), "The Obama Administrative Presidency: Some Late-Term Patterns," *Presidential Studies Quarterly*, vol. 46, December, pp. 868–890.

Ruffin, Herbert (2015), "Black Lives Matter: The Growth of a New Social Justice Movement," http://www.blackpast.org/perspectives/black-lives-matter-growth-new-social-justice-movement (last accessed September 5, 2018).

Savage, Charlie (2015), *Power Wars: Inside Obama's Post-9/11 Presidency* (Boston, MA: Little Brown).

Schier, Steven E. (ed.) (2016), *Debating the Obama Presidency* (Lanham, MD: Rowman & Littlefield).

Sentencing Project (2013), *Report of the Sentencing Project to the United Nations Human Rights Committee. Regarding Racial Disparities in the United States Criminal Justice System,* https://www.sentencing-project.org/wp-content/uploads/2015/12/Race-and-Justice-Shadow-Report-ICCPR.pdf (last accessed November 17, 2019).

Shapiro, Thomas, Tatjana Meschede, and Sam Osoro (2013), "The Roots of the Widening Racial Wealth Gap: Explaining the Black-White Economic Divide," Research Report, Waltham, MA: Brandeis University.

Sides, John and Lynn Vavreck (2013), *The Gamble: Choice and Chance in the 2012 Presidential Election* (Princeton, NJ: Princeton University Press).

Singh, Nikhil Pal (2017), *Race and America's Long War* (Oakland: University of California Press).

Skocpol Theda and Lawrence R. Jacobs (2011), *Reaching for a New Deal: Ambitious Governance, Economic Meltdown, and Polarized Politics in Obama's First Two Years* (New York: Russell Sage).

Skocpol, Theda and Lawrence R. Jacobs (2012), "Accomplished and Embattled: Understanding Obama's Presidency," *Political Science Quarterly*, vol. 127, no. 1, pp. 1–24.

Skocpol, Theda and Vanessa Williamson (2012), *The Tea Party and the Remaking of Republican Conservatism* (New York: Oxford University Press).

Skocpol, Theda et al. (2012), *Obama and America's Political Future* (Cambridge, MA: Harvard University Press).

Skowronek, Stephen (1997), *The Politics Presidents Make: Leadership from John Adams to Bill Clinton*, 2nd rev. ed. (Cambridge, MA: Harvard University Press).

Skowronek Stephen (2011), *Presidential Leadership in Political Time: Reprise and Reappraisal* (Lawrence: University Press of Kansas).

Skowronek, Stephen, Stephen M. Engel, and Bruce Ackerman (eds.) (2016), *The Progressives' Century. Political Reform, Constitutional*

Government, and the Modern American State (New Haven, CT: Yale University Press).

Smith, Mychal D. (2014), "How Trayvon Martin's Death Launched a New Generation of Black Activism," *The Nation*, August 27, http://www.thenation.com/article/how-trayvon-martins-death-launched-new-generation-black-activism/ (last accessed September 5, 2018).

Smith, Robert C. and Richard Seltzer (2015), *Polarization and the Presidency: From FDR to Barack Obama* (Boulder, CO: Lynne Rienner).

Socialist Worker (2014), "What Divides Black America," August 27, http://socialistworker.org/2014/08/27/what-divides-black-america (last accessed September 5, 2018).

Spielman, Fran (2016), "Chicago pays $5.5M in Reparations to 57 Burge Torture Victims," *Chicago Sun Times*, January 4, http://chicago.sun-times.com/chicago-politics/7/71/1225907/chicago-pays-5-5-million-reparations-57-burge-torture-victims (last accessed September 5, 2018).

Squire, Aurin (2015), "The End of Respectability Politics," *The Slice,* February 20, http://talkingpointsmemo.com/theslice/the-end-of-black-respectability-politics (last accessed September 5, 2018).

Starr, Paul (2013), *Remedy and Reaction: The Peculiar American Struggle over Health Care Reform* (New Haven, CT: Yale University Press).

Sugrue, Thomas J. (2010), *Not Even Past, Barack Obama and the Burden of Race* (Princeton, NJ: Princeton University Press).

Sugrue, Thomas J. (2013), "A House Divided," *The Washington Monthly*, January/February, http://washingtonmonthly.com/magazine/janfeb-2013/a-house-divided-2/ (last accessed September 6, 2018).

Talpin, Julien (2016a), *Community Organizing. De l"émeute à l'alliance des classes populaires aux Etats-Unis* (Paris: Raisons d'agir).

Talpin, Julien (2016b), "La représentation comme performance. Le travail d'incarnation des classes populaires au sein de deux organisations communautaires à Los Angeles, USA," *Revue Française de Science Politique*, vol. 66, no. 1, pp. 91–116.

Taylor, Keeanga-Yamahtta (2014), "What Divides Black America," *Socialist Worker*, August 27, http://socialistworker.org/2014/08/27/what-divides-black-america (last accessed September 6, 2018).

Taylor, Keeanga-Yamahtta (2015), "In Baltimore and Across the Country, Black Faces in High Places Haven't Helped Average Black People," *In These Times*, April 29, http://inthesetimes.com/article/17888/baltimore_riots_black_politicians (last accessed September 6, 2018).

Taylor, Keeanga-Yamahtta (2016), *From #BlackLivesMatter to Black Liberation: Racism & Civil Rights* (Chicago: Haymarket).

Tesler, Michael (2016), *Post-Racial or Most Racial? Race and Politics in the Obama Era* (Chicago: Chicago University Press).

Tesler, Michael and David O. Sears (2010), *Obama's Race: The 2008 Election and the Dream of a Post-Racial America* (Chicago University of Chicago Press).

The Guardian (2018), "The Counted: People Killed by Police in the US," https://www.theguardian.com/us-news/series/counted-us-police-killings (last accessed September 6, 2018).

The New York Times Editorial Board (2014), "End Mass Incarceration Now," *The New York Times*, May 24, http://www.nytimes.com/2014/05/25/opinion/sunday/end-mass-incarceration-now.html (last accessed September 6, 2018).

The New York Times Editorial Board (2016), "Voters Tell Prosecutors, Black Lives Matter," *The New York Times*, March 18, http://nytimes.com/2016/03/18/opinion/voters-tell-prosecutors-black-lives-matter.html (last accessed September 6, 2018).

The Washington Post (2015), "Police Shootings," https://www.washingtonpost.com/graphics/national/police-shootings (last accessed September 6, 2018).

Thompson, Heather A. (2010), "Why Mass Incarceration Matters: Rethinking Crisis, Decline, and Transformation in Postwar American History," *The Journal of American History*, vol. 97, no. 3, pp. 703–734.

Thrasher, Steven W. (2015), "'We're winning': Jesse Jackson on Martin Luther King, Obama and #blacklivesmatter," *The Guardian*, August 16, http://www.theguardian.com/us-news/2015/aug/16/jesse-jackson-martin-luther-king-obama-and-blacklivesmatter (last accessed September 5, 2018).

Thurber, James A. (2011), *Obama in Office* (Boulder, CO: Paradigm Publishers).

Thurber, James A. and Antoine Yoshinaka (eds.) (2015), *American Gridlock: The Sources, Character, and Impact of Political Polarization* (New York: Cambridge University Press).

Tometi, Opal (2014), "Staying Focused in the Movement for Racial Justice," *The Huffington Post*, December 22, http://www.huffingtonpost.com/opal-tometi/staying-focused-in-the-mo_b_6366618.html (last accessed September 6, 2018).

Tometi, Opal and Gerald Lenoir (2015), "Black Lives Matter Is Not a Civil Rights Movement," *Time*, December 10, http://time.com/4144655/international-human-rights-day-black-lives-matter/ (last accessed September 6, 2018).

Travis, Jeremy, Bruce Western, and Stevens F. Redburn (2014), *The Growth of Incarceration in the United States: Exploring Causes and Consequences* (Washington, DC: The National Academies Press).

Ture, Kwame (Stokely Carmichael) and Charles V. Hamilton (1967), *Black Power: The Politics of Liberation in America* (New York: Random House).

US Department of Justice (2014), "Investigation of the Cleveland Division of Police," December 4, https://www.justice.gov/file/180576/download (last accessed September 5, 2018).

US Department of Justice (2015), "Investigation of the Ferguson Division of Police," March 4, https://www.justice.gov/sites/default/files/opa/press-releases/attachments/2015/03/04/ferguson_police_department_report.pdf (last accessed September 5, 2018).

Vergniolle de Chantal, François (2016), *L'impossible présidence impériale. Le contrôle législatif aux Etats-Unis* (Paris: Editions du CNRS).

Wacquant, Loïc (2006), *Parias urbains. Ghetto, banlieues, État* (Paris: La Découverte).

Wacquant, Loïc [1999] (2011), *Les prisons de la misère* (Paris: Liber, Raisons d'agir).

Wallace, Sophia J. (2014), "Papers Please: State-Level Anti-Immigrant Legislation in the Wake of Arizona's SB 1070," *Political Science Quarterly*, vol. 129, no. 2, pp. 261–291.

Warren, Dorian T. (2010), "The American Labor Movement in the Age of Obama: The Challenges and Opportunities of a Racialized Political Economy," *Perspectives on Politics*, vol. 8, no. 3, pp. 847–860.

Wenger, Yvonne and Luke Broadwater (2015), "Mayor Calls on Black Men to Do More to Stop Violence," *The Baltimore Sun*, March 9, http://www.baltimoresun.com/news/maryland/politics/bs-md-baltimore-state-of-city-20150309-story.html (last accessed September 5, 2018).

West, Cornel and George Yancy (2015), "Cornel West: The Fire of a New Generation," *The New York Times*, August 19, http://opinionator.blogs.nytimes.com/2015/08/19/cornel-west-the-fire-of-a-new-generation/ (last accessed September 5, 2018).

WeTheProtesters (2014), "The Demands," http://www.wetheprotesters.org/ and http://www.thedemands.org/ (last accessed September 5, 2018).

White, John Kenneth (2012), *Barack Obama's America: How New Conceptions of Race, Family, and Religion Ended the Reagan Era* (Ann Arbor: The University of Michigan Press).

Wilder, Craig S. (2013), *Ebony and Ivy: Race, Slavery, and the Troubled History of America's Universities* (New York: Bloomsbury Press).

Wilkerson, Isabel (2014), "Mike Brown's Shooting and Jim Crow Lynchings Have Too Much in Common," *The Guardian*, August 25, http://www.theguardian.com/commentisfree/2014/aug/25/mike-brown-shooting-jim-crow-lynchings-in-common (last accessed September 5, 2018).

Willer, Robb, Matthew Feinberg, and Rachel Wetts (2016), "Threats to Racial Status Promote Tea Party Support Among White Americans," *Stanford Working Papers* No. 4322.

Wilson, William J. [1978] (1980), *The Declining Significance of Race: Blacks and Changing American Institutions* (Chicago: University of Chicago Press).

Wilson, William J. (1999), *The Bridge Over the Racial Divide: Rising Inequality and Coalition Politics* (Berkeley and New York: University of California Press and Russell Sage Foundation).

Wilson, William J. (2009), *More than Just Race: Being Black and Poor in the Inner City* (New York: W. W. Norton & Co.)

Wilson, William J. [1996] (2012), *When Work Disappears: The World of the New Urban Poor* (New York: Random House).

Wood, Erika (2009), "Restoring the Right to Vote," *Research Report*, New York: Brennan Center for Justice, https://www.brennancenter.org/publication/restoring-right-vote (last accessed July 12, 2016).

Wood, Erika and Rachel Bloom (2008), "De Facto Disenfranchisement," *Research Report*, New York: Brennan Center for Justice, https://www.brennancenter.org/publication/de-facto-disenfranchisement (last accessed July 12, 2016).

Zappi, Sylvia (2015), "Une Marche de la dignité à Paris contre les violences policières," *Le Monde*, October 31, http://www.lemonde.fr/societe/article/2015/10/31/une-marche-de-la-dignite-a-paris-contre-les-violences-policieres_4800681_3224.html (last accessed September 5, 2018).

Zelizer, Julian (ed.) (2018), *The Presidency of Barack Obama: A First Historical Assessment*, (Princeton, NJ: Princeton University Press).

Zetter, Kim (2014), *Countdown to Zero Day: Stuxnet and the Launch of the World's First Digital Weapon* (New York: Crown).

Index

Sotomayor, Sonia, 71
Supreme Court, 62, 66,
    70–1, 73–4, 131,
    136–7, 358, 374, 388,
    399, 411
Sunstein, Cass, 5

Tea Party Movement, 8, 10,
    57, 125, 127, 222, 243,
    251–2, 270, 306, 340,
    371–3, 411
Trump, Donald, 16, 19, 31, 37,
    47–51, 68, 72, 81–3, 120,

125, 133, 135, 137, 170,
171, 202, 250, 253–4,
257–8, 271, 276, 282,
284–5, 306, 352, 368,
375–6, 389, 391, 396–9,
404–6, 410–19

voting rights, 274, 276,
    294, 367

Wall Street reform, 57, 273
Warren, Elizabeth, 45, 418
Wright, Jeremiah, 2

EU representative:
Easy Access System Europe
Mustamäe tee 50, 10621 Tallinn, Estonia
Gpsr.requests@easproject.com

www.ingramcontent.com/pod-product-compliance
Lightning Source LLC
Chambersburg PA
CBHW051947270326
41929CB00015B/2556